T3-BGV-839

Inflation & the Nixon Administration

Volume 2

1972-74

Inflation & the Nixon Administration

Volume 2

1972-74

Edited by Lester A. Sobel

Contributing editors: Joseph Fickes, Mary Elizabeth Clifford, Barry Youngerman, Gerry Satterwhite

FACTS ON FILE, INC.   NEW YORK, N.Y.

Inflation
& the
Nixon
Administration

Volume 2

1972-74

© Copyright, 1975, by Facts on File, Inc.
All rights reserved. No part of this book may be
reproduced in any form without the permission
of the publisher except for reasonably brief
extracts used in reviews or scholarly works.
Published by Facts on File, Inc.,
119 West 57th Street, New York, N.Y. 10019.
Library of Congress Catalog Card No. 74-75153
ISBN 0-87196-276-4

9 8 7 6 5 4 3 2 1
PRINTED IN
THE UNITED STATES OF AMERICA

Contents

Introduction

INFLATION, AN UNWANTED LEGACY of the mid-1960s, battered the economies of the United States and most other nations at an accelerating pace throughout the five and a half years that Richard M. Nixon was President of the U.S.

By the time the Watergate scandal had put an end to the Nixon Administration, the U.S. economy was in the grip of a "double-digit" inflation spurred by quadrupled petroleum prices, world food scarcity, "rising aspirations" and increasing competition for the world's resources. The U.S. consumer price index (sometimes referred to as the "cost-of-living" index) had risen by 3% in 1972 and by 8.8% in 1973. But by May 1974, the 12-month rise in the index had reached a "double-digit" figure—10.7%—for the first time in more than two decades.

The effects of this inflation were grave. Unemployment soared, the rate of production declined, and among many observers the question was whether recession had already arrived or was merely imminent. The situation was described by Prof. Paul A. Samuelson of MIT in a quickly popular term as "stagflation"—economic stagnation coupled with inflation.

The seriousness of the problem is almost universally acknowledged. Dr. Arthur F. Burns, chairman of the Federal Reserve Board, told the graduating class of Illinois College May 26, 1974 that, "if past experience is any guide, the future

1

of our country is in jeopardy. No country that I know of has been able to maintain widespread economic prosperity once inflation got out of hand.... If long continued, inflation at anything like the present rate would threaten the very foundations of our society." Burns said that "in recent weeks, governments have fallen in several major countries, in part because the citizens ... had lost confidence in the ability of their leaders to cope with the problem of inflation."

Burns noted that "except for a brief period at the end of World War II, prices in the United States have of late been rising faster than in any other peacetime period of our history." But he pointed out that "a large part of the recent upsurge in prices has been due to special factors.... [D]uring 1973 a business-cycle boom occurred simultaneously in the United States and in every other major industrial country. With production rising rapidly across the world, prices of labor, materials and finished products were bid up everywhere." Matters were made worse, Burns said, when "disappointing crop harvests in a number of countries in 1972 forced a sharp run-up in the prices of food last year," and "the manipulation of petroleum supplies and prices ... gave another dramatic push to the general price level." These special factors, however, merely magnified "a serious underlying bias toward inflation" whose roots, "ironically,... lie chiefly in the rising aspirations of people everywhere," Burns asserted.

Robert S. McNamara, president of the World Bank, observed Sept. 30, 1974 that the "significant acceleration" in the inflation rate in the developed countries had begun "before the rise in the prices of petroleum and other primary commodities" and was "only partially explainable by them." Speaking before the bank's board of governors, McNamara said that "international prices, which had risen only 6% in the decade prior to 1968—less than 1% per year—have risen at an annual rate of nearly 10% in the five years since." Although "inflation benefits virtually all of the developing countries by reducing the burden of their debt service in relation to the value of their exports," McNamara conceded, he warned that for many such nations "—and especially the poorest—this benefit will be more than offset by the deterioration in their terms of trade." He added that "inflation has already eroded the value of the concessionary aid they receive."

The causes of inflation and the cure for this economic disease are subjects of disagreement among students of the problem. Sen. Harry F. Byrd Jr. of Virginia told the Senate Aug. 5, 1974 that he had discussed the matter with "distinguished economists." He said that "a number" of them were "coming to agree" with him that "massive deficits in the federal budget are the chief cause of inflation" and that, "given the key role of the federal budget, ... it is imperative that Congress and the President work together to cut government spending."

But Walter W. Heller, economics professor at the University of Minnesota and a former Presidential adviser, writing in the *Wall Street Journal* of Sept. 27, 1974, described as "myths" such assertions as (a) "profligate budget expansion has plunged us into this inflation," (b) "huge federal deficits have poured fuel on the fires of inflation," (c) "cutting the budget offers us so much anti-inflationary clout that we should move ahead on it and make fiscal policy even more restrictive than it is" and (d) "the main contribution the federal government can make to the battle against inflation is to tighten its own belt." Heller declared that "skyrocketing food, fuel and commodity prices, coupled with excessive dollar devaluation, accounted for the great bulk of our 1973–74 inflation." He asserted that "recent real budget increases are being held to modest levels: the real volume of total federal spending (in constant dollars) is somewhat *lower* today than it was at the end of 1972."

David I. Meiselman, economics professor at Virginia Polytechnic Institute & State University, had held in an article in the *Wall Street Journal* Sept. 13, 1974 that "the worldwide acceleration of inflation since 1973 resulted primarily from a speed-up in the pace of monetary expansion throughout the world rather than from declines in output stemming from such oft-cited events as the disappearance of anchovies off the coast of Peru or the operations of the OPEC oil cartel...." "Since Federal Reserve actions determined the quantity of money, the Fed rather than the fish in Peru is primarily to blame for our inflation woes," Meiselman declared.

At a summit meeting on inflation held in Washington Sept. 27, 1974, Sen. Mike Mansfield of Montana spoke of the petroleum price and production manipulation as "a major source of inflation." But "as far as the United States is concerned," he added, another "factor is Vietnam.... Its terrible cost will extend far into the first half of the next century...."

Secretary of the Treasury William E. Simon attempted to clarify the situation Dec. 11, 1974 in answering what he described as the most relevant questions on inflation and attendant economic problems. "To my way of thinking," Simon said, "unsound [government] monetary and fiscal policies have been the most fundamental causes of present-day rampaging inflation." Such "unsound" policies, he said, "include our three-year experiment with wage and price controls, which led to severe economic distortions and supply shortages." "Political pressures have long put a premium on excessive consumption," he continued. "Monetary policies have been overly stimulative. And federal budgets have been spurring inflation since the early 1960s." Although high oil prices were "an important factor" in inflation recently, Simon conceded, they accounted directly for only about 15% of the rise in the consumer price index in the previous 12 months and might have been responsible for "as much as one-third of the 20% increase in wholesale prices" in the year.

This book and its predecessor volume—*Inflation & the Nixon Administration, Volume 1, 1969-71*—attempt to provide the essential facts on which these divergent opinions are based. This book records the economic events of the final two and a half troubled years during which the Nixon Administration sought to deal with worldwide inflation and with the condition's associated problems. The material in this volume is taken almost exclusively from the record compiled by FACTS ON FILE in its weekly coverage of current world history. A conscientious effort was made to record all events without bias.

1972

Continuing his reversal of previous policy, President Richard M. Nixon ordered further temporary stimulation of the economy during 1972 as his earlier anti-inflationary actions seemed to be working. The rate of inflation in the U.S. declined from an annual rate of 5.1% during 1972's first three months to 2.7% in the final quarter and worked out to a moderate 3% for the year. Nixon, despite his dislike of economic controls, promised to keep them as long as necessary. The dollar was devalued under legislation raising the price of gold. Food costs continued to rise, but Agriculture Secretary Earl Butz led a defense of U.S. farmers as victims rather than profiteers of the price spiral. In hopes of bringing meat prices down, Nixon abandoned meat import quotas. Price curbs were extended to additional foods. A massive sale of U.S. grain to the Soviets, however, stirred controversy as it stimulated additional food price increases in the U.S. and abroad and as critics charged that the deal had profited only the U.S.S.R. and a few grain dealers.

Government Policy

Pause in Inflation Surge

Although the U.S. rate of inflation measured 5.1% during 1972's first quarter, the increase in prices and wages leveled off during the remainder of 1972. The inflation rate for the full year was only 3%, the lowest figure since 1966.

The following figures for the first quarter of 1972 indicate some of the effects of government and industry decisions and actions taken during 1971.

Price indexes up. The consumer price index (CPI) rose to 123.2% of the 1967 average in January and to 123.8% in February. But March was the first month since November 1966 in which the index failed to rise.

After declining by .2% in January despite a rise of 1.5% in the meat, poultry and fish index, consumer food prices turned upwards in February at a seasonally adjusted rate of 24%.

Food costs, exempt from federal controls, rose 1.7% at their fastest pace since March 1958 and accounted for three-quarters of the overall CPI increase. Over half the CPI increase was ascribed to rising meat prices.

It was reported that of about 100,000 prices checked monthly by the Bureau of Labor Statistics in the sectors subject to the federal controls program, 70% remained unchanged, 22% rose and 8% declined.

Herbert Stein, chairman of the President's Council of Economic Advisers, noted at a news conference March 23 that soaring food prices obscured the statistics indicating a successful stabilization program, e.g. a .1% decline in the average retail price of nonfood commodities. In the consumer services sector, prices rose only .2%, compared with 4.1% a year earlier; it was the lowest annual rate of increase since 1965. In his capacity as co-chairman of the Cost of Living Council (CLC), Stein said the Administration preferred to rely on market forces to restrain food prices and did not plan to adopt controls.

The seasonally adjusted wholesale price index rose .4% in January, .7% in February and .1% in March.

Food prices, which were at the heart of the large February increase, declined on the index for March.

First-quarter indicators. The Commerce Department's composite index of leading economic indicators rose to 134% of the 1967 average in January, to 134.7% in February and to 138.2% in March.

Despite the continued upward trend, the February increase was the smallest monthly gain in the index since September 1971.

Personal income up. Personal income rose $8.1 billion in January, when a $2 billion federal pay hike went into effect. Incomes then climbed by $8.9 billion in February and $3.3 billion in March to a seasonally adjusted annual rate of $905.1 billion.

Consumer credit soars. Outstanding consumer credit rose by a seasonally adjusted $637 million in January, $966 million (the third highest increase so far) in February and a record $1.36 billion in March.

5.9% jobless. The unemployment rate declined slightly to 5.9% in January and 5.7% in February, then rose again in March.

The March increase brought the unemployment figure back to 5.9%, the same level as in January.

But at the same time, the number of Americans holding jobs rose in March by 632,000 to 85.4 million. That was the largest gain in any one month in the past five years.

Herbert Stein, chairman of the Council of Economic Advisers, said that "we have been expecting that it [the unemployment rate] would rise temporarily" after the February decline.

The number of persons unemployed in March totaled 5.2 million. On a seasonally adjusted basis, that figure was 160,000 more than the February number.

GNP up. The U.S. gross national product (GNP) rose at an annual rate of 6.5% during the year's first quarter.

The industrial production index, which measured the output of U.S. factories, mines and utilities, rose .6% in March. Similar .6% increases had been registered in each of the last five months.

The March gain brought the overall index to a seasonally-adjusted 109.6% of the 1967 average. That mark was 4% above a year earlier, but down 2% from the March 1969 level, the high-water mark.

The number of new housing units started set records of 2,471,000 in January and 2,655,000 in February before declining to 2,320,000 in March.

Corporate profits analyzed. Two measures of corporate profits showed that 1972 after-tax profits, when expressed in 1958 dollars, were below the $45 billion peak of 1966 and that net corporate

cash flow, also in 1958 terms, was just above the 1966 high of $66 billion, the Commerce Department reported July 6.

"Real" profits after taxes declined to a $29.6 billion low in the fourth quarter of 1970 and rose only to $37.9 billion in first quarter 1972. Net cash flow, including earnings (after taxes and dividends) plus depreciation showed less decline from 1966 through 1970 and rose to a high in 1972's first quarter of $66.4 billion.

Nixon's Economic Program

Richard M. Nixon outlined his economic program for 1972 and beyond in the traditional key economic messages—the budget message and the Economic Report—which he submitted to Congress in January.

Budget projects large deficit. President Nixon submitted to Congress Jan. 24 a $246.3 billion budget for fiscal 1973 with an estimated deficit of $25.5 billion. Receipts were estimated at $220.8 billion. (A peacetime record deficit of $38.8 billion was projected, incorrectly, for fiscal 1972.)

The central purpose of the new budget, Nixon declared, was "a new prosperity for all Americans without the stimulus of war and without the drain of inflation."

Citing the fiscal 1973 deficit as a $13½ billion reduction from the previous year, Nixon said his new budget "brings us strongly forward toward our goal of a balanced budget in a time of full employment." It "diminishes stimulation as the new prosperity takes hold and, by so doing, acts as a barrier against the renewal of inflation pressure," he said.

The President stressed that the budget was predicated on a "full employment" concept,* with spending and revenue calculated on the basis of an economy operating at a "full employment" level of about 4% unemployment (instead of the expected actual level of unemployment). Nixon urged Congress "to respect the full-employment spending guideline."

---

*In his 1971 State of the Union message, President Nixon had outlined a "full-employment" (no more than 3.8% unemployment) budget "designed to be in balance if the economy were operating at its peak potential."

Deficit spending justified—The big deficit and a request to increase the budget authority for military programs by $6.3 billion, the largest new initiative in the budget, were major features of the new budget.

The President justified both as necessary—deficit spending to increase jobs and spur the economy, a rise in defense fund obligations to modernize the U.S. arsenal.

Deficit spending at this time, he said, was a "strong but necessary medicine" taken "because we need it, not because we like it." As the economy "successfully combats unemployment," he said, "we will stop taking the medicine well before we become addicted to it."

Nixon pointed out that the rate of increase in federal spending was only 4.1% from the previous year, that 71%* of federal spending was "uncontrollable," or built into the budget from ongoing programs enacted by Congress, and that tax revenues were $22 billion less because of reductions for individuals since he assumed office.

Defense priority stressed—In the area of defense, Nixon said "it would be foolhardy not to modernize" at this point. It was a priority of his Administration "to create a peaceful world order," he said, and "we can only negotiate and maintain peace if our military power continues to be second to none."

Stressing the need for "a strong fiscal discipline" in the years ahead, Nixon cautioned Congress not to cut the defense budget, which, he said, represented as submitted "America's actual military needs and offers the best means to secure peace for the coming generations." He urged Congress "not to make the costly mistakes it has made in previous years in its defense cuts" and "to face squarely the difficult questions involved in setting priorities within the overall constraint of a full-employment balance." Again he urged Congress not "to take the dangerous course of trying to match domestic spending increases with cuts in vitally needed defense funds."

New spending programs, he insisted, "must be evaluated against the most stringent of standards: Do they have enough merit to warrant increases in taxes or elimination of existing programs?"

Spending ceiling recommended—In a separate message Jan. 24, the President requested Congress to enact "an absolute limit on spending" for the new budget at the $246.3 billion level, beyond which Congress or the Executive branch could not go. It was vital, he said, that both branches "act together to stop raids on the treasury which would trigger another inflationary spiral."

Basic budget preferences stated—The President stated his "basic preferences" in allocating the national resources: (a) that costs be counted before spending decisions were made, and (b) that "an increasing share of national resources must be returned to private citizens and state and local governments."

Referring to the decreased rate of increase (4.1%) in federal spending and the reductions in recent years of income taxes for individuals ($22 billion), the President noted a "basic shift in the government's fiscal philosophy"—that "the upward curve of federal spending is beginning to flatten out while the federal income tax 'bite' out of the individual paycheck is becoming measurably less."

Largely because of the built-in budget programs, proposed outlays for domestic "human resources" purposes exceeded those for defense, which comprised 31.8% of the new budget. For the first time, the budget for the Department of Health, Education and Welfare ($79 billion) exceeded that for the Defense Department ($76.5 billion). "Income security" payments to people totaled $69.7 billion in the 1973 budget compared with $55.7 billion in fiscal 1971.

In the area of channeling funds to state and local governments, Nixon again put priority on his revenue sharing plan, including $2.5 billion for this in fiscal

---

*A New York Times diagram Jan. 25 depicted the President's budgetary choices as restricted to only 31.3% of total expenditures, with 68.6% of the budget's expenditures required under existing law. In that discretionary area of choice, 20.3% of the expenditures in the new budget were allotted to the military, 11% to civilian purposes.

1972, retroactive to Jan. 1, and $5.3 billion in fiscal 1973. The Administration also shifted from fiscal 1973 to fiscal 1972 a planned welfare payment of $1 billion to state and local governments.

No new tax proposals—There were no new major tax increase proposals in the budget. A request for $300 million in higher taxes on truckers had been presented before and persistently rejected by Congress. A rise in the Social Security tax collection was to be reaped from a proposed increase in the wage base on which the tax was collected. The Presi-

dent proposed that the Social Security-Medicare tax rate, currently 5.2% of wages for both employer and employe, rise to 5.4% Jan. 1, 1973 and the amount of annual income subject to the tax be increased to $10,200, retroactive to Jan. 1, 1972 (it had been raised Jan. 1 from $7,800 to $9,000.)

Some highlights of the budget:

Defense. Although President Nixon requested authority to commit $83.4 billion for defense, a $6.3 billion rise from fiscal 1972, actual spending in fiscal 1973 was budgeted at $76.5 billion, a rise

Budget Receipts

(In billions of dollars for the fiscal year)

	1971 actual	1972 estimate	1973 estimate
Individual income taxes	86.23	86.5	93.9
Corporation income taxes	26.785	30.1	35.7
Social insurance taxes and contributions:			
Employment taxes and contributions	41.699	46.367	55.113
Unemployment insurance	3.674	4.364	5.016
Contributions for other insurance and retirement	3.205	3.361	3.554
Excise taxes	16.615	15.2	16.3
Estate and gift taxes	3.735	5.2	4.3
Customs duties	2.591	3.21	2.85
Miscellaneous receipts	3.858	3.525	4.052
Total receipts	**188.392**	**197.827**	**220.785**

Budget Outlays

(In billions of dollars for the fiscal year)

	1971 actual	1972 estimate	1973 estimate
National defense*	77.661	78.03	78.31
International affairs and finance	3.095	3.96	3.844
Space research and technology	3.381	3.18	3.191
Agriculture and rural development	5.096	7.345	6.891
Natural resources and environment	2.716	4.376	2.45
Commerce and transportation	11.31	11.872	11.55
Community development and housing	3.357	4.039	4.844
Education and manpower	8.654	10.14	11.281
Health	14.463	17.024	18.117
Income security	55.712	65.225	69.658
Veterans benefits and services	9.776	11.127	11.745
Interest	19.609	20.067	21.161
General government	3.970	5.302	5.531
General revenue sharing	------	2.25	5.0
Allowances for:			
Pay raises (excluding Department of Defense)	------	.25	.775
Contingencies	------	.3	.5
Undistributed intrabudgetary transactions:			
Employer share, employe retirement	−2.611	−2.687	−2.893
Interest received by trust funds	−4.765	−5.19	−5.697
Total outlays	**211.425**	**236.61**	**246.257**
Budget deficit	**23.033**	**38.783**	**25.472**

*Includes allowances for military retirement systems reform and civilian and military pay raises for Department of Defense.

of $700 million from the current fiscal year. The balance of the new obligational authority was to be spent as new weapons, the development of which was delayed by costs of the Vietnam war, were produced in future years.

Incorporated into the budget planning was a request, sent to Congress along with the 1973 budget, for a $254.8 million supplemental appropriation to the fiscal 1972 defense budget. The supplemental included more than $100 million for four giant planes as an airborne command post to control strategic forces in a nuclear emergency. It also covered $141 million for research and development, $35 million of which was for a new nuclear submarine, the ULMS (undersea long-range missile system).

The ULMS was being planned as a furtherance of the Polaris-Poseidon missile-firing submarine system. The system's final shape was still in formulation, partly because of program cost estimates, which ranged from $15 billion to $30 billion. The fiscal 1973 budget allotted $942.2 million for ULMS, a rise from $139.8 million in fiscal 1972 funds.

Another big item in the fiscal 1973 budget was $299 million for long-lead material for a fourth nuclear aircraft carrier.

Strategic forces were allotted a total of $8.8 billion in budget authority in fiscal 1973, a $1.2 billion increase. Increases were budgeted for the Safeguard antiballistic missile (ABM) system, up $366.6 million from fiscal 1972 to $1.48 billion; the B1 long-range bomber, up $74.2 million to $444.5 million in fiscal 1973; the AWACS (airborne warning and control system), up $330.6 million to $469.9 million.

New budget authority for research and development on weapons was to rise from $6.2 billion in fiscal 1972 to $7.2 billion, while budget authority for general-purpose forces would decrease slightly from $25.7 billion in fiscal 1972 to $25.6 billion in fiscal 1973. The decline was attributed to cutbacks in Vietnam war costs, which were estimated at $7.1 billion in fiscal 1972 compared with $11.5 billion in fiscal 1971 and $20 billion in fiscal 1970.

By service, the budget provided new spending authority of $25.2 billion for

the Navy, $23.5 billion for the Air Force and $22.1 billion for the Army.

Military manpower was scheduled to total 2,358,000 by June 30, 1973, a decline of 33,000 in one year and of 1,-189,000 from the 1968 war peak. The planned mid-1972 service strengths: Army—841,000 (down 20,000 from the year earlier). Air Force—717,000 (down 13,000). Navy—602,000 (no change). Marines—198,000 (no change).

To advance the services toward an all-volunteer footing, the President requested another military boost Jan. 1, 1973 that would raise basic recruit pay to $332.10 monthly from the current $288. New budget authority of $4.1 billion was requested for higher pay.

Of the new budget authority, $3.6 billion was slated for shipbuilding.

Among individual items in the fiscal 1973 defense budget, in terms of new budget authority (increases and decreases from fiscal 1972 budget):

Airborne Command Post—$141.2 million. Poseidon missile conversion—$404 million (up $21.3 million) for change of subs to the improved Poseidon missile (capable of carrying MIRVs, or multiple independently targetable warheads), $347.4 million (down $35.8 million) for the missiles. Minuteman intercontinental missile system—$837.4 million (down $10.7 million). Nuclear attack subs—$1.04 billion (up $143.7 million).

General purpose destroyers—$612.1 million (up $12.9 million). PF patrol frigates, a new class of small escort ships—$193 million (up $181.7 million) for the first vessel. Patrol hydrofoils—$60.4 million (up $55.1 million).

A small aircraft carrier, to be equipped with vertical takeoff planes and helicopters and planned for use as a sea control ship—$10 million for advanced procurement (a new item). F14A Navy jet fighter plane—$734.8 million (down $296.1 million).

F15 Air Force fighter—$910.5 million (up $490.6 million). F111 Air Force warplane—$165.3 million (down $340.5 million).

C5A giant cargo jet—$207.6 million (down $113.9 million). P3C (landbased) antisubmarine plane—$246.4 million (down $32.1 million). S3A (carrier based) antisubmarine plane—$665.9 million (up $83.4 million). Harrier vertical-takeoff jet—$133.1 million (up $19.4 million). Cheyenne attack helicopter—$53.5 million (up $44.2 million).

Space. Outlays for the National Aeronautics and Space Administration were to remain near the fiscal 1972 level of about $3.2 billion. Construction of a space shuttle formed a major commitment of the budget, with spending to be doubled to $200 million in fiscal 1973 and expected to reach $600 million by fiscal 1974 and $1 billion in 1975.

A cost-cutting item of the space budget would be the ending of the phase-out of the Nerva nuclear energy rocket vehicle program to develop a 75,000-pound-thrust rocket for trips to planets. A smaller rocket with thrust of 15,000-20,000 pounds was to be designed. NASA also was dropping plans for "Grand Tour" flights by unmanned spacecraft to the outer planets in favor of plans for separate flights to Jupiter and possibly Saturn.

Plans to launch a Skylab space station in earth orbit, with flight scheduled for 1973, were funded in the 1973 budget, which also provided for development of a third-generation weather satellite for flight in 1976 and of an orbiting "high-energy astronomy observatory" to study high-frequency radiation from space.

Health. Outlays for research by the National Institutes of Health were to increase by $177 million to a total of $1.4 billion. Major initiatives were planned for cancer research, with a $335 million funding, up $57 million, and for heart and lung disease research, which was allotted $221 million, a $30.6 million increase.

Medicare outlays for health insurance for the aged would rise from $9 billion to $10.4 billion, and the Administration planned some changes in the Medicare program, to provide health benefits for the disabled and to eliminate the monthly premium for coverage of doctor bills.

Another increase was budgeted for Veterans Administration health care spending, a rise of $254 million to a $2.5 billion total.

A major reduction was planned for the Medicaid program of health care for the poor—from a $4.4 billion level to $3.4 billion. But the reduction was offset by an accounting change shifting some outlays into an earlier fiscal year (1972) and enabling a $1 billion advance payment in matching funds to be paid states for Medicaid and welfare cash grants.

The Administration also envisioned a shift of emphasis in the program away from costly hospital treatment to less-expensive outpatient care.

Another major trend covered in the health budget was a spending increase

of 64%, or $70 million, to a $179 million total for Food and Drug Administration, which planned to treble its investigations of product safety and consumer injury in fiscal 1973.

Welfare. Although the budget called for "management initiatives" to curb the rising costs of the federal welfare program—an effort expected to save $400 million in welfare payments and Medicaid funds—federal payments for cash welfare grants would rise an estimated $846 million to $7.6 billion. With Medicaid's health aid to the poor added in, welfare outlays in fiscal 1973 would rise 14.5%. This compared with a 23.5% increase in fiscal 1972 and a 28.6% rise in fiscal 1971, the reduced rate of increase attributed largely to cutbacks by states in their programs and the resulting cutback in federal matching funds.

The welfare system was viewed in the budget as a temporary one to be replaced with the Administration's welfare reform program. A $350 million item was included for preliminary administrative work in setting up the new system.

Education. Education outlays would rise $1.1 billion from the fiscal 1972 level to $15.7 billion in fiscal 1973. A majority of this, $9.4 billion, would be "direct support," of which $5.2 billion —some $400 million more than the year before—would be channeled through the Office of Education and $2.2 billion—an increase of $200 million—would go through the Veterans Administration for schooling under the GI Bill.

An expansion of the grant program for needy students in higher education was projected—to a $671.5 million level in fiscal 1972 to provide help to 1,280,-000 students (up 438,000 in a year). An increase to a $701.8 million level in fiscal 1973 was requested. General-purpose grants to institutions of higher education were not provided in the budget.

An appropriation of $1 billion was requested for aid to school systems undergoing desegregation.

The budget incorporated the Administration's special education revenue sharing plan, funded with $3.2 billion in fiscal 1973, or the same total as the fiscal 1972 total for all current programs.

Community development, housing. A $2.3 billion revenue-sharing program for urban community development was provided in the budget to replace programs for urban renewal, model cities, open space, neighborhood facilities and rehabilitation loans. The budget total for fiscal 1973 was only $1.8 billion, but President Nixon promised to request another $490 million if Congress enacted the plan.

Total fiscal 1973 outlays for the Department of Housing and Urban Development would increase $805 million to $4.8 billion.

The department estimated that 566,-000 subsidized housing units would be started in fiscal 1973.

Commitments to subsidized apartments would be reduced in fiscal 1973 to a $150 million level from the $200 million level in fiscal 1972.

The program was plagued with problems, and the Administration planned to focus on quality rather than quantity. Funds were budgeted to develop a way to counter the growing problem of abandonment of the inner-city housing that was under federal subsidy.

Transportation. Spending of $8.6 billion was proposed for transportation in fiscal 1973. This included Commerce Department maritime subsidies, where the budget contained authorization for construction of 17 high-capacity ships in fiscal 1973, compared with 18 smaller ones in fiscal 1972 and a 30-ship level projected for fiscal 1974, the level set a year ago for fiscal 1973. The new budget's outlays for this program would rise $37 million to $198.4 million in fiscal 1973. For the Coast Guard, $66 million was budgeted toward a second modern icebreaker.

Outlays for highway building were to rise to $4.9 billion ($4.69 billion in fiscal 1972), spending for roadside billboard removal was increased 33%, for improved air traffic-control facilities 7% and grants for airport building rose 69%.

Savings were anticipated in aviation support, largely because of elimination of the supersonic transport program. The Administration planned to propose later a "revised schedule" of aviation user charges and planned to cut back the "sky marshal" program to curb plane

hijackings from a 1,500-man level to 500 by the end of fiscal 1973.

The budget also reiterated Administration requests for increases in diesel-fuel and heavy-truck taxes.

For mass transit, $1 billion was budgeted for fiscal 1973, but actual outlays were set at $280 million in fiscal 1972 and about $390 million the next year. The Administration had released only $600 million of $900 million approved by Congress for fiscal 1972 spending on mass transit.

The budget called for a 46% increase in authority to make new commitments for transportation research and development, to the $666 million level, encompassing projects such as high-speed air-cushioned vehicles and ways to keep drunken drivers off the road.

The budget contained the first presidential endorsement of the Regulatory Modernization Act to "deregulate" freight transportation by easing federal controls.

The environment. The budget request for the Environmental Protection Agency totaled $2.446 billion, about the same as the year before.

More than 80% of the budget—$2 billion, the same amount as requested for fiscal 1972—was for federal grants for sewage facilities, in keeping with the Administration plan for grant commitments of $8 billion over four years. Actual disbursements for treatment plants were estimated at $1.1 billion in fiscal 1973, up from $908 million in fiscal 1972.

To implement the 1970 Clean Air Act in fiscal 1973, the President requested $171.5 million, or $148.5 million less than the Administration had estimated, when the legislation was pending in Congress, would be needed and $128.5 million less than authorized by the act.

For the solid-waste program, for which Congress authorized $238 million by fiscal 1973, the President requested $23.3 million, $11.3 million less than the previous year.

There was also a reduction of $5 million for research and development of improved waste water treatment technology, with more reliance put upon private industry to cope with the problem.

Agriculture. Feed-grain price supports were expected to cost $1.8 billion, a slight rise from the fiscal 1972 level. Dairy products were to be subsidized with $491 million in federal purchases, up $46 million.

Another major method of supporting domestic farm prices, through food-aid shipments, was expected to decrease about $230 million to $1.17 billion in fiscal 1973.

The budget requested expansion of Farmers Home Administration loans for low-to-moderate-income housing, from a loan-level of $1.6 billion in fiscal 1972 to $2.1 billion, which was expected to enable about 142,000 rural families to acquire homes, 30,000 more than the previous year.

Crime. Total spending on federal anti-crime programs was to rise from $1.9 billion to $2.3 billion in fiscal 1973. Outlay for law-enforcement assistance to the states was projected at $595 million, up from $425 million in fiscal 1972 and $33.5 million in fiscal 1969. Funding of the FBI remained around $330 million.

Science research. Budget commitments for scientific research and development were set at $17.8 billion for fiscal 1973, a 9% rise, of which $40 million was directed into the new program to develop high-technology products.

Outlays for general research were budgeted at $16.8 billion, a 4.4% increase.

Foreign aid. A $3.19 billion foreign aid program was projected for fiscal 1973, a decline from a $3.22 billion program expected for fiscal 1972. The new budget allocated $639 million to international financial organizations, $906 million for bilateral economic aid, $796 million for economic supporting assistance and $839 million for the Food for Peace program.

The budget reflected a shift toward channeling more U.S. aid through multinational agencies, providing for commitments of $1.47 billion through the international channel and $1.26 billion through bilateral aid programs.

The Agency for International Development (AID) was to be reorganized, effective Feb. 1, into new bureaus for humani-

FEDERAL RECEIPTS, OUTLAYS, DEFICITS (OR SURPLUSES) & INTEREST ON NATIONAL DEBT 1955–72

[In billions of dollars]

	Receipts	Outlays	Surplus (+) or deficit (−)	Debt interest
1955	58.1	62.3	−4.2	6.4
1956	65.4	63.8	+1.6	6.8
1957	68.8	67.1	+1.7	7.3
1958	66.6	69.7	−3.1	7.8
1959	65.8	77.0	−11.2	7.8
1960	75.7	74.9	+.8	9.5
1961	75.2	79.3	−4.1	9.3
1962	79.7	86.6	−6.9	9.5
1963	83.6	90.1	−6.5	10.3
1964	87.2	95.8	−8.6	10.7
1965	90.9	94.8	−3.9	10.3
1966	101.4	106.5	−5.1	12.0
1967	111.8	126.8	−15.0	13.4
1968	114.7	143.1	−28.4	14.6
1969	143.3	148.8	−5.5	16.6
1970	143.2	156.3	−13.1	19.3
1971	133.7	163.7	−30.0	21.0
1972	148.8	178.0	−29.2	21.8

Source: Office of Management and Budget and Treasury Department.

tarian, security, economic-development and administrative purposes. A 25% reduction in personnel over two years was anticipated, pending new retirement legislation.

Deficits, urban aid cuts scored. Leading Congressional Democrats offered immediate criticism Jan. 24 of the President's new budget.

While House Republican Leader Gerald R. Ford (Mich.) hailed it as a "constructive program to heal the economic wounds of war," House Speaker Carl Albert (D, Okla.) expressed disappointment with the President's prescription for a "sick" economy of less money for economic development, health, housing and education.

Chairman George H. Mahon (D, Tex.) of the House Appropriations Committee accused the President of trying to "sugar coat" even larger deficits and warned that a tax increase was inevitable to avoid "fiscal collapse."

Sen. William Proxmire (D, Wis.), chairman of the Joint Economic Committee, said the proposed increase in the military budget was "indefensible at a time when the incremental cost of the Vietnam war has dropped by $20 billion."

Sen. Edmund S. Muskie (Me.), a leading contender for the Democratic presidential nomination, spoke of the anticipated huge budget deficits in connection with the Nixon Administration's "disastrous management of the economy."

Sen. Edward M. Kennedy (D, Mass.) contrasted the budget "awash in red ink" to the President's request for a "promiscuous increase of billions for defense" when the need was for billions for schools, homes and health.

New York Mayor John V. Lindsay said the budget provided "more to death abroad and less for life at home."

The executive committee of the United States Conference of Mayors Jan. 25 expressed dismay with the budget's "proposed cut of $765 million" in several major urban programs.

Federal subsidies assailed. Sen. William Proxmire (D, Wis.) released a report of his Joint Economic Committee Jan. 10 which indicated that federal subsidies had cost America's taxpayers at least $63 billion in fiscal 1970.

Proxmire called the federal subsidy system "a mindless means of spending taxpayers' money." He added that he thought it "seems to be out of control."

The report by Proxmire's committee represented the first investigation of the overall costs of the government's subsidy operations. The report listed major categories of subsidies, their estimated annual budgetary costs and some of their programs. They were:

■ Cash subsidies of about $10 billion–$13 billion to encourage farmers to produce or not produce crops, help students, sponsor the construction of irrigation systems and build and operate ships.

■ Tax subsidies of about $38 billion to encourage military service, promote home ownership and accelerate the use of certain natural resources.

■ Credit subsidies of about $4 billion–$5 billion to provide low-cost rural electric and telephone service, build hospitals and support higher education.

■ Benefit-in-kind subsidies of about $10 billion to provide goods and services at lower costs.

Food stamp cutback restored. The Nixon Administration Jan. 16 reversed a planned cutback in the food stamp program after the change had drawn protest from senators and governors.

Under 1971 legislation calling for a uniform national eligibility standard, the Agriculture Department had set $360 as the top monthly income limit for participants in the food stamp program. The change would allow an additional 1.7 million persons, mostly in Southern and Western states, into the program while eliminating from it, or reducing benefits to, some 2.1 million persons, mostly in Northeastern states where the cost of living was higher.

The change had been protested Dec. 19, 1971 by 28 senators in a letter to the Agriculture Department.

Sens. George McGovern (D, S.D.) and Clifford P. Case (R, N.J.), in separate statements Jan. 3, warned that they would take legislative action, if necessary, to counter the change.

The protest gained momentum when it was joined by the governors of 15 states and New York Mayor John V. Lindsay, whose representatives met in Hartford, Conn. Jan. 7 to mount an effort to preserve current benefits. They demanded that no family be dropped from the program and that benefits be increased to reflect the cost of an adequate diet.

The New York Times reported from confidential budgetary documents Jan. 12 that the Nixon Administration had impounded $202 million of funds allocated for food assistance, almost 10% of the $2.2 billion appropriated by Congress for the food stamp program. The Administration's budget request for food stamps was $2 billion for fiscal 1972, and Congress had added $200 million to the program.

Sen. Hubert H. Humphrey (D, Minn.) and McGovern protested the impounding Jan. 12. Assistant Agriculture Secretary Frank B. Elliott said that day the $202 million had not been impounded, except in a technical sense, and the money, while not requested by the department for its budget, was "available from the Office of Management and Budget any time we need it."

The policy reversal was announced Jan. 16 by Agriculture Secretary Earl L. Butz, who said he had issued new regulations to insure that "the benefits available to each household are as high or higher than they were under the old regulations." He made clear that the "impounded" funds would be used.

A department report Jan. 1 put enrollment in the food stamp program at 10.9 million persons in November 1971. The combined enrollment in the food stamp program and the program of distributing surplus commodities to needy families was estimated at 14.4 million in November. This compared with a 13.1 million combined enrollment a year earlier and 7.1 million two years previously.

Connally scolds business. Treasury Secretary John B. Connally Jr. defended the budget deficit and scolded businessmen for sitting on the sidelines and complaining about economic uncertainty while the Administration was doing all it could to cope with the problem. Addressing a Washington, D.C. meeting of the U.S. Chamber of Commerce, Connally said, "This administration has defended the American business enterprise of this nation far more than you've defended yourselves."

Commenting that it was "a political world," Connally said he was not a "deficit-spending man," but he asked rhetorically, "What position would we be in if we had a balanced budget with over five million persons unemployed?" Under the circumstances, he said, fiscal stimulus was mandatory. "I understand your concern. But for restoring vitality to the economy, you ought to be applauding it," he said

Connally's last comment was in apparent reference to a speech delivered earlier by Arch N. Booth, the chamber's executive vice president.

Connally said the projected 9% increase in capital spending for new plant and equipment in 1972 did not represent a "banner year" for business confidence. He chastised his audience of more than 1,000 business leaders for not taking greater advantage of the 7% investment tax credit, which they had demanded, the Administration had supported and Congress had passed in 1971.

Both Connally and Price Commission Chairman C. Jackson Grayson Jr., who also addressed the conference, stressed that removal of wage and price controls ultimately depended on the cooperation of business. Connally warned the businessmen to "make up your minds that you can no longer negotiate and expect anybody to support unconscionable and unreasonable wage demands" and "you can't continue to raise your prices in an unconscionable fashion." The audience, said to represent the nation's top 1,500 companies, was told by Connally, "You get special treatment." He said his listeners couldn't count on controls ending just because some small firms had been given exemptions.

Both Connally and Grayson said that wage and price controls would remain in effect until inflation was reduced to a 2%–3% annual rate, the target set by the Administration.

Fiscal 1972 deficit $23 billion. George Shultz, who succeeded Connally as Secretary of the Treasury June 12, reported July 24 that the federal budget deficit for fiscal 1972 (July 1, 1971 through June 30, 1972) was $23 billion. Budget outlays totaled $231.6 billion, receipts $208.6 billion.

On a "full-employment" budget basis, Shultz said, based on revenues and expenditures if unemployment were at a 4% rate, spending totaled $228.6 billion and revenues $225 billion.

Economic Report stresses controls. President Nixon's Economic Report to Congress, delivered Jan. 27, stressed that wage and price controls would be continued until "reasonable price stability can be maintained without controls." The President predicted that the goal of reasonable price stability without controls "can and will be reached." "How long it will take," he said, "no one can say," but he pledged that his Administration would "persevere" until the goal of stability was reached and that controls would not be kept "one day longer than necessary."

The duration of controls was the major topic of his brief Economic Report, as it was of the accompanying annual report of the President's Council of Economic Advisers, which asserted, "Speculation that the Administration will abandon the controls prematurely—out of fatigue, ideological aversion or other causes—is groundless." The current system of controls, it said, "will be adapted as necessary" to achieve the goal of stability. The President. in his report, referred at one point to. the price-wage control system as "still in its formative stage."

Confidence asserted for 1972—The President said the results of the new economic policy announced Aug. 15, 1971 were "extremely encouraging." Nixon asserted that the year "begins on a note of much greater confidence than prevailed six or 12 months ago." The one "great problem" remaining, he said, was to reduce the unemployment rate from its 6% level. He expressed determination "to reduce that number significantly in 1972."

GNP forecast—In its detailed economic forecast, the council estimated that the gross national product (GNP), or total private and governmental output of goods and services, would increase by about 9.5% to $1.145 trillion in 1972, a $98 billion rise from 1971's $1.047 trillion. The growth of "real" GNP was forecast at 6%, compared to a 2.7% increase in physical volume of output in 1971. Inflation was expected to decline to "around 3¼%" in 1972 from the 4.6% inflationary rise in the GNP price index in 1971. (The economy performed even better than predicted. GNP rose by 9.7% in 1972 to a $1.152 trillion level, and inflation dropped to a 3% rate for the year.) Although such anticipated growth in GNP would be "significantly faster" than in 1971, the council cautioned that "the picture drawn here is not one of takeoff into a cyclical boom" and said all such forecasts were "subject to a considerable margin of possible error."

Unemployment rate goal 5%—The possibility that the economy "might lag behind the estimates made today," the council said, "calls for readiness to take additional steps" to achieve the GNP goal and to reduce the unemployment rate to "the neighborhood of 5% by year end."

The council noted, however, that the federal budget was stimulative and, on a "national income accounts" (NIA) basis, which did not include lending operations, would in fact stimulate the economy more than indicated in the regular budget version presented Jan. 24. Federal outlays on the NIA basis were to rise 13% in calendar 1972, or about $29 billion, to $251 billion, with a $36 billion deficit forecast, a rise from $23 billion in calendar 1971.

Other statistical predictions—The biggest item in the GNP, consumer spending, was expected by the council to increase by about 8% from the $662.2 billion total of 1971. The rate of savings was not expected to decline on a sustained basis from the exceptionally high 8% average of the past two years.

A fourfold increase over 1971 was forecast for business-inventory accumulation, to an $8 billion total in 1972, but the council cautioned that such a "substantial" change in business inventory policy was among the "major uncertainties" of the year. An 8% rise in total business-fixed investment in 1972 was predicted, based on a broader survey than the plant-and-equipment survey by which the Commerce Department and Securities and Exchange Commission predicted a 9% increase.

Government purchases, including salaries but not welfare-type payments, were anticipated to grow by 11% (9% at the federal level, 12% for state and local governments), but the figures anticipated enactment of the revenue-sharing program.

For private housing starts, the council forecast 2.2 million units in 1972, a gain from 1971's record 2,048,200.

As for foreign trade, the council said the net balance between exports and imports of goods and services "will probably be close to zero" for 1972 as a whole. It anticipated it would take "some months" to gain impetus away from the $2 billion annual rate of deficit of 1971's fourth quarter.

Free-trade stance—The council favored a free-trade policy and warned that "voluntary" agreements to limit imports, such as those negotiated by the U.S. for steel and textiles, had "serious disadvantages" and could foster "cartels." Two prerequisites were cited for continued progress toward freer trade—a "more flexible" international monetary system and a general "milieu of expanding employment opportunities."

Money-supply requirement noted— Throughout its report, the council stressed the importance of the role of the Federal Reserve Board (FRB) in the planned economic stimulus for 1972. "The steady, strong expansion we seek," it said, "will require support from monetary policy" and "an abundant supply of credit and other liquid assets and favorable conditions in money markets" was necessary. "Steps have already been taken" at the FRB, the council noted, to effect a "more rapid rise of currency and demand deposits than occurred in the second half of 1971" (the money-supply growth rate was at an 0.8% average annual rate over the past five months).

Joint Economic Committee hearings. Congress' Joint Economic Committee, headed by Sen. William Proxmire (D, Wis.), began hearings Feb. 7 on the economic outlook for 1972 based on the annual economic reports to Congress by the President and the Council of Economic Advisers (CEA) Jan. 27.

Proxmire described the CEA report as "very honest, realistic," but expressed reservations about (1) the Administration budget policy, which he did not believe was stimulative enough to cut unemployment adequately, and (2) for the forecast that the unemployment rate would be reduced to "the neighborhood of 5%" of the labor force by the year end.

Testimony covering a wide range of national and international economic problems was heard Feb. 7 from CEA Chairman Herbert Stein and CEA member Ezra Solomon, Feb. 8 from George P. Shultz, director of the Office of Management and Budget (OMB), Feb. 9 from Federal Reserve Board Chairman Arthur F. Burns, and Feb. 16 from Treasury Secretary John B. Connally Jr.

Among the key topics:

Unemployment—The joint prepared statement presented Feb. 7 by Stein and Solomon focused on unemployment. They said, "the choice of means to reduce unemployment must be influenced by the existence of . . . other objectives . . . [including] reasonable price stability, a balance in our international economic position, and an increase in productivity." They forecast a 6% increase in real demand and output between calendar years 1971 and 1972 would reduce the unemployment rate by the end of 1972 "to the neighborhood of 5%."

Much of the joint statement concerned the new concentration of unemployment among women and young persons. Although the reported unemployment rate of persons 16–21 in 1971 was 15%, the proportion of the total population in this age bracket was only 8%, including many in school looking only for part-time work.

Stein said the government planned to spend $5.1 billion on manpower programs in fiscal 1973, a 20% increase over spending in fiscal year 1972 and double the amount spent in fiscal 1970. He opposed a bill backed by House Democrats to create 500,000 public service jobs.

During testimony Feb. 16, Proxmire confronted Secretary Connally with an internal Treasury report authored by Herman Liebling, the Treasury's top staff economic forecaster. The report concluded that "over the next few years the 4% unemployment rate as a national goal is not feasible without significant inflation." Connally stood by the 4% unemployment goal (the level at which the Administration considered the economy to be in a state of "full employment"), although he conceded it would be "extremely difficult" to attain without reviving strong inflationary pressures. He indicated that a 5.3% unemployment rate at the end of 1972 would be satisfactory.

Economic growth—Burns Feb. 9 called for a "resumption of rapid productivity" to spur significant wage hikes, larger profit margins, price declines and a more advantageous competitive position abroad. His assessment of chances for economic recovery in 1972 were generally optimistic. He said "real" economic growth might top Administration forecasts of a 6% improvement and permit unemployment to "diminish" faster than expected.

Countering Proxmire's contention that recent statistics provided no evidence of any "pattern for a vigorous recovery," Connally said Feb. 16 that 1972 would be a "year of strong economic expansion."

Budget deficit—In testimony Feb. 9, FRB Chairman Burns said that the "sheer size" of the projected fiscal 1972 budget deficit of $39 billion "gives me some pause," but he said it was "crucial" to bring future budgets back into a "more balanced fiscal position."

"To maintain the public confidence," Burns said, "that is so vital to the achievement of faster economic expansion, I consider it crucial to make tangible progress toward a more balanced fiscal position in the 1973 budget and beyond . . . I would urge . . . that the Congress impose a rigid ceiling on fiscal 1973 expenditures . . . to be treated as inviolate except in the event of a grave national emergency . . . ."

In view of the large budget deficit projection, Burns counseled that "an unduly expansive monetary policy would be most unfortunate." He nevertheless promised that the Federal Reserve would feed an adequate supply of money and credit into the economy to finance more consumer spending and investment plans as a means to bolster the economy. He said that the Federal Reserve was determined to prevent a "renewed inflationary spiral."

OMB Director Shultz emphasized Feb. 8 the obligation of the legislative and executive branches of government to control spending. He defended the "full employment" budget concept as a means to impose discipline on government outlays: "Fiscal stimulation remains high so long as it is needed. As the need for stimulation decreases, the actual stimulation diminishes. In this way the stimulus remains as long as excessive unemployment persists but is

automatically turned off as soon as the effects of stimulation begin to lead to inflation." He urged Congress to legislate a mandatory ceiling of $246.3 billion on budget outlays. He rejected a proposal that key Congressional committees help decide what items should be cut from the budget if the total exceeded the ceiling, saying the decision should be the sole responsibility of the President.

Wage-price controls—Burns said Feb. 9 that the "special immunities" of labor unions should be curbed. He added he had "most reluctantly" concluded that Congress should legislate compulsory arbitration for labor disputes involving the national interest. He urged the Pay Board to "resist pressures to reach compromises in specific cases that threaten to undermine its overall objective." The Price Commission, however, should retain its flexibility to permit "confident and constructive business behavior."

(According to figures disclosed in testimony by Connally Feb. 16, new wage settlements [not deferred increases or retroactive payments] approved by the Pay Board showed an average increase of 4.5%.)

Interest rates—Burns said Feb. 9 recent Federal Reserve policy to expand bank reserves had helped to push interest rates, especially short-term rates, downward. Both Burns and Stein forecast that short-term rates would begin to rise as the economy picked up. Burns made it clear he did not want to see currently higher long-term rates rise any further. He pledged that the Federal Reserve's interest and dividends committee would continue to "nudge interest rates down" where possible.

Burns criticized former Treasury Undersecretary Robert Roosa who was quoted by The Washington Post earlier in the week as saying that the Federal Reserve had "torpedoed" the Smithsonian monetary accord Dec. 18, 1971. Roosa had accused the Federal Reserve of allowing interest rates to fall too low, lowering incentive to rechannel dollars back to the U.S. from Europe.

Burns conceded that the "re-flow" had been limited, but said the countries participating in the Smithsonian talks understood that they would have to "accumulate additional dollars" since there was to be no dollar convertibility into gold and it "was expected" that the U.S. balance of payments deficit would persist.

Business Council fears inflation. A statement issued Feb. 17 in Washington by economic advisers of the private Business Council voiced "strong concern" that the Administration's present fiscal and monetary policies would stimulate the economy towards "more rapid inflation later this year and in 1973." The economists were connected with companies represented on the council, some 100 major U.S. corporations.

The economists predicted that the real Gross National Product would rise by 5%-6% in 1972 and that inflation would continue at a 3%-4% annual rate.

Martin scores deficit spending. The Administration's fiscal policy came under fire Feb. 24 from the Federal Reserve Board's former chairman, William McChesney Martin Jr. Addressing a meeting of the Conference Board in New York, Martin said, "We have engaged in fiscal stimulus which is so far in excess of any reasonable requirement that it borders on the irresponsible."

Study finds need for tax rise. A Brookings Institution report May 24 found the federal government "overcommitted" in current budget programs and facing a $17 billion shortfall by fiscal 1975 even assuming a prosperous economy. The study concluded that "lasting new federal initiatives can be financed only with a tax increase."

The $17 billion deficit could be expected, according to the study, in the context of a $300 billion federal budget for fiscal 1975 even if Congress enacted only programs proposed by President Nixon and no other additions. Legislation then before Congress for increased Social Security benefits could by itself "use up" regular revenue growth of the budget through fiscal 1977, according to the study.

These conclusions were reached even with possible lower defense spending, the study using a minimum defense budget of less spending than projected by the Administration. According to the Washington Post May 25, the suggested defense cutbacks ranged up to $13 billion a year.

In fact, "the total sums involved [in possible expenditure reductions] are small compared to the cost of new programs" already proposed, the study said. The study pointed out that the prospect of budget reduction was further clouded by Congress' past reluctance to cut back traditional subsidy programs.

Two major pessimistic findings of the study: federal spending on civilian programs had been rising since 1966 faster than revenues, and budget programs for major domestic problems too often led to "dead ends" because of uncertainty about the proper solution and insufficient funding or both.

Neither the Administration plan nor the House Ways and Means Committee plan for revenue sharing, the study found, would confront the main problem of the revenue "crisis" of the central cities, which would receive relatively little help under either plan with funding spread among state and local jurisdictions.

The Brookings study also pointed out that alternatives to the burdensome local property tax, currently financing elementary and secondary schools, were facing an insurmountable problem of finding a fair distribution formula.

Nixon prefers budget discipline—John D. Ehrlichman, the President's chief adviser on domestic affairs, said at a news conference May 25 the Administration was "committed to cutting expenditures rather than increasing revenues through more taxes."

The policy directive from President Nixon, he said, was "to button down." This tack would apply to the fiscal 1974 budget, Ehrlichman said, in stressing the Administration's opposition to any federal tax increase "for the forseeable future." Ehrlichman said some form of taxation, such as a value-added tax, could be substituted, however, for "unfair and regressive" local property taxes.

Ehrlichman said many of the domestic programs begun in the Johnson Administration were "fit for repeal" because they offered little or no "payoff" for the tax dollar. As an example, he cited the Model Cities program.

Ehrlichman cited other budgetary areas where reductions could be made— in social service programs, where costs could be shifted to state and local governments, and in defense programs, in the event a limit on strategic arms was reached.

George P. Shultz struck the same note before the Senate Finance Committee May 25, that the Administration was pushing for budget "discipline" rather than tax increases. "Before we have anything to say about the possibility of higher taxes," he said, "we must do everything we can to bring outlays under control." Shultz appeared at a confirmation hearing on his nomination as Treasury secretary, which the panel endorsed.

Federal debt ceiling raised. The Nixon Administration asked Congress Jan. 25 for a $50 billion increase in the national debt ceiling. Under pressure of the $64.3 billion total budget deficit forecast for fiscal 1972–73, the Treasury requested an increase in the temporary ceiling on the federal debt to $480 billion through June 30, 1973. The current temporary ceiling of $400 billion would be retained.

The actual debt subject to limitation was $426.55 billion as of Jan. 20, and it was expected to total $479.93 billion by the end of fiscal 1973.

The $50 billion increase was the largest ever sought by the executive branch, and Treasury Secretary John B. Connally was challenged on the issue at a House Ways and Means Committee hearing Jan. 31. Members of both parties cited the apparent need to raise federal taxes soon to cover the huge impending deficits. But Connally insisted that a tax increase in 1972 or 1973 was "not inevitable" if Congress would not spend more than proposed by the President in his budget.

The committee Feb. 3 voted unanimously in favor of a $20 billion temporary increase in the debt ceiling, expiring June 30. This decision was approved March 15 by 237–15 House vote and 55–33 Senate vote.

Senate-House conferees had deleted March 9 a Senate provision setting a fiscal 1973 spending limit of $246.3 billion, Nixon's budget estimate, but excluding debt service, Social Security payments and any legislative appropriations exceeding Administration requests.

The Administration June 2 then asked Congress to provide a $465 billion debt ceiling through February 1973. Congress, in a last-minute move June 30, voted instead to extend the $450 billion ceiling until Oct. 31.

Treasury Secretary George P. Shultz and Casper W. Weinberger, director of the Office of Management and Budget, appeared before the Senate Finance Committee June 28 to urge passage of the bill before the deadline. Weinberger said "there is enough disenchantment with public institutions without any kind of spectacle as would be afforded by a country without a debt ceiling" after June 30.

Both the Senate and the House defeated attempts to attach additional riders to the debt ceiling bill. The Senate June 30 defeated efforts to include other limitations on federal expenditures and to force the release of impounded highway construction funds.

Foreign aid. The foreign aid authorization for fiscal 1972 was passed by 203–179 House vote Jan. 25 and signed by President Nixon Feb. 7.

Nixon protested, however, that Congress had set the funding authorizations "below minimum acceptable levels" and had attached to the bill an "unprecedented number of restrictive and nongermane amendments, some of which raise grave constitutional questions."

Congress had approved an authorization level of $2.752 billion for fiscal 1972, of which $1.518 billion was for military assistance. The total was $800 million less than the President's budget request. The bill also authorized $984 million in fiscal 1973 for economic aid.

Further Congressional resistance to the foreign aid program was indicated Jan. 25 by Senate Democratic Leader Mike Mansfield (Mont.), who told a Senate Democratic caucus that the program had become "largely an irrelevant exercise in government spending." The group's policy committee, he said, was "actively considering suggestions which range from reduction to elimination of foreign aid."

The aid measure carried amendments that called, among other things, for (a) a $341 million ceiling on military and economic aid to Cambodia, (b) a ban against aid to Pakistan except for food and humanitarian assistance through international agencies, (c) the earmarking of $250 million for relief of East Pakistani refugees, (d) a curb against aid to Greece without a presidential declaration that it was in the national interest, (e) a 15% cut in U.S. military missions abroad, (f) the recipient nation to pay 10% of the value of aid in its own currency and these funds to be used for educational and cultural exchange purposes, (g) Congress to be notified if the Administration shifted funds from one country to another, and (h) release of some $2.8 billion in impounded funds for domestic programs by April 30 or a withholding of the foreign aid funds.

A bill appropriating $2,618,221,000 for fiscal 1972 foreign aid was passed by 213–167 House vote Feb. 24 and 45–36 Senate vote March 2 and was signed by Nixon March 9.

The bill provided $1.45 billion for military aid programs—$500 million for military grant aid, $550 million for security-supporting assistance and $400 million for military credit sales funds. $50 million in security-supporting assistance and $300 million of the foreign military credit sales funds were earmarked for Israel.

The bilateral economic aid program was funded with a total of $1,168,-221,000.

With $571,216,000 appropriated for related international programs, the bill's total appropriations were $3,189,437,000. The related programs covered the Peace Corps, which received $72 million; the Inter-American Development Bank, which was allotted $211,760,000; and the World Bank, whose share was set at $123,050,000. International organizations were funded at $127 million, including $86 million for the United Nations Development Fund. The final bill also provided $200 million for relief of Bangla Desh refugees and $12,500,-000 for the Overseas Private Investment Corporation.

The $3.2 billion total appropriation was $1.2 billion less than the Administration's fiscal 1972 budget request.

A sense of Congress statement was appended to the bill in favor of having the U.S. share of funds to the International Atomic Energy Agency reduced to no more than 31.5% of total IAEA contributions.

The final version of the bill emerged from a Senate-House conference committee Feb. 22 without the signature of the leader of the Senate conferees, Sen. William Proxmire (D, Wis.), who objected to the military aid figures as too high and the Peace Corps and multilateral assistance figures as too low.

Rural development plan starts. President Nixon sent Congress a special message Feb. 1 proposing a $1.3 billion credit program to foster economic growth in rural America and stem migration to the cities. Despite expenditures of nearly $1 billion annually on rural development programs, the President said, "the problems have continued to grow."

A modified version of the proposal, dubbed the Rural Development Act of 1972, was passed by 339–36 House vote July 27 and unanimous Senate vote Aug. 17 and signed by Nixon Aug. 30.

The bill authorized $500 million in grants and loans for commercial and industrial development in areas with populations under 10,000 and for cost sharing provisions for water quality and conservation measures under the Farmers Home Administration.

Dollar devalued, gold price up. Treasury Secretary John B. Connally Jr. sent Congress legislation Feb. 9 to devalue the dollar by raising the official price of gold from $35 to $38 a fine ounce. The bill had been delayed while the U.S. worked out major trade accords, announced the same day, with the European Common Market and Japan. The U.S. had committed itself to devalue the dollar in the monetary accord reached Dec. 18, 1971.

The measure, dubbed the Par Value Modification Act, was passed by 86–1 Senate vote and 342–43 House vote and was signed by President Nixon April 3.

In his letter to Congress, Connally

noted that the 7.89% devaluation of the dollar (raising the price of gold 8.57%) represented an average 12% depreciation weighted against the new, higher parities and volume of trade with other countries.

Nixon said in a statement released in conjunction with the signing that devaluation "cannot—and does not—stand alone" in the fight to reform the world trade and monetary systems.

He said the devaluation "is a basic point of departure in working toward a new international economic stability . . ." He added that the "strength and competitiveness of our economy also depend on our success in dealing with inflation at home."

The devaluation became official May 8 after the International Monetary Fund (IMF) formally announced the reduction in the parity of the U.S. dollar to 0.818-513 grams of fine gold from 0.888671 grams.

The U.S. Treasury had officially notified the IMF of the reduced official parity of the dollar May 5. The U.S. announcement had been delayed until the Senate May 5 had approved a House-passed bill appropriating $1.6 billion to compensate the IMF and other international financial institutions for the loss in the value of their dollar holdings stemming from devaluation.

Prices, Wages & Controls

AFL-CIO to report all price rises. The AFL-CIO announced Jan. 3 it would report every retail price rise to the Internal Revenue Service for checking out possible stabilization violation.

The federation, which had instituted a "watchdog" operation on pricing, took the action, according to Leo Perlis, head of the operation, because Price Commission rules were "so elusive."

"Employers are seeing to it that wage controls are enforced, but it is easy to evade the price guidelines," he said. "Maybe our action will force the Administration to assign enough people to allow the revenue service to do the job properly."

C. Jackson Grayson Jr., chairman of the Price Commission, proposed Jan. 11 that consumers boycott retailers who violate price controls.

Addressing a meeting in Washington of AFL-CIO price monitors, Grayson said there were "clear indications" that the board's policies had taken hold "to slow inflation down to break the fever."

Price-posting suits filed. The Cost of Living Council (CLC) announced Jan. 22 that the Justice Department had filed suits against 67 companies on charges of failure to post proper lists of the highest prices charged during the wage-price freeze. One suit was later dropped after discovery that the store did not have the annual sales volume necessary to be covered by the requirement.

Another 28 price-posting suits were filed Jan. 30.

The CLC Jan. 18 had announced a drive by the Internal Revenue Service (IRS) to check retail price-posting. It promised legal action against the "bulk" of violators.

In a report from the IRS Jan. 17, "roughly" 60%–70% of 36,000 stores spot-checked since Jan. 1 had been found to be in violation of price posting regulations, failing to display base prices or displaying them incorrectly. But of 1,144 establishments inspected Jan. 17, only 173 "potential" violations were reported.

Part of the reduction in violations from the early spot-checks and Jan. 17, when the violation rate was 15%, was attributed to a Jan. 15 Price Commission ruling exempting retail stores and businesses with annual revenues under $200,-000 from the requirement to post signs listing price information. The requirement for providing price information upon request was not lifted.

Restaurants exempted from posting— The IRS ruled Jan. 18 that restaurants were not required to post base prices since they were "service organizations" rather than retailers of food.

Pay Board rejects aerospace pact. The Pay Board Jan. 5 rejected aerospace contracts on the grounds their 51¢-an-hour (12%) wage increase was "unreasonably inconsistent" with objectives of the Economic Stabilization Act and "contrary" to board standards. The rejection of the aerospace contracts, covering more than 100,000 workers in five companies and two unions, forced them into renegotiation.

The board's action was by a 9–5 vote, with the labor members in the minority. They considered the increase to include 34¢ as a "catch up" due from cost-of-living provisions. A court challenge of the decision was being considered by labor, whose board members in a statement Jan. 5 denounced "certain business and so-called public members of this board" for trying to use the board "to frustrate and destroy the collective bargaining process."

The board Jan. 13 imposed an 8.3% ceiling on the aerospace industry's first-year wage increases. It said that previous cost-of-living agreements in the industry justified an increase in excess of the 5.5% guideline.

The board approved a 34¢ hourly raise the first year as justified by cost-of-living increases since 1968, and it sanctioned payment of the additional 17¢ an hour during the contract's second year. Counting the contracts' provision of a 3% raise in the second year, the increase would total 6.98%. The contracts called for another 3% in the third year.

The board's aerospace decision was by an 8–2 vote with all five labor members abstaining and all five public members supporting the decision. Two business members voted against it.

The presidents of the unions involved in the contracts being considered— Leonard Woodcock of the United Automobile Workers and Floyd E. Smith of the AFL-CIO International Association of Machinists—were members of the Pay Board and abstained in the voting.

The companies involved were North American Rockwell Corp., McDonnell Douglas Corp., Boeing Co., Lockheed Aircraft Corp. and LTV Aerospace Corp.

Recovery of frozen wages. The Pay Board Jan. 13 approved retroactive payment of wage increases frozen during the 90-day wage-price freeze that ended Nov. 14, 1971.

Payment of increases of up to 7% would be permitted in general, and the full increase was authorized if prices or taxes had been raised to cover the wage boosts.

Rail pay increases approved. The Pay Board Jan. 25 approved by an 8–5 vote two pay increases totaling more than 10% for 180,000 members of the United Transportation Union (UTU). The increases, due in April and October, were approved on condition that it could be shown at that time that work-rule changes agreed to by the unions were being put into effect.

On other wage increases due under the UTU pact, the board approved payments of 4% on April 1, 1971 and 5% on Oct. 1, 1971, to be paid retroactively, and took no action on a combined 5% increase due in 1973.

After the board's action, the UTU and the National Railway Conference Jan. 27 signed the contract agreement, which had been reached in August 1971.

U.S. Steel cuts prices. The U.S. Steel Corp. announced Jan. 5 it was rolling back some price increases because of competitive market conditions. In December 1971, the firm had been granted an average price increase of 3.6%. It later raised prices on some products an average 7.7% within the overall 3.6% guideline.

Its key price reduction was $5 a ton less (3%) for hot-rolled and cold-rolled sheets, products used for making automobiles and appliances.

Several other steelmakers indicated later Jan. 5 their intention to remain "competitive" in pricing.

Price-rise approvals for big firms. The Price Commission Jan. 6 detailed a new procedure for price increase approvals for tier one companies, those with sales of $100 million a year or more. Firms with sales of this volume had been required to seek advance approval for price rises. The new rule would permit them to raise prices by 2% or less over a year period with quarterly reports submitted to the commission, which could then apply its guidelines to infractions.

Price Commission officials reported Jan. 7 that 33 of the nation's largest corporations had pledged to hold their average price increases to 2% or less during the next 12 months (and thus were eligible for new simplified reporting procedures).

Later, the Cost of Living Council (CLC) Jan. 18 exempted multi-industry companies with annual sales in a single line of less than $100 million from the requirement to obtain advance approval for price increases.

Mail rates exempted from control. Postal rate increases were exempted from control by the Cost of Living Council Jan. 8. The council approved a Postal Service request for a rise in third-class mail rates of 23.9%, effective Jan. 24.

Future mail rate increases were to be reviewed by the Postal Rate Commission to assure conformity with the council's anti-inflationary standards.

The commission proposed June 5 that a $1.45 billion rate increase, in effect on a temporary basis since May 1971, be reduced by $78.3 million. But the commission let stand the increases requested for first class, airmail and postcards. The rates were made permanent July 6 after the Postal Service announced June 29 that it accepted the commission's recommendations.

The 5.5% cutback would result from a 9% rate reduction in second class mail, an 8% cutback in third class mail costs, a 16% decrease in fourth class mail rates and a refusal to increase postcard costs from 6 cents to 7 cents as requested by the Postal Service. Approval of the largest rate boost in U.S. history left the Postal Service with a fiscal 1972 deficit of $9.9 million, according to the Wall Street Journal June 6.

The Journal reported that magazine and newspaper publishers were especially critical of the second class postal rate increases, which Osborn Elliott, editor of Newsweek magazine, said posed "a threat to the health of many magazines and to the survival of some."

Stephen Kelly, president of the Magazine Publishers Association, and Andrew Heiskell, chairman of Time Inc., called on Congress to set limits on the size of postal rate increases, the Journal reported.

The Postal Service said Aug. 28 that it was dropping a planned $450 million postal rate increase because of a successful cost control program.

The budgeted rate increase would have raised first class postage from 8¢ to 9¢.

Postmaster General Elmer T. Klassen said that a hiring freeze in effect since March and an early retirement program had reduced the work force by 33,000 and saved the mail service more than $300 million.

2nd car-price rise granted. A second round of price increases on 1972 automobiles was approved by the Price Commission Jan. 12 to cover costs of new safety devices and antipollution equipment. Price increase grants included .9% to General Motors Corp., 1.07% to Ford Motor Co. and .83% to American Motors Corp. Chrysler Corp., which had been permitted a 4.5% price rise previously but imposed only 3%, was to raise prices within the remaining 1.5% for the new equipment.

The commission had approved a first round of price rises in November 1971.

Some rental, retail controls lifted. The Cost of Living Council (CLC) exempted from price controls Jan. 19 about 40% of the rental units in the country and 75% of the retail firms, those with annual sales under $100,000. The order did not apply to service establishments. The small firms affected by the order accounted for only 15% of the country's total retail sales.

The rent decontrol also applied to small units. The CLC acted in both instances because the enforcement burden was great and the impact on inflation minimal in these areas. The CLC expected restraint to be imposed on the small units from "competition in the marketplace." The large firms with their great impact on inflation would also come under sharper enforcement scrutiny.

The rental units exempted from price controls were: (a) luxury apartments renting for $500 or more a month; (b) apartment buildings with four or fewer units that were owner-occupied and rented under leases running longer than from month-to-month; and (c) single-family homes renting for longer than month-to-month where the landlord owned four or fewer units.

Witnesses speaking for tenants urged the Rent Advisory Board at its first public hearing on rents April 14 to freeze rent increases because tenants were being squeezed between rent hikes and wage freezes. The spokesmen for the tenants included Sens. Jacob K. Javits (R, N.Y.) and Clifford Case (R, N.J.). Spokesmen for both tenants and landlords testified to the complexity and confusion of the rent guidelines.

Rent rule revised—The Price Commission May 18 issued a new regulation setting a ceiling of 8% on rent increases for certain tenants—those whose leases were for more than a year's period and who signed them since Dec. 29, 1971. The ruling was expected to apply to about 5% of all tenants nationally.

The rule required landlords to offer tenants an option of a new lease of one year with the 8% ceiling or a lease of at least the previous length at the higher rent allowable under the previous rule. The 8% ceiling could be exceeded only to pass on increases in property taxes and municipal service costs.

The Rent Advisory Board announced Aug. 18 that it was setting an Aug. 31 deadline for landlords to offer tenants the option.

Pay policy changes. The Pay Board Feb. 8 revised its policy on merit increases to apply to union as well as nonunion wages. The policy limited annual raises to 5.5%.

The board announced Feb. 9 a requirement for advance notification to it of pay increases due in the second or later years of multiyear labor contracts affecting 1,000 or more workers if the increases exceeded 7%. The notification would have to be accompanied by justification for the excess. The existing contracts would be permitted to take effect unless challenged by interested parties of five members of the board on the ground that the increase was "unreasonably inconsistent" with the board's general guidelines.

Guideline flexed for fringe benefits. The Pay Board announced Feb. 23 it would allow annual increases in fringe benefits equal to .7% of total compensation in

excess of its standard wage guidelines. In cases where fringe benefits had not been raised during the past three years, the board would permit catch-up increases totaling up to 1.5% beyond its basic wage guidelines.

The basic guidelines condoned a 5.5% wage increase and, in some cases, up to 7% annually. Thus, the wage-fringe guideline would permit increases up to 6.2%, 7.7% or 9.2% (the new allowances of .7% plus 1.5% catch-up, starting with the special cases permitted a 7% basic wage raise).

In the catch-up provision, the board would permit employers who had raised fringe benefits less than 1.5% during the past three years to give the difference in added benefits without counting against the guideline.

To encourage fringe benefit plans, the board allowed a further exemption from the general pay guideline in cases where employer expenditures for fringe benefits amounted to less than 10% of total compensation costs. In such cases, additional fringe increments would be allowed within that 10% ceiling, up to a maximum increment of 5%.

The board permitted exemptions from its general guidelines for many employe-incentive plans, such as plant-wide productivity sharing programs and individual incentive plans. Newly instituted plans would have to be reported to the board prior to becoming effective for certification that they properly fell within the exempt category.

The ruling on fringe benefits was adopted without support from the board's five labor members, who abstained from the vote. They were against specifying any curbs on fringe benefit increases.

N.Y. phone strike settlement. A seven-month, statewide strike by plant craftsmen against the New York Telephone Co. ended Feb. 18. About 32,000 workers were involved, members of 23 locals of the AFL-CIO Communications Workers of America which had rejected the union's national settlement with the Bell System in July 1971.

A new three-year pact providing a basic pay raise of 33½%, effective upon the return to work, was ratified by the New York locals Feb. 16. They obtained beyond the national settlement an additional \$1-\$1.50 a week and improvement in various benefits.

The Pay Board April 25 approved the contract's provision of a 15.3% raise in the pact's first year. Although the phone increase exceeded the Phase Two guidelines, it was comparable to the national wage settlement that took effect before the wage freeze.

Dock settlement terms cut. West Coast longshoremen returned to work Feb. 21 and ended a 134-day strike, the nation's longest dock walkout. A tentative settlement had been ratified by members of the striking International Longshoremen's and Warehousemen's Union (ILWU) Feb. 19.

Legislation to end the strike and provide arbitration of the dispute, cleared by Congress Feb. 9, was signed by President Nixon Feb. 21 as a symbolic gesture. The signing, which had been delayed to encourage voluntary agreement, was announced by Labor Secretary James D. Hodgson, who said that "unless unknown or unexpected developments" occurred the legislation would "have no force and effect." The President appealed again for Congress to pass legislation to deal with major transportation work stoppages.

The new contract, extending until July 1, 1973, provided for a total increase in the wage base from \$4.28 to \$5.40 an hour. It also called for a guarantee of 36 hours weekly pay for more than 9,000 full-time workers and 18 hours weekly pay for more than 4,000 part-time workers. Another key item in the pact was a \$1 "tax" paid by the employers for every ton of containerized dock cargo handled by non-ILWU members.

The Pay Board decided March 16 to cut the negotiated wage increases sharply.

The board's decision came in an 8-5 vote, with all five labor members voting against the wage cut.

The board said new calculations showed that the settlement amounted to a 20.9% increase in wages and benefits in the first year of a two-year contract.

Even as they rejected the dock settlement, the board voted their approval of a contractual agreement that would give longshoremen an increase in wages and benefits that totaled 14.9%:10% for pay and fringe benefits and 4.9%

in fringe benefits that were not covered by the board's controls.

Pay Board Chairman George H. Boldt said the rollback was consistent with the drive of "winding down this stubborn inflation."

The labor members of the board denounced the decision as the product of an "unholy alliance" between the board's public and employer members. According to the board's labor representatives, the rejection of the settlement would mean an average loss of \$1,150 to each of 15,000 West Coast dock workers over the next year and a half.

The majority on the board said the 10% increase in pay and benefits reflected "a special exception," with 3% approved to reflect productivity gains made through collective bargaining. The full 4.9% in "excludable fringes" was approved, the majority said, because it was needed to help promote the workers' on-the-job efficiency.

The Pay Board decision was accepted by the ILWU and Pacific Maritime Association May 15.

In another action affecting dockworkers, the Pay Board, with only labor's representative in opposition, had voted by 6-1 May 8 to trim a 15% wage increase negotiated for East and Gulf Coast longshoremen to raises ranging from 9.8% to 12.1%.

About 50,000 longshoremen would be affected by the board's decision. Specifically, the board's order meant they would be allowed increases of up to 55¢ an hour instead of the 70¢ negotiated in their new contracts with the shippers.

The board's decision meant the Eastern dockers would get a 35¢ hourly raise plus the fringe benefits negotiated in their new contract with the shippers. The 35¢ boost and the fringe benefits, the board said, amounted to a 9.8% raise.

The board gave the New Orleans dockworkers a 12% boost. Dockers working on Gulf ports further west got an 11.4% raise.

The variations in the raises resulted in differences in current salary scales among East and Gulf port dockworkers.

The Pay Board June 6 refused an International Longshoremen's Association (ILA) appeal of the wage ruling; however, the board voted 4–2 to accept the second year pay raises of 5.7%–5.9% for East Coast dock workers on condition that union work rules were changed and the administration of the union's guaranteed annual income program was tightened.

The ILA ultimately accepted the cut.

Construction raises put off. The chairman of the Construction Industry Stabilization Committee indicated March 5 that the panel was holding up "hundreds" of deferred pay raises for construction industry workers so that it could set noninflationary patterns on a city-by-city basis throughout the U.S.

John Dunlop said, however, that it was not possible to apply the Pay Board's general limit of 5.5% for new pay raises to the construction industry.

Before President Nixon ordered a freeze on wages and prices, wages in the construction industry had been increasing by about 18% a year. Since mid-August 1971, when the freeze was implemented, the stabilization panel had cut construction industry wage increases sharply, but the raises approved were still higher than the Pay Board's 5.5% standard.

The higher-than-average construction wage increase had prompted some members of the Pay Board to express concern that continued high wage boosts approved by the stabilization committee could undermine the entire anti-inflation program.

Dunlop had said his committee's policies "as a whole represent to a corresponding degree the policies of the Pay Board." He added, however, that several factors made it impossible to impose "a set of qualitative rules on the construction industry."

Abel attacks stabilization panel— I. W. Abel, president of the United Steelworkers of America, had sent a telegram Feb. 22 to the other 14 members of the Pay Board complaining that the stabilization committee was approving wage increases for construction workers that went beyond the board's 5.5% guidelines.

In his telegram, Abel noted that while the Pay Board had set a 5.5% guideline for wage increases in 1972, the stabiliza-

tion panel had recently approved a 53% wage increase spread over three years for a painters' union in Harrisburg, Pa. Abel said "such a double standard is indefensible."

Abel said it was "absolutely essential" that the Pay Board take action "to insure quality for all sectors" in the application of wage controls.

*Detroit workers get new pact—*Construction workers in Detroit Feb. 28 accepted a two-year multicraft contract providing for wage and benefit increases of $1 an hour. That pay raise represented a 4.5% wage boost over the two years of the contract.

The two-year agreement covered 16 trades with 30,000 workers and 19 employer associations.

Price controls eased. Regulations were announced by the Price Commission March 9 to help low-profit companies improve their economic picture by raising prices at a controlled level.

Under the new guidelines, companies with sales of $1 million or more annually could raise their prices to achieve a profit of between .2% and 3% of sales, depending on each firm's capital turnover. There were 14,000–15,000 companies in that category.

In the second category, companies with sales of under $1 million could increase prices to realize a margin of profit of up to 3%, regardless of their capital turnover.

The commission did, however, put some curbs on price increases. Even if a company was suffering a loss or had low profits, the commission said, it could not raise the price of any individual product or service by more than 8%.

Price Commission tightens curbs. The Price Commission March 15 began a series of steps designed to make more restrictive the controls on prices.

Following a review of staff studies projecting the results of current price policies, the commission indicated more restrictive controls were needed to insure that its anti-inflationary goals were met.

At the center of the tighter controls was the commission's decision to reduce to 1.8% from 2% the maximum average price increase allowed over a 12-month period to large "tier one" companies that entered long-term price agreements with the commission.

Since its inception in December 1971, the term pricing system had enabled companies with sales of $100 million or more a year to agree to an average increase over a 12-month period rather than to apply to the Price Commission every time they sought to raise the price of an individual product. To date, 120 of the nation's largest concerns had agreed to hold their average price increases to 2% or less over the next year.

The new change in the term pricing system meant that all companies now choosing to enroll in the program had to limit their average price increases to 1.8%.

The commission made its decision after reviewing reports by one of its research units on the impact on the consumer and wholesale price indexes of prices not covered by the controls and of prices of utilities and other services.

Utility rate guidelines. New guidelines for regulating utility rate increases were announced by the Price Commission March 17. The commission's chairman, C. Jackson Grayson Jr., said it had been established in recent hearings that "many rate increases, some of them substantial, would clearly be necessary in order to supply continuing adequate, safe and pollution-free services."

Under the new guidelines, supervision of utility rate increases would remain with state or federal regulatory agencies. But the agencies were to develop specific stabilization regulations, based on rates of return and cost factors, that would require approval by the commission, which would then issue certificates of compliance to permit the agencies to approve the increases without review. The commission would monitor the performance of the regulator agencies and review, within a 60-day period, noncertificated rate increases granted.

The Price Commission Feb. 10 had suspended for 30 days all rate increases by privately-owned companies whose fees or schedules were set by state or federal

regulatory agencies. The ruling, applying to utilities, telephone companies and airlines, stemmed largely from public concern with rising utility rates. Since the new guidelines had not been issued within this freeze period, the commission March 8 had extended the freeze until March 25.

In a corresponding ruling, the commission also suspended a $160 million increase granted the New York Telephone Co. Feb. 3. Bell telephone companies were reported to have requested $920 million in rate increases from state regulatory panels and the parent company, American Telephone and Telegraph Co., had a $540 million increase pending before the Federal Communications Commission.

Labor Vs. Administration

AFL-CIO attacks Nixon policies. The AFL-CIO Executive Council, at its mid-winter meeting in Bal Harbour, Fla. Feb. 14–21, denounced the Nixon Administration's foreign and domestic policies.

In its economic statement adopted Feb. 19, the council said the Nixon Administration's "remedy for . . . [the] prolonged economic mess is optimistic rhetoric combined with trickle-down policies of increasing government subsidies for big business." It said the Administration a year ago had promised a "sharp" upturn but what happened was "the highest unemployment in 10 years [and] a 4.3% rise in living costs." While productivity rose, with the increase in unit labor costs "cut in half," it said, the rise in the price level continued "with only little abatement and the lion's share of the productivity gain went to profits" and other business income.

The council advocated an expanded public service employment program, a higher federal minimum wage, tax reform (it opposed a value-added tax) and a revamping of wage-price controls, which it considered too tough on wages and too easy on prices.

In a statement approved Feb. 14, the council had attacked the control program as "unfair" and "weighted" against workers, especially lower-paid workers.

AFL-CIO President George Meany criticized the Pay Board Feb. 17. He said the public was not represented on it, and he warned that there might be new dock strikes if the recently negotiated dock settlements were reduced by the board.

Labor leaders quit Pay Board. Four of the five labor members of the Pay Board resigned March 22–23. President Nixon March 23 then changed the tripartite board into a single unit with seven public members.

Announcing the change, Nixon assailed the labor leaders' walkout as "selfish and irresponsible."

Three of the labor chiefs quit March 22. They were AFL-CIO President George Meany, I. W. Abel, president of the United Steelworkers of America, and Floyd Smith, president of the International Association of Machinists.

Leonard Woodcock, president of the United Automobile Workers, joined them March 23.

Frank E. Fitzsimmons, president of the International Brotherhood of Teamsters, was the only labor member to remain on the board. Fitzsimmons said March 22 that he would stay on to "work within the system."

Nixon reacted to the labor leaders' defections by issuing an executive order restructuring the Pay Board, formerly composed of five members representing organized labor, five representing business, and five representing the public.

Under the new set-up, the five public members of the board, among them Board Chairman George H. Boldt, would remain. Fitzsimmons would also remain on the board, joined by one of the five business representatives now on the board, as yet unnamed. The other four would be dropped.

Nixon would pick the business member from among these members of the old board: Virgil B. Day, vice president of the General Electric Company; Rocco C. Siciliano, president of the T. I. Corporation, a holding company; Leonard F. McCollum, chairman of the Continental Oil Company; Benjamin F. Biaggini, president of the Southern Pacific Railroad, and Robert C. Bassett, chairman and president of the Bassett Publishing Company.

The five public members forming the nucleus of the revised board were Boldt,

Arnold R. Weber, former executive director of the Cost of Living Council; Kermit Gordon, president of the Brookings Institution; William G. Caples, president of Kenyon College, and Neil H. Jacoby, professor at the University of California, Los Angeles.

Nixon's order indicated that the labor and business members would be regarded as public members of the revised Pay Board.

Announcing the change, Nixon alluded to his past remarks that "fighting inflation must be everybody's job." "Yesterday," he said, "George Meany walked off the job." Nixon said he respected Meany as "a powerful spokesman for the nation's largest labor organization." But he pointed out that Meany's AFL-CIO accounted for only 17% of America's wage earners. Nixon then said:

"It is my responsibility to act and speak for all the people and I shall meet that responsibility. As President I cannot permit any leader representing a special interest, no matter how powerful, to torpedo and sink a program which is needed to protect the public interest."

Following Nixon's announcement, the White House released a prepared statement on the changes in which Nixon said that "all rules and regulations [of the Pay Board] remain in full force."

Nixon termed the labor walkout "a disservice to the American people." He noted that shortly after Meany and the others quit the board, the AFL-CIO Executive Council expressed dissatisfaction with the board's rejection of the West Coast longshoremen's contract settlement. The President pointed out that the Pay Board had approved a 14.9% wage increase for the dock workers, "even though it was more than double the general limit which the board had set.

"The Pay Board," Nixon said, "was right and Mr. Meany was wrong on this issue."

Nixon also rejected some labor leaders' assertions that the board's recent decisions were politically motivated. "Although a few labor leaders have chosen to reject their public responsibility and have sought to justify their action with standard political rhetoric, this Administration will not accept an 'anti-labor' label, Nixon said. "On the contrary—there can be no more 'pro-labor,' 'pro-workingman' stand than a firm decision to protect the buying power of the wage earner's dollar."

Statements on labor walkout—The three labor leaders declared March 22 that they had quit the Pay Board because it offered labor "no hope for fairness, equity or justice." At a news conference at the AFL-CIO's Washington headquarters, Meany denounced the Administration's economic policy as unfair. He accused the Administration of "flagrant favoritism" toward "big business and the banks."

President Nixon's immediate reaction came in a statement released March 22 by White House Press Secretary Ronald L. Ziegler. Nixon said he would not allow "a few labor leaders to sabotage his fight against inflation."

The resignations also prompted an immediate response from Pay Board Chairman George H. Boldt. He took issue with Meany's statement and denied there had been any attempt by the Administration to influence the board's public members. The board's record, he said, showed that there was no "sinister plot" against workers.

At the March 22 news conference, Meany announced that the federation's Executive Council had voted unanimously to end labor's participation on the board. Meany said, "we will not be a part of the window dressing for this system of unfair and inequitable government controls of wages for the benefit of business profits." "I am sure," he added, "they [the Administration] will use us as a scapegoat for the collapse of their policy." Meany said the board had been neither tripartite nor independent.

Citing labor's grievances with the board, he specifically pointed to its recent rejection of the West Coast longshoremen's contract.

A statement released by the AFL-CIO Executive Council March 22 without reservation backed the walkout of Meany, Smith and Abel. The council said that because of its "deep disbelief in and distrust of" the Nixon Administration's economic policy, it would free the AFL-CIO representatives "from any grounds for the inference of complicity in the formulation or execution" of that policy.

Leonard Woodcock, the fourth labor leader to quit the board, called on Congress March 23 to investigate what he called the "scandalous and unfair" administration of the Economic Stabilization Act. Woodcock emphasized that he was not quitting the board solely because some of its decisions had gone against labor, but because of continued inflation and Administration policy. "The Nixon game plan is to take worker money and place it in the pockets of employers through both action and inaction," he said.

Nixon said at a news conference in his office March 24 that the war on inflation "will succeed" with the cooperation of Meany and his friends "if possible, but without it, if necessary."

On the matter of Meany's resignation from the Pay Board, Nixon "respectfully" suggested he "overstepped" and possibly a majority of AFL-CIO members realized "that wage increases that are eaten up by price increases are no wage increases at all." They would remember he said, that in the past six months since Phase Two began "we have had an increase in real wages." "While we have had this one month of bad figures," he added, "and believe me I am not satisfied with bad figures, I want these food prices down—nevertheless, our wage-price controls are working. We are going to reach our goal . . . or are going to come very close to it, cutting the rate of inflation in half."

Siciliano remains on Pay Board. President Nixon completed the roster of the revised Pay Board March 28 by naming Rocco C. Siciliano, a holdover from the original board, as the sole business representative and seventh member.

Inflation Rate Declines

The Nixon Administration was able to report at least some temporary success for its anti-inflation program as the rate of inflation declined from 5.1% in 1972's first quarter to 1.8% in the second. The gross national product, adjusted to eliminate the effects of inflation, grew at a 6.5% rate in the first quarter, while in the second quarter the rate of "real" GNP was given as 9.4%, the highest rate in almost seven years. Personal income was at an annual rate of $914.7 billion in the first half of 1972, up 8% from the first half of 1971.

Price indexes up. The consumer price index rose moderately to 124.3% of the 1967 average in April, to 124.7% in May and to 125% in June.

The .1% rise of the consumer price index in June was the smallest increase since March.

The prices of several items on the index, which measured the prices of all the goods and services that an average wage earner bought in a month, rose in April, but mostly by small amounts. Food prices, for the most part, showed no change from the March levels. On a seasonally adjusted basis food prices dropped .1%. Beef and veal prices declined for the first time in four months.

Among the items that registered price rises on the April index were used automobiles, men's clothing, electricity bills, alcoholic beverages and restaurant meals.

Declining with food prices were gasoline prices and mortgage interest rates.

In May the food price index declined .1% from April but was based on a survey made in the first week of May before meat prices began to increase. However, fruit, vegetable and wholesale food price increases were reflected in the CPI rise.

Increases in clothing, used car and gasoline prices contributed to the .6% CPI rise in nonfood items. The cost of services increased .2% while the increase in property taxes was the smallest in almost a year.

Food prices were up .2%, with meat, fresh fruits and vegetables showing rises; nonfood items registered no increase in June. Service charges rose .3%.

Wholesale prices rose .3% in April, .5% in May and .5% in June to 118.8% of the 1967 average.

Industrial commodity prices, which were seen as the key barometer of inflation within the overall index, also rose .3% in April. That was a little less than the increase in February and March when industrial prices climbed .4%.

Speaking at a press conference May 5, Herbert G. Stein, chairman of the President's Council of Economic Advisers, said that movements in industrial wholesale prices constitute "the real core" of price trends. He added, "here we see just the beginning of a little tapering off" in the pace of price increases.

The rise in the overall index came despite a drop in food prices. Among the food prices that fell at the wholesale level in April were those for eggs, meat and poultry.

Industrial commodity prices rose .4% in May, paced by a 1.7% increase in lumber and wood products and a 2% hike in hides, skins and related products. The industrial commodities index, due to price hikes for lumber and hides (which were not subject to price controls until processing began) and gasoline, rose .4% in June, as it had throughout 1972.

Second-quarter indicators. The Commerce Department's composite index of leading economic indicators rose to 139.7% of the 1967 average in April, went up another 1.4% in May and reached 142.1% in June.

Seven of the eight indicators on the index available for April showed gains. Improvements were registered by stock prices, industrial-materials prices, new factory orders for durable goods, building permits, new orders for plants and equipment, the average workweek and initial claims for unemployment insurance (treated inversely).

The indicator showing negative movement was the ratio of price-to-unit labor costs, which declined for the fourth consecutive month.

Six of the 12 indicators deteriorated in May: average workweek, initial unemployment insurance claims (treated inversely), new factory orders for durable goods, contracts and orders for plant and equipment, average stock prices, and the price-labor cost ratio in manufacturing.

Consumer credit increases. Consumer installment credit climbed a record $1.44 billion in May, exceeding both April's gain of nearly $1.1 billion and the previous record high set in March of $1.36 billion, the Federal Reserve Board announced July 5.

Consumer installment credit rose by $1.33 billion in June, the fourth consecutive month of increases greater than $1 billion.

Jobless rate drops. The unemployment rate fell .4%, the greatest monthly drop since February 1965, to a seasonally adjusted 5.5% in June, the lowest rate since October 1970, the Labor Department reported July 7. (The rate had been 5.9% in March, April and May.)

Ezra Solomon, a member of the President's Council of Economic Advisers, said the improving labor pattern, caused by a smaller than anticipated increase in the size of the labor force, was spread through virtually all categories of workers by age, sex, race and occupation, a statement disputed by Sen. William Proxmire (D, Wis.), chairman of the Joint Economic Committee, who saw no job gains for the over-25 age group.

The monthly unemployment rate had also fallen in June 1971 but increased again when jobseekers just out of school were included in the index. Solomon said the employment trends were more accurately reflected in an unemployment rate drop of .2% since fourth quarter 1971.

Productivity index rises. The Labor Department announced July 27 that productivity in the nation's private sector rose at a seasonally adjusted annual rate of 6% during the second quarter. This increase brought the index of output per man hour to 112.5% based on 1967 levels.

Gains in the nonfarm sector were 5% at a seasonally adjusted annual rate. Factory productivity rose only 3.7%, a slight decrease from the 4.5% pace in the first quarter.

Construction increases. Construction contracts in May rose to a record $9.1 billion, a jump of 28% over May 1971, F. W. Dodge, a McGraw-Hill Co. division, reported June 29. The seasonally adjusted figures reached 165 based on a 1967 level of 100.

Residential building, especially in multifamily housing, showed the largest gain of 35% from the previous year but nonresidential construction was up 33%.

Dodge reported July 18 that new construction contracts at midyear were valued at $86 billion, up 8% from 1971 figures.

Economic Controls in Action

Views differ on controls. Herbert Stein, chairman of the President's Council of Economic Advisers, told the Joint Congressional Economic Committee April 14 that price-wage controls had "dramatically reduced the anxiety in the country" and had a significant impact on inflation. However, Stein conceded to the committee, which was conducting hearings on Phase Two of the Administration's economic stabilization program, there was "apparently good reason to believe that in a large number of cases the price increases have permitted an increase of profit margins beyond the standards of the [controls] system."

The committee's chairman, Sen. William Proxmire (D, Wis.), told Price Commission Chairman C. Jackson Grayson Jr. April 18 that the Phase Two program was "almost a total failure." Proxmire asserted that wholesale prices had gone up 1.8% in the six months prior to the 90-day Phase One price freeze instituted Aug. 15, 1971 and 3.5% since the Phase Two program began after the freeze.

Grayson replied that both phases of the control program must be considered together and that the rate of inflation in that time had been slowed appreciably.

New regulations to curb increases— Grayson asserted April 18 that the commission was putting new regulations into effect that would, he expected, reduce price increases by major firms by about 30%. Under rules previously used by the commission, claimed cost increases were adjusted—and generally reduced—for productivity gains, or output per man-hour. Under the new rules, to go into effect May 1, the productivity deduction would be figured on an industry-wide basis according to statistics of the Bureau of Labor Statistics.

Grayson told the committee that 95% of the firms requesting price raises had shown productivity gains smaller than the BLS figures.

According to Price Commission Executive Secretary Louis P. Neeb April 18, the panel had approved as of March 30 price increases averaging 3.2% for companies with $250 billion in annual sales. The average permissible price increase was expected to be reduced to about 2.2% under the new regulations.

The commission had issued regulations April 15 to curb the "windfall" profits of some companies and contractors. The new rules were directed at firms that had raised prices in anticipation of wage increases in labor contracts already signed, and at firms that had realized profits from reductions in labor costs.

AFL-CIO President George Meany had requested the Price Commission in a letter March 31 to require employers to reduce consumer prices by any amount of profit gained from wage cutbacks imposed under the stabilization program. At a Joint Economic Committee hearing April 20, Meany urged the Administration to impose effective controls on all prices, including food prices, or "get rid" of the current program, which was a "shambles," and limit controls "to the areas of monopoly power and a few areas of supply shortage."

Donald Rumsfeld, executive director of the Cost of Living Council, revealed April 11 that more than 20% of the firms with annual sales of more than $50 million were in apparent violation of price control regulations. The figure was based on a survey of quarterly reports that had turned up 24 possible violations out of 105 reports. Rumsfeld said unjustified increases would be subject to rollbacks and court action.

Price rollbacks ordered—Grayson disclosed April 24 that the commission had begun ordering "hundreds of millions of dollars" in price cuts after processing the reporting · firms' quarterly reports on their profit margins. In a speech before a New York meeting of the Associated Press, held in connection with the annual American Newspaper Publishers Association convention, Grayson said about 25% of the reports processed showed profit ceilings had been exceeded, and about 50% of the reports had been returned because they were incorrectly filled out. He urged those firms in violation of the profit restrictions to cut prices "voluntarily before we have to order them."

Panel sees controls failing—The Joint Economic Committee of Congress criticized the wage and price control program as ineffective and unfair May 21. Although the Republican members in a minority report found that, "on the whole

the new economic policy is succeeding," the majority of the panel concluded that the "cure is worse than the disease," that inflation was not only not being effectively curbed but built-in economic inequities were being perpetuated and augmented.

The majority said the controls program suffered from "excessive secrecy" that undermined public confidence in its effectiveness. It recommended more public hearings and release of more data submitted to the control agencies.

The majority urged removal of controls in areas "where a reasonable degree of competition prevails," except in a few areas, such as health services, where demand exceeded supply. Exemption from controls also was recommended by the panel for all concerns employing fewer than 1,000 workers and for the working poor. The committee deplored the stabilization program's $1.90-an-hour poverty wage level as too low and recommended a freeze on total executive compensation, including bonuses and stock options, of more than $200,000 a year.

It said the rent control program should either be revised or abandoned.

Productivity commission criticized—A report issued by the Joint Economic Committee July 9 charged that the National Commission on productivity had accomplished little in its two-year existence.

The report, entitled "American Productivity: Key to Economic Strength and National Survival," defined productivity as "the relation of expansion in output to the increase in inputs of resources," as well as the more standard definition of output per manhour.

In a statement accompanying the report, Sen. William Proxmire (D, Wis.), chairman of the Congressional committee, said that "since 1966, when inflation set in and policies were belatedly directed to its containment, growth in productivity—output per unit of input—has fallen to 1% compared with a growth rate of 2.6% in the preceding decade." Proxmire attributed the decline to continued high unemployment.

Administration sees controls success. The Cost of Living Council (CLC) May 20 reported progress on the economic stabilization front. It said the controls program seemed to be moving toward the Administration's goal of lowering the rate of inflation to 2%–3% by the end of 1972.

The report, an assessment of the program in the first quarter of 1972, was accompanied by a statement from President Nixon noting the "encouraging evidence that the nation continues to make progress in the battle against inflation" and "some evidence" that the bulge of inflation "was tapering off" and the impact of controls "becoming more evident."

CLC Director Donald Rumsfeld, in issuing the report, emphasized the progress during the quarter "despite food prices and the walkout by some members of the Pay Board." He said there were encouraging trends in consumer and wholesale prices, growth of workers' take-home pay and growth of employment.

OECD sees U.S. economic upturn. In a study issued July 20, the Organization for Economic Cooperation and Development (OECD) predicted a slowdown in the U.S. rate of inflation due to wage and price controls, unemployment leveling off at 5% by mid-1973 and a "significant" improvement in the balance of payments.

The semiannual study, entitled "The Economic Outlook," analyzed the economic prospects for the OECD's 23 member nations. It concluded that the opportunities for growth were "quite favorable" for most nations as a result of increased business confidence following the Smithsonian Agreements.

Energy rate curbs. The Price Commission April 5 approved average price increases of 2% for four major oil companies, with the maximum single-product increase held to 8%. The companies: Standard Oil Co. of California, Standard Oil Co. (Ohio), Continental Oil Co. and Humble Oil & Refining Co.

In a controversial move, the Federal Power Commission (FPC) announced April 6 that it would permit natural-gas producers to increase prices, particularly on new supplies, to spur exploration and offset the current short supply. An increase

in the natural gas price was endorsed April 10 by Interior Secretary Rogers C. B. Morton, who told the House Committee on Interior and Insular Affairs "we are facing a fuel and power crisis." Undersecretary of State John N. Irwin ·2d told the panel that the U.S. faced the prospect of importing half the oil it used by 1980. The new policy was adopted by the FPC Aug. 3.

The Federal Power Commission announced Dec. 12 that it would not raise the ceiling rate for natural gas sold on the interstate market. The commission instead urged producers to utilize the "optional pricing procedure" that the FPC had promulgated in August.

The FPC's policy of allowing free market forces to drive up the price of natural gas in an attempt to foster exploration and development of the fuel appeared to parallel an Administration position.

An earlier FPC decision rendered Dec. 7 limited the commission's jurisdiction over synthetic gas. The agency declared that its regulatory power over the interstate price of synthetic gas extended only to cases where natural gas had been mixed with a synthetic fuel, such as liquid naphtha.

The Federal Power Commission May 19 gave approval to a voluntary settlement by the Tennessee Gas Pipeline Co., a division of Tenneco, Inc., and its customers and state regulatory commissions, rolling back a wholesale natural gas rate increase by nearly $46 million a year. The FPC staff and the General Services Administration had contested the settlement. An increase to $140 million a year had been requested in August 1970 and put in effect March 1971. The approved rate increase to $94.3 million represented a 19.8% hike and was opposed by two FPC members as a violation of Price Commission guidelines.

Electricity costs climbing—In its annual report, issued Sept. 17, the FPC found that electricity costs for the average homeowner were higher in 1970 than at any time before 1940 and were 6% higher than 1969 costs.

Although actual costs per kilowatt hour declined from 2.7¢ to 1.53¢ from 1926–

1968, heavy electrical usage caused consumers' bills to rise.

ITT unit in violation. The Price Commission April 12 ordered Aimco Industries, Inc., a subsidiary of the International Telephone and Telegraph Corp., to refund $75,000 in price increases deemed to have exceeded allowable profit margins on its brake-shoe products. Two other firms also were ordered to roll back price increases—Browning-Ferris Industries, Inc., a solid-waste processing company in Houston, and Harvest Markets, Inc., a supermarket chain in Buffalo, N.Y.

The rollbacks were the first ordered by the commission for violations of base-profit-margin regulations.

The commission April 13 denied price increases to two other ITT companies— the ITT lamp division, which had requested an increase of 13.67%, and the Continental Baking Co., which had requested raises of 13.5% on bread and cake products.

The commission did approve April 13 six increases for other ITT units, ranging from an average .55% on auto parts for Thompson Industries to an average 5.43% on Continental's cake products sold in the Midwest and East.

Ford, Woolworth denied hikes—The commission April 24 denied, because of the profit factor, a 4.45% increase requested by Ford Motor Co. on prices for its general parts division, industrial and chemical product division, glass division and its imported Capri car line.

On April 25, the commission ordered the F. W. Woolworth Co. to roll back its restaurant and lunch counter prices to levels charged before the August, 1971 freeze. It ordered price rollbacks for the Simpson Timber Co. on the West Coast and denied a request by Sonesta International Hotels Corp. to increase prices in four of its hotels.

Other price cuts ordered—The commission ordered price cuts April 27 by a food chain, a wholesale grocery company, a supermarket and discount drug chain, and a retail drug chain; April 28 by the Continental Can Co. and American Can Co.; May 2 by a printing firm, an electronic firm and a snowmobile manufacturer.

The can company decision was a rescission of price increases previously approved by the commission, which expressed concern about the effect of rising can prices on food prices. The food chain was ordered to put into effect a triple price reduction to provide compensation to customers in the company's new fiscal year. The companies covered by the May 2 action were required to provide refunds to customers.

Rail freight rise suspended. The Price Commission asked the Interstate Commerce Commission (ICC) April 18 to suspend, pending a study, a $489 million freight-rate increase scheduled to go into effect May 1 for the nation's railroads. The ICC complied April 24, suspending the increase pending an investigation while continuing a 2.5% surcharge previously granted pending action on the higher increase.

Court upholds Pay Board ruling. U.S. District Court Judge C. Stanley Blair in Baltimore April 19 upheld a Pay Board regulation and fined a company and a union for implementing a wage agreement exceeding the board's standards. The disputed contract was between the Great Atlantic and Pacific Tea Co., Inc. and a local of the AFL-CIO Amalgamated Meat Cutters union. Both were fined the maximum federal civil penalty of $2,500. The suit, filed Feb. 24, was the first legal action brought by the Justice Department to enforce Pay Board regulations.

The wage agreement had called for wage increases of 15%–22%, and the board had ruled the increases would have to be cut back to 7%. The settlement involved 77 workers.

Controls lifted on small firms. Donald Rumsfeld, director of the Cost of Living Council, announced May 1 that business and government units with fewer than 60 employes would be exempt from Phase Two wage and price controls.

The exemption affected about 5 million firms accounting for 28% of the nation's sales and employing 19 million persons, about 26% of the nation's payroll work force. In the local government area, the exemption covered 83% of the total such units and some 7% of the total employment.

Rumsfeld said the action was taken to "eliminate unnecessary red tape" in administration and enforcement of the stabilization program and to permit the program to focus more on large units with major economic impact.

The exemption did not apply to units in the construction industry or the health services, where controls were tightened, Rumsfeld said, because of the "serious inflationary impact" from these areas. Construction firms with annual sales of $50 million or more and health-service units with sales of $10 million or more would be required to obtain prior approval from the Price Commission for price rises, a Tier One requirement heretofore applicable only to companies with sales of $100 million or more. The number of health-care firms in the Tier One category was thus increased from two to 54 and construction firms from 35 to 79.

In addition, construction firms with annual sales ranging from $25 million to $50 million and health-care firms with sales ranging from $5 million to $10 million were required to report price and wage actions and justify profit margins within the stabilization program's guidelines.

Rumsfeld also announced other steps to firm up the control program: a 34% boost in Price Commission staff to 595 persons and a 27% increase in Pay Board staff to 174 persons; a reallocation of Internal Revenue Service manpower to detail 51%, instead of the current 21%, of the 3,000 IRS agents to monitor compliance with stabilization regulations.

AFL-CIO scores exemptions—A spokesman for the AFL-CIO executive council May 2 called the exemptions for small businesses "outrageous." "It is the poor who will have to shop in exempt stores," he said, "just as it is the poor who are living in housing that was exempted previously."

Exemptions denied—The CLC May 17 denied requests from industry and union groups for exemptions from wage-price controls for broadcast advertising rates, musicians' wages and building service contractors.

CLC exempts athletes—The CLC announced its decision July 21 to exempt professional athletes, team managers and coaches from wage controls. The decision was made to avoid complications arising from teams located in Canada and "to correct the inequities which arise from imposing controls on the short earning lives which professional athletes experience relative to wage earners in other sectors of the economy."

Raises barred unless profit reported. The Price Commission May 3 suspended all price increases for about 1,500 major concerns that had not submitted profit margin reports as required. Firms with annual sales of $50 million or more were required to report their earnings regularly or certify that prices had not been raised.

The delinquent companies were given five days to comply with the reporting requirement or be subject to a rollback order from the commission for any price increases, even those already approved by the commission. Civil penalties also would be sought.

The commission also gave notification that future requests for price increases would not be considered by the panel if the firm had not submitted "acceptable profit margin reports."

The Price Commission July 30 announced plans to exempt from profit margin restrictions companies that agreed to rollback price increases imposed since the Phase One freeze and also agreed to refund the amount to customers.

$1.90 pay ceiling rejected. A federal district court in Washington, D.C. ruled July 14 that the Cost of Living Council (CLC) acted "in excess of agency authority" and in violation of the intent of Congress by exempting only wages below $1.90 an hour from Pay Board controls. The CLC had adopted the $1.90 exemption ceiling Jan. 29; it arrived at the figure by starting with a Bureau of Labor Statistics standard of an adequate annual budget in 1970—$6,690—for an urban family of four with the wage earner between 35 and 54 years, then applying adjustments for cost of living, an average of 1.7 workers per family, an average family size of 3.6, and other factors. The $1.90 figure by an 8-5 Pay Board vote Jan. 19. According to the majority opinion, the $1.90 figure was "inconsistent" with the purposes of the Economic Stabilization Act, which required action to insure that wage increases would not be denied to anyone whose earnings were substandard or who was "a member of the working poor."

The suit, affecting 14 million workers, was brought by the AFL-CIO and its affiliate, the International Union of Electrical, Radio and Machine Workers, Feb. 3.

Judge William B. Brown said that the Economic Stabilization Act of 1971, from which the CLC derived its regulatory authority, was not intended to freeze workers' wages at the poverty level. The court did not set a new floor for regulated wages, but referred to a level of $3.35 an hour, a figure selected by the Bureau of Labor Statistics as providing an adequate minimum income for an urban family of four in 1970. Organized labor had said in its brief that it was the implicit intent of Congress to exempt wages below $3.35 an hour from controls, although no specific figure was included in the legislation.

According to the Washington Post July 15, CLC selection of the $1.90 figure came after the Pay Board was unable to agree on one. The CLC decision was based partly on the fact that the $1.90 limit would exempt from controls only nine million employees, or 21% of the nonsupervisory work force, while a $3.35 cutoff would exempt 23 million workers, or more than 50% of the workforce.

CLC sets $2.75 wage ceiling—The CLC announced July 25 that wage controls would be lifted for workers earning less than $2.75 an hour, thereby exempting 10 million additional employees.

CLC Director Donald F. Rumsfeld said at a news conference that the higher exemption cutoff reflected moderate increases in the cost of living since controls were first imposed and an expectation that the minimum wage would be raised.

The International Union of Electrical, Radio and Machine Workers said July 25 that the new CLC figure was too low and that it would ask the court to set the exemption figure "in the vicinity of $3.80 an hour."

The $2.75 cutoff would release 43% of the nation's nonfarm, nongovernmental workers from the Pay Board's wage control program. When combined with the CLC's earlier exemption of workers employed in small firms, the total number exempted was 32.5 million or 56%.

Burns see stiffer curbs—In testimony before the Congressional Joint Economic Committee July 26, Federal Reserve Board Chairman Arthur F. Burns warned that it might be necessary to lower the Pay Board's 5.5% ceiling on wage increases.

Burns said inflation could be spurred by the large numbers of labor contracts to be renegotiated in 1973 and by a large deficit in fiscal 1973. Pay Board Chairman George Boldt had indicated in a speech to the National Press Club June 30 that the Board had begun a review of its policies that could lead to a tightening of the guidelines.

(The Labor Department said July 27 that average annual wage and benefit increases negotiated during the first half of 1972 declined to 7.7% from the previous level of 8.7% for all of 1971.)

Pay Board retains 5.5% limit—The Pay Board announced Aug. 14 that, after six weeks of study, it would retain its 5.5% wage increase guideline.

The Pay Board said that since November 1971 the weighted average increase of wages and salaries for nearly 13 million employes was 5%. But major unions, such as the auto workers and the steel workers, were not bargaining during 1972, and major contracts exceeding the wage raise limit were still awaiting Pay Board action and did not appear in their statistics, the New York Times reported Aug. 13.

Wage-price decontrols urged. The Committee for Economic Development recommended July 20 that the Cost of Living Council (CLC) develop guidelines and procedures for selective termination of wage-price controls.

The committee, representing large manufacturers, financiers and educators, suggested that business, labor and other groups be permitted to petition for decontrols based on the performance of wages, prices, profits and the elimination of obstacles to competition.

The committee's report, entitled "High Employment without Inflation," supported greater control of government spending and endorsed continuation of "stand-by authority for compulsory controls" in "a few sectors in which cost-push pressures are especially virulent—for example, construction."

The report said only a zero rate of inflation would be economically acceptable and recommended that limits for price increases be less than 2.5%. Among efforts to promote wage and price competition, the committee recommended that protectionism be avoided, price support for agricultural goods be replaced by direct assistance to farmers, and corporate mergers promoting productivity be permitted under an altered antitrust policy.

Lumber controls reimposed. Wage and price controls were ordered reimposed July 17 on 62,000 lumber companies that had been exempted on May 1 on the ground that they were too small. In announcing the decision, to take effect July 31, CLC Director Donald Rumsfeld said that Internal Revenue Service surveys indicated that prices charged by small manufacturers, wholesalers and retailers, who accounted for 30% of all lumber sales, had increased "considerably more rapidly" than those in big companies. Raw timber prices remained exempt from controls.

Lumber prices rose 14% during 1972 and accounted for one-fourth of the increase in the Wholesale Price Index's June rise in industrial commodities, Rumsfeld said.

Rumsfeld Oct. 3 announced "a multipurpose drive against rising lumber prices," which included antitrust investigations, Internal Revenue Service studies of pricing and profit margins of "large and small dealers" and the filing of detailed quarterly reports by lumber companies with sales above $5 million. (The usual cutoff for filing requirements was $50 million in sales.) The new filing practices would raise the number of reporting firms from 21 to 583, 30% of the industry.

Rumsfeld admitted that previous CLC action had failed to slow the lumber price rise and added, "The pressure of increased home building is driving up prices of the present limited supply of lumber to a point at which the cost of new dwellings is seriously affected."

In the first Price Commission briefing called on problems of a single industry, officials announced Nov. 20 that an investigation of 350 lumber and wood products companies was under way because evidence indicated that 30% of lumber companies with sales in excess of $5 million were illegally raising prices.

Spokesmen said the commission had also rejected a proposal that would have granted special profit margin provisions to lumber companies that had been exempt from controls during the period May 1–July 17.

The commission announced Dec. 4 that it was revoking a term-limit price agreement with a large lumber company, Southwest Forest Industries, because of violations under the price pact.

The revocation order, the first such government action regarding the commonly used pricing agreements, would require the company to roll back prices and make refunds totaling up to $1 million.

Car prices. Despite record automobile sales, the four major car makers were seeking Price Commission approval of proposed price increases. They cited rising costs caused by federally mandated pollution control devices and improved bumpers.

General Motors Corp. requested a 2% price rise, and 5% increases had been sought by American Motors Corp., Ford Motor Co. and the Chrysler Corp.

But Sen. William Proxmire (D, Wis.) said in a letter to Price Commission Chairman C. Jackson Grayson July 9 that the commission's "stubborn refusal" to obey the Economic Stabilization Act, which required public hearings on major price increases significantly affecting the economy, could result in the car price increases being declared illegal and "subject the auto industry to a rash of litigation and potential liability in excess of $1 billion."

The pending price increases were formally suspended Aug. 24. At the same time, the Price Commission approved selective price adjustments to cover the cost of optional equipment that would be standard in '73 model cars.

Grayson, in court Aug. 11, had promised public hearings on car prices. He made this pledge in response to a suit brought July 26 in federal district court in Washington by Ralph Nader and Consumers Union. The suit, which was dismissed following Grayson's disclosures, would have required the commission to hold open hearings before approving the car price increases. No public hearings had been held previously, although the Price Commission had held that authority since December 1971, according to the Washington Post Aug. 15.

The United Auto Workers (UAW) joined the consumer activists' suit Aug. 16. The UAW charged that industry productivity and profits were up sharply while unemployment in Michigan was at 10.7% in July.

UAW President Leonard Woodcock told a news conference, "We deny that labor cost-push is responsible for inflation and we would welcome public proceedings to prove that point." Woodcock also was critical of Chrysler Chairman Lynn A. Townsend's contention Aug. 16 that price rollbacks would reduce "employment in both the automobile companies and related supplier firms."

Woodcock replied, "Higher prices mean reduced sales and reduced production, and this means fewer jobs for auto workers."

At a White House news conference Aug. 18, CLC Director Donald Rumsfeld said that the Price Commission would not reach a decision on car prices until "well into October at the earliest," although new cars were scheduled to appear in mid-September.

Rumsfeld justified the Administration's action in light of its concern "not only about the specific inflationary impact" of a car price rise, but also its effect on "the public's expectations about inflation."

Under questioning, Rumsfeld indicated that the President was asserting a right to block increases that might possibly be justified under the Price Commission's guidelines.

Rumsfeld had met with representatives of the car makers in the White House Aug. 14-15 to "talk them out of price increases." The jawboning session was only partially successful, however, and forced the Administration to take its subsequent tougher stand. Chrysler Corp. and American Motors Corp. had refused Aug. 16 to withdraw their planned price increases.

Chrysler, which had asked for a $110 increase for its '73 models, charged that the Administration's efforts to obtain a price rollback were "an arbitrary and discriminatory request" that was not "compatible with the law."

American Motors refused to withdraw "voluntarily" its proposed $78 increase for federally required safety and anti-pollution equipment, although it had been reported Aug. 16 that the company would reduce by $68 its original request for a $146 price rise.

General Motors Corp. (GM) announced Aug. 17 it would reduce its requested price rise from $90 to $59, but GM Chairman Richard C. Gerstenberg said the company might be forced to apply to the Price Commission for additional increases at the end of 1972. An Administration spokesman called the GM action a "partial victory."

Of the $59 proposed increase, $54 of it would go toward the cost of federally mandated emission control devices, stronger bumpers and fire resistant fabrics. GM had separately filed with the Price Commission for another $5 increase to cover the cost of making standard equipment that had been optional. Gerstenberg claimed that GM anticipated a $200 jump in costs to the manufacturer for the new models.

The Ford Motor Co. reduced its price increase Aug. 19 from an estimated $92 to $59, following the lead of GM. But Lee A. Iacocca, Ford president, warned that "substantial upward adjustments in our price structure will be required in the near future."

Iacocca echoed other auto industry spokesmen when he declared, "What is really at stake here is how long even the healthiest company can withstand a set of government actions designed to tell you what to do, how to do it, how much time to take, and, finally, how to price it."

Chrysler reacted sharply to the GM and Ford price rollbacks. A company official said Aug. 19, "If the government was trying to turn the entire automobile business over to General Motors, this is the way to do it." He referred to the need for other car manufacturers to remain competitive in the price field, even should their larger price increases be approved by the Price Commission.

The Labor Department's Bureau of Labor Statistics (BLS) gave some support to the auto industry in a report issued Aug. 18. The BLS said the retail value of safety and quality improvements in the 1973 models was $123.80.

Sen. Robert P. Griffin (R, Mich.), a supporter of the auto industry, upheld the White House call for a price rollback. In an open letter to President Nixon, reported by the Wall Street Journal Aug. 16, Griffin cited the advantage gained in the repeal of the auto excise tax as one reason why the manufacturers should absorb some extra costs.

The Price Commission Aug. 29 rejected GM's and Ford's request for price increases on 1973 autos. The commission held that the increases could raise profit margins above the government-imposed ceiling.

Under the profit margin test, companies could pass on cost increases to customers only if the price rises did not result in higher profit margins than those of the base period, which was the average of any two of a company's last three fiscal years ending before Aug. 15, 1971.

Grayson said that Chrysler and American were not in violation of the profit margin test with their requested increases. Ford and GM were told that their first half period profits exceeded the guidelines and after seasonal adjustments, their profits, while legally acceptable, were too close to the limit to justify a price rise.

The commission Oct. 17 approved increases of 1.92% for Chrysler and 5.3% for American.

Citing competitive pressures, Chrysler said its actual car price increase would average only $20 a unit, although the company had been permitted a $60.10 hike. American announced a $38 estimated increase. The firm had been authorized to raise prices $144.28. (But Chrysler announced Dec. 6 that it would raise its markup to the full $60.10 allowed.)

The commission also ruled that the price rise was applicable only to those cars that left the factory after Oct. 16.

At public hearings Sept. 12–15, Chrysler had sought a price boost of 2.98%. American had requested a 5.5% rise.

The government acted to allow the car manufacturers to cover the costs of federally required safety and antipollution features; American was also allowed an increase to cover ordinary manufacturing costs.

Ralph Nader appeared before the hearing Sept. 14 to charge the four major car manufacturers with exaggerating the costs of installing the required safety and pollution control devices.

The Price Commission Dec. 1 authorized increases averaging $54 for GM and about $63 for Ford.

The authorization, which took effect Dec. 2, was granted on the basis of increased costs necessitated by federal standards requiring installation of new pollution control and safety devices.

Ford was denied the full $92 price increase it had requested because the added amount was also intended to cover higher general manufacturing costs. GM, whose price application did not include those extra costs, won the entire increase it had requested.

GM's first request for a price increase had been rejected by the Price Commission, which claimed the price hike would cause the company's profit margin to exceed allowable limits; however, Oct. 27 GM reported a 44% decline in profits for the third quarter ending Sept. 30, prompting the renewed request.

GM's net income for the first nine months of 1972 was $1.5 billion, 7% above 1971 levels. Company spokesmen claimed that the domestic pretax profit margin for the January-September period was below the ceiling established by the Price Commission.

In announcing the $54 requested price hike, which was intended to cover the cost of federally mandated pollution control and safety equipment, GM officials said it was willing "to forgo until January 1973 any price increase to recognize other cost increases such as labor, material, etc."

Ford had reported Oct. 27 a third quarter profit gain of 9.3% to $94.4 million, up from $86 million in September 1971. Net income (worldwide) for the January-September period increased 39% to $629.6 million from $453 million.

Although the profit margin for the first nine months of the year exceeded Price Commission limits, Ford officials denied that the profits for the full year would violate the allowable limits "even if the company was permitted to increase prices."

Chrysler Corp. Oct. 23 reported its highest third quarter profits since 1950. Earnings climbed from $6.2 million in 1971 to $31.9 million at the end of September 1972.

Net income for the first nine months was $136.1 million, up from $48.4 million reported in the same period of 1971.

American Motors Corp. announced Dec. 13 it was raising its car prices another 1.1%, an action which had already won Price Commission approval.

The Price Commission announced Dec. 14 that it was indefinitely suspending Chrysler's request to raise 1973 car and truck prices an average of 3.04%. The commission Dec. 18 also suspended GM's request of a 3% raise.

Both postponements were taken to examine the companies' cost-price data. Chrysler and GM had sought the increases to cover general economic costs for labor and materials. All four car manufacturers had received government authorization to raise prices in order to cover federally-mandated safety and antipollution features.

Canada scores GM prices—Canada's minister for industry, trade and commerce, Alastair Gillespie, charged that prices for American-and Canadian-made GM cars were 9% higher than in the U.S., while Canadian-made cars were cheaper for Americans than for Canadians to buy, according to the Wall Street Journal Dec. 6.

Gillespie asked that General Motors of Canada, Ltd., a subsidiary of the Michigan-based car manufacturer, "reconsider" its 1973 price hikes and, in a veiled threat, reminded company officials of Ottawa's proposal to reduce the corporate tax rate on manufacturing operations from 49% to 40%. The tax cut was an effort aimed ultimately at "the elimination of price differentials," Gillespie said.

Imported car prices raised—The two major importers of cars to the U.S. announced price rises for 1973 models. Volkswagenwerk AG reported Oct. 16 an increase averaging 1.7% for most cars. The $30–$110 rise was cleared by the Price Commission, company officials said.

Toyota Motor Sales, USA, Inc., a division of Toyota Motor Works, Ltd., announced price increases of $42–$155 on its 17 models of cars and trucks Nov. 19, but said it was eliminating a suggested $50 dealer preparation fee on individual cars. According to the company, the increases were within federal price control guidelines.

Ceiling on dividend hikes. The Administration announced July 27 that a 4% ceiling would be placed on increases for corporate dividends in 1973. However, firms that increased dividends by less than 4% in 1972 could add that unused sum to the 1973 increase. The rule would apply to corporations subject to the Securities and Exchange Commission with $1 million in assets and 500 common stockholders and to insurance companies with capital stock.

Inflation Growth

The U.S. seemed to be losing ground in the battle against inflation during 1972's third quarter. The inflation rate increased from a 1.8% level in the April–June period to a 2.4% rate in July–September. The growth of the gross national product, after adjustment to remove the effects of inflation, declined during the same period from 9.4% to 6.3%.

Price indexes climb. The consumer price index climbed to 125.5% of the 1967 average in July, to 125.7% in August and to 126.2% in September.

Food costs increased during July at a higher rate than other costs.

Eggs, raw fruits and vegetables, which were not subject to economic controls, rose in price. Non-food commodities increased .3% and the service price index rose by the same amount.

The price of meat rose 2.8%, up 10.1% over July 1971. But Edgar R. Fiedler, assistant secretary of the Treasury for economic affairs, predicted that meat prices would soon show a reduction because of a 13% drop in cattle prices since mid-July.

The Wall Street Journal disputed this forecast Aug. 18 and warned that meat prices would be higher by the end of 1972, despite a temporary decline in prices. The Journal said an anticipated, but temporary, drop in the retail price of meat would be due to a 14% increase over 1971 in the number of cattle being slaughtered during July and August.

According to the Journal, the recent suspension of the beef import quota had no effect on the increased supply of cattle because foreign nations were already exporting as much meat as was available. Instead, the increase in cattle was attributed to animals being sent to slaughter prematurely to take advantage of the high price of meat. Supply also grew because droughts had forced ranchers to cut back the size of herds. But recent rain and the continued high price of meat were causing cattlemen to rebuild the size of herds and keep animals off the market, the Journal said.

The Department of Labor reported that an average worker's real spendable earnings for a week increased .5% in August to $96.16 in 1967 dollar terms. The 4.1% gain in purchasing power over Aug. 1971 was a record high. Real spendable earnings were up .5% in September to $97.58 a week, an increase of 4.5% from the year before.

The wholesale price index, seasonally adjusted, rose to 119.7% of the 1967 average in July, to 119.9% in August and to 120.2% in September.

Indicators decline. The composite index of leading business indicators rose by 2.6% during August but then dropped by .2% in September. This was the first decline in two years.

Productivity growth slows. The Labor Department reported Oct. 27 that the productivity rate for the third quarter improved by 3.7% at a seasonally adjusted annual rate, a slower rate than in the second quarter, when the improvement in output per man hours was 6.2%.

Jobless rate steady. The unemployment rate continued at 5.5% in July, rose slightly to 5.6% in August and then declined to the 5.5% level in September. The 5.6% rate for 1972's third quarter compared with the second quarter's 5.7% level.

There were 4.7 million workers without jobs and 82 million employed during September. The number of people at work increased by 250,000.

Arthur Okun, an adviser for Democratic presidential candidate George McGovern and former chairman of the Council of Economic Advisers, said the unemployment figures represented "an intolerable level of joblessness" which was especially acute for skilled workers.

The National Labor Committee for the Election of McGovern-Shriver, in a statement issued Oct. 6, noted that the unemployment rate was 3.3% when the Nixon Administration took office and added, "This is a fact that should not be fuzzed over in the Administration glee over a .1% drop in unemployment one month before the presidential election."

Median family income tops $10,000. The median income of U.S. families was $10,285 in 1971, the Census Bureau announced July 17. The figure, based on a March 1972 national survey, exceeded $10,000 for the first time, but the report showed that the $418 increase over 1971 was erased by inflation. The 1970 median income figure of $9,867, adjusted by "constant dollars" of equal purchasing power in 1971 terms, was $10,289, four dollars more than a year later. Between 1961 and 1971, the median income rose 79% from a base of $5,737.

The Census Bureau also reported that the number of persons classified as poor in the U.S., 25.6 million, remained unchanged from 1970. In 1971 13% of U.S. families had incomes below the official poverty level of $4,-137 for an urban family of four, about the same percentage as in 1970.

A gain was reported in the number of families earning more than $15,000, a rise from 19% in 1970 to 25% in 1971. About 5% of all families earned more than $25,000 and less than 1% earned in excess of $50,000 in 1971.

No change from 1970 was recorded in the earning ratio of full-time, all-year working men and women; the figures were $9,630 for men, $5,700 for women. The median family income where the head of the household worked full-time, year-round was $12,-440.

State budgets show deficits. State government spending in fiscal 1971 exceeded revenues by $1.6 billion, the first budget deficit in more than 10 years, the Census Bureau reported July 17. Although revenues were 9.3% higher than in fiscal 1970, expenditures rose 16.2%.

The states' largest expenditure, $35.1 billion, went to education, but spending for welfare, $16.3 billion, showed an increase of 23.3% over 1970. Highway and hospital spending comprised the third and fourth largest bloc of outgoing funds.

Policy & Politics

Congress urged to curb spending. President Nixon urged Congress in a special message July 26 to resist the "temptations to overspend for desirable social programs or to spend for partisan political advantages" and abide by a $250 billion spending limit for the fiscal 1973 federal budget. He warned he would veto "excessive" spending bills.

Congress had already exceeded his fiscal 1973 budget requests by $7 billion, he said, and warned that further action "appears to be on the way." The "inevitable result" of such action, Nixon said, would be higher taxes and higher prices. "I am convinced," he said, "the American people do not want their family budgets wrecked by higher taxes and higher prices and I will not stand by and permit such irresponsible action to undermine the clear progress we have made in getting America's workers off the inflation treadmill of the 1960s."

At a briefing on the President's message, John D. Ehrlichman, his adviser on domestic affairs, said, "We have what you would call a credit card Congress that is in the process of running up a big bill on a sort of spending-now, tax-later basis."

Federal Reserve Board Chairman Arthur F. Burns also urged Congress July 26 to "put our fiscal house in order." He told the Joint Economic Committee that if the budget deficit grew at a time when the economy was expanding "briskly," it would "add explosive fuel to the fires of inflation." Burns advocated the $250 billion spending ceiling.

The same theme was sounded by other spokesmen for the Administration. Caspar W. Weinberger, director of the Office of Management and Budget, told the committee July 27 that Congressional budget excesses could "force a huge tax increase." If Congress wanted new programs it would have to make "some deletions" elsewhere in the budget, he said, and added that "we ought to have learned by now that throwing the taxpayers' money at social problems isn't the way to solve them."

Herbert Stein, chairman of the Council of Economic Advisers, told the Congressional panel July 24 the way to prevent an "explosion of demand" was to keep "the budget from exploding."

Economists oppose spending limit— Three leading Democratic economists, in testimony before the Joint Economic Committee July 27, offered qualified praise for the Administration's economic stabilization program but opposed its proposed spending limit of $250 billion as a premature attempt to slow economic recovery.

Walter W. Heller of the University of Minnesota, Paul A. Samuelson of the Massachusetts Institute of Technology and John Kenneth Galbraith of Harvard University, all former economic advisers to the Kennedy and Johnson Administrations, appeared before the committee's hearings on midyear economic conditions.

The three economists also called for tax increases by 1974 in order to offset possible inflationary trends when full employment was restored. Although favoring greater "equity" in the tax system, the group agreed that the closing of loopholes alone would not raise sufficient additional federal revenues after 1973 to cover deficit spending.

Heller, Samuelson and Galbraith also favored more stringent price and profit controls and maintenance of some form of control mechanism when the current economic stabilization program expired in April 1973.

Samuelson testified that the Administration "can stand everything but success. In the summer of our healthy advance, they look forward to the winter of our excess." He warned of repeating the "mistakes of the sorry Eisenhower decade" when fiscal and monetary restraints were applied before economic expansion was fully underway.

Heller termed the proposed spending ceiling "economically counterproductive." Galbraith criticized the Administration for its "unconcealed preoccupation with the performance of the economy not over the indefinite future but in the last week of October and the first week of November."

The economists joined Committee Chairman William Proxmire (D, Wis.) in refuting the Administration charge that the Democratic-controlled Congress "is engaged in an orgy of profligate spending," as Proxmire declared. Heller added that the Administration had contributed to the nation's budgetary problems by its 1971 approval of $12 billion in permanent tax cuts "that the country could ill afford."

Party platforms. 1972 was a presidential election year, and both national parties included detailed statements on inflation in their election platforms.

Among excerpts from the Democratic platform, which was adopted July 11–12:

The Nixon Administration has deliberately driven people out of work in a heartless and ineffective effort to deal with inflation. Ending the Nixon policy of creating unemployment is the first task of the Democratic Party.

■ The Nixon "game plan" called for *more* unemployment. Tens of millions of families have suffered joblessness of work cutbacks in the last four years in the name of fighting inflation . . . and for nothing.

■ Prices rose faster in early 1972 than at any time from 1960 to 1968.

■ Today there are 5.5 million unemployed. The nation will have suffered $175 billion in lost production during the Nixon Administration by election day. Twenty percent of our people have suffered a period without a job each year in the last three.

■ Business has lost more in profits than it has gained from this Administration's business-oriented tax cuts.

■ In pockets of cities, up to 40 percent of our young people are jobless.

■ Farmers have seen the lowest parity ratios since the Great Depression.

■ For the first time in 30 years, there is substantial unemployment among aerospace technicians, teachers and other white-collar workers.

■ The economic projections have been manipulated for public relations purposes.

The current Nixon game plan includes a control structure which keeps workers' wages down while executive salaries soar, discourages productivity and distributes income away from those who need it and has produced no significant dent in inflation, as prices for food, clothes, rent and basic necessities soar. . . .

Economic Management. Every American family knows how its grocery bill has gone up under Nixon. Every American family has felt the bite of higher and higher prices for food and housing and clothing. The Administration attempts to stop price rises have been dismal failures—for which the working people have paid in lost jobs, missed raises and higher prices.

This nation achieved its economic greatness under a system of free enterprise, coupled with human effort and ingenuity, and thus it must remain. This will be the attitude and objective of the Party.

There must be an end to inflation and the ever-increasing cost of living. This is of vital concern to the laborer, the housewife, the farmer and the small businessman, as well as the millions of Americans dependent upon their weekly or monthly income for sustenance. It wrecks the retirement plans and lives of our elderly who must survive on pensions or savings gauged by the standards of another day. . . .

A first priority of a Democratic Administration must be eliminating the unfair, bureaucratic Nixon wage and price controls.

When price rises threaten to or do get out of control—as they are now—strong, fair action must be taken to protect family income and savings. The theme of that action should be swift, tough measures to break the wage-price spiral and restore the economy. In that kind of economic emergency, America's working people will support a truly fair stabilization program which affects profits, investment earnings, executive salaries and prices, as well as wages. The Nixon controls do not meet that standard. They have forced the American worker, who suffers most from inflation, to pay the price of trying to end it.

In addition to stabilizing the economy, we propose:

■ To develop automatic instruments protecting the livelihood of Americans who depend on fixed incomes, such as savings bonds, with purchasing power guarantees and cost-of-living escalators in government social security and income support payments.

■ To create a system of "recession insurance" for states and localities to replace lost local revenues with federal funds in economic downturns, thereby avoiding reduction in public employment or public services.

■ To establish longer-term budget and fiscal planning, and

■ To create new mechanisms to stop unwarranted price increases in concentrated industries. . . .

International Economic Policy

In a prosperous economy, foreign trade has benefits for virtually everyone. For the consumer, it means lower prices and a wider choice of goods. For the worker and the businessman, it means new jobs and new markets. For nations, it means greater efficiency and growth.

But in a weak economy—with over five million men and women out of work—foreign imports bring hardships to many Americans. The automobile or electrical worker, the electronics technician, the small businessman—for them, and millions of others, foreign competition coinciding with a slack economy has spelled financial distress. Our national commitment to liberal trade policies takes its toll when times are bad, but yields its benefits when the economy is fully employed.

The Democratic Party proposes no retreat from this commitment. Our international economic policy should have these goals: To expand jobs and business opportunities in this country and to establish two-way trade relations with other nations. To do this, we support the following policies:

■ End the high-unemployment policy of the Nixon Administration. When a job is available for everyone who wants to work, imports will no longer be a threat. Full employment is a realistic goal, it is a goal which has been attained under Democratic Administrations, and it is a goal we intend to achieve again;

■ Adopt broad programs to ease dislocations and relieve the hardship of workers injured by foreign competition;

■ Seek higher labor standards in the advanced nations where productivity far outstrips wage rates, thus providing unfair competition to American workers and seek to limit harmful flows of American capital which exploit both foreign and American workers;

■ Adhere to liberal trade policies, but we should oppose actions and policies which harm American workers through unfair exploitation of labor abroad and the encouragement of American capital to run after very low wage opportunities for quick profits that will damage the economy of the United States and further weaken the dollar;

■ Negotiate orderly and reciprocal reductions of trade barriers to American products. Foreign nations with access to our markets should no longer be permitted to fence us out of theirs;

■ Support reform of the international monetary system. Increased international reserves, provision for large margins in foreign exchange fluctuations and strengthened institutions for the coordination of national economic policies can free our government and others to achieve full employment;

■ Support efforts to promote exports of American farm products; . . . .

Among excerpts from the Republican platform, adopted Aug. 22:

The goal of our Party is prosperity, widely-shared, sustainable in peace.

We stand for full employment—a job for everyone willing and able to work in an economy freed of inflation, its vigor not dependent upon war or massive military spending.

Under the President's leadership our country is once again moving toward these peacetime goals. We have checked the inflation which had started to skyrocket when our Administration took office, making the difficult transition from inflation toward price stability and from war toward peace. We have brought about a rapid rise in both employment and in real income, and laid the basis for a continuing decline in the rate of unemployment.

All Americans painfully recall the grave economic troubles we faced in January 1969. The Federal budget in fiscal 1968 had a deficit of more than $25 billion even though the economy was operating at capacity. Predictably, consumer prices soared by an annual rate of 6.6% in the first quarter of 1969. "Jawboning" of labor and business had utterly failed. The inevitable tax increase had come too late. The kaleidoscope of "Great Society" programs added to the inflationary fires. Our international competitive position slumped from a trade surplus of $7 billion in 1964 to $800 million in 1968. Foreign confidence in the value of the dollar plummeted.

Strategies and Achievements. Our Administration took these problems head on, accepting the unpopular tasks of holding down the budget, extending the temporary tax surcharge, and checking inflation. We welcomed the challenge of reorienting the economy from war to peace, as the more than two and one-half million Americans serving the military or working in defense-related industries had to be assimilated into the peacetime work force.

At the same time, we kept the inflation fight and defense employment cuts from triggering a recession. The struggle to restore the health of our nation's economy required a variety of measures. Most important, the Administration developed and applied sound economic and monetary policies which provided the fundamental thrust against inflation.

To supplement these basic policies, Inflation Alerts were published; a new National Commission on Productivity enlisted labor, business and public leaders against inflation and in raising real incomes through increased output per worker; proposed price increases in lumber, petroleum, steel and other commodities were modified. A new Construction Industry Stabilization Committee, with the cooperation of unions and management, braked the dangerously skyrocketing costs in the construction industry.

Positive results from these efforts were swift and substantial. The rate of inflation, more than 6% in early 1969, declined to less than 4% in early 1971.

Even so, the economic damage inflicted by past excesses had cut so deeply as to make a timely recovery impossible, forcing the temporary use of wage and price controls.

These controls were extraordinary measures, not needed in a healthy free economy, but needed temporarily to recapture lost stability.

Our mix of policies has worked. The nation's economic growth is once again strong and steady.

The rate of increase of consumer prices is now down to 2.7%.

On the employment front, expenditures for manpower programs were increased from $2.3 billion to a planned $5.1 billion; new enrollees receiving training or employment under these programs were increased by more than half a million; computerized job banks were established in all cities; more than a million young people received jobs this summer under Federal programs, 50% more than last year; engineers, scientists and technicians displaced by defense reductions were given assistance under the nationwide Technology Mobilization and Re-employment program; 13 additional weeks of unemployment compensation were authorized; and a Special Revenue Sharing Program for Manpower was proposed to train more people for more jobs—a program still shelved by the opposition Congress.

Civilian employment increased at an annual rate of about 2.4 million from August 1971 to July 1972. Almost four and one-half million new civilian jobs have been added since President Nixon took office, and total employment is at its highest level in history.

The total productive output of the country increased at an annual rate of 9.4% in the second quarter of 1972, the highest in many years.

Workers' real weekly take-home pay—the real value left after taxes and inflation—is increasing at an annual rate of 4.5%, compared to less than 1% from 1960 to 1970. For the first time in six years real spendable income is going up, while the rate of inflation has been cut in half.

Time lost from strikes is at the lowest level in many years.

The rate of unemployment has been reduced from 6.1% to 5.5%, lower than the average from 1961 through 1964 before the Vietnam buildup began, and is being steadily driven down.

In negotiation with other countries we have revalued the dollar relative to other currencies, helping to increase sales at home, and abroad and increasing the number of jobs. We have initiated a reform of the international monetary and trading system and made clear our determination that this reform must lead to a strong United States position in the balance of trade and payments.

The Road Ahead. We will continue to pursue sound economic policies that will eliminate inflation, further cut unemployment, raise real incomes, and strengthen our international economic position.

We will fight for responsible Federal budgets to help assure steady expansion of the economy without inflation.

We will support the independent Federal Reserve Board in a policy of non-inflationary monetary expansion.

We have already removed some temporary controls on wages and prices and will remove them all once the economic distortions spawned in the late 1960's are repaired. We are determined to return to an unfettered economy at the earliest possible moment.

We affirm our support for the basic principles of capitalism which underlie the private enterprise system of the United States. At a time when a small but dominant faction of the opposition party is pressing for radical economic schemes which so often have failed around the world, we hold that nothing has done more to help the American people achieve their unmatched standard of living than the free enterprise system.

It is our conviction that government of itself cannot produce the benefits to individuals that flow from our unique combination of labor, management and capital.

We will continue to promote steady expansion of the whole economy as the best route to a long-term solution of unemployment.

We will devote every effort to raising productivity, primarily to raise living standards but also to hold down costs and prices and to increase the ability of American producers and workers to compete in world markets.

In economic policy decisions, including tax revisions, we will emphasize incentives to work, innovate and invest; and research and development will have our full support. . . .

We will pursue the start we have made for reform of the international monetary and trading system, insisting on fair and equal treatment.

Since the 1930's, it has been illegal for United States citizens to own gold. We believe it is time to reconsider that policy. The right of American citizens to buy, hold, or sell gold should be re-established as soon as this is feasible. Review of the present policy should, of course, take account of our basic objective of achieving a strengthened world monetary system.

Taxes and Government Spending. We pledge to spread the tax burden equitably, to spend the Federal revenues prudently, to guard against waste in spending, to eliminate unnecessary programs, and to make sure that each dollar spent for essential government services buys a dollar's worth of value.

Federal deficit spending beyond the balance of the full employment budget is one sure way to refuel inflation, and the prime source of such spending is the United States Congress. Because of its present procedures and particularly because of its present political leadership, Congress is not handling Federal fiscal policies in a responsible manner. The Congress now permits its legislative committees—instead of its fiscal committees—to decide, independently of each other, how much should be devoted to individual programs. Total Federal spending is thus haphazard and uncontrolled. We pledge vigorous efforts to reform the Congressional budgeting process.

As an immediate first step, we believe the nation needs a rigid spending ceiling on Federal outlays each fiscal year—a ceiling controlling both the executive branch and the Congress—as President Nixon strongly recommended when he submitted his fiscal 1973 budget. Should the total of all appropriations exceed the ceiling, some or all of them would be reduced by Executive action to bring the total within the ceiling. . . .

Taxes and government spending are inseparable. Only if the taxpayers' money is prudently managed can taxes be kept at reasonable levels.

When our Administration took office, Federal spending had been mounting at an average annual rate of 17%—a rate we have cut almost in half. We urge the Congress to serve all Americans by cooperating with the President in his efforts to curb increases in federal spending—increases which will ordain more taxes or more inflation.

Since 1969 we have eliminated over $5 billion of spending on unneeded domestic and defense programs. This large saving would have been larger still, had Congress passed the Federal Economy Act of 1970 which would have discontinued other programs. We pledge to continue our efforts to purge the government of these wasteful activities. . . .

International Economic Policy. In tandem with our foreign policy innovations, we have transformed our international economic policy into a dynamic instrument to advance the interests of farmers, workers, businessmen and consumers. These efforts are designed to make the products of American workers and farmers more competitive in the world. Within the last year we achieved the Smithsonian Agreements which revalued our currency, making our exports more competitive with those of our major trading partners, and we pledge continuing negotiations further to reform the international monetary system. We also established negotiations to expand foreign market access for products produced by United States workers, with further comprehensive negotiations committed for 1973.

As part of our effort to begin a new era of negotiations, we are expanding trade opportunities and the jobs related to them for American workers and businessmen. The President's summit negotiations, for example, yielded an agreement for the Soviet purchase, over a three-year period, of a minimum of $750 million in United States grains—the largest long-term commercial trade purchase agreement ever made between two nations. This amounts to a 17% increase in grain exports by United States farmers. A U.S.-Soviet Commercial Commission has been established, and negotiations are now under way as both countries seek a general expansion of trade.

As we create a more open world market for American exports, we are not unmindful of dangers to American workers and industries from severe and rapid dislocation by changing patterns of trade. We have several agreements to protect these workers and industries—for example, for steel, beef, textiles and shoes. These actions, highly important to key American industries, were taken in ways that avoided retaliation by our trading partners and the resultant loss of American jobs.

As part of this adjustment process, we pledge improvement of the assistance offered by government to facilitate readjustment on the part of workers, businessmen and affected communities.

In making the world trading system a fairer one, we have vigorously enforced anti-dumping and countervailing duty laws to make them meaningful deterrents to foreign producers who would compete unfairly.

The growth of multinational corporations poses both new problems and new opportunities in trade and investment areas. We pledge to ensure that international investment problems are dealt with fairly and effectively—including consideration of effects on jobs, expropriation and treatment of investors, as well as equitable principles of taxation. . . .

We pledge increased efforts to promote export opportunities, including coordination of tax policy and improved export financing techniques—designed to make America more competitive in exporting. Of critical importance will be new legislative proposals to equip American negotiators with the tools for constructing an open and fair world trading system.

We deplore the practice of locating plants in foreign countries solely to take advantage of low wage rates in order to produce goods primarily for sale in the United States. We will take action to discourage such unfair and disruptive practices that result in the loss of American jobs. . . .

House kills works bill. In its first major action after the recess for the Democratic National Convention, the House defeated July 19, by a largely partisan 206–189 vote, a Democratic-sponsored bill for an 18-month, $5 billion program of grants for local water and sewer projects, designed to provide at least 500,000 new jobs.

The vote came after an amendment was passed by a 205–192 vote to suspend any grants in years in which the federal budget deficit was $20 billion or more.

The fiscal 1973 budget deficit was currently estimated as at least $27 billion.

During debate, Republicans charged that the bill was inflationary, a duplication of water pollution measures already approved and an attempt to embarrass President Nixon in an election year.

Nixon claims economic successes. President Nixon assessed the results of his year-old New Economic Policy Aug. 12 and declared that the stabilization program had produced "tangible pocketbook progress."

Despite his forecast of continued economic improvement, Nixon termed the budget situation critical and reiterated his warning that Congressional failures to adhere to his $250 billion spending limit could result in "big increases in the cost of living, or big new taxes—or the first followed by the second."

The President's remarks were contained in an introduction to a report issued by his Council of Economic Advisers (CEA), which was an updated version of its testimony before the Joint Economic Committee of Congress July 24.

Nixon cited six economic improvements: the "rate of increase in the cost of living, which had been cut by one-third before the freeze, has now been cut in half"; civilian jobs grew by 2.5 million; unemployment decreased from 6% to 5.5%; the Gross National Product increased by nearly 9%; real spendable earnings rose 4%, and this was "three times the average rate from 1960-68"; trade agreements would "substantially help us to improve our international competitive position as well as help other countries strengthen their economies."

A more extended evaluation of the economy's performance since August 1971, when Phase One was instituted, was offered by Cabinet secretaries and Administration economic advisers at a day-long briefing for reporters Aug. 10. News from that press conference was embargoed until 6 p.m Aug. 12.

Despite the President's claim of having slowed inflation, CEA Chairman Herbert Stein said at the briefing that consumers could expect "considerably more rapid increases in the Consumer Price Index for a couple of months" caused by recent higher wholesale food prices.

Donald Rumsfeld, director of the Cost of Living Council (CLC), reflected the Administration's concern that consumers were unaware of a slowed rate of inflation and a rise in real purchasing power. Rumsfeld said he had told his wife that "food was up zero point zero (0.0%), and she said, 'Do me a favor. Don't ever say that in public. No one will believe it.'"

Democratic presidential nominee George McGovern reacted sharply to the Administration's claims, the New York Times reported Aug. 12, in a statement comparing the state of the economy with a man who found his lost wallet with the money gone but the identification intact. "At least he got his drivers' license back but he would rather not have lost it in the first place."

McGovern said Nixon's policies had achieved a mini-recovery "and the Administration is entitled to take credit for it—as long as it takes the blame for the maxi-recession which it had previously engineered."

The Joint Economic Committee of Congress, also issued a rebuttal to Nixon's remarks, charging that the economic advances registered in the past few months were only a relative improvement compared with the "prolonged recession" of the last three years, the Washington Post reported Aug. 13.

The committee declared that the Administration's policies were "unduly influenced by a fear of inflation and by a stubbornly held, but erroneous, belief that the way to control inflation is to restrict the growth of output and employment."

Unemployment "can and should" be reduced to 4% within 18 months, the committee said, and fiscal and monetary stimulus "will continue to be needed," the Wall Street Journal reported Aug. 14.

Defense spending defended. The Pentagon, in a sweeping defense of its economic policies, struck back at its critics Aug. 10 in a report it said was designed to "debunk the view" that defense spending excessively strained the nation's budget.

The 193-page report, entitled "The Economics of Defense Spending—A Look at the Realities," was compiled by Robert C. Moot, comptroller of the Defense Department.

At a press conference following release of the report, Moot said his work "is an attempt to provide the facts for those who want to look it up and check the accuracy of what they read. It is intended to debunk the view that defense spending is the big problem child" in distribution of government spending. Defense Secretary Melvin R. Laird, who also attended the press conference, said the report was "an attempt to explode a lot of myths that have developed."

Included in the report was the disclosure that the extra cost of the Vietnam war, resulting from the increased military actions of U.S. forces in response to the North Vietnamese spring offensive, would be $1.1 billion. That was less than Laird had estimated in earlier reports.

According to the report, the estimated "incremental" cost of the war in the current fiscal year was $5.8 billion. That was $1.1 billion above the $4.7 billion figure estimated in January, before the North Vietnamese drove southward. The total cost of the war in the current fiscal year was put at $7.1 billion, also up $1.1 billion from the January estimate.

In other parts of the study, Moot reported:

■ Once the effects of inflation were calculated, particularly on military pay, defense spending was at its lowest point in 21 years.

■ Defense presently accounted for 20% of all government spending—federal, state and local—and about 30% of all federal spending.

■ Defense now accounted for a smaller portion of the nation's manpower than at any other time since 1953. The report said it was figuring into that proportion military personnel, civilian Defense Department personnel and industrial workers producing defense equipment.

■ In terms of current dollars, weapons procurement now was $300 million more than eight years ago, before the Vietnam war. Weapons procurement represented a little more than 25% of the total defense budget.

Without identifying him by name, Laird again attacked Sen. George McGovern, the Democratic Presidential nominee, for his views on defense spending. Laird said "the American people are not going to be taken in by politicans who advocate a $30 billion cut in defense spending."

HEW, Labor funds vetoed. President Nixon vetoed a $30.5 billion appropriations bill for fiscal 1973 for the Departments of Labor and Health, Education and Welfare (HEW) Aug. 16. That same day the House voted 203–171 in favor of overriding the veto, but fell short of the necessary two-thirds margin.

Nixon had threatened July 6 to veto any bill that exceeded his budget requests.

In his veto message, Nixon termed the appropriations bill, which would have provided $1.76 billion more than requested, "a perfect example of that kind of reckless spending that just cannot be done without more taxes or more inflation, both of which I am determined to avoid."

House and Senate conferees had approved a joint version of the appropriations bill Aug. 1 providing $5.1 billion to the National Institutes of Health and to the Health Services and Mental Health Administration, which was $900 million more than the Administration requested. Appropriations for education totaled $4.1 billion, exceeding the Administration budget by $800 million.

The Labor Department would have received $3 billion, slightly less than the Administration figure. A House amendment introduced by Rep. Carl T. Curtis (R, Neb.) and accepted by the Senate Aug. 10 would have barred Labor Department funds for inspection of businesses employing 15 or fewer persons under the provisions of the Occupational Health and Safety Act. The amendment would have exempted 86% of the nation's employers and 25% of the workers from the act's enforcement provisions.

Senate Democratic leader Mike Mansfield (Mont.) said the bill's $1.76 billion in excess of the Administration's request almost equalled the $1.7

billion in foreign military aid funds proposed by the Administration but defeated in the Senate. He said the fate of the two measures demonstrated the sense of priorities in the Congress.

"The issue of where the government spends its money is one I think the Congress is willing to take to the country," Mansfield declared Aug. 10.

Blue collar wage hike approved. President Nixon signed a bill Aug. 21 that would permit a 4% pay raise for many of the government's blue collar workers by April 1973.

The House had approved the wage bill Aug. 15 on a voice vote. The Senate had passed the bill Aug. 7, also on a voice vote.

The bill would create a fourth and fifth wage level in the blue collar job ladder of the Civil Service Commission (CSC), and would add an estimated $181 million to the federal payroll.

President Nixon had vetoed a smaller wage hike bill in 1971, saying it would fuel ":the fires of inflation."

Federal wage hike delayed. President Nixon acted Aug. 31 to postpone a 4.4% pay raise for 3.6 million federal employes until January 1973. The pay raise, authorized by the 1970 Pay Comparability Act to maintain comparable salaries between government workers and privately employed individuals, was due to to take effect Oct. 1.

Nixon cited the Economic Stabilization Amendments Act of 1971, which barred raises greater than 5.5% a year. Federal employes were permitted a Pay Board-approved salary increase in January.

The 1970 act required the President to submit an alternative wage plan to Congress if the Administration decided not to authorize the semi-automatic pay increases due under the law. Congress could overturn the President's decision to delay the raise by rejecting the alternative plan. Nixon offered no other pay recommendation to Congress.

Minimum wage bill dies. The House Oct. 3 refused to send its version of a minimum wage bill to a conference committee where differences with a Senate-passed bill could be reconciled. The vote was 196–188.

Rep. Carl D. Perkins (D, Ky.), sponsor of the House bill, had also failed to move the legislation into conference with the Senate Aug. 1.

The movement to block passage was supported by Republicans and the Administration. They feared that House Democratic liberals, who were in the majority among House conferees, would abandon the more conservative House wage bill in favor of the more generous Senate version, the New York Times reported Oct. 3.

The House, by 330–78 vote May 11, had passed a GOP-sponsored bill to raise the minimum wage for most workers from $1.60 an hour to $1.80 in 1972 and to $2 in 1973. This would apply to most manufacturing and retail jobs.

A $1.70 minimum wage, rising to $1.80 in 1973, was set for most employes of schools, colleges, laundries, hotels and restaurants. The agricultural wage minimum would rise from $1.30 an hour to $1.50 and to $1.70 one year later. For persons under 18 and students under 21 the minimum would be $1.60 an hour in nonagricultural jobs and $1.30 in farm jobs.

The bill, backed by many Southern Democrats as well as Republicans, was approved after the House rejected, by a 218–192 vote, a Democratic bill that would have expanded coverage of the minimum wage legislation to many workers currently not covered, such as maids and other domestic workers and employes of state and local governments. The Republicans argued that extension of the current coverage would be unwise in a time of high unemployment.

The GOP bill did not include other provisions of the Democratic bill to allow the president to impose higher import quotas or tariffs on foreign products made by workers earning much less than the U.S. minimum wage, to prohibit the government from buying such products in large amounts and to require equal pay for women in executive, professional and outside sales jobs.

The Senate, by 65–27 vote July 20, had passed a Democratic-sponsored bill to raise the minimum to $2.20 an hour by 1974. The bill also extended coverage to 7.5 million additional workers, including domestics and Civil Service employees.

Earlier in the day, the Senate had rejected a subsitute bill proposed by the Administration that would have increased the minimum wage from the present $1.60 an hour to $2 an hour by 1973 and that did not include any broadened coverage.

The Republican sponsored bill was defeated 47–46, with Sen. George McGovern (D, S.D.) casting the decisive vote. McGovern had flown to Washington from South Dakota, where he was vacationing. McGovern's action was seen as an election year bid for support from organized labor, according to the New York Times July 20. The Washington Post reported July 21 that the Democrats had a margin greater than one vote assured to defeat the Republican bill but staged the close vote to dramatize McGovern's role.

The Senate's Democratic bill would have raised the minimum wage to $2 in 1972 and to $2.20 in 1974 for most workers in maufacturing and retail jobs. Maids, gardeners and other domestics eligible for minimum wages under the Senate bill would not be entitled to overtime payment, but government employees, also covered by the bill, would receive overtime pay.

Congress rejects spending curb, extends debt ceiling. Before adjourning Oct. 18, Congress Oct. 17 rejected Nixon's demand that it place a $250 billion limit on federal spending in fiscal 1973. But Congress Oct. 18 passed, at Nixon's request, a bill raising the national debt ceiling from $450 billion to $465 billion and extending this temporary ceiling to June 30, 1973. The spending curb had been attached as an amendment to the debt ceiling bill.

The defeat of the proposed spending curb was part of a Congressional response to a legislative challenge in which Nixon had linked his veto of a landmark water pollution bill to his demand for a ceiling on Congressional spending.

John D. Ehrlichman, assistant to the President for domestic affairs, sat in the diplomatic gallery of the Senate Oct. 17 as the chamber voted 39–27 to reject a compromise version of the Administration's spending proposal. Erlichman returned to the White House for a press conference where he announced the water pollution bill's veto, which had been prepared in advance of the Senate vote on the spending ceiling measure.

In a statement released to the press, Nixon said, "I have nailed my colors to the mast on this issue" of higher prices and higher taxes. "The political winds can blow where they may." Within two hours, Congress reacted by voting to override the veto.

The spending ceiling compromise rejected Oct. 17 had been worked out in conference committee after the House Oct. 10 had voted, 221–163, to approve a new debt ceiling of $465 billion through June 30, 1973 and at the same time gave its approval to the bill's amendment authorizing a $250 billion spending limit for fiscal 1973.

House passage of the bill, to give the President unrestricted power to cut back federal programs of his own choosing, was considered a victory for the Administration and the bill's major supporter, House Ways and Means Committee Chairman Wilbur D. Mills (D, Ark.), and a defeat for the House Democratic leadership.

A substitute spending cut proposal, offered by House Appropriations Committee Chairman George H. Mahon (D, Tex.), had been defeated earlier Oct. 10 by 215–167 vote.

The Mahon measure would have required the President to submit to Congress by Jan. 2 any recommended spending cuts. The new Congress would then act on the Administration requests, denying the President unlimited authority to make selective appropriations cutbacks.

Mills urged passage of the spending curb saying, "If you kill this, my Democratic colleagues, you can kiss Democratic control of the Congress goodby" because "the people are tired of inflation."

Despite a Nixon threat to hold Congress responsible for any future tax increases if the spending curb were not passed, opponents of the measure contrasted the issues of inflation and fiscal crisis with the constitutional question of a usurpation of Congressional authority by the executive branch of government.

Speaker Carl Albert (D, Okla.), who normally did not take part in House debate, declared, "Undoubtedly we need to curtail spending. But it is less important that we may make a mistake in the fiscal policies of this country than that we transfer authority that the Constitution had bestowed on Congress."

The Senate Oct. 13, by 62–10 vote, had then approved its own debt-ceiling bill and spending-ceiling amendment.

The amendment prohibited cutbacks on an explicit list of government programs—military pay, interest on the public debt, veterans' benefits and services, Social Security payments including Medicare, Medicaid, public assistance, social service grants, the food stamp program and judicial salaries. The amendment also required proportional reductions on the remaining federal programs. This restriction was intended to force cutbacks in the Pentagon budget as well as social welfare measures which were targeted for reduction by the President.

In addition, the Senate amendment permitted a maximum cut of only 10%—totaling $7.5 billion—in the allowable areas.

The amendment, which had been proposed by Sen. Len B. Jordan (R, Ida.) and included seven Republicans among the 12 co-sponsors, was aimed at preserving the authority over power of the purse granted Congress by the Constitution.

The conference committee version of the spending limitation retained some restrictions on the President's discretionary powers to make funding cuts.

The compromise, worked out Oct. 15 in consultation with Treasury Secretary George P. Shultz and Caspar W. Weinberger, director of the Office of Management and Budget, retained bans on appropriation reductions for certain programs, such as military pay, Social Security payments, public assistance and judicial salaries, but permitted presidential cuts of up to 20% in 50 broad functional categories, such as national defense, agriculture and pollution control. No restrictions were put on spending cuts made within individual programs in those categories.

The proposal was acceptable to the Administration, but was rejected by

Sen. Majority Leader Mike Mansfield (D, Mont.), who declared Oct. 15, "It just digs a little deeper into the Constitutional prerogatives of Congress."

Supporting the conference report was Senate Finance Committee Chairman Russell B. Long (D, La.), who said Oct. 15 that the compromise "would only make legal what presidents since Thomas Jefferson have done by usurpation" by impounding and not spending funds already appropriated by Congress.

The Democratic leadership in the Senate refused to bring the conference report to a vote until the President revealed his intentions regarding the water-pollution bill. Nixon had until midnight Oct. 17 to veto the bill before it became law without his signature.

Campaign pressures for adjournment forced a Senate vote Oct. 17 when the chamber rejected the spending - ceiling compromise and detached it from the debt-ceiling bill. The latter measure was approved by voice vote in both houses Oct. 18.

Presidential reaction—President Nixon Oct. 19 reacted to his defeat over the spending-curb amendment by revealing that he intended to impound funds already appropriated by Congress in order to remain under a spending limit of $250 billion for fiscal 1973.

Treasury Secretary George P. Shultz disclosed the plans after a meeting with the President, Ehrlichman and Weinberger.

Nixon vetoes 11 bills as too costly. President Nixon reported Oct. 27 he was pocket vetoing* nine bills that had authorized or appropriated more funds than he had requested, in order "to avoid the need for a tax increase next year." Nixon announced two more pocket vetoes Oct. 30, of bills to aid the elderly.

The most crucial of the bills vetoed Oct. 28 was a $30.5 billion appropriation for the Departments of Labor and Health, Education and Welfare (HEW). The President had also vetoed an earlier version of the bill, and he said in his

_____
*The pocket veto is the president's constitutional authority to kill legislation after Congress adjourns simply by failing to approve within 10 working days.

"memorandum of disapproval" Oct. 27 that the new bill "contains the same face amount" as the old, and would cause a $531 million "overspending" in the current fiscal year. The new bill had contained a proviso giving the President authority to reduce actual expenditures to $29.3 billion, but Nixon had requested about $28.8 billion.

Despite the veto, the two executive departments would operate at previous budget levels until Feb. 28, 1973 under a "continuing resolution" approved by Congress, which covered agencies whose appropriations bills might not be enacted. The resolution provided, however, that an increase to $1.5 billion in black-lung benefits to miners be implemented even if the Labor-HEW bill were vetoed.

In his veto message, Nixon cited his "promise to the American people" not to increase taxes, and said he still intended to limit spending to $250 billion in the current, 1973 fiscal year. The bills vetoed Oct. 27, he said, would "breach the budget" by $750 million in fiscal 1973 and by $2 billion in fiscal 1974.

Nixon blamed Congress for forcing his hand by failing to grant him overall authority to cut back spending programs at his own discretion. John Ehrlichman, assistant to the President for domestic affairs, said Oct. 27 that Nixon would veto or impound (withhold) about $10 billion in appropriations to meet the $250 billion limit. Since the vetoed bills added up to a savings of far less than $10 billion, most of the savings would have to be achieved by impounding.

Economic Control Developments

CLC exemptions. The Cost of Living Council (CLC) exempted movie and television producers and distributors from price controls, the Wall Street Journal reported Aug. 14, because base period prices and proper cost justifications were difficult to ascertain in the "boom or bust business."

The Journal also reported that the CLC had lifted controls from the sale of live garden plants.

The CLC had disclosed in an announcement Aug. 10 that silver was excluded from price curbs. The CLC said it acted at the request of three Idaho mining companies because newly mined silver was being hoarded or exported for sale at higher prices on international markets where the metal sold for $1.81 an ounce. The domestic price was $1.61. The CLC said that the lower U.S. price level was "discouraging domestic production and jeopardizing the health of the U.S. silver industry."

Pay Board activity. The Pay Board announced the following pay increases: a 13.2% raise for 3,600 hard coal miners under terms of the first year of a wage contract, Aug. 21; a 9.5% increase for 2,000 coal mine construction workers, Aug. 23; a 9.1% pay and fringe benefit increase for 3,000 workers at the Pratt & Whitney Aircraft division of United Aircraft Corp., Aug. 26; an 8.5% raise for employes at the Washington Post and the Washington Evening Star-Daily News, Sept. 12; and a 5% wage boost for rail industry employes, giving them a combined total for 1972 of 10%, Sept. 19.

The CLC said Sept. 21 that employes of all local governments, regardless of size, would be subject to Pay Board rules.

The council reimposed the wage standards on government units of 60 or fewer persons despite its May 1 exemption for small employe groups, to equalize pay disparities for teachers, policemen and other civil servants.

The Pay Board reported Oct. 3 that a second year 7% wage and benefit increase, won by the United Mine Workers as part of a three-year contract, could take effect in November.

The board ruled Nov. 9 that merit raises must be within the 5.5% limit. The regulation took effect Nov. 14 and superseded a previous ruling, which had allowed workers an additional 1.5% merit wage boost over the 5.5% limit.

The Pay Board Nov. 14 ordered that pay raises of 11% for the major New York City area newspapers, deferred since March as the third portion of a three-year contract, be reduced to 8%. The Price Commission then ordered that advertising rate increases previously authorized at those papers be cut back 12%–25%.

The wage-price rulings also affected commercial printers in the area whose 11% raises were rolled back three points. Their previously approved price increases were also ordered reduced.

The Pay Board Dec. 26 cut back the pay increase due 400,000 members of the Teamsters Union Jan 1, 1973 an average 5¢ an hour.

Limit on legal fees. The Price Commission Sept. 6 imposed a 2.5% ceiling on increases in fees charged by law firms having 60 or more employes.

Price Commission Chairman C. Jackson Grayson Jr. cited a "13% jump in the cost of legal services" in justifying the fee limit. Grayson warned other fee-based professions that "we are monitoring prices of other professional services for any similar indications of inflationary trends."

The 13% fee increase was based on the legal services component of the Consumer Price Index between June 1971 and June 1972. But the index measured only the fees charged for the drawing up of wills, and was seen by some observers not to be representative of the trend in fees for all legal services, the New York Times reported Sept. 6.

Profit margin rule discredited. A confidential study made for the Federal Reserve Board revealed that the Price Commission's profit margin rule was ineffective in restraining price increases in the major manufacturing and mining companies, the New York Times reported Sept. 14.

The unofficial survey, made in August by McKinsey and Co. of 114 companies, predicted the guideline would not have a "significant impact" on price stabilization before the April 1973 expiration date of wage-price controls.

The information was disclosed by unidentified Democrats who hoped to discredit the Administration program, according to the Times.

Price Commission actions. The Price Commission issued its first subpoenas Oct. 4 to compel two companies, which sell cement-making equipment, and a trade association to appear at hearings about cement prices.

The commission released new regulations Oct. 4 which modified profit margins rules for companies that had changed their corporate structures through mergers, spinoffs, acquisitions and divestitures.

Time Inc.'s request to raise its magazines' advertising and circulation prices an average 5.6% was denied Sept. 29, the commission reported.

Universal Container Corp. won commission approval to increase prices up to 8% for all its domestic operations, according to the Wall Street Journal Sept. 28.

The commission announced Sept. 28 that S. E. Rykoff & Co., a Los Angeles-based food wholesaler, had reduced its revenues an estimated $3.5 million. The cutback, ordered by the commission because the company exceeded profit margin restrictions, was the largest reduction during the period of price

The American Bakers Association reapplied Nov. 11 for an industry-wide bread price increase of 2¢ a loaf, effective by the spring of 1973. The association predicted wheat prices would continue to rise because of recent U.S. sales of grain to the U.S.S.R.

The Price Commission had rejected the industry's first bid for a price hike Oct. 24, ruling that any price increases would be considered only on a company-by-company basis.

The commission had approved an estimated 2.5% increase for the price of bread produced by the International Telephone and Telegraph Corp.'s subsidiary, Continental Baking Co., Nov. 2 and 6. Pillsbury Co., was allowed an average 11.2% increase on the price of flour Nov. 6.

The commission Nov. 20 allowed Standard Oil Co. of California to raise the price of low sulphur fuel used by electrical utilities by up to 9.2% in California and by up to 23.9% in Hawaii.

Texaco Inc. also was granted permission for an 8.3% price increase for fuel oil.

Three large national baking companies were allowed scaled down price increases of 2.3%-5.9%.

In action Dec. 5, the Price Commission approved a 2.9% advertising rate increase for Dow Jones & Co., publishers of the Wall Street Journal.

Price increases top wage gains. The Labor Department reported Oct. 27 that wages increased only 60% as fast as prices in the first year of the economic controls program, when prices rose 2.2% in the private sector and unit labor costs rose 1.3%.

Real compensation per man hour—wages plus fringe benefits measured after inflation—advanced 2.6%.

In another report issued Oct. 28, the Labor Department reported that nearly 1.5 million workers received average wage increases of 6.6% under contracts negotiated during the first nine months of the year. Contract settlements had risen by 8.1% in all of 1971.

Steel price hike set. U.S. Steel Corp. announced Nov. 17 that it would raise prices an average 2.7%, effective early in 1973.

The company based its increase on an authorization to raise steel prices an estimated 3.6% granted by the Price Commission in December 1971.

U.S. Steel had not utilized the full extent of the increase during 1972 and spokesmen said the new price rise would fall within the previously approved limit.

Bethlehem Steel Corp. announced Nov. 21 that it planned two rate boosts which would raise net income by 1.8%. The first price hike, effective Jan. 1, 1973, affected such steel products as pilings, shapes, rails and plates. The second, requiring Price Commission approval, applied to tin mill goods and was scheduled to take effect Feb. 16, 1973.

Pay Board rules recodified. The Pay Board issued a revised set of regulations Nov. 23. Among the changes:

■ A new flexible size for money pools in incentive compensation plans which could grow or shrink as the number of participants changed. A fluctuating size for stock option grants was also allowed as the number of participating executives changed. The base period for calculating the number of shares was lengthened to cover the years the compensation plan had been in operation.

■ Consulting or advisory services, awarded employes as a loophole to avoid the 5.5% wage limit, were termed "job perquisites" and included within the 5.5% ceiling.

■ Tandem wage boosts were permitted if the raise took effect within six months of the "lead" pact's increase.

FCC approves AT&T increase. The Federal Communications Commission (FCC) Nov. 22 approved an estimated 2% rate increase for the American Telephone & Telegraph Co. (AT&T) which would insure the company a revenue return of 8.5%–9% or $145 million a year in pretax profits.

AT&T criticized the 5–2 ruling as inadequate. The company had sought a return of 9.5% in its 1971 request to the FCC. Increases permitted the company by the regulatory agency in the past 22 months totaled $395 million.

The rate increase was higher than recommended by the FCC's own staff report and by its hearing examiner. According to agency officials, AT&T had revenue returns of 7.75% for the first nine months of 1972 and was currently earning 8%. The FCC decision would require Price Commission approval.

Commissioner Nicholas Johnson, who dissented from the ruling, termed the decision an "unsupportable outrage" which violated federal price control guidelines. "AT&T has today been handed a blank check by the FCC, drawn on the account of the American consumer," he said.

AT&T announced Dec. 1 that business calls would be primarily affected by the projected increase. Of the expected $145 million revenue increase, $124 million would come from higher costs for interstate calls made during the day with operator assistance, $11 million from higher rates for wide-area telecommunications services (WATS lines) and $22 million from cost savings offset by $12 million in higher settlements to independent telephone companies.

Colorado rate boost contested—The federal government filed suit in Denver Nov. 30 to block an 8.6% rate increase allowed the AT&T unit Mountain States Telephone & Telegraph Co. by the Colorado Public Utilities Commission.

The Justice Department acted on behalf of the Defense Department and other federal installations in the state, alleging that the increase violated federal price control limits.

Inflation Rate Gains

The inflation rate continued to gain, from a level of 2.4% in 1972's third quarter to a 2.8% annual rate in the October–December period. The growth in the gross national product also increased. After adjustment to eliminate the effects of higher costs, the GNP growth rate rose from 6.3% in the third quarter to 8% in the final period.

The purchasing power of the dollar declined from 82.4¢ in 1971 to 78.9¢ in 1972, as measured by consumer prices and using 1967 as base.

Price index rise continues. The consumer price index rose from 126.6% of the 1967 average in October to 126.9% in November and 127.3% in December.

The wholesale price index rose from 120% of the 1967 average in October to 120.7% in November and 122.9% in December.

Incomes up. The total national income rose from $859.4 billion in 1971 to $941.8 billion in 1972. The seasonally adjusted annual rate in 1972 ranged from $911 billion in the first quarter to $978.6 billion in the fourth quarter.

Total compensation of employes rose from $644.1 billion in 1971 to $707.1 billion in 1972.

Spendable earnings drop. The Labor Department reported Dec. 22 that real spendable earnings for a typical family of four fell .5% in November, the first decrease since May. A worker's pur-

GOVERNMENT POLICY

57

chasing power for a week was put at
$96.78, but it remained 4% above the 1971
level.

Bank rates down & up. Bankers Trust
Co. of New York led the nation's
commercial banks Jan. 4 in paring their
prime (or minimum) interest rates
charged on corporate loans from 5.25%
to 5%. The initial move toward a 5%
prime rate was made by Irving Trust Co.
Dec. 31, 1971, but the reduction did not
become industry-wide until the move by
Bankers Trust. A 5% prime rate was last
effective from Dec. 6, 1965–March 10,
1966. The cut Jan 4 was the fourth reduction since October 1971 when the prime
rate stood at 6%.

The First National City Bank (N.Y.)
cut interest on savings accounts by
.5% to 4%, effective Feb. 1. It was the
first reduction of the key interest rate
by Citibank since 1938. A cut in the
bank's prime rate from 5% to 4.75% took
place simultaneously.

Toward mid-1972, however, eight of
the nation's leading banks announced
that prime lending rates would be increased to 5.25%.

The First National City Bank and the
Irving Trust Co., whose rates floated in
relation to the money market, and
Marine-Midland Bank-New York,
Chemical New York, the Bank of New
York and the First Pennsylvania Banking & Trust Co., which maintained
fixed rates, were among the banks to
act June 23.

First National Bank of Boston and
Mellon National Bank & Trust Co.,
Pittsburgh raised the rate June 27. Mellon also announced adoption of the floating prime rate.

The New York Times June 24 attributed the credit curb to higher competing rates in the money market rather
than to a strong corporate demand for
loans.

The First National City Bank of New
York and the Mellon National Bank &
Trust Co. of Pittsburgh announced
Dec. 22 that they were raising their prime
interest rates from 5¾% to 6%. Other
major banks followed Dec. 26, despite
Administration pressure to keep the
business lending rate down.

Money supply tightened. The Federal
Reserve Board's Open Market Committee voted Sept. 19 to further slow the rate
of growth of the nation's money supply, it
was announced Dec. 18.

The decision, affecting checking account funds and currency in circulation,
was made provided that such actions
would not cause disturbances in the
money market, such as sharply increasing
short term interest rates.

The money rate grew by an adjusted
annual rate of 8.5% during the second
quarter of 1972, but slowed to 3.5% by
October.

Dow-Jones closes above 1000. The
Dow-Jones Index of 30 major industrial
stocks closed above the 1000 mark on
the New York Stock Exchange for the
first time in history Nov. 14.

The closing average was 1,003.16,
which represented a gain of 6.09 points
for the day. At its highest point, the
index climbed to 1,006.92. The final
figure marked an increase of 8½ points
during the last month reflecting optimism
in the market based on prospects for

GROSS NATIONAL PRODUCT (GNP) & PER CAPITA GNP IN CONSTANT DOLLARS

	GNP in constant 1958 dollars (billions)	Percent change from preceding period	Per capita GNP in constant 1958 dollars (dollars)
1950	355.3	9.6	2,342
1951	383.4	7.9	2,485
1952	395.1	3.0	2,517
1953	412.8	4.5	2,587
1954	407.0	−1.4	2,506
1955	438.0	7.6	2,650
1956	446.1	1.8	2,652
1957	452.5	1.5	2,642
1958	447.3	−1.1	2,569
1959	475.9	6.4	2,688
1960	487.7	2.5	2,699
1961	497.2	1.9	2,707
1962	529.8	6.6	2,840
1963	551.0	4.0	2,912
1964	581.1	5.4	3,028
1965	617.8	6.3	3,180
1966	658.1	6.5	3,348
1967	675.2	2.6	3,398
1968	706.6	4.7	3,521
1969	725.6	2.7	3,580
1970	722.5	−.4	3,526
1971	745.4	3.2	3,600
1972	790.7	6.1	3,787

Source: Office of the Secretary of the Treasury, Office of Debt Analysis, Nov. 21, 1973.

peace in Indochina and President Nixon's re-election. The index closed at a record high Nov. 17—1,005.57 after falling below the 1,000 mark Nov. 15 but ending at 1,003.69 Nov. 16.

The index had reached its lowest 1972 point Jan. 26, when it fell to 889.15. It then rose steadily until May 26, when it reached 971.25. It fell slightly during June and July but had been rising since it had registered 910.45 July 20.

Jobless rate down. The unemployment rate remained at the 5.5% level from June through October, then dropped to 5.2% in November and 5.1% in December.

47 cities at 6% unemployment—Four cities, whose jobless rates fell below the level of 6%, were removed from the Labor Department's list of areas with "substantial unemployment" Oct. 31.

With the removal of Pittsburgh, Baton Rouge, La., Racine, Wis. and the Gary-Hammond-East Chicago area of Indiana, the department listed 47 cities with high unemployment, the lowest level in 20 months.

Administration drops jobless target—Herbert Stein, chairman of the Council of Economic Advisers, told the Joint Economic Committee of Congress Oct. 26 that the Administration had abandoned the goal of a 4% unemployment rate.

Stein said any target would be "counterproductive" because of the "wide range of opinion about what the target rate of unemployment should be in today's context." The 4% figure had been set in 1962 as an interim level, although the jobless rate did not fall below 4% until 1966.

Economic control program evaluated. The Joint Economic Committee of Congress began three days of hearings Nov. 13 to consider an extension of wage-price controls as Phase Two of the economic stabilization program ended its first year of operation.

The White House refused to allow Cost of Living Council Director Donald Rumsfeld to appear before the Con-

gressional committee because the President had not yet decided whether to ask for an extension of Phase Two regulations, according to the Wall Street Journal Nov. 14.

Administration officials had expressed satisfaction with the wage-price program during a news conference Nov. 11. They declined to say when the restrictions would be lifted, but acknowledged that an extended evaluation of the controls program was occurring that would determine its future beyond the April 30, 1973 deadline.

Sen. William Proxmire (D, Wis.), chairman of the Joint Economic Committee, had predicted in an interview Nov. 12 that Congress would not authorize an extension of wage-price controls without certain changes, including the exemption of companies with annual sales below $100 million.

Such an exemption would affect 1,720 firms but, subject to Congressional veto, the President would have the power to impose controls on those companies if acute cost-price pressures arose.

Proxmire ruled out any exemptions for the construction and health care industries and said he did not favor a specific limit on corporate profits. Instead, Proxmire said he preferred granting the President the authority "to step in and roll back prices" in the event of windfall profits.

During the first day of committee testimony Nov. 13, two economists, Barry Bosworth and Robert R. Nathan, urged a minimum one-year extension of the controls program and called for tightened restrictions on prices.

Pay Board Chairman George H. Boldt assured the group that no reduction in the 5.5% mandatory wage standard was being considered.

Proxmire was critical of the testimony delivered Nov. 14 by the chief economist of the U.S. Chamber of Commerce, Carl H. Madden, who said he supported the extension of wage-price controls beyond April 1973 because of increased union power, the loss of spending control by Congress and worldwide inflation.

Proxmire responded to those remarks by quoting a statement made by President Nixon Nov. 5; Proxmire, however, applied it to businessmen: "If ... you make him completely dependent and pamper him and cater to him too much, you are going to make him soft, spoiled and eventually a very weak individual," Proxmire said.

"Your support of these price and wage controls," he declared, "makes me wonder if the controls aren't really becoming a shield for business which protects them from having to rely on competition and from having to rely on their own initiative in negotiating with labor."

Price Commission Chairman C. Jackson Grayson Jr. appeared before the committee Nov. 15 but refused to say when he thought the economic restrictions could be lifted. However, he had said Nov. 6 in an interview with the magazine U.S. News and World Report that he opposed the extension of wage-price limits after price stability had been attained.

Grayson told the committee that the controls program had reduced the rate of inflation by 1.5%–2%, compared with an uncontrolled economy.

Walter W. Heller, a Democratic economic adviser, testified Nov. 15 that he supported continuation of Phase Two until unemployment dropped to 4%.

Wage-price control extension sought. Treasury Secretary George P. Shultz said Dec. 11 that President Nixon had decided to ask Congress for an extension of wage-price controls beyond the April 30, 1973 deadline,

Other anti-inflation measures announced by the Administration were a freeze on federal hiring and promotion until the end of January, when the budget would be submitted to Congress, and a salary freeze at the "executive levels," including members of Congress and the judiciary, for all of 1973.

Shultz said the President was confident his fiscal 1974 budget sent to Congress early in 1973 would be "within full employment revenues," that is, the budget would be derived from revenues generated by an economy operating at 4% unemployment.

Nixon "now feels sure," Shultz added, that total spending for fiscal 1973, which would end June 30, 1973, could be

restricted to the Administration goal of $250 billion.

In a separate statement, Nixon declared, "No federal program, no matter how attractive they may be individually, can have a higher priority than the protection of the purchasing power of all the people."

Shultz said there would be "early consultations" with business and labor groups and the federal agencies currently administering the stabilization program. In a statement issued Dec. 12, AFL-CIO President George Meany said the "first priority" in drawing up new controls should be making them "fair, equitable, effective and across the board on all prices, costs and incomes, including profits. . . . If that equity is not achieved, we believe controls should be abolished."

$10 billion budget cut sought. The Administration was seeking to cut $9.5 billion–$10 billion from the fiscal 1973 budget spending programs authorized by Congress, Caspar W. Weinberger said Dec. 6. Appearing in New York before the 24th national conference of the Tax Foundation, the federal budget director said the recently adjourned

DISPOSABLE PERSONAL INCOME (DPI) IN CONSTANT DOLLARS

Period	Total in 1958 dollars (billions)	Per capita in 1958 dollars (dollars)	Per capita DPI, change from preceding period (percent)
1950	249.6	1,646	6.4
1951	255.7	1,657	.7
1952	263.3	1,678	1.3
1953	27ɔ.4	1,726	2.9
1954	278.3	1,714	−.7
1955	296.7	1,795	4.7
1956	309.3	1,839	2.5
1957	315.8	1,844	.3
1958	318.8	1,831	−.7
1959	333.0	1,881	2.7
1960	340.2	1,883	.1
1961	350.7	1,909	1.9
1962	367.3	1,969	3.1
1963	381.3	2,015	2.3
1964	407.9	2,126	5.5
1965	435.0	2,239	5.3
1966	458.9	2,335	4.3
1967	477.5	2,403	2.9
1968	499.0	2,486	3.5
1969	513.6	2,534	1.9
1970	534.8	2,610	2.6
1971	554.9	2,680	2.7
1972	577.9	2,767	3.3

Source: Office of the Secretary of the Treasury, Office of Debt Analysis, Nov. 21, 1973.

Congress had authorized spending programs of about $260 billion, $10 billion more than the $250 billion spending ceiling advocated by the Administration.

The larger figure "would have provided a full-employment deficit of totally unacceptable size, and clearly inflation-producing," he said. The "full-employment" reference was to a target budget considered to be in balance when outlays equaled what federal revenues would be with all but 4% of the labor force employed. If outlays exceeded revenues in the 4% unemployment situation, the "full-employment" deficit would exist.

The $250 billion spending ceiling had been "chosen specifically," Weinberger

noted, "with the idea of trying to get back to a figure that would leave us some reasonable safety margin against the production of more inflation by our own activities." And a $250 billion figure, he said, "would still have a full-employment deficit of somewhere in the $3.5 billion range, and we think that is right out at the extreme margin of safety."

Weinberger expressed confidence "we can come very, very close" to a $250 billion spending total for fiscal 1973, although the $9.5 billion–$10 billion in cuts would have to be made from a limited area of about $40 billion of the budget considered by the Administration to be controllable, or susceptible to reduction.

Food Prices Continue Up

Farm-&-Food Cost Controversy

The cost of food continued to rise during 1972 despite occasional brief pauses in the upward spiral.

Retail prices of food rose from 118.4% of the 1967 average in 1971 to 123.5% in 1972. Consumer costs of meats, poultry and fish climbed from 116.9% of the average in 1971 to 128% in 1972.

Wholesale prices of farm products, acting in the same manner, went up from 112.9% of the 1967 average in 1971 to 125% in 1972. Wholesale livestock prices rose from 118.3% to 142.5% in the same period.

The rise in food prices and consequent hardship suffered by workers and other low-income consumers led to a search for culprits. Farmers were frequently criticized as profiteers, but they were defended by their supporters as suffering as much as any group from inflation.

Prices received by farmers for all farm products rose from 285% of the 1910-14 average in 1971 to 320% in 1972. The prices they received for crops during this period went up from 242% to 261%, while their prices for meat animals climbed from 402% to 494%. The prices farmers paid for all commodities, services, interest, taxes and wage rates rose at this same time from 410% to 432%, and their parity ratio from 69 to 74.

Farmers defended, curbs opposed. Secretary of Agriculture Earl L. Butz campaigned in farm areas in February against imposing controls on rising food prices. Raw farm product prices, exempt from Phase 2 controls, rose 3% in January and 2% in February.

In speeches Feb. 7 in Fargo, N.D. and Feb. 11 in Des Moines, Iowa, Butz warned farmers to prepare to resist pressures for such controls from consumers and the news media. Butz said Feb. 7, "I want to remind you that as your prices improve and begin to reflect in markups at retail counters, we may have a fight on our hands."

Butz assured farmers that the prices they received were justified. Speaking at a meeting of the Tennessee Livestock Association in Nashville Feb. 16, Butz blamed rising supermarket prices on higher family incomes, food stamps, and higher labor costs.

Key officials involved in the Administration's wage-price program had expressed concern at rising food costs, particularly for meat. Donald Rumsfeld, executive director of the Cost of Living Council, told newsmen Feb. 11 that the council was working on recommendations with respect to meat prices, but he refused to specify what action the council would take. He acknowledged that an increase in meat import quotas was "among the more likely" steps. The Washington Post reported Feb. 13 that Price Commission Chairman C. Jackson Grayson Jr. had cautioned that price controls on foodstuffs might cause farmers to stop bringing their goods to market.

Addressing cattleraisers in Houston, Butz predicted March 14 that federal price controls on beef would lead to meat rationing and empty meat counters.

Grayson March 17 deplored Butz' continued calls for higher farm prices.

Grayson said he realized Butz was "speaking to his constituency" but cautioned that if "the leader of every sector of the economy did that, the efforts to achieve price stability would be wrecked."

Referring to the argument that some workers needed wage raises to "catch up" with the income of others, Grayson said, "the name of the 'catch up' game is inflation."

Grayson warned that if the rising trend continued for the prices of raw agricultural products, which were exempt from controls, "then we will recommend action to the Cost of Living Council or take action ourselves."

Butz replied later March 17 the farmer received only 38¢ of the food dollar and "you can't accuse farmers of causing inflation with those kind of figures."

Repeating this theme at the Southern Regional Republican Women's Conference in Atlanta March 25, Butz said, "Never has the consumer bought food so cheaply as he does now."

He noted: "The American consumer is going to buy his food with 15.6% of his take home pay. Last year it was over 16% and two years ago it was 23%." Butz defended the farmer, pointing out that farm prices were only 7% higher than 20 years ago.

Instead of blaming farmers for inflated prices, Butz said, something should be done about the greed of organized labor.

Mrs. Virginia Knauer, the President's consumer adviser, differed from the agriculture secretary's assessment of food prices. She urged shoppers March 25 to buy more meat substitutes and less precooked frozen or other processed foods until grocery prices leveled off.

Rep. Ed Edmondson (D, Okla.) defended the farmers against charges of profiteering. In a statement in the March 30 Congressional Record, Edmondson said:

The Department of Agriculture revealed that meat products this month rose above parity for the first time since 1910, for a parity ratio slightly above the depression day ratio. For the first time in 62 years, the meat producers are getting a return nearly equal to that of the rest of the economy.

Beef producer prices only now are recovering to the levels of 20 years ago—and those levels are not taking into account a depreciated dollar. During this 20 years, other wages have more than doubled and supplements and fringe benefits have multiplied sevenfold.

Farm food prices are up 7 percent in the past 20 years; wholesale food prices are up 22 percent; retail food prices are up 44 percent. During 1971, the retail cost of a typical market basket of food increased $21—the farmer received $1 and the other $20 increase was absorbed by middlemen. Yet, during these years since 1951, production costs to the farmer have nearly doubled; hired help wages have doubled; real estate taxes, farm machinery prices, and indebtedness are all up. But farmworker's output is more than three times as great as it was 20 years ago.

Our farmers can hardly be accused of profiteering. The farmer's share of each food dollar is 38 cents, compared with 49 cents of each food dollar 20 years ago. His income after taxes is 75 percent of the income of nonfarmers. His 7-percent increase in prices over two decades cannot be considered inflationary. . . .

Meat import quota raised—President Nixon signed a proclamation that in effect raised by 7% the U.S. meat import quota for 1972, the White House announced March 9.

Meat imports would increase by 80 million pounds to 1.24 billion pounds, compared with the 1971 quota of 1.16 billion pounds. The new import level was set by Secretary of Agriculture Earl L. Butz.

Connally meets supermarket heads—Rising meat prices were the focus of a meeting in Washington March 29 between Treasury Secretary John B. Connally Jr. and the heads of 12 major supermarket chains.

At a news conference following the two-hour meeting, Connally said no action compelling retailers to lower their prices was planned. The retailers, he said, were asked to monitor their profit margins and submit a weekly report on meat prices to the CLC.

The Agriculture Department reported March 31 that price mark-ups by meat packers had risen 7% in the year ending in February compared to supermarket mark-ups of 24.3% in the same period.

Nixon deplores February rise. President Nixon said at his news conference March 24 that the Administration was "particularly disappointed" at the 1.7% rise (24% at an annual rate) in consumer food prices in February. He warned that if "...those food prices do not start to move down, then another action will have to be taken. I am prepared to have such other action taken."

Nixon indicated that the target of any future action he might initiate would be the profit margins of middlemen and retailers who he believed were responsible for the widening "spread between what the farmer receives and what the consumer pays in the grocery store and the supermarket."

Noting that farmers took home one-third the price of food, Nixon said it would be "totally unfair to make the farmer the scapegoat for the high meat prices and the high food prices."

Farm prices off. A decline in livestock prices contributed to a 2% drop in the index of farm prices in February, according to the Agriculture Department March 30.

The decline was the first after five consecutive months of increases.

Much of the decline was attributable to a 3% drop in livestock prices. Prices for beef cattle averaged $32.40 a hundred-weight, down 20¢ from the record level of $32.60 set in January.

Overall, meat prices were then 19% above the March 1971 level.

Retail food prices down—Retail food prices dropped .4% in March, marking their first downward movement in five months, the Agriculture Department reported April 26.

Noting that consumer prices had risen .2% before adjustment, the department attributed the difference to the fact that its report covered the entire month of March while the Consumer Price Index covered only the first week of the month. The department added that a decline in the prices of beef and pork accounted for much of the different between the two indexes.

Food prices investigated. At Price Commission hearings March 28 on the effectiveness of current controls, AFL-CIO President George Meany presented surveys, part of a nationwide AFL-CIO monitoring program, on selected food products in 20 urban areas that showed rapid price increases between Jan. 5 and March 15.

Concerned with rising wholesale and consumer price indexes, Meany said, "One hundred per cent of a worker's paycheck is controlled but 21% of the Consumer Price Index—what a worker's paycheck must buy—is not controlled." Meany produced a sample of products that he said were selling at the same price in food stores but with less quantity representing a price increase.

At the hearings March 29, Harvard University economist Otto Eckstein urged the CLC to impose controls on raw agricultural products. Eckstein said the consumer was at least a partial victim of the Administration's strategy to gear its agricultural policy to generate quick income for the farmers "after three years of neglect."

At Price Commission hearings April 12, three New York Democratic Congress members, Reps. Bella Abzug, Benjamin Rosenthal and Lester L. Wolff, urged a freeze on raw food prices.

Food-price investigations were also being conducted by the Internal Revenue Service and a House Agriculture subcommittee headed by Rep. Graham Purcell (D, Tex.). The Purcell panel heard testimony April 10 from meat packers and cattle raisers who denied responsibility for high meat prices. A food-chain spokesman told the subcommittee April 11 that retail beef prices had escalated early in the year because of a temporary shortage and not because of profiteering by retailers.

'Food watch' unit established. The Price Commission announced May 3 it was forming a "food watch" unit to monitor supply and demand in the food industry and analyze inflationary trends. The panel also planned to meet periodically with food retailers and wholesalers to keep abreast of market conditions. Other stabilization units were to monitor Phase Two compliance of the wholesalers and retailers, profit margins and raw-food prices.

Price Commission Chairman C. Jackson Grayson Jr. said no direct action to control food prices was planned at this time because there had been "a sufficient easing of food prices."

Food prices head upward again. The retail price of farm-produced foods showed a .4% rise in May following two months of decline, the Agriculture Department announced June 23. This report contrasted with the Consumer Price Index (CPI) retail food price figures for May, which indicated only a .1% increase.

The difference resulted from the Agriculture Department's sampling of prices throughout the month and the CPI's reflection of prices only at the beginning of May.

The food price jump was attributed to pork and fresh fruit and vegetable price increases. While the prices of beef, eggs and fryer chickens declined, officials noted that beef and pork prices "were trending upward toward the end of the month."

The Price Commission had noted June 21 that high food prices were not the result of noncompliance with price regulations and excessive profit margins by retail food chains.

The recent increase in overall food prices was caused by an alternative markup of nonmeat products where price increases were not included in the retail sale of meat, and by a drought in the West causing fruit and vegetable shortages, according to the New York Times June 16.

A report on the farm-retail price spread, which declined by 1.4% from April to May, indicated that middlemen were absorbing some of the price increases. But Mark Frederiksen of the Center for the Study of Responsive Law,

an aide to consumer advocate Ralph Nader, charged June 23 that retailers had maintained higher price margins for beef and other foods since Phase Two began.

The AFL-CIO June 22 called for a rollback to the August 1971 levels of wholesale and retail food prices.

Retail food prices were up .9% in June, led by price rises for beef, pork, frying chickens, fresh fruits and vegetables, the Agriculture Department reported July 26.

The market basket index registered the largest increase since February. All of the price rises went to farmers, with middlemen reducing their income from price hikes. The index stood at a record $1,299 for annual food costs for a family of four.

The market basket index rose another 1.8% in July (reported Aug. 24).

Of the $23 monthly increase, $16 was attributed to higher farm prices, paced by record prices for beef and pork.

The cost of feeding a family of four for a year declined $1 in August to $1,322.

Meat Supply & Price

Action weighed in food price rise. President Nixon, acknowledging that meat prices were "beginning to rise again and rising very fast," announced June 22 that he was considering a temporary suspension of meat import quotas to ease the high demand for meat, which was in short supply. Answering questions at his news conference, Nixon said that the suspension would "not affect the problem immediately but at least it would affect it over the next few months."

He also directed the Cost of Living Council (CLC), which met June 22, to draw up further options available to the Administration to control all food prices. The Price Commission had recommended June 21 that the CLC take "firm and immediate action" in adopting price controls over raw agricultural products.

Price Commission chairman C. Jackson Grayson said June 15 that stabilization actions under consideration were "so undesirable that they will only be taken as a last resort." Possible options included a temporary freeze on food prices and a rationing program if meat shortages persisted.

Agriculture Department officials reported that meat prices were high on foreign markets according to the New York Times June 22.

A spokesman for the Australian Trade Commission, representing a major exporter of meat to the U.S., said in the same Times report that "there has been an unfortunate idea that meat imports are like a faucet that you can turn on and beef will pour out. There may be some increase in beef shipments, but I doubt there will be any deluge."

Livestock prices climb—The Agriculture Department reported June 30 that livestock prices rose 3% in the month (or 31 days) that ended June 15. The increase brought the meat price index to 24% above the June 1971 level. Beef and hog prices were at record levels of $34.20 a hundredweight and $25.40 a hundredweight.

Timothy D. McEnroe, public relations director for the National Association of Food Chains, said June 15 the higher meat prices were caused by a relative shortage of beef and a continued high demand but, he said, "We know the retailers will be blamed for it; it happens every time."

Meat quota lifted. The lifting of all meat import quota restrictions, effective immediately for the remainder of 1972, was announced by the White House June 26.

Shultz was not able to promise a reduction in meat prices as a result of the action taken by the President. "What we are trying to do is stabilize" prices, Shultz said.

The White House announcement repeated President Nixon's June 22 warning that elimination of the meat quota would not immediately increase the supply of beef in the U.S. "I can't say we will get a huge surge of imports," Shultz said, because world demand and world prices for beef remained high.

Treasury Secretary George Shultz said at a press briefing that no freeze on food prices was being considered. Raw agricultural products remained exempt from stabilization controls.

C. Jackson Grayson, chairman of the Price Commission which met in an unusual Sunday session June 25 to review the economic controls program, said he was "very pleased" with the President's action but was not confident of meeting the goal of reducing inflation to 3% by 1972.

Dr. Lawrence W. Van Meir of the National Canners Association, said June 26 that "the meat prices causing the most concern are fresh, choice beef and imports are not going to have much importance as far as those prices are concerned." (Imported beef was frozen and canned lean, tough meat used in commercial hamburgers and frankfurts.)

An Agriculture Department report in the Wall Street Journal June 26 indicated that as of June 1 the number of marketable hogs and pigs declined by 7% from 1971 and that the hog crop would continue to fall through mid-1973. The number of beef cattle was up 12% over 1971, the New York Times reported June 26, but meat prices had risen 19% in the year ending in March.

Packers and retailers generally greeted the President's announcement with skepticism, the New York Times and the Journal of Commerce reported June 27. Joseph Belsky, president of the Amalgamated Meat Cutters and Butcher Workmen, said June 26, "With equal effect the President might have sought to cut the price of Cadillacs by encouraging the import of bicycles."

Sen. George McGovern (D, S.D.) said in Atlanta, Ga. June 28 that the President's action was "ersatz baloney" which would not slow food price increases.

Ambassadors of 12 meat-exporting nations met at the U.S. State Department in Washington, D.C. July 12 and heard Administration spokesman Charles W. Bray 3rd say that the American meat market was "wide open and we will take all you can send."

The envoys, from Australia, New Zealand, Mexico, Ireland, Guatemala, El Salvador, Honduras, Nicaragua, Costa Rico, Panama, the Dominican Republic and Haiti, conferred with Treasury Secretary George P. Shultz,

Acting Secretary of State John N. Irwin 2nd and representatives from the Department of Agriculture, the Cost of Living Council, the President's Council of Economic Advisers and the Office of Consumer Affairs.

EEC raises beef prices. The ministers of agriculture of the six European Economic Community (EEC) nations July 17-18 agreed to raise beef prices by an additional 4%, effective Sept. 15. An earlier 4% price increase had been decided on in March. The ministers postponed a decision on an EEC Commission proposal, strongly backed by France, for subsidies to encourage animal production.

Beef price watch ordered. Although the wholesale meat price index declined slightly during August, according to the Labor Department, Cost of Living Council (CLC) Director Donald Rumsfeld Sept. 7 ordered the Internal Revenue Service to monitor meat prices at 100 large food chains.

Rumsfeld said the difference between the carcass price of beef and its retail price was 37¢ a pound, compared with 28.4¢ during August 1971.

In a letter to Price Commission Chairman C. Jackson Grayson Jr., Rumsfeld also suggested that the Price Commission "consider possible changes in the existing regulations" which allowed retail stores to maintain artificially high prices for beef.

CHOICE STEER PRICES
(Annual average per 100 pounds, Omaha market)

1950	$28.88		
1951	34.92	1962	26.45
1952	32.37	1963	22.70
1953	22.77	1964	22.21
1954	23.45	1965	25.12
1955	22.16	1966	25.69
1956	20.09	1967	25.27
1957	22.61	1968	26.83
1958	26.39	1969	29.66
1959	26.93	1970	29.33
1960	25.18	1971	32.03
1961	23.78	1972	35.83

Farm-to-consumer gap widens—The Agriculture Department's August market basket report of retail food prices, which was issued Sept. 28, indicated that middlemen were not passing along to consumers the increasingly cheaper farm prices for beef.

During August, retail beef prices dropped 1.5¢ a pound while cattlemen lowered prices 8.4%. Packers and retail stores widened their margins 12.6%.

The spread between the farm value and the retail price of beef increased from 39.8¢ a pound to a record 44.8¢ a pound during the month.

Sen. Clifford P. Hanson (R, Wyo.) inserted in the Congressional Record (of May 4) data on how "the consumer's beef dollar" was "divided by the beef industry." The material, based on Agriculture Department figures as presented by M. J. Hankins, a Nebraska livestock-feeders spokesman, at a Price Commission hearing:

Example—1,100-pound choice steer dressing 63 percent yields a 693-pound carcass of beef—491.3 pounds less trimming waste.

The rancher receives $270.20. (700 pounds feeder steer at $38.60. This for all expenses of raising the steer.)

The feeder receives $98.27. (This for 400 pounds of grain with high grain rations. About five months time required in the feedlot.)

The packer receives $37.34. (491.3 pounds at 7.6 cents. This includes slaughtering and preparing the carcass for the retailer.)

The retailer receives $163.11. (491.3 pounds at 33.2 cents—up 24.3 percent from last year. This covers such items as cutting and wrapping and displaying for self-service.)

The consumer pays $568.92. (491.3 pounds retail cuts at an average of 115.8 cents.)

Hog prices soar—Hog prices reached record levels of $34 a hundred weight in the Midwest Dec. 21. The Agriculture Department also reported that prices for all of 1972 would be 13% higher than the previous year.

1973 meat import quota lifted. Treasury Secretary George P. Shultz announced Dec. 21 that President Nixon had extended the suspension of meat import quotas for all of 1973.

Shultz said the action, which was aimed at the "maintenance of price stability," would increase meat imports by 10%.

Larger supplies of foreign meat would add to the total supply of meat in the U.S. by less than 1%, after an expected 3% gain in domestic production, according to the Wall Street Journal Dec. 22.

Meat imported during 1972 totaled 1.3 billion pounds, according to Shultz. That figure was only slightly higher than the allowable quota level of 1.24 billion pounds.

Two further government actions were taken against rising meat prices. The Price Commission announced Dec. 21 that it was suspending a special pricing arrangement with the nation's 18 largest processors of soybean. Soybean meal, a major component of livestock feed, had risen 100% in the past year, the commission reported.

The Cost of Living Council announced Dec. 23 that it was ordering its first rollback of retail meat prices. Four small grocery store chains agreed to comply after an investigation of their prices.

Curbs on More Food

Food price controls extended. Price controls were imposed on unprocessed agricultural products and seafood at the wholesale and retail levels effective July 16, the White House announced June 29.

Prices for fresh fruit, vegetables, eggs and raw seafood were stabilized by the President's action but prices for grains, soybeans and livestock continued to be exempt from controls until food processing began, at slaughtering in the case of animals.

Cost of Living Council Director Donald Rumsfeld, who announced the President's orders, estimated that $12 billion in food sales, which represented 11% of an average family's grocery budget, would be included under the Price Commission's margin control regulations.

Prices at the farm production level remained exempt from stabilization. Rumsfeld said the new controls did not represent a freeze on profits or on prices and were not designed to reduce consumer food prices. The President's aim was to control the "costs of those prod-

ucts which historically show supply and demand volatility as they pass through the merchandising pipeline," Rumsfeld said.

At a meeting of the Cost of Living Council (CLC) and supermarket executives July 5, Treasury Secretary George P. Shultz predicted a "downturn" in meat prices within weeks.

In the first of a series of meetings with farmers, canners, meat exporters and others, Shultz, who was also CLC chairman, asked the food chain officials to reflect drops in wholesale meat prices at the retail level "without a lag" that typically occurs in the markdown process. The groups also proposed to increase the food distribution industry's productivity and to provide greater publicity for the Agriculture Department's "best buy" notices to encourage nonmeat purchases by consumers.

Stein defends food price policy. Herbert Stein, chairman of the President's Council of Economic Advisers, addressed the American Political Science Association Sept. 8 and said "the food price situation is not critical."

Stein observed: "The Bureau of Labor Statistics spends $2.5-million a year calculating the Consumer Price Index. And yet any housewife can stand up and assert that the index is wrong and her unsupported recollections and spotty impressions will be accepted as refuting the result of all this thought and effort. I hope I will not be accused of male chauvinism if I accept the findings of the statisticians."

Stein claimed that "the average worker's ability to buy food has increased substantially in the past year" when food prices rose 3.7% and after-tax earnings rose 7.2%.

Farm prices set record. The price of raw farm products, led by cattle and hog increases, rose a record 1.5% in July for the second consecutive month, the Agriculture Department reported July 31. Farm prices were 13% above those measured in July 1971. Farm expenses increased by 1% in July, up 6% from the previous year.

The farm price index rose 1% the following month.

Although beef cattle prices fell for the first time in four months, the prices of hogs, wheat and other raw agricultural products not subject to economic controls increased.

The farm price index was unchanged in September but rose 1% monthly in October and November.

Wheat prices were at a nine-year high of $1.97 a bushel Nov. 15 but beef cattle prices fell to the lowest level in six months in November.

Retail food prices rose from 124.6% of the 1967 average in August to 124.8% in September, 124.9% in October, 125.4% in November and 126% in December.

Grain Sale to U.S.S.R. Stirs U.S. Controversy

The negotiation of a massive sale of U.S. grain to the Soviet Union in July produced a brief spurt of praise for the Nixon Administration policy of ending Cold War antagonisms and promoting trade and good relations with the Communist world. But this short period of euphoria was quickly followed by a burst of angry criticism as it was charged that the U.S.S.R. had out-bargained the U.S. in a deal that would enrich a few grain dealers, give the Soviets low-price grain to make up for their own crop failures and cost Americans heavily in higher food prices, credit financing and tax-paid subsidies.

Soviets to buy U.S. grain. President Nixon announced July 8 that the U.S. had concluded a three-year agreement for the sale of at least $750 million of American wheat, corn and other grains to the Soviet Union.

It was the biggest grain transaction in history between two countries.

Some Administration officials said they expected actual Soviet purchases of American grain to be considerably higher than $750 million. Secretary of Agriculture Earl L. Butz said repeatedly at a White House briefing that the $750 million figure represented only "a minimum."

The agreement was signed for the U.S. by Butz and Commerce Secretary Peter G. Peterson. Mikhail R. Kuzmin, first deputy minister for foreign trade, signed for the Soviet Union.

Under the agreement, the Soviet Union would purchase grain on the commercial market from private grain dealers in the U.S.

As a result of the agreement, U.S. agricultural exports would increase by 17% over the next three years.

Also included in the agreement was a U.S. pledge that it would provide long-term credits to the Soviet Union from the Agriculture Department's Commodity Credit Corporation. At the White House briefing, Peterson said the total amount of credit outstanding to the Soviet Union would not be allowed to exceed $500 million.

In cash terms, the Soviet Union would purchase $200 million worth of American wheat for delivery during the first year of the agreement—Aug. 1 through July 31, 1973. Loans from the Commodity Credit Corp., which the Soviet Union would use to finance the purchases, had to be repaid within three years of delivery.

Subsidy guarantee ended. The Agriculture Department ended its guarantee Aug. 25 of a sliding scale of subsidies to pay the difference to U.S. wheat exporters between the domestic and the lower world price for the grain.

The action had the effect of limiting exports and averting a U.S. wheat shortage. Assistant Secretary of Agriculture Carroll Brunthaver said the new subsidy policy was not aimed at reducing the domestic price of wheat, but it could prevent a further price rise.

Conflict of interest charged. Charges made Aug. 30 by Consumers Union that two Agriculture Department officials violated federal conflict of interest laws in connection with the recent sale of wheat to the Soviet Union escalated Sept. 8 when Democratic Presidential nominee George McGovern charged that the Nixon Administration and large grain exporters and speculators engaged in a "conspiracy of silence" to exploit U.S. grain farmers.

Consumers Union asked the Justice and Agriculture Departments to investigate the role in the grain deal of Clarence D. Palmby, formerly assistant agriculture secretary for international affairs and chief negotiator with the Soviets, and Clifford G. Pulvermacher, a former general manager of the Export Marketing Service in the Agriculture Department (USDA).

Both had resigned their federal posts in June after taking part in April credit negotiations with the Soviet Union related to the forthcoming wheat sale,

Their present employers, Continental Grain Co. and Bunge Corp., participated as grain exporters in the U.S.-Soviet wheat deal

The Consumers Union complaint cited a federal law prohibiting former federal employes from representing anyone other than the U.S. in matters in which they had a personal and substantial role while in government. Another federal law required a one-year ban against the handling by former federal employes of private parties' matters that were under their previous official purview.

The General Accounting Office (GAO) announced Sept. 6 it would investigate related charges brought by Rep. Pierre S. du Pont 4th (R, Del.) that exporters benefitted from the wheat sale by acquiring inside information of the transaction, thereby purchasing grains at low cost and defrauding farmers of a rightful share in profits from the Soviet transaction, and by obtaining heavy subsidies for their subsequent sales.

Du Pont said he also questioned whether the government's policy of regulating world wheat prices under the subsidy plan was "detrimental to the American consumer."

A Senate Agriculture Committee staff memo noted that its investigations uncovered a "coziness between the Department of Agriculture and private grain exporters" that "is clearly working out as both a windfall for the Russians and exporters at the direct expense of the U.S. taxpayer."

Rep. Graham Purcell (D, Tex.), chairman of the House Agriculture Subcommittee on Livestock and Grain, asserted Sept. 1 that a majority of producers of hard red winter wheat would show fewer overall 1972 profits than in 1971 and fewer profits from the Soviet trade than if the deal had not been made.

Farmers sold grain to the exporters at lower prices before the Soviet wheat purchases were known and the subsequent rise in price then reduced wheat subsidies by $100 million, Purcell said.

The Washington Post reported Aug. 26 that 400,000 bushels or one-quarter of the total crop had been sold to the Soviet Union since July, while domestic prices rose from $1.50 a bushel to $2. The New York Times reported Aug. 2 that the 1972 wheat crop was 6% smaller than a year ago.

McGovern sees conspiracy—Speaking to farmers in Wisconsin Sept. 8, McGovern charged that the wheat deal was "another example of the big business favoritism and inside deals that have come to characterize the Nixon Administration."

"Richard Nixon's Department of Agriculture is on loan to the giant grain companies," McGovern declared. He accused Palmby and Pulvermacher of abuse of trade information gained while employed in the USDA and noted that Brunthaver, Palmby's successor in the department post, left Cook Industries to join the USDA early in the Nixon Administration. Cook sold soybeans to the Soviet Union under the recent trade agreement, according to the New York Times Sept. 8.

The Post Aug. 27 also identified two other Administration officials who were former employes of firms which benefitted from the grain sale. George Shanklin, assistant general manager of the USDA Export Marking Service since January, had been the Bunge Corp.'s representative in Washington. (Pulvermacher had retired as general manager of the USDA service to take Shanklin's lobbying job.)

The second official was William Pearce, who had been deputy special representative of the White House for trade negotiations since December 1971. Before that time, he was a vice president of Cargill Inc., a major supplier of corn to the Soviet Union in the recent transaction.

In his speech in Superior, Wis., McGovern contended that "there is now evidence that these big grain companies had quietly gone into the open market during July to buy up as much wheat as possible at the lowest domestic prices before the farmers could get wind of the magnitude of the Russian deal."

McGovern claimed that when terms of the U.S.-Soviet transaction were announced July 8, farmers thought the purchases would be spread evenly over three years and that grains other than wheat would comprise the bulk of the transaction.

"Many unsuspecting farmers from early harvest states sold their wheat at July prices, about $1.32 per bushel, unaware that if they held their production, prices would rise to current levels of around $1.65."

The National Farmers Union Sept. 10 corroborated McGovern's charges of heavy losses taken by farmers who had no prior knowledge of the impending Soviet purchases.

McGovern also charged that under a special one-week grace period between Aug. 25 and Sept. 1, exporters were able to get certification of grain subsidies on proposed sales to the Russians at the 47¢ a bushel rate, which was being discontinued.

"That one deal cost the American taxpayers more than $128 million alone," McGovern declared.

(The 47¢ level was based on the difference between the domestic wheat price of $2.10 a bushel Aug. 24 and the $1.63 basic export price. Exporters registered 280 million bushels for the subsidy during that week, according to the Times Sept. 10.)

Assistant USDA secretary Brunthaver admitted to reporters Aug. 26 that the department had assured grain exporters that the U.S. would raise the export subsidy if necessary so that they could sell at the then price of $1.63 per bushel for wheat, even if the sale to the Soviets pushed up the domestic purchase price of wheat and increased the exporters' costs.

Butz replies—Agriculture Secretary Earl L. Butz Sept. 11 challenged McGovern to produce a "shred of evidence" that there was inside information available to grain exporters of the impending Soviet sale.

Butz termed McGovern's charges that the Soviet transaction was worked out three months in advance of the public announcement "a bald-faced lie." According to the Times Sept. 10, McGovern had charged that the actual grain deal was arranged in April when Butz, Palmby and Pulvermacher were in Moscow to settle credit terms.

Butz said Sept. 9 he had asked the Justice Department to investigate the conflict of interest charges, which, he said, impugned his own and President Nixon's "personal integrity."

House inquiry. The House Subcommittee on Livestock and Grains opened hearings Sept. 14 on the Soviet grain deal. Agriculture Secretary Earl Butz and Assistant Agriculture Secretary for International Affairs Carroll G. Brunthaver denied knowledge of telephone calls placed to the grain exporting companies by a USDA official telling of an impending change in the export subsidies affecting the Soviet wheat sale.

Charles W. Pence, director of the Grains Division in the USDA's Export Marketing Service, admitted to reporters Sept. 14 that he had placed those calls early Aug. 24 at Brunthaver's instructions.

Before the subcommittee Sept. 18, Pence said he had called the six exporters involved in the deal, but said the exporters could not have profited from the information because the subsidy change was effective retroactively to Aug. 23, the day before the phone calls.

According to a USDA statement Sept. 15 acknowledging Pence's action, the department claimed that although the cutoff day for the subsidy change was at first set for Aug. 23, the deadline was moved up to Aug. 24 after officials decided Aug. 25 that "some exporters might not have received word on Thursday, Aug. 24, and therefore might have continued selling wheat under the earlier payment policy."

(Under a one-week grace provision, grain deals concluded before 3:30 p.m. Aug. 24 were eligible for registration under the higher subsidy rates.)

Subcommittee members questioned why the exporters' subsidy information was not given to grain producers as well. Brunthaver replied Sept. 18 that the news would have been "market sensitive" if disseminated to farmers because it would indicate the department's "bearish" intention to drive down the domestic price of wheat, thereby reducing the subsidy.

But this information given to exporters was not "market sensitive" when given to exporters, Brunthaver contended.

(The New York Times had reported Sept. 15 that the Louis Dreyfus Corp., which had announced Sept. 13 a 15 million bushel wheat sale to China, was eligible for a $5.8 million subsidy under the one-week grace period.

(Dreyfus claimed the transaction was completed by Aug. 24, although verifying data on the sale was not filed with the USDA until Sept. 11, the last day of the grace period, discounting weekends and holidays. The subsidy was roughly double what the company would expect under the subsidy policy then in effect.)

Butz admits report withheld—Agriculture Secretary Butz acknowledged before the House hearings Sept. 14 that a report by the USDA's Economic Research Service (ERS), which could have driven up the domestic price of wheat, was withheld from the public because it was considered "too controversial."

The mid-August ERS report analyzed Soviet crop conditions and concluded that the department had overestimated Soviet wheat production.

The study, which was classified confidential, would have provided farmers with some evidence of the magnitude of the Soviet purchases through U.S. exporters. Instead of the 7 million tons of wheat originally thought to be needed by the Soviet Union, the report predicted 11 million tons would be bought. In making the July 8 credit announcement, the Administration had said U.S. farmers could expect initial wheat sales of 1.3 million tons. The USDA Aug. 26 had estimated total Soviet wheat purchases to date at 10.4 million tons.

The Wall Street Journal reported Sept. 14 that a McGovern supporter, John Schnittker, a former Johnson Administration official in the USDA, charged that the U.S. agriculture attache in Moscow had filed reports in June and August that had also indicated the worsening prospects for Soviet grain harvests.

The reports were suppressed, Schnittker said. USDA officials confirmed that the studies were labeled confidential and were not available to the public.

Butz said Sept. 15: "The facts are that this is the greatest transaction of its kind in world history—that wheat has gone up 50¢ a bushel—that nobody, including the Russians themselves, realized how great their need for wheat would be until their crop reports started coming in during July, after the government negotiations had been completed and announced."

Palmby rejects charges—Clarence D. Palmby, ex-USDA official currently a vice president of Continental Grain Co., Sept. 19 denied "categorically" that he had taken part in his company's negotiation with the Soviet Union after he left the government in June.

In testimony before the House subcommittee, Palmby protested the "shameful defamation" of character he had undergone and claimed he had not even discussed the grain transaction with company officials because of possible conflict of interest violations.

Palmby said it was an "outright lie" that he had carried inside information on the transaction to his new employer. But he also disclosed that Continental contracted to sell 4 million tons of wheat and 4½ million tons of feed grains to the Russians July 5, three days before the Administration announced the credit arrangements permitting further grain purchases.

Another contract for a million tons of wheat was let on July 11. The Continental transactions comprised nearly half the total Soviet purchases of wheat.

Palmby said the export company knew nothing of the pending credit agreement with the Soviets, and that Continental kept its own transaction of July 5 secret from the Agriculture Department.

Later Sept. 19, W. B. Saunders, vice

president of Cargill, Inc., another exporter, testified at the hearings that his company had sold 2 million tons of wheat to the Soviets, half July 10 and half Aug. 1.

Palmby and Saunders declined to reveal the price paid to farmers for early grain purchases to cover the impending sales.

Subcommittee Chairman Rep. Graham Purcell (D, Tex.) declared, "I see nothing to indicate Palmby's activities were anything but proper," but said he would reserve judgment on the Agriculture Department's handling of the transaction.

Palmby had said he agreed with subcommittee member Rep. Melcher that the government's July 8 announcement regarding estimated purchases by the Russians was "misleading" to the farmers in light of Continental's just concluded transaction.

Palmby told the head of the subcommittee Sept. 25 that he purchased a large New York cooperative apartment April 3 or 4, just before leaving for Moscow to start preliminary negotiations on credit terms for the Soviet grain sale, and several weeks before May 12, when he informed Agriculture Secretary Earl L. Butz of his plans to resign and join Continental.

Palmby revealed the information, what he called "supplemental details," in a letter to Rep. Graham Purcell.

Palmby said he bought the apartment, which would sell for about $100,000, as a "gamble" and had not yet decided to accept the Continental job offer. The exporting company's office was located in New York.

As a USDA official, Palmby earned $38,000 annually. Currently he earned in excess of $100,000, according to the Washington Post Sept. 26.

Of his six credit references for purchase of the apartment, Palmby listed four Continental officials.

Palmby said he had received the job offer "in early March," and did not accept it until May 11. In earlier testimony, Palmby had told the subcommittee that he had not taken "very seriously" a job offer made in early March and that during that time, his contacts with Continental officials were "very limited," the Post reported.

Palmby had also said Continental's "firm offer came finally along—as I recall, somewhere around the first part of

May, in that area," according to the Post.

FBI inquiry set. President Nixon Sept. 20 ordered an investigation by the Federal Bureau of Investigation (FBI) to determine whether U.S. grain exporters made "illegal excess profits" from the recent sale of wheat to the Soviet Union.

The White House announcement followed a statement by Vice President Agnew Sept. 19 that an investigation by the FBI's "business fraud and business practices unit" was "in progress."

According to Rep. John Melcher (D, Mont.) Sept. 20, a member of the House Agriculture subcommittee that was investigating the wheat deal, Agnew's announcement "came as a complete surprise to the White House, but a decision was made, with the Department of Agriculture [USDA] agreeing, that he had to be taken off the hook and backed up."

In making the inquiry announcement, White House Press Secretary Ronald L. Ziegler disclosed that a separate investigation by the USDA's Commodity Exchange Authority had "turned up no impropriety whatsoever."

Three other inquiries into the wheat sale were under way:

■ The General Accounting Office (GAO) was conducting its study of the USDA and grain exporters on the request of Rep. Pierre S. du Pont 4th (R, Del.).

■ Another probe, according to The New York Times Sept. 20, was requested by Rep. Benjamin S. Rosenthal (D, N.Y.). It involved the Justice Department in a study of possible violations of conflict of interest laws by ex-USDA officials Clarence Palmby and Clifford Pulvermacher.

■ A third investigation referred to by Ziegler, by the USDA's Commodity Exchange Authority, was trying to discover whether grain exporters profited from inside information about the trade deal before it was announced July 8.

USDA ends wheat subsidy. The Agriculture Department (USDA) announced Sept. 22 that it was eliminating the export subsidy by setting the payment rate at zero because of the "strong demand for wheat and supplies."

Dropping the subsidy had the effect of raising the export price of wheat 14¢, the difference between the world price and the domestic price. The domestic price also rose 4¢, bringing the export price to $2.44 a bushel, up 18¢ from the world price of $2.26 on Sept. 22.

The General Accounting Office Nov. 3 released preliminary findings from its investigation of the grain sale.

The agency reported that the USDA "may" have paid excessive subsidies for wheat.

Exporters seek tax benefit. The Treasury Department made public Sept. 27 a request by Continental Grain Co., for tax forgiveness on half the profits already made under the Russian wheat purchase.

The Department also released correspondence from Sen. Russell B. Long (D, La.) and Sen. Herman E. Talmadge (D, Ga.), chairmen of the Senate Finance and Agriculture Committees, supporting the tax break for Continental and other grain exporters.

The department Sept. 29 issued a proposed ruling denying the tax-forgiveness request.

The government released the correspondence at the urging of Tax Analysts and Advocates, a Washington public interest law firm, which had said it would seek a court order for the information if the Treasury Department did not make it public.

The exporters sought relief under the 1971 tax bill which encouraged companies to establish Domestic International Sales Corporations (DISCs) for the conduct of their export businesses. Under the law, taxes on half the profits earned by DISCs could be deferred as long as the profits were returned to the export business or remained in the U.S. as "producer's loans."

The law provided, however, that the secretary of the Treasury could deny DISC tax benefits if the profits derived from sales were "accomplished by a subsidy granted by the U.S. or any instrumentality thereof."

The exporters claimed exemption from the subsidy provision, citing a Senate Finance Committee report on the tax bill which said the subsidy clause was inapplicable when a subsidy program was "designed to subsidize both domestic and foreign markets of U.S. products (such as general [farm] price support programs)."

Sen. Harry F. Byrd Jr. (Ind., Va.), a member of the Senate Finance Committee, wrote the Treasury Department Sept. 28 expressing opposition to a stated department position of Aug. 20, when a spokesman said the government was "leaning toward acceptance" of the exporters' interpretation of the tax law.

A favorable tax ruling for the exporters would cost the Treasury Department $100 million, Byrd said.

(The new ruling did not affect the exporters' undisputed eligibility for preferential tax treatment for profits earned since the termination of the wheat subsidy program.)

The Washington Post reported Nov. 14 that the USDA had recommended the requested tax forgiveness.

Cargill claims loss. Replying to the proposed Treasury ruling, Cargill, Inc. asserted Nov. 2 that it had lost $661,386, or .9¢ a bushel, on its sale of nearly 74 million bushels of wheat to the Soviets.

In making its first financial disclosure in company history to counteract charges of windfall profits, Cargill attributed the loss to "the need to purchase the wheat at rapidly rising prices and, at the same time, failure of the government's export differential [subsidy] to keep pace with those rising prices."

Cargill denied that it had received inside information regarding Soviet intentions to purchase huge supplies of grain and said it had not begun to make large purchases of grain until after its second deal with the Russian negotiators Aug. 1, when the price of wheat had started its rise.

According to Cargill, the firm was committed to supplying 30 million bushels of wheat more than it held in storage after the first contract was signed with the Russians July 10. After the second deal Aug. 1, spokesmen claimed the company was short more than 60 million bushels.

The company claimed that its purchase price of wheat averaged $2.009 per bushel, while its sale price was an estimated $1.621 per bushel. Cargill said it received an average subsidy payment from the USDA of 33.4¢ per bushel and denied that it had waited until the end of August to apply for most of its federal subsidy when the support price had reached a record high of 47¢.

Shippers eligible for grain subsidy. The Commerce Department revealed that costs to taxpayers over the next three years for the subsidy paid U.S. ship owners for transporting grain to the Soviet Union could total $50 million, according to the New York Times Sept. 29.

The Maritime Administration had announced Sept. 29 that it would pay U.S. shippers the difference between the U.S. costs of $21 a ton and the current world charter rates of $8 a ton.

Wheat prices set records. The Agriculture Department reported Sept. 29 that the price of wheat rose 22¢ in September to $1.73 a bushel, equaling a record bushel price set in 1963. The monthly increase was the largest in 25 years.

The price of corn, which was also affected by large Soviet purchases, increased 7¢ to $1.22 a bushel.

Total grain sale loss estimated. The Washington Star News Nov. 1 estimated the net loss to U.S. taxpayers as a result of the Soviet purchase of grain at $27 million.

Taxpayer Gains (In Millions)

Rise in value of surplus wheat	$183.5
Cut in 1972 farm subsidy	$120.
Cut in 1973 farm subsidy	$189.
Storage and interest savings	$ 73.
Total Gains	$565.5

Taxpayer Costs

Rise in bread price	$178.5
Rise in flour price	$ 20.
Wheat export subsidy	$300.
Shipping subsidy	$ 40.
Subsidy cost to farmers who sold early	$ 54.
Total Costs	$592.5

Millers seek price rise—Six of the major flour mills asked the Price Commission Sept. 28 to approve 8.9%–12% increases in the price of home baking flour. The millers based their claims on the increased price of wheat.

U.S. bakers had asked the Price Commission Aug. 24 to permit a 1¢–3¢ per loaf increase in the retail price of bread, saying that recent large sales of wheat to the Soviet Union had reduced the domestic supply and caused wheat prices to rise.

The CLC Sept. 7 rejected a request from the American Bakers Association that bread prices be exempt from price controls because of rising wheat prices.

Grain ship rate rises. The first U.S. ship carrying 36,500 tons of wheat to the Soviet Union docked in Odessa Dec. 20 after negotiations deadlocked over shipping rates were settled Nov. 22 in Washington.

A complex agreement covering only the period until Jan. 25, 1973 was arranged by Assistant Secretary of Commerce Robert J. Blackwell on the basis of a sliding scale of $10.34–$9.90 per ton of grain.

Another pact was signed Dec. 20 setting the carrier rate at $10.34 per ton until July 1, 1973.

Renewed shipping talks had become necessary after world charter rates climbed following conclusion of a U.S.-Soviet maritime agreement Oct. 14.

Third nation carriers had already shipped 3 million of the 17 million tons of grain bought by the Soviet Union, according to the Commerce Department Nov. 22.

USDA corn subsidy attacked. The Agribusiness Accountability Project released a report Oct. 7 which was critical of the USDA subsidies given to Continental Grain Co. and Cargill Corp. for the 1971 sale of corn to the Soviet Union.

The nonprofit research group, which was funded by the Field Foundation Inc., entitled the report, 'The Great Grain Robbery and Other Stories.'

The study contended that the controversial government subsidy to U.S. wheat exporters during 1972 was part of standard USDA policy. That policy of favoring exporters began with the Nixon

Administration "gutting the International Grains Agreement," the study stated.

In late 1971, according to the report, the USDA bought barley "at inflated prices" of $1.18 or more per bushel, and sold it to Cargill and Continental for 83¢ to 91¢ per bushel. The export companies then sold the barley to the Soviet Union.

The USDA defended the barley sale, the report said, as a necessary inducement to encourage Soviet purchases of corn, which was also in surplus. The report pointed out, however, that Louis Dreyfus Co. subsequently sold corn to the Soviet Union without special conditions and that the USDA permitted exporters to fulfill contracts with corn, half of which was taken from U.S. stocks.

The report also examined the ownership and activities of the major exporting companies. Most exporters were not subject to Securities and Exchange Commission regulations because the firms were internationally owned and privately held.

A secondary source of corporate power, research indicated, was exercised in the exporters' ownership of shipping lines and massive storage facilities, which were used by the government.

(The Wall Street Journal had reported Oct. 2 that cash prices for corn were 30% above 1971 levels despite two years of bountiful harvests.)

Soviet & U.S. grain harvests. Soviet officials making Moscow . television speeches in connection with annual Farmers Day celebrations Oct. 8 estimated that the Soviet Union's 1972 grain supply would reach planned levels if foreign purchases were added to the domestic crop.

According to the New York Times Oct. 9, officials expected domestic grain production to reach 167 million metric tons. Added to the approximately 20 million tons purchased abroad, this would bring the total disposable grain supply to almost 190 million tons, the level of production planned for 1972.

Vladimir V. Matskevich, the agriculture minister, had declared Oct. 4 that although the recent drought was the worst "in 100 years of recorded meteorological history" there would be "no question of starvation."

The U.S. Agriculture Department Dec. 12 made public data revealing that the 1972 U.S. wheat crop exceeded a 25-year record in reaching sales of $3.4 billion. Total production was 1.54 billion bushels worth an average of $2.23 a bushel, up from $1.89 a bushel in 1971.

China buys U.S. wheat. U.S. Agriculture Secretary Early L. Butz said Sept. 14 that China had placed an order for wheat with the U.S. subsidiary of a French-based company.

Later Sept. 14, an official of the Louis Dreyfus Corp., the New York branch of the French firm Societe Anonyme Louis-Dreyfus et Cie., said the Chinese had agreed to purchase 18 million bushels of soft red wheat. The U.S. firm would "de-Americanize" the grain by selling it first to the parent firm in France for "business reasons."

The spokesman declined to discuss prices and other market details of the agreement.

International Trade, Payments & Monetary Problems

U.S. Trade Deficit

In 1971 the U.S. suffered its first trade deficit in 83 years, and its payment deficit reached a record height. The poor trade and payments record, further weakening the value of the dollar, was a serious complication in the U.S. struggle against inflation.

First trade deficit since 1888. The U.S. suffered a $2.047 billion trade deficit in 1971, the Commerce Department reported Jan. 25. It was the first time imports had exceeded exports since 1888.

The seasonally adjusted figures:

	Exports	Deficit (-) or Surplus (†)	Imports
1971	$43.56 billion	-$2.047 billion	$45.6 billion
1970	$42.66 billion	†$2.71 billion	$39.95 billion

The weak rise in exports in 1971 was caused, a Commerce Department official said, by a "slowdown of economic activity and increasing idle capacity in other major industrial countries" at a time when U.S. demand for foreign goods rose sharply.

Harold C. Passer, assistant secretary for economic affairs, said realignment of the world's currency exchange rates and current negotiations to pull down barriers to U.S. exports made him optimistic about improvement in the U.S. trade position in 1972.

The U.S. foreign trade deficit soared to a record $6.34 billion in 1972.

The 1972 deficit reflected currency revaluations undertaken at the Smithsonian meeting in December 1971 as well as the recent upturn in the domestic economy.

For 1972, imports totaled $55.56 billion, up 22% from 1971. Exports gained 13% to reach $49.12 billion.

Preliminary reports indicated that import prices rose 7% during 1972 while export prices were 3% higher than in 1971.

'71 payments deficit a record. Preliminary figures issued by the Commerce Department Feb. 15 on the basis of one of its four balance of payments measurements showed that the U.S. had suffered its worst payments imbalance in its history in 1971. The "official reserve transactions" ("official settlements") measure showed a deficit of $29.63 billion (seasonally adjusted) nearly triple 1970's deficit of $9.82 billion.

The official settlements measurement reflected losses of U.S. monetary reserves, accumulations of dollars by foreign central banks and immediate foreign exchange market pressures on the dollar. The figures showed a further buildup of $27 billion in foreign central banks and a $2.5 billion decline in U.S. reserve assets.

Two measures of the nation's balance of payments showed improvement during the fourth quarter of 1972 and for the year as a whole, according to the Commerce Department.

The deficit, gauged by "official reserves transactions" which reflected capital movements, was $1.4 billion in the final quarter and $10.11 billion during the year.

Measured on a "net liquidity" basis, which indicated the dollar outflow from private and governmental sectors of the U.S. economy, the deficit declined to a fourth quarter level of $3.98 billion. For the entire year, the deficit was $13.78 billion.

A factor in the payments improvement was an increase in foreign purchases of U.S. stocks. Investment was up from $379 million to $1.14 billion during October-December 1972, and up from $849 million in 1971 to $2.37 billion during the past year.

Measured as the balance on current accounts, the fourth quarter deficit was $1.61 billion compared with $1.77 billion during July–September 1972. A year's total of the current accounts deficit was a record $7.98 billion, reflecting a deterioration in the export-import trade.

Textile trade deficit. The U.S. suffered its worst textile trade deficit in modern times in 1971, the Commerce Department reported Feb. 8. The 1971 textile trade deficit was $1.99 billion, up from 1970's $1.54 billion deficit. The U.S. had suffered textile trade deficits annually since 1961. Textile imports totaled $2.76 billion in 1971, while exports were $770.9 million. Japan and other Asian nations had agreed to limit exports to the U.S.

Japan, Europe to cut steel exports to U.S. Agreement by Japanese and major European steel producers to limit steel exports to the U.S. in 1972–74 was announced by White House Press Secretary Ronald L. Ziegler May 6. The agreement, covering about 85% of steel exports to the U.S., followed nearly 18 months of negotiations between the U.S. and the heads of steel associations in Japan and in the European Coal and Steel Community and Britain.

President Nixon, in a statement is-

sued from his Camp David, Md. retreat, said the accord represented "a substantial improvement" over the voluntary quotas that went into effect in 1969 and would help save "the jobs of American steel workers."

The agreement would reduce from the current 5% to 2.5% the average annual growth rate of steel exports to the U.S.; set specific limits on exports of stainless, tool and other alloyed and high value steel products; impose greater curbs on the shifting of steel exports within the limitations; restrict geographic distribution to prevent concentration in markets; and limit for the first time exports of some fabricated structural steel and cold finished steel bars.

The accord was expected to limit total steel exports to the U.S. to 16.5 million tons, approximately 10% less than in 1971. The curbs would cut the foreign steel products share of the U.S. market to about 14.5% compared with 17.9% in 1971.

The agreements were contained in letters addressed recently to Secretary of State William P. Rogers, the New York Times reported May 7.

Nathaniel Samuels, deputy undersecretary of state for economic affairs, who had headed the U.S. negotiating team, indicated May 6 the foreign steel producers had agreed to restrict their exports to ward off enactment of tougher protectionist measures by the U.S. Congress. He also said "there's no evidence" the agreement would result in steel price increases despite the competitive loss of the lower priced foreign steel.

Wide April trade deficit. The U.S. recorded its second-largest foreign trade deficit in April with imports exceeding exports by a seasonally adjusted $699.4 million, the Commerce Department announced May 26. That gap was surpassed only by the $821 million deficit in October 1971.

The April figures brought the total deficit for the first four months of 1972 to $2.2 billion.

Exports fell off in April 3.4% from a seasonally adjusted $3.89 billion in

March to $3.76 billion in April.

Imports in April were also down, slipping .3% from $4.47 billion in March to $4.46 billion in April.

Payment deficit narrows. The Commerce Department reported May 16 that the U.S. balance of international payments, measured by two of the four yardsticks used, showed a marked improvement in the 1st quarter of 1972. But despite the improvement, the U.S. still faced a substantial payment deficit.

On the "official reserve" basis, the first quarter deficit was a seasonally adjusted $3.5 billion. That was down from $6.3 billion in the 4th quarter of 1971 and the massive $12.2 billion of the 3rd quarter, when the dollar outflow reached its peak prior to devaluation.

The net liquidity deficit in the 1st quarter was $3.2 billion, down from $4.3 billion in the 4th quarter of 1971 and the record $9.3 billion in 1971's 3rd quarter.

The Commerce Department estimated the total net "liquid private capital outflow" from the U.S. in the 1st quarter at $275 million, substantially lower than the $1.9 billion figure in the 4th quarter of 1971.

Smaller trade deficit in May. The Commerce Department reported June 26 that the May trade deficit, the smallest since January, was $552.4 million, down from $699.4 million in April. Although the trade gap narrowed, it remained far above the $200.6 million deficit registered in May 1971. (All figures were seasonally adjusted.)

Exports in May, largely in foodstuffs and civilian aircraft, were up $175 million or 4.1% from April to a $3.91 billion total. Imports increased only .1% or $6 million in May to $4.47 billion.

Import trade developments. Between March and May the Administration took stringent measures on a number of import trade issues regarding establishment and enforcement of import quotas on fuel products, steel, earthenware, and textiles and the enforcement of the antidumping and countervailing duty statutes.

Eugene T. Rossides, assistant secretary of the Treasury for enforcement, tariff and trade affairs, at a meeting in Los Angeles April 18, disclosed that the Treasury was planning to apply antidumping regulations with more stringency than in the past. He added that in order to enforce the regulations prohibiting import sales at "less than fair value," "amendments of our antidumping act and countervailing duty statute may be required to achieve freer and fairer competition in international trade."

In keeping with this new policy, Rossides issued instructions May 23 directing the Customs Bureau to establish a monitorship over steel import quotas, notifying the State Department and participating foreign steel concerns of any violations of the agreement, announced May 6, limiting steel imports.

The Tariff Commission, in a 4–0 vote (2 abstentions) April 20, held that large power transformers exported to the U.S. from France, Great Britain, Italy, Japan, and Switzerland were being dumped in the U.S. at prices less than those of their respective home markets.

Deputy White House Press Secretary Gerald Warren reported April 24 that Nixon had ordered increased tariff rates on imported ceramics and earthenware, signing a proclamation April 20 raising duties on such goods by 8.5% of value.

The Wall Street Journal reported May 2 that Nixon rejected the Tariff Commission's proposal to increase the present duties levied on imported glass in order to protect the domestic industry, and ordered that the duties on such imports be reduced from 20.9% to the pre-1962 rates of 15% by April 30, 1974. The U.S. imported glass from Belgium, Greece, Italy, Japan, Poland, Taiwan, and West Germany.

Nixon May 11 ordered a 15% increase in the crude oil import quota, Canadian imports increasing from 540,000 to 570,-000 tons a day, Venezuelan and Middle East imports rising from 965,000 to 1,-165,000 tons a day. George A. Lincoln, director of the Office of Emergency Preparedness, said May 11 the "supply-demand balance . . . showed that under present conditions, domestic production would not meet the anticipated demand throughout the year without added imports." In a May 11 speech in New York, Assistant Secretary of the Interior Hollis M. Dole reported that in the past the oil import quotas were designed to guarantee a surplus of oil east of the Rockies. However, he said since that surplus stock has now been exhausted, the "new emphasis on the program will be to permit imports to fill the gap between demand and production."

The New York Times reported May 23 that the American Textile Manufacturers Institute indicated that U.S. textile imports had slowed since an agreement to limit quotas was reached with Japan, Hong Kong, South Korea, and Taiwan in October 1971.

U.S. investments abroad up. The Commerce Department reported Nov. 2 that foreign investments by U.S. companies rose $7.8 billion in 1971 to $86 billion, setting a record for a year's total figure.

U.S. investment in Europe was $27.62 billion; Canada, $24 billion; Japan, $1.8 billion; Australia, New Zealand and South Africa, $4.88 billion.

In developing countries, direct investment totaled $23.34 billion, including $15.76 billion in Latin America.

Income from the investments was $9.45 billion, a gain over the 1970 level of $7.9 billion.

Investments in the U.S. made by

foreign businessmen also increased during 1971 to $13.7 billion from $13.27 billion. Earnings were at $1.11 billion, up from $854 million.

Common Market Enlarged

The six-nation European Economic Community (Common Market) agreed in January to admit four additional European nations to membership. But in September the voters of one of the four, Norway, vetoed Norway's entry. The enlargement of the Common Market potentially enabled Western Europe to unify and use its economic strength more effectively in fighting inflation and in dealing with such major economic powers as the U.S. and the Soviet Union.

10 countries sign Treaty of Accession. Ten Western European nations signed the Treaty of Accession in Brussels Jan. 22 to create an enlarged European Economic Community (EEC). The occasion, marked by a televised ceremony in Brussels' Egmont Palace, represented a successful outcome to nearly 19 months of intensive negotiations.

The documents comprising the treaty were the brief treaty providing for the entry of Denmark, Ireland, Norway and Great Britain into the EEC and to the European Atomic Energy Community; a decision taken earlier Jan. 22 by the six members of the EEC Council of Ministers on the entry of the four applicant nations into the European Coal and Steel Community; and the draft accord setting out the conditions of entry and the transitional arrangements by which the four would adapt to the EEC rules.

Signing for the four applicant nations were Prime Ministers Edward Heath of Great Britain and John Lynch of Ireland, and Premiers Jens Otto Krag of Denmark and Trygve Bratteli of Norway. Britain's chief market negotiator Geoffrey Rippon also signed a document incorporating an exchange of letters in 1971 on the gradual phase-out of sterling's role as an international reserve currency.

In his address delivered at the cere-

WORLD TRADE
(In billions of dollars)

EXPORTS.	1970	1971	1972
Total	*129.6	188.5	416.5
United States	20.6	27.5	49.8
European Community	42.3	64.7	154.9
Of which: United Kingdom	10.6	13.7	24.3
Japan	4.1	8.5	28.6
Other developed countries	19.5	29.0	66.9
Less developed countries	26.9	35.7	71.7
Communist countries	16.2	23.1	44.6
China	2.0	2.0	3.1
U.S.S.R.	5.6	8.2	15.4
Other	8.6	12.9	26.1

IMPORTS			
Total	135.8	198.7	431.2
United States	16.4	23.2	59.0
European Community	45.1	69.2	154.5
Of which: United Kingdom	13.0	16.1	27.9
Japan	4.5	8.2	23.5
Other developed countries	23.8	37.4	76.9
Less developed countries	29.6	37.6	71.4
Communist countries	16.4	23.1	45.9
China	2.0	1.8	2.8
U.S.S.R.	5.6	8.1	16.0
Other	8.8	13.2	27.1

monies, Heath noted "this ceremony marks an end and also a beginning: An end to divisions which have stricken Europe for centuries. A beginning of another stage in the construction of a new and a greater united Europe."

The treaty would go into effect Jan. 1, 1973, subject to ratification by the four applicant nations.

Norway vetoes entry—In a national referendum held Sept. 24–25, the Norwegian electorate rejected entry into the EEC.

Government leaders of the six present EEC member nations expressed regret at the referendum's outcome Sept. 26, and the EEC Commission called it a "defeat of 'Europe' " and "a step backwards on the path toward European unity." The Commission rejected Norway's request for immediate negotiation of a free trade agreement similar to those recently signed by the EEC and members of the European Free Trade Association not seeking market membership.

The campaign leading up to the referendum had been bitter, with the electorate sharply divided.

The pro-market coalition included industrialists, bankers, and almost all labor leaders, major political parties and newspapers.

Those opposed to entry included fishermen who feared it would insure EEC members' access to Norwegian waters; farmers who thought they would lose income with EEC pricing policies; conservative nationalists; young radicals who opposed capitalist domination; and left-wing trade unionists who wanted closer ties with communist East Europe.

Ireland's entry into the EEC had been approved in a national referendum May 10. Britain's entry was approved by the House of Commons July 13 and the House of Lords Sept. 20. Danes, in a binding referendum Oct. 2, approved Denmark's entry by a 63.5%-to-36.5% margin.

In contrast to the Norwegian referendum, Danish farmers voted massively in favor of membership, primarily because they did not want to be cut off from their biggest customer, Great Britain, which was to join the market in 1973. Other pro-market groups included industrialists, financiers and most newspapers. Membership foes included small farmers, radical intellectuals, youth organizations, rightist and leftist splinter groups and the two largest unions—the metal workers and semi-skilled workers.

Economy Minister Per Haekkerup warned Sept. 21 that rejection of EEC membership would lead to "a very considerable devaluation of the kroner."

U.S.-EEC accord. U.S. Treasury Undersecretary Volcker said Feb. 9 that the U.S. had won substantial trade concessions from the European Economic Community in an agreement completed by negotiators in Brussels Feb. 4 and accepted by the U.S. and the EEC members Feb. 8.

The EEC's acceptance had been held up when France insisted Feb. 7 that the pact be made contingent on future concessions from the U.S. The U.S. negotiator, William Eberle, had rebuffed French demands for U.S. concessions on imports of French cheese and cognac. The other EEC countries persuaded France to accept a compromise by which the EEC would orally request U.S. concessions on certain EEC exports when the accord was signed.

The terms were made public Feb. 11 after formal approval of the accord by the EEC Council of Ministers.

The pact gave the U.S. short-term trade concessions on its agricultural exports. The Common Market agreed (1) to add 1.5 million tons of surplus wheat during the 1972–1973 crop year to its wheat stockpile, rather than sell it in competition against the U.S., (2) to lower tariffs on certain citrus fruit imports in 1972 and 1973, (3) to apply export subsidies to grains to prevent "trade diversions" favoring the EEC, (4) to make proposed taxes on tobacco "neutral" as between domestic tobacco and imports and consult with the U.S. before putting the taxes into effect.

In return for the concessions won from the EEC, the U.S. agreed not to plant 26 million acres of wheat and feed grains during the 1972–1973 crop year.

Economic union plans approved. Foreign and finance ministers of the six EEC members March 21 formally approved plans, agreed on by the finance ministers March 7, to form a West European economic and monetary union.

The monetary plan ratified by the ministers provided for the reduction, effective July 1 on an experimental basis, of the fluctuation margins among EEC currencies from the present 2.25% to 1.125% above or below the parity rate. The wider margin—totaling 4.5%—that was agreed on in December 1971 would remain in effect between European and non-European currencies.

Currency margin cut set. The six central bank governors of the European Economic Community (EEC) agreed April 10 to reduce fluctuation margins among EEC currencies from the current 2.25% to 1.125% above or below parity rates, effective April 24.

A statement on the decision noted that the central bank governors of the four candidates for EEC membership—Britain, Ireland, Norway and Denmark—had participated in the meeting and had "stated that they hoped to participate in the narrower bands scheme as soon as possible and on the same terms as those agreed by Common Market members."

Agriculture accord. The EEC agriculture ministers March 24 agreed on a program that would raise farm prices and implement the Mansholt plan for modernising the EEC farming system.

Under the accord, the guaranteed prices for the 1972–73 crop year would rise 4%–5% for grain and 8% for dairy products. Beef prices would rise 4% immediately, with additional increases to be worked out later. The increases largely followed a compromise recommended by the EEC Commission, but were lower than the average 8% rise in cereal prices and 12% rise in milk product prices demanded by farmers' organizations.

The major price dispute was between France and West Germany, with France urging higher prices for beef than for crops to encourage animal production and West Germany seeking to protect its grain farmers with higher grain prices.

The ministers also agreed on proposals to increase farm efficiency, but allocated only $285 million a year for this purpose.

The ministers had also agreed March 16 to peg the farm price standard, known as the unit of account, to the value of the U.S. dollar before the devaluation agreed on in December 1971. The purpose of this price-dollar link was to head off an inflationary round of food price increases.

West German farmers protest—More than 300,000 West German farmers had demonstrated throughout West Germany Feb. 11 against the EEC Commission's price increase proposals. The farmers demanded agricultural price increases of at least 12%, compared to the Commission's proposals for increases averaging 8%.

'71 wage costs increased. Industrial wage costs rose sharply in 1971 in the EEC nations, according to a provisional EEC report released April 11.

The report said wage costs per unit of industrial output rose by 14.5% in Italy, 9% in Belgium, 8% in West Germany, 7.5% in the Netherlands and 6% in France. The U.S. rate of increase was 2.5% in 1971.

The European wage cost rise reflected both actual pay increases and a slowdown in industrial expansion.

Monetary Policy

Dollar weakens. The U.S. dollar fell to its parity floors against other currencies Feb. 2. As a result, there was substantial supportive intervention by European central banks. The renewed speculation raised some doubts about viability of the December 1971 international currency realignment.

In Frankfurt, the dollar closed near its floor of 3.15 marks at 3.186 marks, and the West German Bundesbank was forced to buy an estimated $250 million to prevent the dollar from falling below its parity floor. It was the bank's first intervention since the currency realignment.

Dollar purchases by the Bank of England swelled its gold and convertible currency reserves beyond $6.96 billion Feb. 2. British reserves had climbed $398 million since December 1971.

In Belgium, the central bank was forced to buy dollars Feb. 2 and cut its discount rate from 5% to 4½%. (The Netherlands Central Bank had made a similar reduction effective Jan. 6, and Denmark's National Bank cut its discount rate from 7½% to 7% effective Jan. 10.)

Gold nears $50 per ounce. The price of gold passed $49 an ounce on the London and Zurich markets Feb. 2. Gold closed in London at $49.25, a gain of $1.00 an ounce from the previous day and $5.55 an ounce since the beginning of the year. In Zurich, the closing price was quoted in a range of $49.20–$49.70 an ounce, after closing at $48.10–$48.40 Feb. 1.

Gold had sold briefly at $55 an ounce in Paris in January 1949, and as high as $112 an ounce in Paris in January 1946.

Under the March 1968 two-tier gold pricing system, central banks had agreed to trade gold among themselves at the official U.S. price of $35 an ounce, while other purchasers could buy and sell gold in free markets at whatever the market would bear. When the U.S. suspended the dollar's convertibility into gold in August 1971, the central banks had stopped trading in gold.

The speculation was also linked to a renewed run on the dollar in European money markets and to the Nixon Administration's refusal to send formal dollar devaluation legislation (raising the official price of gold to $38 an ounce) to Congress until the U.S. had received satisfactory trade concessions from the Common Market, Japan and Canada.

The gold rush apparently abated late Feb. 2 after the U.S. Treasury Department announced that the Administration would submit the devaluation bill in the near future without change.

U.S. policy. The U.S. Federal Reserve System disclosed in minutes released Feb. 7 that its Open Market Committee had voted Nov. 16 and Dec. 14, 1971 to promote a "greater growth" in the nation's money supply. An amendment to the Dec. 14 action, adopted Dec. 20, provided for more flexible open market operations to handle any upset in U.S. financial markets following the world monetary accord.

According to the Dec. 14 minutes, the money supply (private demand deposits plus currency in circulation) showed little change from October to November and "had not grown on balance since August."

Europeans criticize U.S. policy. Alleged U.S. indifference to the international monetary impasse drew sharp criticism from European leaders, especially the French finance minister, Valery Giscard d'Estaing.

Speaking at the end of a three-day meeting of European and U.S. business leaders in Versailles March 3, Giscard d'Estaing conceded the U.S. should not have to shoulder all the burden of a return to dollar convertibility and he said that Europe was prepared to assume some of the burden. However, pending an improvement in the U.S. balance of payments, he called on the U.S. to limit capital outflows.

French President Georges Pompidou, speaking at a news conference in Paris March 16, said he felt optimistic about the monetary situation because Congress was acting on the dollar-devaluation bill, interest rates in the U.S. were beginning to rise and a new expansion of the U.S. economy should attract dollars from Europe.

(Herbert Stein, chairman of the President's Council of Economic Advisers, speaking in New York March 9, had rejected proposals that the U.S. raise interest rates to protect the value of the dollar. He asserted that foreign exchange markets were reflecting "unjustified anxiety" about the dollar and the latest monetary disturbance was only temporary.

(The First National City Bank in New York raised its floating prime lending rate from 4⅜% to 4.5% March 12 and to 4.75% March 16. Irving Trust Co. of New York also raised its prime rate to 4.75% March 16. But Bank of France reduced its discount rate from 6% to 5¾% April 6.)

Burns on U.S. plans. Federal Reserve Board Chairman Arthur F. Burns conferred with central bankers from Western Europe, Japan and Canada in Basel, Switzerland March 11-12 and reportedly gave assurances that the U.S. was prepared to begin talks on reform of the world monetary system and, presumably, the restoration of the dollar's convertibility to gold. The private weekend talks, held under the auspices of the Bank for International Settlements (BIS), came after the dollar had again declined sharply in foreign exchange markets March 8-9.

The New York Times reported March 13 that the central bankers had reached general agreement that: (1) they would defend the Dec. 18 Smithsonian currency accord by supportive purchases of dollars to prevent the dollar from falling below its parity floor; (2) foreign exchange curbs introduced in Europe and Japan were reducing the usefulness and attractiveness of the dollar abroad; and (3) the gap was narrowing between high European interest rates and lower U.S. rates, making it more attractive for dollars to return to the U.S. The Times' informants said Burns had reassured his overseas counterparts that U.S. interest rates had reached their low point and would begin to rise.

Connally on new talks. A few days after the Basel meetings, in a speech March 15 to the Council on Foreign Relations in New York, Treasury Secretary John B. Connally Jr. said he had assigned Treasury Undersecretary Paul A. Volcker to initiate talks with other countries on a new forum for discussion of monetary reforms. He stressed that no "American plan" would be presented until the government had completed its policy studies on the subject.

Connally indicated that the Group of Ten industrial nations, the most recent forum on world monetary issues, was unsatisfactory for further talks because its membership was limited and it had no authority to settle the trade matters that were an essential part of the talks. As an alternative, Connally suggested a Group of 20 nations be set up on the representational pattern of the IMF Executive Board. (Connally elaborated further on the issue of a new forum in an interview with the Wall Street Journal published March 20. He proposed three simultaneous negotiations by the Group of Ten, a new Group of 20 and another new grouping representing major power blocs).

Connally stated that the problems involved were complex and that the U.S. government was ill-equipped to cope with them because of its "ponderousness, division of responsibility, rivalry, and, in some sectors, innocence." He declared the U.S. would resist foreign pressures to make "premature" commitments, especially on the issue of dollar convertibility.

In the Wall Street Journal interview, Connally also noted that the U.S. did not have enough gold to buy back surplus dollars from Europe. He suggested that countries that had regular balance of payments surpluses should be required to allocate part of their excess monetary reserves to a special fund from which deficit countries could borrow.

Volcker on monetary reform—U.S. Treasury Undersecretary Paul A. Volcker called on Japan April 15 to join in establishing new international trade and monetary machinery "under which the system would force an equilibrium" between surplus and deficit nations. Volcker's statement was made at a news conference following two days of talks in Tokyo with Japanese Finance Ministry officials.

Volcker offered no suggestions for the type of mechanisms he had in mind, but said the various options should form part of the discussions for monetary and trade reform.

Volcker also expressed the hope that

an "international consensus" would emerge "within the next month or so" on the "forum or forums" to be used for future trade and monetary talks. He suggested the possibility of "a combination of forums, some combination of new and old" to replace past reliance on the Group of Ten industrial nations.

In related developments, Volcker held secret talks on monetary and trade issues with leading European officials near Oxford, England, April 23, the New York Times reported April 29.

Treasury Deputy Undersecretary Jack F. Bennett said May 8 the U.S. was "consciously refraining" from presenting proposals on the "detailed mechanics" of world monetary reform until agreement was reached on some basic principles. The principles, enunciated in a speech to the Bankers Association for Foreign Trade delivered in Colorado Springs, touched on the questions of foreign government subsidies for producers of commodity exports and import substitutes; the use of barriers to prevent borrowing and raising capital abroad in order to "buttress export-subsidizing undervalued exchange rates"; and the choice between most-favored-nation trade rules or discrimination erected by regional blocs.

Bennett also reiterated U.S. demands for the phasing out of gold from its central role in the international monetary system; a more rapid adjustment among currency exchange rates "to differential rates of growth in productivity and inflation among nations"; and provision of "international pressure on a transgressing nation" in monetary and trade issues.

EEC backs wider monetary forum. The finance ministers and central bank governors of the six European Economic Community (EEC) member and four candidate nations met in Rome April 24–25 to discuss world monetary reform.

Italian Finance Minister Emilio Colombo, chairman of the meeting, said April 25 the group favored creation of a new 20-nation body, within the framework of the International Monetary Fund (IMF), to hold monetary reform discussions. The proposal diverged from the informal U.S. position,

which backed the establishment of a new monetary forum modeled after, but separate from, the 20-member IMF executive board.

Colombo also said the EEC recognized that trade issues were linked to monetary problems, but felt trade negotiations should continue within the General Agreement on Tariffs and Trade (GATT). This position was opposed to U.S. demands that trade as well as monetary reform talks be held within the proposed new forum.

Burns proposes monetary plan. U.S. Federal Reserve Board Chairman Arthur F. Burns, a longtime friend and confidant of President Nixon, proposed a 10-point program for the reform of the world monetary system at a session of the American Bankers Association (ABA) international monetary conference in Montreal May 12.

Burns' proposals included a call for a "continued but diminishing role" for gold as a reserve asset, with a corresponding increase in the importance of the International Monetary Fund's (IMF) Special Drawing Rights (SDRs or "paper gold"); restoration of some kind of dollar convertibility in the future; "symmetrical" division of responsibilities between creditor and debtor nations in adjusting trade imbalances and maintaining international monetary order.

The impact of Burns' program was tempered by Paul A. Volcker, U.S. Treasury undersecretary, who said May 12 in Montreal that Burns was "not speaking for the United States government." Volcker, who was attending the bankers' conference, said the U.S. would be "firm on some matters—such as reinforcing the trend toward de-emphasizing of gold —and open-minded on others, such as the role for reserve currencies."

OECD meeting stalemated. The 11th annual ministerial meeting of the Organization for Economic Cooperation and Development (OECD) ended in Paris May 26 without breaking the stalemate between the U.S. and European nations on coordination of monetary and trade negotiations.

The final communique issued May 26, at the end of the three-day OECD meeting, said the 23 member nations "recognized that some important issues arise" from the "interrelationship" between monetary and trade questions. However, the ministers had rejected May 25, at a closed session, a U.S.-backed proposal made by OECD Secretary General Emile van Lennep for creation of a small "umbrella" OECD committee to coordinate trade and monetary reform talks to be held within the General Agreement on Tariffs and Trade (GATT) and the proposed "Group of 20."

The ministers agreed only to authorize van Lennep to offer suggestions for adapting the OECD's existing committees to aid study of the reform issues. The opposition to the creation of a new coordinating committee was led by France, which reportedly saw the plan as aimed at extracting trade concessions in return for progress on monetary reform.

Gold prices soar. The price of gold rose to a recent high of just under $60 an ounce on European markets May 31, an increase of about six dollars in three weeks.

The price hit $60 an ounce on the London and Zurich markets at one point, but immediately declined. In London, the closing price was quoted at $59.45 an ounce, a 90¢ increase over the previous day. In Frankfurt, the price rose by $1.07 an ounce to $59.63; in Zurich it rose to a range of $59.20 bid and $59.60 asked, an increase of 60¢-70¢ for the day.

The Bank of France and the Bank of Japan were said to have intervened in the foreign exchange market to buy dollars and halt the increases in the dollar rate of the franc and the yen, the New York Times reported June 1.

The wave of speculation was fed by a report that U.S. Treasury Undersecretary Paul A. Volcker had refused to rule out a second dollar devaluation to Geneva newsmen May 30. Volcker immediately said the report had misconstrued his comments.

The basic reason for soaring gold prices was thought to be South Africa's decision to cut gold sales to the free market, a policy disclosed May 16 by the governor of the South African Reserve Bank, Theunis De Jong. He attributed the decision to South Africa's improved balance of payments situation.

Eurocurrency growth strong. The Bank for International Settlements (BIS) said in its annual report issued June 13 that the Eurocurrency market continued to expand strongly despite a lack of demand from U.S. banks for Eurodollar funds.

The BIS, which was owned by the world's 30 leading central banks, put external assets in foreign currencies reported by the eight largest West European countries at $100.4 billion, an increase of $22.2 billion. Liabilities totaled $97.9 billion. Outstanding foreign currency credits rose from $57 billion to $71 billion and its dollar component increased from $46 billion to $54 billion.

Pound Sterling Freed

Britain floats pound. The British Treasury announced June 23 it was freeing the pound sterling from its official parity rate of $2.6057 and letting it float temporarily in the international money market to a new level determined by supply and demand.

The surprise move, following a week of heavy speculation against sterling, would constitute a de facto devaluation and ended Britain's efforts to maintain the pound to within 2.25% above and below (a total margin of 4.5%) the fixed parity price agreed by the Group of 10 industrial nations at the Smithsonian Institution in Washington in December 1971.

The move also cut Britain loose from the European Economic Community's (EEC) policy of adhering to a narrower 1.125% margin above and below (2.25% total) the parity rates among current and future members' currencies.

In a speech to the House of Commons later June 23, British Chancellor of the Exchequer Anthony Barber said the immediate cause of the float was the massive speculation against the pound that had forced Britain to use its reserves and had led to intervention by Europe's central banks to maintain the official rate. He said "if this had continued at the rate of the last few days, we might have found that in due course our reserves had been greatly diminished . . . I was determined that we should not revert to this situation where we would have to borrow substantial sums." Barber said the government intended "to return as soon as conditions permit" to a fixed parity rate.

The interventions by the Bank of England and other European central banks had reportedly totaled about $2.6 billion in the past two weeks, according to official sources cited in the London Times June 24. Britain would have to repurchase the sums lent by the other central banks within a month, which would have quickly exhausted London's $7.1 billion in official reserves.

Barber also announced the extension of exchange controls to capital transactions in the overseas sterling area, a move designed to prevent British citizens from circumventing controls over capital movements of the pound.

Immediately following the initial London announcement, Britain, Italy, Denmark, the Netherlands and Belgium closed their foreign exchange markets. France, West Germany and Switzerland opened their markets, only to experience a speculative run on the dollar, forcing the central banks to intervene in support of the official parity rates. The deluge of dollars caused all the remaining West European markets and most of the Middle East, Asian and South African exchanges to close within a few hours.

West German Economics and Finance Minister Karl Schiller said June 23 that the German central bank had bought $878 million and the French central bank $146 million before the markets closed that day.

On the New York foreign exchange market, one of the few remaining open June 23, the pound dropped to a recent low of $2.46, but recovered toward the close of trading to $2.53, still considerably below the official rate.

The float affected the gold markets, which had remained open June 23, raising the gold price in London to $65 an ounce briefly, to close at $63.25, a $1.40 increase over the previous day.

Rumors of a pound devaluation had led June 16 to a pound selling spree that forced the central banks of West Germany, France and Belgium to buy sterling.

The rumors of devaluation intensified June 19 with an address by Denis Healey, the British Labor party's finance spokesman, who said in Parliament that he expected a devaluation of sterling in July or August. Despite denials later that day by Barber that the pound's parity rate was "unrealistic," the Healey comment set off a new wave of speculative selling that led to further intervention by the European central banks.

The increase by the Bank of England June 22 of its bank rate from 5% to 6% failed to stem the selling and by the night of June 22, the eve of the float, the pound had fallen 2.5¢ from its official parity rate of $2.6057.

(Britain's official reserves of gold and convertible currencies had dropped by $185 million to $6.965 billion in June, the first such decline in the reserves since September 1970, according to British Treasury figures cited in the London Times July 5. The decrease did not include the sales of EEC currencies, to be repaid by Britain, in support of sterling prior to the closure of foreign exchange markets following the pound float.)

The pound continued to decline in London from about $2.50 after the reopening of its foreign exchange market June 27 to $2.44 July 5, a de facto 5.59% devaluation of the pound from its former official parity rate' of $2.6057. The pound had dipped briefly to $2.419 July 4.

Foreign exchange markets exhibited uncertainty over the course of the dollar, with the West German central bank and other European central banks reportedly buying dollars July 3-4 to maintain the official parity rate of the dollar within the agreed fluctuation margins. The Swiss central bank had bought small amounts of dollars July 3 for the first time since the floating of the pound, enabling the dollar to close at 3.7525/40 francs, within the selling and buying range authorized by the official parity exchange. The dollar's official "floor" rate within the currency fluctuation margin was 3.7535 francs.

Monetary Reform Pressed

World monetary reform group chosen. The International Monetary Fund (IMF) announced June 26 the formation of a "Committee of 20" to negotiate world currency reform and "related issues." The U.S. and underdeveloped nations had pressed for a new and enlarged organization to take over the negotiations begun by the Group of 10, which comprised the leading Western industrialized nations.

U.S. Treasury Undersecretary Paul A. Volcker, in testimony June 22 before a House banking subcommittee, predicted that basic agreement on the principles of monetary reform could be reached in two years. Volcker emphasized that monetary reform undertaken by the Committee of 20 would not be a "patch-up of Bretton Woods," the basic international monetary agreement reached in 1944.

The scope of the proposed talks included international trade issues, capital flow, investment, development assistance and preferential trade pacts, such as those provided by the European Economic Community. The inclusion of trade rules in the currency negotiations was considered a victory for the U.S. which had maintained that international trade issues could not be isolated from reform of world monetary systems.

Volcker noted that a "fundamental issue" before the Committee of 20 would be the balance of payments "adjustment process." The U.S., Volcker said, favored "more flexibility in exchange rate practices" and greater "incentives or penalties" to reduce large payment surpluses and deficits worldwide. The growing U.S. trade deficit had contributed to the 1971 breakdown in the fixed exchange rate system.

Under the IMF resolution creating the Committee of 20, the U.S., Britain, France, West Germany, Japan and India would have one representative each. Clusters of smaller countries would select the remaining 14 representatives.

EEC to defend currency rates & margins. The EEC finance ministers, meeting in Luxembourg June 26, agreed to defend the Smithsonian accord's fixed currency parities and fluctuation margins, with more purchases of dollars if needed, and to maintain the narrower fluctuation band among EEC currencies introduced April 24.

But the ministers also agreed to tighten exchange controls, with the French and West German governments determined to try to keep dollars from swamping their foreign exchanges.

To maintain a common monetary front, the EEC ministers were forced to grant concessions to Italy, which had wanted to pull out of the narrower EEC margin system. They agreed to a complicated formula under which weak-currency countries like Italy would be permitted to repay in dollars its debts resulting from the central banks' support operations. The traditional EEC arrangement provided for currency debts to be repaid according to the composition of the nations' reserves, which in Italy's case would have threatened its gold holdings.

The Danish government, which like Britain had adhered to the EEC's narrow fluctuation margins in May, announced June 27 it would temporarily pull out of the EEC 2.25% margin range, but would remain within the Smithsonian 4.5% band. Danish Economics and Budget Minister Per Haekkerup disclosed that the EEC finance ministers in Luxembourg had not offered Denmark sufficient credit facilities to remain within the narrower margin band. The Danish central bank also announced June 27, effective the following day, an increase in its bank rate from 7% to 8% and curbs on private banks' credit facilities in the central bank.

Bonn sets exchange controls. The West German Cabinet, overruling dissenting Economics and Finance Minister Karl Schiller, decided June 29 to impose foreign exchange controls to prevent an inflow of unwanted speculative currencies in the wake of the floating of the British pound.

The measures, effective July 1 along

with previously decided increases in domestic minimum reserve requirements for banks, were ordered at a meeting begun June 28 and resumed early June 29. During the session, Schiller, Bonn's chief advocate for unrestricted monetary flows, had repeatedly threatened to resign. (He ultimately did resign, effective July 7.)

U.S. shores up the dollar. The Federal Reserve Bank of New York, acting as the agent for the Federal Reserve System, intervened in foreign exchange markets July 19 by selling German marks, Dutch guilders and other currencies to protect the value of the dollar, the first such government action since August 15, 1971.

The Federal Reserve move was not officially announced but Chairman Arthur F. Burns acknowledged the action. Burns said the U.S. wanted to assure other nations that it would assume responsibility for maintaining the interim Smithsonian Agreements, which had set current exchange rates as a step toward full-scale international monetary reform.

That agreement was thought to have been placed in jeopardy when Britain allowed the pound to float.

The new U.S. policy appeared to be a reversal of former Treasury Secretary John B. Connally's views, the New York Times reported July 20. Connally had held that it was up to other nations to defend the dollar because any dollar depreciation would prove a boon to U.S. exports. But to counter the U.S.'s seeming unwillingness to act, other nations had imposed increasing control over capital movements.

The Treasury Department said July 20 that the intervention decision indicated "absolutely no change" in basic U.S. international monetary policy. But spokesmen said that the U.S. would continue to intervene at "strategic" moments to help combat short-term speculative movements of funds "on whatever scale and whenever intervention was seemed desirable."

The bank's action, which caused foreign currencies to decline in value while the dollar rose, was accomplished by reactivating swap lines, or short-term renewable loans of one nation's currency for another. The reciprocal borrowing arrangements had not been in use since August 15, when President Nixon acted to cut the gold and dollar tie. In the past, swap lines had been used to protect U.S. gold reserves and the FRB had not intervened itself in the foreign exchange market. But under the new policy, the FRB could utilize swap lines to intervene, according to the New York Times July 20.

The FRB announced Sept. 7 it had sold $31.5 million in foreign currencies during July and August to defend the dollar's value established by the 1971 Smithsonian Agreement.

It was also reported Sept. 7 that the FRB had repaid more than $1 billion of $2.8 billion owed to foreign central banks. The debts, incurred under swap line agreements, originated prior to August 1971, when President Nixon had suspended the use of swap lines. The debts were repaid at a loss because of the 1971 devaluation of the dollar, spokesmen said.

Soviets revalue ruble. The U.S.S.R. announced an upward revaluation of the ruble July 4. The U.S. dollar fell in value from 82 rubles 30 kopeks per 100 to 82 rubles.

Monetary reform aims set. The finance ministers of the six EEC members and four candidate members agreed July 17 on eight main objectives for the long-term reform of the international monetary system. The agreement came at the beginning of two days of talks in London, the first to be held outside the existing community.

Anthony Barber, British chancellor of the exchequer, who served as chairman of the meeting, announced the agreed objectives: the new system should be based on fixed but adjustable parities; free convertibility between currencies should be restored; the supply of world liquidity should be internationally regulated; nations should promptly adjust their balance of payments problems; the destabilizing effects of short-term capital flows should be reduced; the principle of equal rights and obligations of surplus and deficit countries should be established; interests of developing countries should be taken into account; the above principles posed no conflict with the EEC's objective of economic and monetary union.

The ministers agreed to stand by their previous decision to defend the existing currency parities of the Smithsonian Agreement, countering rumors that the EEC was ready to launch a joint float of their currencies against the dollar.

Ministers agree to monetary fund—The finance and foreign ministers of the 10 nations then agreed in principle Sept. 11–12 to set up a European monetary fund and formulate concerted anti-inflationary measures. The two groups of ministers met separately and jointly in Rome Sept. 11 and in Frascati, near Rome, Sept. 12.

The agreement in principle to establish a European monetary fund with powers and funds to settle European currency debts was adopted by the finance ministers Sept. 11 and formally approved at a joint meeting of finance and foreign ministers in Frascati Sept. 12. The fund would coordinate daily operations of the central banks in maintaining the 2.25% currency fluctuation margin among EEC members and arrange multilateral intervention to support the parities of EEC currencies. The fund would settle transactions in the EEC's "unit of accounts," each of which was equivalent to one dollar before the recent devaluation.

Anti-inflationary budgets urged—The EEC Commission, in its annual report released Sept. 12, urged member governments to adopt national budgets designed to reduce consumer price increases to 3.5% in 1973. The report suggested that the six present EEC member governments limit public expenditure increases to 9% to 10.5% and adopt more cautious credit policies to limit the current "excessive growth" in liquidity.

Currency exchange rate changes. The IMF announced July 31 that 15 countries in the sterling zone would follow the British lead and allow their currencies to float with sterling: Barbados, Botswana, Fiji, The Gambia, Guyana, India, Ireland, Jamaica, Lesotho, Malawi, Mauritius, Sierre Leone, South Africa, Swaziland and Trinidad and Tobago.

Those countries in the sterling zone that were maintaining a previously existing peg to gold or the U.S. dollar were: Australia, Ghana, Iceland, Jordan, Kenya, New Zealand, Nigeria, Pakistan, Tanzania, Uganda, Western Somoa and Zambia.

Cyprus, Kuwait, Malaysia, Oman and Singapore discontinued their pegs to sterling and maintained parity with gold or the dollar. Iraq, though not a formal member of the sterling zone, took similar action in discontinuing its June 1972 tie to sterling. Hong Kong maintained a temporary tie to the U.S. dollar.

Sri Lanka, previously pegged to the dollar, was pegged to sterling and thus floated its currency.

U.S. firm on money reform, gold. Paul A. Volcker, Treasury undersecretary for monetary affairs, told the Alpbach European Forum, meeting in Austria Sept. 4, that the U.S. would resist efforts by European nations to impose their monetary system on the rest of the world.

Volcker said that the use of gold as a monetary metal "will have to go the way of silver." In the meantime, the U.S. would not increase the official price of gold from the present $38 an ounce, he declared.

In testimony Sept. 11 before the Joint Economic Committee of Congress, Volcker reaffirmed the Treasury's view that the role of gold "should and must continue to diminish" and said it was a "dangerous illusion" that an increase in the price of gold would solve basic monetary imbalance questions.

Volcker also rejected intervention by the Federal Reserve Board (FRB) and the Treasury in foreign exchange markets "to artificially prop up the dollar counter to any basic balance of payments trends." However, occasional government action would continue to be taken to combat speculative pressures, Volcker said.

U.S. dissents on money, trade report. An Organization for Economic Co-operation and Development (OECD) report issued Sept. 5 in Paris called for the reorganization of trade and monetary organizations such as the International Monetary Fund, the OECD and the General Agreement on Tariffs and Trade nations, leading to closer cooperation between the groups.

The paper, prepared by a 12-member committee on trade, also established the basis for further negotiations on the subjects of money and trade by setting out the major contrasting positions taken by the U.S. and European countries.

President Nixon's special representative for trade negotiations, William D. Eberle, who was a member of the committee, criticized aspects of the report in an attached addendum.

The committee's recommendations were too cautious on monetary issues and agricultural trade liberalization, Eberle said. The report reaffirmed the principle of fixed exchange rates for currencies, established at the Bretton Woods meeting in 1944.

The committee also accepted the principle that agriculture trade should be liberalized, but the proposal fell short of the U.S. view that agricultural products should be traded as freely as industrial commodities.

Eberle had urged that European countries replace price support subsidies or border levies with direct income payments to farmers.

Committee Chairman Jean Rey, former president of the European Economic Community Commission, said the report represented a compromise position and that it would have reflected stronger views if the group had known that Eberle would include a dissenting report with the compromise, to which he had been a party.

Rey said the French positions—that monetary reforms were needed to correct trade deficits and that deficit countries bore the major responsibility for monetary adjustments—predominated in the study group.

The U.S. had held that freer trade measures were required to correct monetary imbalance and that countries with a trade surplus should act to restore currency equilibrium, the New York Times reported Sept. 5.

IMF annual report. The International Monetary Fund (IMF) called on the U.S. Sept. 10 to raise its short term interest rates as an interim measure to attract capital and realign its foreign trade imbalance.

The IMF urged Japan and those European countries with large payment surpluses, economic slack and unemployment to adopt expansionary monetary policies aimed at bringing down interest rates.

The recommendations, published in the IMF's 1972 annual report, followed extensive study of the impact of the Smithsonian Agreement of December 1971, which had realigned world currency rates.

The report concluded that although there would be little improvement in the world wide balance of payments problem during 1973, "it can be expected that the realignment will, in due course, lead to the restoration of international payments equilibrium—unless [the Smithsonian Agreement's] intended effects are blunted or frustrated by inappropriate national policies."

Underdeveloped countries, with the exception of oil-producing nations, were not adversely affected by the currency realignment, the report found.

The IMF foresaw "a very difficult situation" for industrial nations because of a "climate of deep-rooted inflationary psychology and widespread inflationary expectations based on the experiences of recent years."

Government action to combat inflation in the form of "incomes policies" had not proved very successful, the IMF reported.

Currency reform report—In a separate report on monetary reform issued Sept. 6, the IMF concluded that any future currency system should be more "symmetrical" than the old, in which the U.S. dollar was the dominant influence.

The group suggested that in the future, the U.S. could settle its balance of payments deficit by paying out reserve assets, such as gold, U.S. holdings of foreign currencies, special drawing rights (SDRs) and the U.S. quota in the IMF, instead of financing the deficit through the issuance of more dollars.

There were also recommendations for clearer criteria for parity changes, an increased role for SDRs, greater freedom for the U.S. to change the value of its currency and smaller, more frequent changes in currency values.

The IMF was unable to obtain a consensus on the role and price of gold, the role of the IMF in initiating parity changes and the desirability of greater controls on capital movement.

Trade & Policy

U.S. violation of GATT charged. The British government accused the U.S. July 3 of violating the General Agreements on Tariffs and Trade (GATT). In a note, Britain alleged that the U.S. had granted its manufacturers an export subsidy in the form of tax advantages under the 1971 Revenue Act.

The Act set up Domestic International Sales Corporations (DISCS) for the purpose of managing manufacturers' export businesses. DISCs were permitted a 50% indefinite tax deferrment provided the profits were reinvested in export activities.

U.S. curbs hide exports. U.S. Commerce Secretary Peter G. Peterson July 15 announced a quota on cattle hide exports to ease "inflationary pressures" on U.S. prices of shoes and other leather goods.

The quota, imposed under the Export Administration Act, would limit exports to the 1971 record level of 16 million hides. Peterson said the quota would be in effect through November when the supply and price situations would be re-examined.

The Washington Post reported July 16 that the price of hides had doubled between October 1971 and July 1972.

The Price Commission had acted in May to prevent shoe manufactuers from adding normal percentage markups to the higher leather prices.

Trade gap worsens. The Commerce Department reported July 27 a trade deficit in June of $590.3 million, seasonally adjusted.

The monthly figure, the third largest on record, brought the midyear trade gap to $3.34 billion, the largest in history. The deficit for the second quarter also was at a record high of $1.93 billion.

U.S. imports in June totaled $4.5 billion, exceeded only in January following the end of the dock strike. U.S. exports for the month were $3.9 billion. Compared with 1971 figures, imports during the first six months of 1972 rose 18% while exports increased 9%.

The trade deficit dropped to $542.2 million in July.

Exports rose 2.9% to $4.02 billion but imports jumped 1.5% to a record level of $4.56 billion.

The January–July trade deficit total was $3.88 billion, which was a larger figure than any past deficit measured in a 12-month year. The U.S. deficit had persisted for 15 of the past 16 months, primarily due to trade imbalance with Japan and Canada.

The deficit for August, however, was only $462.6 million, the lowest figure in eight months.

Payments deficit improves. The second quarter deficit in the U.S. international balance of payments was reduced to a seasonally adjusted level of $831 million on the official reserve basis, the best showing since the first quarter of 1969, according to the Commerce Department Aug. 15.

Officials attributed the improvement to a net inflow of an estimated $1.5 billion in liquid private capital, largely in Eurodollars.

There was less improvement in the net liquidity balance which showed a deficit of $2.32 billion.

Japan third in exports. A Japanese white paper on foreign trade published June 27 said Japan was the third largest exporting country in the world in 1971, outranked only by the U.S. and West Germany. The previous year's exports totaled $24 billion, representing an annual growth rate of more than 20% over the 1970 figure.

The report also said that Japan was the fifth largest importing nation in the world in 1971, with nearly $20 billion worth of goods brought in from other nations.

U.S.-Japanese summit talks. U.S. President Richard M. Nixon and Japanese Premier Kakuei Tanaka ended two days of summit talks in Hawaii Sept. 1 with agreement on short-term measures to reduce the huge U.S. trade deficit with Japan.

A joint communique issued Sept. 1 announced anew the Japanese government's intention to promote imports from the U.S. and to "reduce the [trade] imbalance to a more manageable size within a reasonable period of time." The general nature of the statement indicated Nixon's failure to obtain a specific commitment for a substantial reduction of the U.S. trade deficit with Japan, which was expected to total $3.8 billion in 1972.

A separate statement on trade announced an agreement under which Japan would buy about $1.1 billion worth of American goods over the next two years as a step toward the reduction of the trade imbalance between the two nations. The accord provided for purchase of $390 million worth of U.S. agricultural, forestry and fishery products; $50 million worth of special grain purchases; $320 million in civil aircraft; $20 million worth of helicopters and aviation-related facilities; and $320 million in uranium enrichment services.

(Most of the economic package had been negotiated in recent weeks by U.S. Ambassador to Japan Robert S. Ingersoll and Deputy Vice Foreign Minister Kiyohiko Tsurumi, the New York Times reported Sept. 2. Ingersoll said Sept. 1 a few final details were resolved at the summit talks.)

U.S.-Soviet deals made. International Harvester Co. would supply the Soviet Union with $40 million worth of tractors and equipment by the end of 1973, it was announced Aug. 16 by the company's executive vice president, Omer G. Voss, and by Vladimir Sushkov, head of the Soviet delegation to the International Trade Fair in Seattle.

The large tractors, the International TD-25C, were to be used to construct natural gas pipelines.

The deal was one of a number of U.S.-Soviet arrangements being encouraged as part of a program for expanding U.S. imports in an attack on inflationary trends.

U.S. and Soviet officials disclosed Aug. 24 a series of agreements between the two countries to exchange technological processes. The accords were revealed at a joint news conference at the National Press Club in Washington by Boris E. Kurakin, a spokesman for Licensintorg, the official Soviet buyer and seller of technology, and Henry Shur, president of Patent Management, a U.S. patent and transfer firm that had signed six agreements with Licensintorg.

East-West trade expansion urged. The Committee for Economic Development (CED) Sept. 11 urged the U.S. to remove all restrictions on nonmilitary exports to the Soviet Union, China and other Communist nations, with the exception of North Vietnam, North Korea and Cuba.

The CED, a nonprofit, nonpolitical research organization representing 200 leading businessmen and educators, made its recommendations in conjunction with similar groups in Great Britain, West Germany, France, Japan and Sweden.

The groups proposed that credit terms be liberalized for Eastern bloc countries; that the U.S. and Communist countries extend reciprocal most favored nation trade agreements; that the U.S. permit American companies to invest and enter co-production agreements in Communist countries; and that the Western nations consider at their forthcoming International Monetary Fund meeting in Washington various ways to make the ruble and other Communist currencies convertible on the world money market.

The CED also proposed that an international organization, representing Eastern and Western bloc nations, be formed to establish ground rules to facilitate the expansion of trade.

Communist countries should provide antidumping commitments, the CED said, and adhere to the provisions of the General Agreement on Tariffs and Trade (GATT).

'Significant progress' reported. A joint communique released Sept. 14 by the U.S. and the Soviet Union stated that talks held in Moscow Sept. 11–13 between Soviet officials and Henry A. Kissinger, President Nixon's national security adviser, had produced "significant progress" toward a comprehensive trade agreement between the two countries.

The statement said that during his visit Kissinger had held "frank and constructive" discussions with Leonid I. Brezhnev, the Soviet Communist party leader, and with Foreign Minister Andrei A. Gromyko.

"Special attention was given to the status of commercial relations," the dispatch said, and progress "was made on several issues of principle."

The officials also "agreed to conclude promptly" a maritime agreement that would allow U.S. and Soviet ships to carry cargoes to each other's ports.

ASP repeal accord dropped. The foreign ministers of the nine future members of the European Economic Community (EEC) decided in Brussels Dec. 19 to drop a long-pending agreement that called for the U.S. to end the "American Selling Price" (ASP) system of protecting chemical imports and ·for the EEC, in return, to reduce certain trade barriers. The accord had not been implemented because of the refusal by the U.S. Congress to end the ASP, under which tariffs on certain foreign chemical ·products were calculated on the basis of higher priced equivalent U.S. products.

14 nations sign trade pacts. Representatives of 14 West European nations Dec. 21 signed in Brussels the final documents creating a single free trade area embracing the six original EEC members, the three incoming members and five members of the European Free Trade Association. The latter would have free trade with EEC members. The EFTA signers were Austria, Portugal, Sweden, Switzerland and Liechtenstein.

Iceland and Finland—who had also negotiated EFTA free trade pacts with the EEC—did not sign the final documents.

Progress in Monetary Reform

Nixon pledges action. President Nixon addressed the opening session of the International Monetary Fund (IMF) and World Bank annual meeting Sept. 25 in Washington and committed the U.S. to efforts to achieve a "thoroughgoing reform of the world monetary system." He asserted that reform measures should center on "prompt and orderly adjustments" in balance of payments problems encountered by individual nations.

Nixon reiterated the U.S. position that a modernized currency system could only form part of a "total reform of international economic affairs, encompassing trade and investment opportunities, as well."

Nixon called on "our trading partners to help bring about equal competition." "I will not condone the exporting of jobs out of the U.S. caused by an unfairness built into the world's trading system," he asserted.

The U.S. favored monetary reform not only because it was in "our national self interest," but because "we must make certain that international commerce becomes a source of stability and harmony rather than a cause of friction and animosity," Nixon said.

The President emphasized the key monetary problem—adjustment of payments balances. "No nation," Nixon said, "should be denied the opportunity to adjust, nor relieved of the obligation to adjust."

Shultz outlines U.S. plan—Treasury Secretary George P. Shultz presented the U.S.' specific reform proposals Sept. 26 in an address to the joint Washington meetings.

The Administration plan, which won generally favorable acceptance, included the following major points:

■ A set of rules, based on whether a country was losing or gaining international monetary reserves, would determine whether the currency's basic exchange rate should be altered or the country should take other actions to adjust its balance of payments.

■ Penalties, such as a general import surcharge, should be imposed on countries refusing to change exchange rates or make other adjustments.

■ After a transitional period, when the U.S. achieved payment surplus or equilibrium, it would restore the convertibility of the dollar into monetary reserves, although probably not simply into gold, as in the past.

■ Ordinary trading of currencies should be permitted to fluctuate in wider bands than was presently the case—up to 4.5% on either side of par, instead of the 2.25% established under the Smithsonian Agreement.

■ A "diminishing role for gold" should be paralleled by an increasingly greater role for Special Drawing Rights (SDRs), which eventually would replace the dollar as the monetary system's "numeraire" or unit by which other currencies were measured.

■ Because of the link between currency reform and trade, there should be a "harmonizing" of the rules of the IMF and the General Agreement on Tariffs and Trade (GATT).

■ "Controls on capital flows should not be allowed to become a means of maintaining a chronically undervalued currency."

Shultz said the proposals did not constitute a "detailed blueprint" for monetary reform, but he called on members to prepare "the main outlines of a new system" for the 1973 IMF and World Bank meeting in Nairobi, Kenya.

In speeches later Sept. 26, Great Britain's Chancellor of the Exchequer, Anthony Barber, welcomed the Shultz plan as a "major contribution" to the discussion of monetary reform. But, like Koshiro Ueki, Japan's minister of finance, Barber questioned the value of "objective indicators" to trigger adjustments in exchange rates.

Giscard presents French plan—The French Finance Minister, Valery Giscard d'Estaing, proposed a three stage program for monetary reform at the meeting Sept. 27. The first stage would involve an agreement, to be reached by the next annual meeting in Sept. 1973, on exchange rate mechanisms.

In calling for rapid agreement on currency reform, Giscard again stated a long standing French position that monetary talks should not be delayed by discussions of the trade problem. Joined by Canada later Sept. 27, Giscard argued against any "automatic" formula for determining when a country's exchange rate should be adjusted, a major aspect of the U.S. plan.

(Shultz had said Sept. 26, "I believe disproportionate gains or losses in reserves may be the most equitable and effective single indicator we have to guide the adjustment process.")

Also in opposition to the U.S. position, Giscard said that France preferred the use of a gold "numeraire," instead of a paper gold, or SDR, standard of value.

Other monetary plans. Four other plans dealing with the U.S. and internation monetary and trade difficulties were issued before the IMF meeting opened.

A plan drawn up by C. Fred Bergsten, a former member of Presidential adviser Henry Kissinger's staff, was published by the Council on Foreign Relations Sept. 18. Bergsten, a senior fellow at the Brookings Institution, was quoted by the New York Times Sept. 19 as saying the choice facing the major financial powers was whether "the reform will be negotiated and rational, or result solely from the interplay of market forces and the uncoordinated exercise of national economic and political power." Several points in the proposal were similar to the Shultz plan, including the emphasis on the use of SDRs and wider bands within which currency values could fluctuate.

A study released Sept. 20 by the International Economic Policy Association, representing major U.S. corporations active in trade abroad, concluded that a devaluation of the dollar would not give the U.S. equilibrium in its balance of payments situation "because of the limited volume of trade which is price sensitive." The group suggested that the trade imbalance problem could be solved only by further actions, such as a new international agreement on sharing the balance of payment costs of U.S. troops abroad, tieing all foreign aid and U.S. payments to the World Bank and other international lending institutions to U.S. goods and services and the creation of a public development corporation for long term borrowing of dollars held by foreign governments. States and localities could then reborrow these dollars at low rates for public projects.

The Monetary Committee of the Atlantic Council of the U.S., headed by former Treasury Secretary Henry H. Fowler and including many former high government officials, issued a reform plan Sept. 17. Several aspects of the proposal resembled the Shultz plan, such as penalties for countries refusing to alter exchange rates under new rules and the return of convertibility of the dollar into monetary reserves, although not to gold, after the U.S. balance of payment deficit was overcome. The group suggested an interim pact to assure the exchange rates established under the Smithsonian Agreement be continued through the purchase of dollars, that the U.S. minimize its intervention in foreign exchange markets and that the U.S. guarantee countries holding dollars against loss in event of the dollar's further devaluation.

Henry C. Wallich, a Yale University professor, addressed the IMF Sept. 24 before the meeting's formal opening. Wallich urged the group to adopt a system based on the concept of "effective" exchange rates, determined in part by the exchange rates of a country's major trading partners.

The international monetary system currently utilized a "parity" system of currency values. The Smithsonian negotiation, Wallich said, "brought home the obvious fact that the parity of any one country is a point in a vacuum, of little economic meaning when numerous other countries are changing their parities."

He summarized his plan as one that "leaves major decisions concerning exchange rates to national authorities, delegates minor decisions to the IMF, and thereby seeks to achieve prompt rate changes, consistent rate movements, protection against anticyclical misuse of rate changes and a reduction of speculation."

Changes in gold system urged. A subcommittee of the U.S. Congressional Joint Economic Committee unanimously recommended Nov. 19 that the 1968 international agreement which had established a two-tier gold system be abolished.

In its place, the subcommittee, chaired by Rep. Henry S. Reuss (D, Wis.) urged that central banks and the IMF be permitted to sell gold on the open market (although still be barred from buying it) in order to "help ease the apprehension that currently exists about the viability of the Smithsonian monetary arrangements," to encourage the use of gold by central banks in "international settlements" and to aid in the long-term U.S. goal of "phasing out gold as a monetary reserve asset."

With the end to the two-tier gold system, the subcommittee recommended that private American citizens be allowed to buy, sell and hold gold, a practice forbidden by law since 1933.

Other subcommittee suggestions included:

■ Replacing the current IMF requirement that certain transactions by member states be made in gold, with a provision allowing the full use of "paper gold," Special Drawing Rights (SDRs).

■ Allowing the IMF agreement to purchase gold from South Africa to expire "naturally" in 1971.

■ Permitting a "nominal" issue of SDRs in 1973 and 1974 to prevent their "falling into disuse," and providing that a larger proportion of SDRs be allotted underdeveloped states.

Contrary to the Administration position, the Reuss subcommittee claimed that the role of gold could be further limited before negotiations on other major monetary reform questions were completed.

World monetary talks begin. Deputies of the International Monetary Fund's (IMF) Committee of 20 met in Washington Nov. 26–29 to begin negotiations for reform of the world monetary system.

The U.S. outlined a proposal Nov. 28 calling for an "objective test" to determine when nations should act to restore balance to their payments systems.

The U.S. plan, which was intended to help deal with chronic money deficits and surpluses, suggested that the IMF establish a "normal" figure for each nation's monetary reserves, taking into account estimated "normal" growth, based on its role in the world economy.

Deviations from this "normal" indicator, reflected as changes in the monetary reserve assets, would constitute a signal for prompt action requiring the upward revaluation or devaluation of a nation's currency.

Total U.S. reserves gain. The nation's international reserve assets gained $980 million in 1972 to reach a level of $13.15 billion at the end of the year.

U.S. Gold Holdings, Total Reserve Assets & Liquid Liabilities to Foreigners

[Selected periods in billions of dollars]

	Gold holdings	Total assets	Liquid liabilities
End of World War II	20.1	20.1	6.9
Dec. 31, 1957	22.8	24.8	15.8
Dec. 31, 1970	10.7	14.5	43.3
Dec. 31, 1971	10.2	12.2	64.2
Dec. 31, 1972	10.5	13.2	79.0

Source: U.S. Treasury Department.

Treasury Department officials, who released the figures, attributed the increase to the implementation of dollar devaluation in May 1972. The action also caused the U.S. gold stock to rise in value by $828 million to $10.49 billion.

U.S. holdings in Special Drawing Rights, or "paper gold," totaled $1.96 billion. The nation's ability to draw foreign currencies from the International Monetary Fund was $464 million at the end of the year.

Action Against Inflation

EEC ministers adopt plan. The six finance ministers of the European Economic Community (EEC), meeting in Luxembourg Oct. 30–31, adopted a non-binding anti-inflationary program aimed at reducing price increases from an average 6% annually to 4%.

The ministers of the three future EEC members—Britain, Denmark and Ireland—associated themselves with the objectives of the plan, but said they would decide on how to enact the measures only after taking into account their respective internal situations after entry.

In addition to the declaration of intention to hold price increases to the 4% rate, the ministers agreed to: restrict the growth in money supplies to the increase in the real gross national products of each member state, plus the allowed 4% price rise; hold government spending rises to the GNP rates of increase; and urge "concerted action" against inflation between government, labor and industry in each nation. These decisions were only advisory, and actual implementation would depend on approval by each government.

The ministers also halved the tariffs on beef until Feb. 1, 1973; abolished import quotas on potatoes for a year, effective Dec. 15; and decided in principle to stimulate competition and attack concentrations of industrial power.

Sicco Mansholt, president of the EEC Commission, said Oct. 31 he was "disappointed" by the program and asserted "We need more rigorous policy which is convincing." Singling out the decision on beef tariffs, Mansholt asked "How

8

can I now face my wife, tell her ... we refuse to abolish tariffs while there is a shortage of beef in the world?" The EEC had suspended tariffs on beef for a short period in the summer.

The EEC Commission had proposed total abolition of beef tariffs, an across-the-board 15% tariff reduction on other products for a six-month period, effective Jan. 1, 1973; and a 20% increase in industrial import quotas except textiles, to last six months.

A spokesman for the West German delegation expressed particular disappointment over rejection of an across-the-board tariff cut. The French had fought the proposal, arguing that adoption of unilateral tariff concessions now would weaken the EEC position in the forthcoming world trade negotiations.

Report on inflation—Inflation was increasing at an average annual rate of 6% in the EEC through the summer, according to a report released by the EEC Commission Oct. 13. Food prices rose by 7.4% in France and by at least 6% in the other five EEC nations, the report said. It also listed sharp increases in wages—13.3% in Belgium, 11.2% in France and 9.2% in West Germany.

Paris, Bonn raise bank rates—The French and West German central banks raised their discount rates Nov. 2 in an attempt to stem inflation. French Finance Minister Giscard d'Estaing said his government's move was "a European decision," a reference to the EEC plans to combat sharply rising prices and restrict the growth of money supplies.

The Bank of France increased its bank rate from 5 3/4% to 6 1/2%. The German Bundesbank raised its rate from 3 1/2% to 4%. The German bank also increased its Lombard rate—Central Bank charges to member banks on loans based on securities—from 5% to 6%.

A vice president of the German Bundesbank, Otmar Emminger, told a news conference in Frankfurt Nov. 2 that Germany intended to lower the rate of its expansion in the money supply from the current more than 15% to 9% in 1973.

Britain freezes wages & prices. Prime Minister Edward Heath imposed an im-

mediate 90-day freeze on wages and most prices, rents and dividends Nov. 6. Announcing the program in the House of Commons, Heath said he had been forced to adopt statutory measures following the rejection by Britain's labor unions of government proposals for voluntary wage and price curbs.

Heath said the temporary freeze was the first stage of his anti-inflationary program and he indicated it would be followed by a more sophisticated set of controls if the government failed to reach agreement with the unions on voluntary curbs.

The bill to make the freeze statutory, called the Counter-Inflationary (Temporary Provisions) Bill, was published later Nov. 6. It provided for the freeze to become effective immediately and to last for 90 days after Parliament approved the legislation and the queen gave her assent. It also gave the government the option to extend the freeze for an additional 60 days.

Exempted from the freeze were fruit, vegetables, meat, fish and imported raw materials, in addition to rent increases already ordered for public housing and rents in furnished apartments.

Businessmen and workers had rushed to beat the expected announcement of the mandatory freeze. Shortly before Heath's speech, four automobile manufacturers announced price increases and more than one million workers, 950,000 of them municipal laborers, had obtained pay increases.

Heath had presented his proposal of a voluntary wage and price restraint program Sept. 26 in the latest session of the tripartite talks between the government, the Trades Union Congress (TUC), representing labor, and the Confederation of British Industry (CBI), representing management.

The proposals, which Heath subsequently presented at a press conference, asked for a maximum 5% retail price increase, with a 4% price increase ceiling on manufactured goods, and a flat £2 ($4.90) a week limit on pay increases over the next year. The program pledged the government to aim for a 5% economic growth rate for the next two years and envisaged some type of threshold agreement to cover retail price increases that would result from Britain's entry into the European Economic Community in 1973. It suggested creation of a new body to help low-pay industries achieve efficiencies that would enable them to pay higher wages.

Heath noted that the flat pay rise ceiling, which would apply to all wage and salary earners, would provide a proportionately larger benefit to the lowest paid workers than to top management. He said the ceiling would apply immediately to all government workers.

The proposals were unanimously rejected by the TUC General Council Sept. 27 as "totally unacceptable." However, the council left the door open for further talks to work out an alternative plan. CBI representatives expressed reservations the same day about the price restraint proposals, but the CBI ultimately accepted them.

Following additional talks, the TUC Nov. 2 rejected the government plan.

1% of bank deposits frozen—In an attempt to curb the growth of money supply as part of the government's anti-inflationary program, the Bank of England ordered banks Nov. 9 to deliver to it 1% of their deposits held Nov. 15.

Bonn curbs foreign loans. In another attempt to halt the mounting inflation, the West German government Dec. 6 ordered restrictions on borrowing abroad.

A Cabinet decree, effective Jan. 1, 1973, would reduce the amount of unconditional foreign loans available to German business abroad from 500,000 marks ($156,000) to 50,000 marks. Companies borrowing more than the 50,000 marks would have to deposit the equivalent of half the additional sum in the German Bundesbank (central bank).

The government's council of advisers, in its annual report, proposed the adoption of an income tax surcharge to curb inflation in 1973. The council also called for reduced government spending and moderation in wage and price increases.

France fights inflation. In another attack on France's inflationary spiral, the

government announced Dec. 7 a new program that called for temporary cuts in the value-added tax and a $1 billion state bond issue.

Announcing the plan to the National Assembly Finance Commission, Finance Minister Valery Giscard d'Estaing said the 7% value-added tax on meat would be dropped for six months. The value-added tax on manufactured goods would be cut by 2%, the tax on pharmaceutical goods by 3% and that on pastry by 10%. Giscard d'Estaing appealed to businessmen and industrial leaders to pass on to consumers the full savings from the tax cuts.

In an attempt to stem the potential inflationary effect of the tax cuts, the Finance minister announced the sale of a 15-year state bond issue worth approximately $1 billion. He also announced a $\frac{1}{4}$% increase in interest rates on savings accounts and warned banks to respect existing credit restraints or face stern government penalties.

Ruling out a wage and price freeze at present, Giscard d'Estaing said the government would nevertheless recommend that employers and unions hold wage hikes to 6% and price increases to 4% in 1973.

The new anti-inflationary moves followed the announcement Nov. 27 that the cost-of-living index had risen by .9% in October, compared to .6% in September. Officials said prices had increased by 6.6% in the year ending in October.

The government Nov. 30 had reduced potato prices and released 70,000 tons of butter to the market at reduced prices.

The Bank of France raised from 15% to 33%, effective Nov. 21, compulsory reserve deposits on loans made by commercial banks since March. A spokesman had said earlier that the move would freeze about $740 million in bank assets.

The government raised the guaranteed hourly minimum wage by 5.8% to 4.55 francs Oct. 31. The increase would benefit some 700,000 workers, 200,000 of them agricultural laborers, raising their pay to at least 787 francs a month for a 40-hour workweek and to 892 francs for a 44½-hour week.

1973

Most mandatory wage and price controls were ended by President Nixon in January 1973, and Phase 3's voluntary methods were substituted as the anti-inflationary strategy for the first half of the year. With fewer controls, however, prices continued to go up. The rise in the "cost of living" increased from the 3.4% of 1972 to 8.8% in 1973. A temporary freeze on consumer prices, announced in June, helped slow the price spiral. The freeze was followed by Phase 4, which reinstituted mandatory controls but under which price increases were authorized to a far greater extent. Nixon's budget for 1974 proposed curtailing or ending several federal programs as a means of fighting inflation. Investigators charged that the controversial 1972 sale of U.S. wheat to the U.S.S.R. had been unjustly expensive to U.S. farmers, taxpayers and consumers and an additional cause of high food prices. Energy costs, led by escalating oil prices, continued to rise and acted as a major spur to international inflation. Although world trade grew during 1973, much of the increase was attributable to inflation, and the U.S. share of the trade total dropped because of discriminatory trade practices. A surplus was recorded in the U.S. balance of trade in 1973 (after a deficit in 1972), and the deficit in the U.S. balance of payments declined. These improvements, however, were not sufficient to curb inflation or to halt speculative attacks on the U.S. dollar. Gold prices soared both before and after the U.S. devalued the dollar in February.

Government Policy

Nixon Ends Most Mandatory Wage & Price Controls

Early in 1973, with the rise in prices and wages apparently slowing down, the President ordered an end to most price and wage controls and instituted the voluntary Phase 3 stage of his anti-inflation "game plan." This change, however, took place just at a time when inflation was beginning to accelerate. Consumer ("cost-of-living") prices rose from 125.3% of the 1937 average in 1972 to 133.1% in 1973. During 1973, the consumer price index rose by a 6.1% annual rate (seasonally adjusted) in the first quarter, an 8.4% rate in the second, 9.1% in the third and 9.9% in the final quarter.

Percent rise in cost of living

Year:	
1960	1.5
1961	.7
1962	1.2
1963	1.6
1964	1.2
1965	1.9
1966	3.4
1967	3.0
1968	4.7
1969	6.1
1970	5.5
1971	3.4
1972	3.4
1973	8.8

Phase 3 begins immediately. President Nixon terminated mandatory wage and price controls Jan. 11 except in the "problem areas" of food, health care and construction.

In an Executive Order effective immediately upon its announcement, the President abruptly shifted the Administration's economic stabilization program into Phase 3, voluntary compliance with federal standards toward a national anti-inflation goal. In a message to Congress, the President stated that his ultimate goal was "a further reduction in the inflation rate to 2½% or less by the end of 1973." The previous goal was a 2%-3% rate by the end of 1972.

The President told Congress he had taken the step after conducting extensive consultation to help assess "the place of controls in the future." More than 400 individuals representing "a complete spectrum of interests" had been consulted in 63 meetings. The Administration's finding from this, Nixon said, was "that the burdens of a control system will mount in the coming period if the present system continued for long unchanged in an expanding economy."

Phase 1, a 90-day wage-price freeze, had been initiated Aug. 15, 1971. Phase 2, which was being discontinued, had begun Nov. 14, 1971.

Text of President's Message to Congress on Phase 3

During 1969, the annual rate of inflation in the United States was about 6%. During my first term in office, that rate has been cut nearly in half and today the United States has the lowest rate of inflation of any industrial country in the free world.

In the last year and a half, this decline in inflation has been accompanied by a rapid economic expansion. Civilian employment rose more rapidly during the past year than ever before in our history and unemployment substantially declined. We now have one of the highest economic growth rates in the developed world.

In short, 1972 was a very good year for the American economy. I expect 1973 and 1974 to be even better. They can, in fact, be the best years our economy has ever experienced—provided we have the will and wisdom, in both the public and private sectors, to follow appropriate economic policies.

For the past several weeks, members of my Administration have been reviewing our economic policies in an effort to keep them up to date. I deeply appreciate the generous advice and excellent suggestions we have received in our consultations with the Congress.

We are also grateful for the enormous assistance we have received from hundreds of leaders representing business, labor, farm and consumer groups, and the general public. These discussions have been extremely helpful to us in reaching several central conclusions about our economic future.

One major point which emerges as we look both at the record of the past and the prospects for the future is the central role of our Federal monetary and fiscal policies.

We cannot keep inflation in check unless we keep government spending in check. This is why I have insisted that our spending for fiscal year 1973 not exceed $250 billion and that our proposed budget for fiscal year 1974 not exceed the revenues which the existing tax system would produce at full employment.

I hope and expect that the Congress will receive this budget with a similar sense of fiscal discipline. The stability of our prices depends on the restraint of the Congress.

As we move into a new year, and into a new term for this Administration, we are also moving to a new phase of our economic stabilization program. I believe the system of controls which has been in effect since 1971 has helped considerably in improving the health of our economy.

I am today submitting to the Congress legislation which would extend for another year—until April 30 of 1974—the basic legislation on which that system is based, the Economic Stabilization Act.

But even while we recognize the need for continued government restraints on prices and wages, we also look to that day when we can enjoy the advantages of price stability without the disadvantages of such restraints.

I believe we can prepare for that day, and hasten its coming, by modifying the present system so that it relies to a greater extent on the voluntary cooperation of the private sector in making reasonable price and wage decisions.

Under Phase 3, prior approval by the federal government will not be required for changes in wages and prices, except in special problem areas. The federal government, with the advice of management and labor, will develop standards to guide private conduct which will be self-administering.

This means that business and workers will be able to determine for themselves the conduct that con-

forms to the standards. Initially and generally we shall rely upon the voluntary cooperation of the private sector for reasonable observance of the standards.

However, the federal government will retain the power—and the responsibility—to step in and stop action that would be inconsistent with our anti-inflation goals.

I have established as the overall goal of this program a further reduction in the inflation rate to 2½% or less by the end of 1973.

Under this program, much of the federal machinery which worked so well during Phase 1 and Phase 2 can be eliminated, including the Price Commission, the Pay Board, the Committee on the Health Services Industry, the Committee on State and Local Government Cooperation, and the Rent Advisory Board.

Those who served so ably as members of these panels and their staffs—especially Judge George H. Boldt, chairman of the Pay Board, and C. Jackson Grayson Jr., chairman of the Price Commission—have my deep appreciation and that of their countrymen for their devoted and effective contributions.

This new program will be administered by the Cost of Living Council. The council's new director will be John T. Dunlop. Dr. Dunlop succeeds Donald Rumsfeld who leaves this post with the nation's deepest gratitude for a job well done.

Under our new program, special efforts will be made to combat inflation in areas where rising prices have been particularly troublesome, especially in fighting rising food prices. Our anti-inflation program will not be fully successful until its impact is felt at the local supermarket or corner grocery store.

I am therefore directing that our current mandatory wage and price control system be continued with special vigor for firms involved in food processing and food retailing. I am also establishing a new committee to review government policies which affect food prices and a non-government advisory group to examine other ways of achieving price stability in food markets.

I will ask this advisory group to give special attention to new ways of cutting costs and improving productivity at all points along the food production, processing and distribution chain.

In addition, the Department of Agriculture and the Cost of Living Council yesterday and today announced a number of important steps to hold down food prices in the best possible way—by increasing food supply.

I believe all these efforts will enable us to check effectively the rising cost of food without damaging the growing prosperity of American farmers. Other special actions which will be taken to fight inflation include continuing the present mandatory controls over the health and construction industries and continuing the present successful program for interest and dividends.

The new policies I am announcing today can mean even greater price stability with less restrictive bureaucracy. Their success, however, will now depend on a firm spirit of self-restraint both within the federal government and among the general public.

If the Congress will receive our new budget with a high sense of fiscal responsibility and if the public will continue to demonstrate the same spirit of voluntary cooperation which was so important during Phase 1 and Phase 2 then we can bring the inflation rate below 2½% and usher in an unprecedented era of full and stable prosperity.

Initially, the wage-price standards for Phase 3 would be those in effect under Phase 2. The essential difference was that they would now be "self-administered" by business and labor, who were expected "to determine by themselves what conduct conforms reasonably to the guides" without requiring prior approval from the government. "Voluntary behavior consistent with the standards and the goal will be expected," according to a White House explanation released by Treasury Secretary George P. Shultz, who announced the Phase 3 program.

The government was retaining the power, "and the responsibility," the President emphasized in his message to Congress, "to step in and stop action that would be inconsistent with our anti-inflation goals." Acting under the Economic Stabilization Act, the President requested Congress to extend that legislation for a year beyond its scheduled expiration April 30. Retention of the threat of federal intervention was "the stick in the closet," Shultz said, to insure voluntary compliance with the anti-inflationary goal.

As part of Phase 3, all federal rent controls were abandoned and no formal standard for restraining increases was retained. The President urged landlords "to exercise restraint" themselves. This sector was viewed by the Administration as stable in that there was an expanding supply of rental units, increasing vacancy rates and a modest rate of inflation. Less than 30% of all residential rental units had been covered under Phase 2.

In other revisions, the Pay Board and Price Commission were abolished. The Cost of Living Council was retained, and a new director, John T. Dunlop, a labor relations consultant, was appointed. Dunlop would leave his post as chairman of the government's Construction Industry Stabilization Committee.

A new Labor-Management Advisory Committee to the Cost of Living Council was also appointed to advise on whether the stabilization standards should be changed "and, if so, how," according to the Administration. The membership of the advisory group included five representatives from business and five from labor, including AFL-CIO President George Meany, who described Phase 3 as "a step in the right direction." The other labor members were union presidents I. W. Abel of the AFL-CIO United Steelworkers of America; Frank Fitzsimmons of the International Brotherhood of Teamsters; Paul Hall of the AFL-CIO Seafarers' International Union; and Leonard Woodcock of the United Auto Workers.

Business members were Stephen Bechtel Jr., president of Bechtel Corp.; Edward Carter, board chairman of Broadway-Hale Stores, Inc.; R. Heath Larry, vice chairman of the board of U.S. Steel Corp.; James Roche, member of the board of directors of General Motors Corp., and Walter Wriston, chairman, First National City Bank, New York.

The Cost of Living Council (CLC), receiving some of the staff from the abolished pay and price boards, also would continue work with the monitoring staff from the Internal Revenue Service, but the staff of about 3,000 assigned to this was expected to be reduced by half. The working force of the entire stabilization program was expected to decline also by half to about 2,000 persons.

The CLC itself was amplified by the additions of the secretary of health, education and welfare and Mrs. Anne Armstrong, counselor to the President.

The Construction Industry Stabilization Committee and the current voluntary stabilization program on interest and dividends were to be continued.

In the health care sector, the President directed that a sub-group of the CLC and an outside advisory group probe ways to restrain the strong upward cost thrust.

In the volatile food-price category, the President also was creating a new advisory group "to give special attention to new ways of cutting costs and improving productivity at all points along the food chain," he said. Shultz also said the government planned to sell its grain

RISE IN PRICES INDEXES, 1973				
[Seasonally adjusted annual rate by quarters in percent]				
Type	1st	2d	3d	4th
All consumer prices_____	6.1	8.4	9.1	9.9
Food prices_____	18.6	20.2	24.6	14.5
Energy prices_____	8.2	11.6	5.7	27.0
All other prices_____	2.5	4.1	4.7	6.8
Wholesale industrial prices_	6.5	15.2	6.5	20.5
Energy prices_____	12.8	41.3	22.2	133.2
Other prices_____	5.9	12.6	4.9	11.3

stocks. "We expect to empty the bins and put this on the market," he emphasized. The effort to restrain rising food prices "will be stepped up," he said.

The CLC would maintain pay and price divisions during a 90-day transition period to handle the backlog of existing cases, which would be decided upon Phase 2 standards.

There was some revision of Phase 2 standards. The profit-margin test would be waived in Phase 3 for companies with average price increase for all products not exceeding 1½% in a year. As a concession to labor, companies with fewer than 1,000 employes would no longer be required to keep records of wage increases. The previous small-business exemption covered companies with fewer than 61 employes.

As a result of the abandonment of most mandatory controls, companies with annual sales of $100 million or more would no longer be required to provide "pre-notification" of price increases. Companies in the $50 million sales category would be required to keep records of their price and profit margin changes; those in the $250 million sales category would have to file quarterly reports on such changes. Smaller companies would be exempt from all such requirements.

Employe units of 1,000 or more would be required to maintain records of wage rate changes, units of 5,000 or more to file reports.

White House Summary on New Controls Program

The General Standards

As a general guide for prices, increases of prices above presently authorized levels should not exceed increases of costs. Even where costs have increased, prices should not be increased if the firm's profit margin exceeds the firm's base-period profit margin. Alternatively, a firm may increase prices to reflect increased cost without regard to its profit margin if the firm's average price increases would not exceed 1.5% in a year. The definition and measurement of costs, price, profits, etc., can be guided by the regulations already established by the Price Commission, which are presumably known to the firms involved.

The base period for calculation of the profit-margin guide is revised to permit inclusion of any fiscal year that has been concluded since Aug. 15, 1971.

The existing general standards of the Pay Board can be taken for the present as a guide to appropriate maximum wage increases unless and until they are modified. A labor-management advisory committee

is being established to advise the Cost of Living Council [CLC] on whether the standards should be modified and, if so, how. Certain minor modifications are being announced at this time and published in the Federal Register.

The details of the Phase 3 program are briefly summarized below:

Monitoring

The Cost of Living Council staff and the Internal Revenue Service under the direction of the Cost of Living Council will monitor performance through:

■ Reviewing reports received from firms and employe units.

■ Spot checks and audits of firm records.

■ Use of government and trade data price reporting and record keeping.

With the exception of firms subject to special rules (food and health) or exceptions:

■ All firms with sales of more than $50 million (approximately 3,500 firms) are required to keep records of profit margin changes as well as price changes which will permit the computation of weighted average price increases. Firms will have the obligation of producing these upon request.

■ All firms with sales of $250 million or more (approximately 800 firms) are required to file quarterly reports concerning any weighted average price change and their profit margin.

■ Regulated industries will be guided by the general criteria listed in present Price Commission regulations and restraint is expected to be reflected in their actions and the actions of the regulatory agencies.

■ Requirements will not apply to rental units not already exempt under the present program. Landlords are expected to exercise restraint but no standards or binding requirements will be issued. This step is taken in view of the expanding supply of rental units, increasing vacancy rates and the modest rate of inflation shown in this sector. It is estimated that the present program affects less than 30% of residual rental units.

Wage Reporting and Record Keeping

With the exception of units subject to special rules (food, health and construction) or exceptions:

■ All employe units of 1,000 or more will be required to keep records of wage rate changes. They will have the obligation of producing these upon request.

■ All employe units of 5,000 or more will be required to file reports with CLC indicating wage rate changes.

Reserve Authority and Action of the Cost of Living Council

The Cost of Living Council reserves the authority to establish mandatory standards where that is necessary to assure that future action in a particular industry is consistent with the national goal.

Upon learning through its monitoring of prices and labor negotiations that action has been or is about to be taken that is not consistent with the standards or the goals of the program, the Cost of Living Council can use its authority to issue a temporary order setting interim price and wage levels. This would allow the council to:

■ Require parties to supply information and assurances demonstrating that their actions are not or will not be inconsistent with the standards or goals of the program.

■ Hold public hearings.

■ Issue a special rule or order of the council setting out a specific legally binding level for proposed price or pay action that would restrain an industry or firm from that point on. Such a rule or order could include the requirement to roll back already effected price or wage increases.

Food

Food processors will be required mandatorily to comply with present regulations, somewhat modified, including pre-notification and approval of cost-justified price increases. Food retailers will be held to present margin markups.

Minor administrative modifications will be made. Pay units in the food processing and retailing industries will continue to be covered by present regulations.

A committee drawn from the Cost of Living Council will be established. It will be chaired by the chairman of the Cost of Living Council and composed of the chairman of the Council of Economic Advisers, Secretary of Agriculture, director of the Office of Management and Budget, and director of the Cost of Living Council. The committee's purpose will be to review and recommend appropriate changes in government policies having an adverse effect on food prices.

Health

The present controls applicable to this sector will be continued until appropriate modifications are recommended by the committee described below.

A committee drawn from the Cost of Living Council will be established. It will be chaired by the director of the Cost of Living Council and composed of the chairman of the Council of Economic Advisers, the director of the Office of Management and Budget and the Secretaries of the Treasury and Health, Education and Welfare. (The Secretary of Health, Education and Welfare is being added to the Cost of Living Council.)

The committee's purpose will be to review and make appropriate recommendations concerning changes in government programs that could lessen the rise of health costs.

An advisory committee composed of knowledgeable individuals outside the federal government will be established. It will have a broad mandate and will advise the Cost of Living Council on such matters as the operation of controls in the health industry and changes in government programs that could help alleviate the rise of health costs.

This committee will also work to mobilize insurance companies and other third-party payers to use their influence to curb the rise in health costs.

Construction

The present Construction Industry Stabilization Committee will continue its work with the twin goals of improving the bargaining structure in the industry and achieving additional progress in bringing the rate of wage growth in this sector into line with the general wage growth in the economy.

Rules are provided to insure that modifications in the wage growth rate can be reflected by adjustments in construction prices.

Interest and Dividends

The present highly successful voluntary program will be continued under the direction of the Committee on Interest and Dividends chaired by Dr. Arthur Burns of the Federal Reserve.

Structure

The Cost of Living Council will be continued and its membership expanded to include:

■ The secretary of health, education and welfare.

■ Mrs. Anne Armstrong, counselor to the President.

The Price Commission and Pay Board and all advisory committees will terminate effective not more than 90 days from the date of the executive order or such earlier date as the CLC chairman determines. The Price Commission and Pay Board authority and staff will be transferred to the Cost of Living Council.

The following units will be established or re-established by a new executive order:

The Cost of Living Council.
Labor-Management Committee.
Cost of Living Council Committee on Food.
Food Industry Advisory Committee.
Cost of Living Council Committee on Health.
Health Industry Advisory Committee.
Construction Industry Stabilization Committee.
Committee on Interest and Dividends.

It is estimated that the economic stabilization program personnel will be decreased from the present [total of] about 4,000 to about 2,000 positions.

Transition

New regulations and requirements will take effect immediately.

Parties covered by present program rules will be required to comply with all such rules up to the effective date of the new regulations. Price-wage changes or profit developments occurring at a time when they are subject to present program rules will be subject to review and enforcement even after the new regulations have taken effect. Parties required to report under present rules will be obligated to report in the regular manner all developments occurring under these rules prior to this date.

While the Price Commission and Pay Board will terminate operations, their staffs will immediately be assigned to the Cost of Living Council to handle the orderly disposition of pending matters including the application of present regulations to matters occurring while they were in effect, particularly annual profit margin reports.

A major program of placement will be undertaken by the director's office of the Cost of Living Council to assist Pay Board and Price Commission and Advisory Committee employes in finding suitable employment as the workload decreases.

The Legislation

A one-year extension of the present Economic Stabilization Act is requested.

Reaction. The Dow Jones industrial stock price average set a record high of 1,-051.70 at the New York Stock Exchange close Jan. 11 in response to the partial decontrol announcement. But the market then declined sharply Jan. 12, and the D-J closed at 1,039.36, its largest drop since Dec. 18, 1972 when Vietnam peace talks broke down.

AFL-CIO President George Meany termed the Administration action "a step in the right direction" but reserved the right to oppose continuation of the economic stabilization program after April 30, when Phase 2 would expire.

(United Auto Workers President Leonard Woodcock announced Jan. 16 that his union would fight any extension beyond the April deadline; however, Meany and Woodcock agreed to serve on the Administration's new labor management advisory commission, the Washington Post reported Jan. 17.)

The New York Times reported Jan. 12 that Nixon's decision to drop direct wage-price restrictions resulted in part from Meany's talks with Treasury Secretary George P. Shultz. Shultz agreed to a voluntary controls program, according to the Times, in return for labor's pledge to participate in the stabilization program and to cooperate in seeking non-inflationary wage hikes during 1973 bargaining sessions.

The Times quoted an unidentified union official who described Phase 3 as a "joint Shultz-Meany victory."

Labor spokesmen were pleased with the appointment of John T. Dunlop as director of the new Cost of Living Council, because of his long experience in labor-management relations and his flexible approach to Phase 2 contract disputes, the Times reported.

Walter W. Heller, Gardner Ackley and Arthur M. Okun, economists who were the last three chairmen of the Council of Economic Advisers under Democratic administrations, reacted favorably Jan. 12 to the proposals for Phase 3, although each warned that the voluntary control structure required vigorous use of "standby" government authority when necessary to control inflation.

Congressional reaction was partisan. Rep. Wright Patman (D, Tex.) announced Jan. 11 that the House Banking and Currency Committee would hold hearings on the President's proposals. "The consumer may suffer from this premature move to permissiveness," Patman declared.

Sen. William Proxmire (D, Wis.), chairman of the Joint Economic Committee, said Jan. 11 that he would introduce stronger stabilization guidelines because the program "hasn't worked so far. It shouldn't be easier, it should be harder."

Republican lawmakers and the U.S.

Chamber of Commerce, welcomed the Phase 3 announcement Jan. 11 as heralding the eventual removal of all wage-price controls.

In a letter sent to Nixon Jan. 15, the American Medical Association (AMA) asked that the medical profession be exempted from "special regulations under Phase 3."

The Administration had announced that the food, construction and health industries would remain under direct wage-price controls.

The letter warned that physicians would "not accept such discriminatory treatment."

The AMA claimed that doctors' fees rose 1.7% during Phase 2 under conditions of "voluntary compliance"; however, the Cost of Living Council (CLC) issued figures showing a 2.1% increase during Phase 2 when mandatory controls were in effect. From 1960–1970, the CLC claimed that physicians' office visit fees climbed 61.5% while the consumer price index gained 31.1%.

'72 wage-benefit gains reported. The restraining influence of Phase 2 caused average annual wage and benefit increases in major labor settlements to decline from 8.8% in 1971 to 7.3% in 1972, according to the Labor Department Jan. 27.

The first year of contracts showed that wage and benefit increases rose 8.4% in 1972, compared with 13.1% in 1971. Wage settlements alone rose 6.4% in 1972 over the life of the contract, compared with 8.1% in 1971. In 1972, first-year wage hikes were 7% while 1971 increases were 11.6%.

The average duration of contracts negotiated in 1972 was 25.2 months, compared with 28.4 months under 1971 arrangements.

The contracts, applying to 5,000 or more workers, reflected 592 bargaining settlements for 2.1 million employes.

Discrepancies between the Labor Department's figures and those released by the Pay Board, which had reported an average 5.5% contract raise, were attributed to the Pay Board's inclusion of smaller and nonunion contracts, according to the Wall Street Journal Jan. 29.

Phase 2 costs reported—The Cost of Living Council reported Jan. 15 that the cost of administering Phase 2 was $95 million during the 14 months the wage-price controls were in effect. The Phase 1 freeze period had cost an estimated $1.3 million.

Tough Phase 3 stand promised. At swearing-in ceremonies Feb. 7 for the new Cost of Living Council director, John T. Dunlop, President Nixon promised to use a "very big stick" in dealing with violators of Phase 3 regulations.

In the most determined expression of Administration economic policies, the President referred "to those few who may get out of line" and told Dunlop, "When they do, you let me know."

At Senate Banking Committee hearings Feb. 7 to consider the President's request for a one-year extension of the economic controls program, Federal Reserve System Chairman Arthur F. Burns said he had Nixon's assurance that "enforcement will be very tough indeed" during Phase 3; however, Burns recommended inclusion in the bill of a measure giving the President standby authority, subject to Congressional review, to impose mandatory wage-price controls, a proposal not included in the Administration's bill extending the Economic Stabilization Act beyond the April 30 deadline.

Burns also suggested that Congress insert another Phase 2 requirement deleted from the Nixon legislation—that business and labor give the government advance notice of wage and price increases.

Sen. William Proxmire (D, Wis.), chairman of the Congressional Joint Economic Committee, Feb. 6 expressed skepticism regarding the President's stabilization proposal. "Phase 3 is a feeble, ineffective program" with the force of a "butterfly's hiccup. . . . The public just doesn't believe that you have an effective anti-inflation program," Proxmire told members of the Council of Economic Advisers who were appearing before the committee.

CLC rulings. The Cost of Living Council (CLC) ruled Feb. 8 that during Phase 3, 175 of the nation's largest companies would be required to adhere to term limit pricing agreements already negotiated under the Phase 2 program.

The effect of the ruling was to impose mandatory pricing controls on the firms, whose revenues represented an estimated 10% of total U.S. corporate sales.

Under the agreements, adopted to ease the administration of Phase 2 controls, companies could make price adjustments without seeking advance authorization, provided the weighted average of the increases did not exceed 2% over a 13-month period.

The companies would also remain subject to Phase 2 profit margin restrictions for the duration of the pricing agreements, according to the CLC.

Ninety-one of the long-term pricing agreements were due to expire by April 30, when the "self-administering" Phase 3 regulations would take effect.

In another ruling Jan. 26, the CLC extended the food industry's mandatory wage-price restrictions to include large restaurants, caterers and vending machine operations under the Phase 3 program.

Firms with 60 or more employes, and those companies deriving 20% of total revenues or $50 million from food operations, were affected by the decision.

In wage actions, the CLC declared Feb. 9 that wage cutbacks ordered by the Pay Board under Phase 2 on multiyear contracts could not be altered during Phase 3.

The policy was made explicit in the case of an appeal by the West Coast longshoremen to overturn the Pay Board's rejection of a 30¢-an-hour wage increase. What the CLC did was to uphold the Pay Board's ruling, thereby denying the dockers any wage boosts until June 30, when the two-year contract would expire.

The agency also said any unions or employers that had submitted pay increases to the Pay Board before Jan. 10 could not withdraw them to take advantage of Phase 3's quasi-voluntary controls. Any Pay Board decision rendered after Jan. 10 regarding contracts submitted before Jan. 10 would also be "effective for the entire period specified."

The Pay Board Jan. 31 ordered the 12.3% first year increase won in 1972 by 1,-600 Northwest Airlines pilots reduced to 6.2%; and a 1972 contract negotiated by more than 10,000 Eastern Air Lines mechanics, calling for an 8.9% first year pay hike, was cut to 7% with the difference added to the second year of the contract.

An 8.3% wage and benefit increase won by 33,000 employes of New York City area voluntary hospitals was rolled back to 5.5% by the CLC Jan. 25.

5.5% wage limit in doubt. Treasury Secretary George P. Shultz and John T. Dunlop, director of the Cost of Living Council (CLC), announced Feb. 26 that Phase 2's 5.5% wage guideline would be retained; however, another Administration statement, which did not refer to the 5.5% figure, indicated that a more flexible wage standard had been adopted.

In a paper drafted by Dunlop and released Feb. 26, the Labor Management Advisory Committee declared, "No single standard of wage settlement can be formally applicable at one time to all parties in an economy so large, decentralized and dynamic."

AFL-CIO President George Meany, a member of the advisory panel, said Feb. 26 that he had been assured by Administration officials that the 5.5% limit would be relaxed soon and eventually discarded. Meany interpreted the remarks by Shultz and Dunlop as efforts to "soften the action of the advisory committee."

The Labor Management Advisory Committee had held a private session Feb. 23 in Bal Harbour, Fla.

James M. Roche, former chairman of General Motors Corp. and another member of the labor management group, Feb. 26 cited the 5.5% ceiling as an "overall objective" for 1973. Other government officials predicted that the CLC would conduct case-by-case examinations of bargaining agreements instead of applying a more rigid approach.

Further clarification of the Administration position was provided Feb. 28 at a press briefing conducted by Dunlop. He refused to be identified or quoted directly, but emphasized that the CLC would utilize a flexible approach in applying wage standards to 1973 settlements.

(White House aide John Ehrlichman had told a Detroit businessmen's meeting Feb. 26 that the "5.5% guideline was being gently but firmly removed from the folklore of wage and price controls.")

Dunlop admitted that the specific 5.5% figure had been mentioned in his Feb. 26 news conference in order to counteract other press reports that the ceiling was being abandoned.

Dunlop asserted that the consequences of such a renunciation would have a highly destabilizing effect on wage behavior during Phase 3.

Meany cites 7½% pay-rise guideline— Before attending the advisory committee meeting with Dunlop, George Meany held a news conference Feb. 23 and rejected the current 5.5% wage guideline as "not realistic." If there had to be a figure, he said, it should be at least 7.5% as long as food prices continued to climb. He preferred no guideline for Phase 3.

Meany's AFL-CIO executive council, which was holding its annual mid-winter meeting in Bal Harbour, was critical of the Administration's economic policies Feb. 23. The council objected to the "inequities" in the economic stabilization program and warned that imbalances in the nation's economy, if continued, could lead to "a sharply slowing pace of general economic expansion with a renewed rise of unemployment" by the end of the year.

The council emphasized the need for tax reform and called for elimination of "major loopholes of tax privilege for corporations and wealthy families." It called upon Congress to reject President Nixon's budget proposals for curtailing or ending what it considered many essential programs.

In a statement Feb. 20, the council had protested the "dismantling of essential programs," which it felt was not justified by the "inevitable" administrative inefficiencies and overlappings created from the rapid growth of federal programs in the 1960's.

"The federal government's commitment to help solve the nation's major domestic problems is seriously in danger," the council warned, because of "a combination of presidential vetoes, the impoundment of appropriated funds, program reductions and terminations and revenue sharing."

In a statement Feb. 24, the council called for a comprehensive new trade and international finance policy to halt the eroding U.S. role in world economy. Putting the major blame on the expanding foreign investment by American corporations and banks, it called for a "full-dress Congressional investigation" of such firms, which, it charged, "sell their country short in order to enhance their profits."

As for profits at home, the council said Feb. 25 that business' current boom status was "utterly unfair and inequitable" in light of controls on wages. It recommended an excess profits tax and an end to the business investment tax credit.

2nd Nixon inauguration. Richard M. Nixon was inaugurated for his second term as President Jan. 20.

In his inaugural address, Nixon stressed self-reliance by nations abroad and individuals at home as "we stand on the threshold of a new era of peace in the world."

It was the most expensive inauguration in U.S. history, estimated to cost more than $4 million.

Nixon said in his address:

At home, the shift from old policies to new will not be a retreat from our responsibilities, but a bettter way to progress. . . .

Just as building a structure of peace abroad has required turning away from old policies that failed, so building a new era of progress at home requires turning away from old policies that failed. . . .

Abroad and at home, the time has come to turn away from the condescending policies of paternalism—of "Washington knows best."

A person can be expected to act responsibly only if he has responsibility. This is human nature. So let us encourage individuals at home and abroad to do more for themselves and decide more for themselves. Let us locate more responsibility in more places. Let us measure what we will do for others by what they will do for themselves.

That is why I offer no promise of a purely government solution for every problem. We have lived too long with that false promise. In trusting too much to government, we have asked of it more than it can deliver. This leads only to inflated expectations, to reduced individual effort and to a disappointment and frustration that erode confidence both in what government can do and in what people can do.

Government must learn to take less from people so people can do more for themselves. . . .

Budget for 'Leaner' Government

The second Nixon term opened with the submission of a budget that cut or dropped many existing programs in the interests of fighting inflation by producing a "leaner" bureaucracy.

No major new programs planned. President Nixon submitted to Congress Jan. 29 a $268.7 billion fiscal 1974 budget designed to avoid higher taxes and inflation and drastically revamp the structure of federal programs. No major new programs were requested, although the structural revision presented was considered unprecedented in scope.

Some 112 programs, among them major antipoverty efforts and landmark education-aid legislation, were to be eliminated or reduced. Another 70 programs were to be replaced and encompassed under four special revenue sharing plans, with a total funding of $6.9 billion, covering education, law enforcement, manpower training and urban community development.

And, despite the negotiated ceasefire in the Vietnam conflict, the budget did not reflect any war-end dividend. Defense spending was budgeted at $81.1 billion for fiscal 1974, almost a third of the total budget and $4.7 billion of the $18.9 billion total budget increase from fiscal 1973 to 1974. The President said the defense increase was necessitated by military pay raises toward a volunteer army and general price increases.

The remainder of the budgetary increase from fiscal 1973 to 1974 was brought about by increasing payments for Social Security ($5.7 billion), Medicare and Medicaid ($3.4 billion) and interest on the national debt ($1.9 billion). The latter four items consumed over one-third of the budget.

The programs slashed included many Great Society programs of the Johnson Administration, such as Model Cities, mental health clinics, war on poverty's local action agencies, the public service jobs program, and aid to depressed areas (except Appalachia). The programs affected, the President said, were marked by "disappointments and failures." The cuts included major programs instituted by previous administrations going back to President Harry S. Truman—farm subsidies and vocational education, school district aid and space shuttle development. Most further commitments of federal housing funds were put under a freeze of indefinite length.

The President also requested imposition of higher charges for Medicare and did not earmark funds in fiscal 1974 for national health insurance.

Some budgetary increases—However, there were increases, aside from the mandatory boosts. Despite the rise in defense spending, defense expenditures would drop below 30% of the total budget for the first time in more than two decades.

Among the budgetary increases were funds for a program of direct federal cash grants to needy college students, more than quadrupling to $948 million. Pollution control also was allotted a budgetary increase, although it still was

Budget Receipts

(In billions of dollars for the fiscal year)

	1972 actual	1973 estimate	1974 estimate
Individual income taxes	94.737	99.400	111.600
Corporation income taxes	32.166	33.500	37.000
Social insurance taxes and contributions:			
Employment taxes and contributions	46.120	55.610	67.866
Unemployment insurance	4.357	5.262	6.267
Contributions for other insurance and retirement	3.437	3.667	4.029
Excise taxes	15.477	15.970	16.798
Estate and gift taxes	5.436	4.600	5.000
Customs duties	3.287	3.000	3.300
Miscellaneous receipts	3.633	3.975	4.122
Total receipts	**208.649**	**224.984**	**255.982**

Budget Outlays

(In billions of dollars for the fiscal year)

	1972 actual	1973 estimate	1974 estimate
National defense*	78.336	76.435	81.074
International affairs and finance	3.726	3.341	3.811
Space research and technology	3.422	3.061	3.135
Agriculture and rural development	7.063	6.064	5.572
Natural resources and environment	3.761	.876	3.663
Commerce and transportation	11.201	12.543	11.580
Community development and housing	4.282	3.957	4.931
Education and manpower	9.751	10.500	10.110
Health	17.112	17.991	21.730
Income security	64.876	75.889	81.976
Veterans benefits and services	10.731	11.795	11.732
Interest	20.582	22.808	24.672
General government	4.891	5.631	6.025
General revenue sharing		6.786	6.035
Allowances for contingencies and civilian agency pay raises		.500	1.750
Undistributed intragovernmental transactions:			
Employer share, employe retirement	-2.768	-2.980	-3.157
Interest received by trust funds	-5.089	-5.401	-5.974
Total outlays	**231.876**	**249.796**	**268.665**
Budget deficit	**23.227**	**24.812**	**12.683**

*Includes allowances for All-Volunteer Force, retirement systems reform and civilian and military pay raises for Department of Defense.

Source: Office of Management and Budget

lower than authorized by Congress. Other areas granted budgetary increases were energy research, drug abuse control, civil rights enforcement, rural development, law enforcement, mass transit aid to cities, loans to minority business, aid to Indians, cancer and heart research, food for the elderly poor and consumer safety.

Curb on spending stressed—The President stressed in his budget message the need to hold down government spending at all levels and to avoid a tax increase. Only two tax proposals were made in the budget, involving a $600 million revenue loss to the Treasury in fiscal 1974—an income tax credit for tuition paid to parochial and other nonpublic schools, and a liberalized tax deduction for retirement funds set aside by individuals.

The goal, Nixon said, was high employment prosperity without inflation and without war. His budget proposed, he said, "a leaner federal bureaucracy, increased reliance on state and local governments to carry out what are primarily state and local responsibilities, and greater freedom for the American people to make for themselves fundamental choices about what is best for them."

He noted that the economic climate differed from that of the past two years, when the economy was operating below capacity and the threat of inflation was apparently receding. However, with the economy rising and the threat of inflation as its rider, "the budget must now guard against inflation," the President said. "The surest way to avoid inflation or higher taxes or both is for the Congress to join me in a concerted effort to control federal spending."

He proposed that Congress establish, before approving any spending bills, "a rigid ceiling" on spending limiting total fiscal 1974 outlays to the $268.7 billion recommended in his budget. He also recommended that Congress eliminate annual authorizations in specific amounts, "accept responsibility for the budget totals and . . . develop a systematic procedure for maintaining fiscal discipline," and enact appropriation

bills before the beginning of the fiscal year.

In calculating his spending ceilings, the President utilized again, as he had in the past, the "full-employment" budget concept to hold spending to the revenue level that would exist at full employment, which the Administration figured to be a jobless rate averaging 4% of the work force.

The new budget showed a surplus of $300 million measured on the full-employment basis.

The budget totals—The actual difference between revenues and outlays was projected to be a $12.7 billion deficit for fiscal 1974, which would be about half the $24.8 billion deficit currently foreseen for fiscal 1973 ending June 30. Budget receipts were projected to rise $31 billion, or 13.8%, to a total of $256 billion for fiscal 1974. But, reflecting the effort to curb spending, the outlay request of $268.7 billion for fiscal 1974 was a rise of $19 billion, or about 8%, from fiscal 1973's anticipated level of $249.8 billion.

To stress his point of curbing expenditures, the President projected beyond fiscal 1974 to forecast, for the first time in a budget presentation, details of the budget one year beyond fiscal 1974. A look at fiscal 1975, he said, revealed "very little room for the creation of new programs and no room for the postponement of the reductions and terminations proposed in this budget."

Outlays of $288 billion were projected for fiscal 1975 and revenues of $290 billion, for a "full-employment surplus" of $2 billion. The economy was expected to grow near "full employment" by that time, he said. Therefore, the budget for fiscal 1975 was expected to be very close to actual balance.

If he had not taken action to cut the current budget, Nixon warned, fiscal 1973 spending would total $261 billion instead of $249.8 billion, and "the ballooning effect of one year's expenditures on the next would in turn have meant that 1974's expenditures would be about $288 billion, far beyond full employment revenues, and 1975's expenditures would be approximately $312 billion, leading to a huge, inflationary deficit."

If Congress abided by his budget recommendations, Nixon said, and if a "disciplined approach to federal spending" were taken, it would be possible to avoid a tax increase "for the foreseeable future."

If Congress exceeded the budgeted outlays, he warned, it would face "the alternative of higher taxes, higher interest rates, renewed inflation, or all three." "Should the Congress pass any legislation increasing outlays beyond the recommended total," he said, "it must find financing for the additional amount." Otherwise, he added, the legislation would be inflationary and subject to veto.

The $11.2 billion reduction in fiscal 1973 outlays had been achieved by "impoundments" of appropriated funds and cutbacks of programs ($4.2 billion), a Congressional ceiling enacted on the open-ended program of "social services" grants to the states ($2.3 billion), deferral of a general revenue sharing payment ($1.5 billion) and higher than expected receipts from offshore oil leases.

Federal debt—The total federal debt would rise to more than half a trillion dollars by the end of fiscal 1974—$505.45 billion, from a $473.33 billion level estimated for the end of fiscal 1973. Its interest costs would mount from the $20.58 billion at midyear 1972 to $22.81 billion by mid-year 1973 to $24.67 billion the next year.

Defense. Defense outlays of $79 billion were requested, a $4.2 billion rise from fiscal 1973 and the highest Pentagon budget since the World War II record of $79.9 billion in fiscal 1945. The increase over the previous year was attributed to military and civilian pay increases and inflation.

Vietnam war costs, not reflecting the cease-fire agreement, were put at $2.9 billion in fiscal 1974 ($6.2 billion in fiscal 1973). The $2.9 billion included $1.9 billion for military assistance to Free-World forces in South Vietnam and Laos and $1 billion to support the U.S. forces in

Budget Deficits & Interest on National Debt

[In millions of dollars]

Fiscal year	Receipts	Outlays	Surplus or deficit	Debt interest
1956	74,547	70,460	+4,087	6,787
1957	79,990	76,741	+3,249	7,244
1958	79,636	82,575	−2,939	7,607
1959	79,249	92,104	−12,855	7,593
1960	92,492	92,223	+269	9,180
1961	94,389	97,795	−3,406	8,957
1962	99,676	106,813	−7,137	9,120
1963	106,560	111,311	−4,751	9,895
1964	112,662	118,584	−5,922	10,666
1965	116,833	118,430	−1,596	11,346
1966	130,856	134,652	−3,796	12,014
1967	149,856	158,254	−8,702	13,391
1968	153,552	178,833	−25,161	14,573
1969	187,784	184,548	+3,236	16,588
1970	193,743	196,588	−2,845	19,304
1971	188,392	211,425	−23,033	20,959
1972	208,649	231,876	−23,227	21,849
1973	232,225	246,526	−14,301	24,167

Source: Budget of the U.S. Government, fiscal year 1975 Office of Management and Budget, and the Treasury Department.

Southeast Asia—naval units in the South China Sea, air units in Thailand and the ground forces remaining in Vietnam.

Manpower costs were said to have been stabilized in the fiscal 1974 budget at 56% of outlays. An armed forces personnel reduction of 55,000, to a total of 2,233,000 in the active forces, was budgeted. The goals for the end of the fiscal year (1974), were: Army 804,000 (a cut of 21,000); Air Force 666,000 (26,000 fewer); Navy 566,000 (7,-000 fewer); Marines 196,000 (1,000 fewer).

In conventional forces, the budget would support 13 Army divisions and three Marine divisions, 21 Air Force tactical wings, 14 Navy air wings and three Marine air wings and a Navy fleet of 523 vessels (down 63). The cost would be $26.4 billion in fiscal 1974, up $700 million from 1973.

The Navy share of the fiscal 1974 budget was estimated at $26.4 billion, the Air Force at $24.6 billion, the Army at $21.2 billion.

The budget for the strategic forces would remain the same in fiscal 1974 $7.4 billion.

National Guard and reserve forces were budgeted at $4.4 billion in fiscal 1974, a rise of $400 million.

Foreign aid. The budget estimate for foreign aid and conduct of international affairs was $4.6 billion in fiscal 1974, which included $791 million for military aid and credit sales to Israel. The total was $500 million higher than the previous year's budget estimate but only $150 million higher than actual expenditures in fiscal 1972. The new total reflected a drop of $361 million in the amount of proprietary receipts returning to the U.S. from Marshall Plan loans and military sales.

The budget request for fiscal 1974 included $1.553 billion for development assistance (up $10 million), $1.5 billion (up $200 million) for international security assistance (military aid plus funds to promote "political and economic stability in countries of foreign-policy importance" to the U.S.), $766 million for Food for Peace (down $81 million), $312 million (up $18 million) for foreign information, educational and cultural exchange activities and $77 million (down $6 million) for the Peace Corps. The level of activity for the Food for Peace and Peace Corps programs was to remain stable despite the fund decreases because of increased returns from loans and contributions from host countries.

Multilateral aid through international organizations, as distinguished from bilateral aid from the U.S. to the recipient country, was to comprise 44% of total outlays in fiscal 1974, a rise from 37% in fiscal 1973.

Space. Expenditures for the space program administered by the National Aeronautics and Space Administration (NASA) were increased in the fiscal 1974 budget by about $75 million to $3.1 billion. There were no new cutbacks in programs beyond those previously announced, such as for the space shuttle and astronomy observatory.

Outlays for the space shuttle were to rise $143.5 million to a level of $377 million for fiscal 1974, looking toward a first flight by 1978. The current fund slowdown in effect was expected to delay the project only by nine months.

Poverty and welfare. The budget called for a final dissolution of the Office of Economic Opportunity (OEO), the coordinating agency for antipoverty programs

since the Johnson Administration, ending the $384 million community action program. Some OEO programs would be transferred to other agencies, while legal services for the poor would be reorganized as an independent agency, funded at $71.5 million.

The budget justified the community action cutoff by a lack of evidence that the program was "moving substantial numbers of people out of poverty on a self-sustaining basis."

OEO's migrant programs would go to the Labor Department, its Indian and health programs would go to HEW, and its community economic development programs would move to the Office of Minority Business Enterprise.

The budget did not mention a Family Assistance Plan to replace the welfare system, but HEW officials said a proposal was in the works. Meanwhile, the Administration hoped to save nearly $600 million in welfare payments through management reforms and removal of ineligibles from the rolls. HEW planned to add 700 enforcement employes.

HEW said expenditures on social services for welfare recipients, which Congress had limited at $2.5 billion a year, could be further limited to $1.8 billion. The services included counseling and day care.

Education. The budget once again requested special revenue sharing for primary and secondary education, combining 32 separate programs into a system of block grants totaling $2.5 billion, some $500 million less than originally requested in 1971. The decrease would largely reflect the Administration's proposal to limit the impact program, which aided districts with high proportions of children whose parents worked at federal facilities, to districts where the parents actually lived on federal property. Aid to disadvantaged students under Title I of the Elementary and Secondary Education Act, running at $1.5 billion a year, would have to remain under the $2.5 billion limit.

The budget included no funds for several higher education programs approved by Congress, including operating subsidies and construction loan subsidies for colleges. Officials said many campuses were already overbuilt. A new program of "basic opportunity grants" to 1.5 million needy college students would be funded at $948 million, but two other student aid programs, National Defense Education loans at $290 million and a $210 million Supplemental Opportunity Grant Program aiding 303,000 students in fiscal 1973 would be ended.

The budget revived an Administration proposal for tax credits to parents of nonpublic school children, estimated to reduce revenues by $300 million. $202 million was earmarked to aid schools being racially desegregated.

The budget allocated no new funds for teacher training, in line with the Administration's claim that there were already 75,000 more certified teachers than jobs. Construction and operation funds for public or school libraries was eliminated, as was aid to state education departments, the Follow-Through program to extend Head Start to later years, a university-community services program, and aid for experimental programs under the Elementary and Secondary Education Act.

Health. The budget provided for significant fund increases for Medicare, as mandated by Congress, and for research into cancer and heart disease, but reduced or eliminated programs of hospital construction and maintenance and training of medical personnel, and called for a $700 million increase in payments by Medicare benificiaries.

Total Medicare payments would rise 20% to $12.1 billion, to cover care for 11.6 million people and hospitalization for about 5 million. The budget proposed changes in the Social Security law to require Medicare patients to pay 10% of hospital charges after the first day of hospitalization, at a total cost of $345 million. Officials of the Department of Health, Education & Welfare (HEW) said the change would help create "a cost awareness on the part of the medical care consumer which, besides its effect on over-utilization, should inhibit hospital price increases." Indigent patients could recover the costs through Medicaid, HEW said. Increased payments under the Medicare supplemental doctor's fee plan were also requested.

The 26-year-old Hill-Burton hospital construction act would be allowed to expire, since, the Administration said, hospital beds were already in oversupply, causing low occupancy rates and higher costs, and since hospitals received capital funds from depreciation payments under Medicare and Medicaid.

HEW planned to abandon the regional medical program for heart disease, stroke and cancer. HEW said the centers had failed to coordinate medical resources or disseminate research developments rapidly. HEW would continue to maintain some 515 community mental health centers, but would not expand the network to 2,000 centers as originally planned. Eight Public Health Service hospitals would be turned over to local control.

Training programs for doctors and dentists would continue to be fully funded because of shortages, but reductions were planned in training programs for nurses, pharmacists, veterinarians and other medical personnel. HEW said it would cease support for training research scientists, since federal aid had already increased their numbers massively, and since their earning potential enabled them to finance their own education. The program had previously cost $150 million a year.

Cancer research was budgeted for $445 million, up $91 million, and heart and lung research was scheduled for a $28 million increase to $250 million.

Community development. The budget called for a complete overhaul of all federal housing and urban development programs, previously announced by the Administration, with new commitments for most projects suspended.

A moratorium on new public housing and housing subsidy programs had been announced Jan. 8. This would continue in the new fiscal year, although previous commitments would be carried out, allowing 270,000 subsidized units to be started in calendar 1973, compared with 250,000 in 1972. Fiscal 1974 expenditures would be about $2 billion.

The budget called for an urban development revenue sharing bill, to replace seven federal programs at a rate of $2.3 billion a year beginning in fiscal 1975. The programs would continue in the interim based on previously appropriated but unspent funds, and included $137.5 million in new urban renewal funds for earlier projects. The seven programs were urban renewal, model cities, open space, neighborhood facilities, water and sewer systems, rehabilitation loans and public facility loans.

Several other Housing and Urban Development Department (HUD) programs would end, including public facility grants for new communities, college housing and public housing modernization, allowing a decline of about 2,000 from HUD's current 16,000 employes.

The budget announced that the Economic Development Administration (EDA), the Johnson Administration agency intended to stimulate growth in depressed rural and urban areas, would be phased out, although some of its programs would continue under the Agriculture Department and the Small Business Administration, which would increase its business loan program by $600 million. The Administration said the EDA had had little success in dealing with unemployment nationally.

Civil rights. The Administration requested a $629 million increase to a funding level of $3.21 billion for civil rights activities carried out by several departments. The bulk of the increase would go to the minority business program. In the only program cutback, spending for the Justice Department's Community Relations Service, created under the 1964 Civil Rights Act, was reduced $4 million to $12.8 million.

The department's civil rights division sought a $300,000 expenditure rise to $7.1 million. The Civil Rights Commission would get a 13% spending increase to $5.7 million in order to carry out its new responsibility for fighting sex discrimination. Also charged with that authority and slated for funding hikes were the Equal Employment Opportunity Commission and the Civil Rights Office in the Department of Health, Education and Welfare (HEW).

The President said he planned to reestablish the semi-private Legal Services Corp. at nearly the same funding level—$70 million — but the agency would be housed under HEW after the planned dismantling of the Office of Economic Opportunity was completed.

Crime and drug abuse control. The budget called for a 7.5% increase in anti-crime spending and requested an additional $64 million for drug abuse programs, which would total 719 million.

The Justice Department's entire operating budget was set at $1.8 billion with a large part of that allocated to the Law Enforcement Assistance Administration's (LEAA) efforts to aid crime prevention at the state and local level. LEAA's requested $891 million was 15 times the size of its 1960 funding level and $35.7 million higher than the previous year's request.

The budget included a $16 million increase in Federal Bureau of Investigation (FBI) spending to a total of $266.5 million.

Federal prison construction expenditures were reduced to $14.8 million from fiscal 1973's $42 million in order to explore the feasibility of joint prison management programs with state and local governments.

Other Justice Department agencies seeking expenditure increases were the Bureau of Narcotics and Dangerous Drugs and the Office of Drug Abuse Law Enforcement.

Environment. Although the budget requested a substantial increase in environmental spending, the totals were still far below what Congress appropriated.

Contract authorization for new grants to local sewage treatment plants would increase from $2 billion to $3 billion, compared with Congressional appropriations of $5 billion and $6 billion. Actual payments for construction grants would rise from $727 million to $1.6 billion, but more than half of the increase would go to repay localities for earlier projects they had built in expectation of federal aid.

The budget drastically reduced requests for solid waste control, from $30 million in fiscal 1973 to $5.8 million. Environmental Protection Agency (EPA) Administrator William D. Ruckelshaus said the EPA had already researched a variety of recycling techniques, leaving implementation to local government and industry.

The EPA operating budget would increase by $44 million to $515 million, to administer a variety of clean air, toxic waste disposal and noise control programs.

Construction funds for water projects by the Army Corps of Engineers and the Bureau of Reclamation were cut, from $1.2 billion to $859 million for the corps and from $520 million to $387 million for the bureau. The reduction was in part an economy move, but the budget said that proposals for water project cost-sharing, being developed by the National Water Commission, "will receive full consideration" when completed.

Energy. The budget provided for increased research and exploration to increase the energy supply, in reaction to the winter energy shortage.

Some 3 million acres of Gulf of Mexico offshore oil and gas land would be leased in three regions ranging from Texas to Florida, although bonus payments from the sales were estimated at only $1.8 billion, $300 million less than in the current fiscal year, when more promising parcels were leased.

The Interior Department would receive $129 million for research on exploitation of fossil fuel, up from $107 million. A special $25 million research fund would be set up, to study potentially more abundant or less polluting energy sources such as liquified coal, solar heat and geothermal steam.

The Atomic Energy Commission (AEC) planned to increase research on nuclear power by $171 million to $974 million, including work on a fast breeder demonstration power plant. The AEC would increase permit and license charges to utilities from $18.4 million to $32.1 million.

Agriculture. The new budget incorporated previously announced cuts in crop, rural housing and other programs, for a half-billion drop in the Agriculture Department budget to $9.6 billion, or $2 billion less than what full funding would cost, according to the budget.

Crop related programs would be cut by $1.2 billion, including cuts in direct payments to farmers and export subsidies, and increased interest rates on crop loans. The soil conservation program would be almost eliminated, dropping from $182 million to $10 million.

Rural housing loan subsidies, previously budgeted at $842 million, would be suspended pending re-evaluation of all federal housing programs, and rural electrification loan subsidies would be halted.

The school milk program would be slashed by $72 million, leaving only $25 million in payments to schools without federally supported lunch programs.

The Forest Service would no longer build roads for timber production, reducing the forest road and trail budget from $160 million to $97 million.

Agriculture Department jobs would be reduced by 4,600 to 78,800 through attrition.

Manpower. President Nixon planned a 9.2% reduction, from a current $5.3 billion level to $4.81 billion, in federal manpower programs in fiscal 1974. It would be the first cutback in manpower spending since job-training was initiated in 1962. A shift of authority over major manpower programs from the federal government to the states and localities was also planned.

A large part of the fund reduction would come from phasing out the public service jobs program enacted in 1971, which was running at about a $1 billion-a-year level. The phasing out was "consistent with the increase in new jobs in the private sector," the President said. Fiscal 1974 spending on the program would total $574 million, which was already appropriated.

A 15.7% cut to $1.16 billion was budgeted for the basic manpower training programs run by the Labor Department, including on-the-job and classroom training, summer jobs for youth and subsidies for employers hiring the long-term unemployed.

It was in this area that the President planned to initiate a manpower revenue-sharing plan of block grants to cities and states, a plan Congress had been requested to pass and did not. The President intended to take administrative action, under the 1962 Manpower Development and Training Act and the 1964 Economic Development Act—to initiate the revenue sharing plan himself during the next two years. According to the budget's terminology, "administrative requirements under existing law will be modified to allow the states and localities to group manpower services in ways that best meet local needs and to choose the organizations to operate these programs."

About 75% of the $1.16 billion involved was to go into the revenue sharing funnel to mayors and governors. The remainder was to be retained for "programs requiring national supervision."

Total average enrollment in manpower programs was expected to fall from the 528,600 level of fiscal 1972 to 405,400 in fiscal 1973 and 363,100 in fiscal 1974.

Transportation. Spending on highways was budgeted at $4.53 billion, a 4% decline from fiscal 1973, and mass transit outlays would rise 30% to $494 million. But the spending on highways constituted 57½¢ of the federal transportation dollar, spending on mass transit 6¢ of that dollar. The Administration reaffirmed its commitment to tap the highway trust fund, derived from gasoline taxes, to help pay for mass transit projects.

Spending on highway safety was to increase. So was spending on highway beautification, which was set at $55 million, a $15 million rise, of which $50 million would go toward removing billboards.

The National Railroad Passenger Corp. (Amtrak) was to receive $93 million in fiscal 1974 compared with federal grants totaling $210 million for fiscal 1972–73 plus loan guarantees of $200 million.

The Transportation Department budget of $8.2 billion included $1.8 billion for the Federal Aviation Administration. Outlays for airport grants would climb $14 million to $234 million, airway facilities and equipment would climb $30 million to $252 million.

Shipbuilding subsidies were scheduled to rise from $182 million in fiscal 1973 to $213 million the next year, subsidies to offset operating losses from $215 million to $247 million.

Nixon radio appeal. President Nixon had unveiled his budget proposals in a nationwide radio address Jan. 28 when he called on the public to support those legislators "who have the courage to vote against higher spending."

Nixon forecast a new "era of prolonged and growing prosperity" beginning with 1973 but he declared, "The greatest threat to our new prosperity is excessive government spending."

To justify his sweeping cutbacks in federal programs "that have outlived their time, or that have failed," Nixon cited the "sky-rocketing" budgetary costs in recent years. Since 1952, the budget had doubled every 10 years, he said. He predicted that by the 1990s, it could reach "over a trillion dollars."

Nixon offered three reasons for resisting this expansionary fiscal trend: to prevent a tax increase, to offset inflation and to reduce the size of government.

Nixon concluded that what was at stake in his budgetary proposal to Congress was "your job, your taxes, the prices you pay, and whether the money you earn by your own work is spent by you for what you want, or by government for what someone else wants."

Nixon gave three examples of federal programs which had become "sacred cows . . . no one dared to touch." They were the hospital construction legislation first voted in 1946, "disappointing" urban renewal programs and aid to schools located near federal facilities.

Congressional reaction. Congressional leaders met with President Nixon at the White House Jan. 26 to be briefed on budgetary plans. They gave him bipartisan support to hold spending at the $268.7 billion level, but Sen. Mike Mansfield (D, Mont.) predicted after the meeting that his cutback priorities would not "coincide" with those of the President.

House Speaker Carl Albert (D, Okla.) was critical of another Administration form of cost reduction—the impounding of funds for programs already approved

Declining Dollar Value, Fluctuating Federal Deficit

Year	Decreased purchasing power of dollar (percent)	Value of dollar	Federal deficit (billions)
1940	0	$1.00	−$2.7
1941	−4.9	.95	−4.7
1942	−9.7	.86	−19.3
1943	−5.8	.81	−53.8
1944	−1.6	.80	−46.1
1945	−2.2	.78	−45.0
1946	−7.8	.72	−18.2
1947	−12.6	.63	+6.6
1948	−7.2	.58	+8.8
1949	+1.0	.59	+1.0
1950	−1.0	.58	−2.2
1951	−7.4	.54	+7.5
1952	−2.2	.53	+.49
1953	−.8	.52	−.52
1954	−.4	.52	−1.1
1955	+.3	.52	−3.0
1956	−1.5	.52	+4.0
1957	−3.4	.50	+3.2
1958	−2.7	.48	−$2.9
1959	−.8	.48	−12.8
1960	−1.6	.47	+2.69
1961	−1.1	.47	−3.4
1962	−1.1	.46	−7.1
1963	−1.2	.46	−4.7
1964	−1.3	.45	−5.9
1965	−1.6	.44	−1.5
1966	−2.8	.43	−3.7
1967	−2.8	.42	−8.7
1968	−4.0	.40	−25.1
1969	−5.1	.38	+3.2
1970	−5.6	.36	−2.8
1971	−4.1	.35	−23.0
1972	−3.2	.33	−23.2
1973	−5.9	.31	−14.3

Source: U.S. Bureau of Labor Statistics, U.S. Office of Management and Budget.

by Congress. "The question is whether they're legislating or we are when they abolish a whole program," Albert declared.

But Sen. Minority Leader Hugh Scott (R, Penn.) warned the Congress Jan. 29 that if the budget's spending limit were exceeded, "this will invite vetoes and if the vetoes are overridden, this will invite impoundments."

While conservatives in both parties generally applauded the President's budget message, some Democrats were critical of the planned reductions, claiming that the "brutally misplaced priorities of this Administration" were "good news for the big defense contractors and bad news for the average citizen," according to the Washington Post Jan. 30.

Arthur Okun, a former chairman of the Council of Economic Advisers under the Johnson Administration, Jan. 29 summed up the quandary of legislators, saying that the Nixon budget "repre-

sents impeccable economic policy and intolerable social policy."

Federal deficit declines. The federal deficit in the year ended June 30 dropped to $14.4 billion, some $10.4 billion less than forecast in January, according to the White House July 26. Reasons cited for the deficit decline were a gain in tax receipts and a White House limit on spending.

The Administration reported that the government spent $246.6 billion in the fiscal year, below the Administration's target ceiling of $250 billion established in 1972. Spending for "social service" grants to the states fell $831 million short of the estimate since the "previously anticipated level of state activity did not materialize," according to the official account.

Treasury Secretary George Schultz called the smaller deficit a "welcome result" citing the "determination" of President Nixon to hold down spending, combined with Congressional support for that objective.

Data From Administration

Congress gets economic report. The President's Council of Economic Advisers (CEA) predicted Jan. 30 that strong expansionary forces in the economy during the next year would be reflected in a "very high rate of growth over the first half of 1973," after which "it is both probable and desirable that the rate of expansion will and should abate."

The annual forecast to Congress anticipated that the inflation rate would be held at 3% but only on the condition that Congress adhered to the President's budget limits, that the food price spiral slowed and that "a high degree of compliance" was achieved regarding the Phase 3 stabilization regulations.

In his message accompanying the economic report, Nixon claimed that 1973 could be a "great year" for the nation's economy and added, "The problem . . . will be to prevent this expansion from becoming an inflationary boom."

"Nothing," he said, "is easier or more pleasant, at least for a bureaucracy, than to spend money. But beyond some point, which our budget plans already reach, everything that the government gives out with one hand it must take back with the other, in higher taxes or more inflation or both. Spending proposals must be looked at in this way, by asking whether they are worth either of these costs. Much government spending fails this test."

The President also warned Congress of the need to "manage our fiscal affairs prudently" and served notice on business and labor that the Administration possessed the authority and the will "to intervene where necessary to stop action that is unreasonably inconsistent with [Phase 3] standards."

Other major points in the CEA report:

The "real" Gross National Product (GNP) rate, a figure for the total national output in goods and services after eliminating the effects of inflation, would be 6.75%. A total expansion in the index was expected to reach nearly 10% or $1.267 trillion.

The inflation rate goal, measured by the price index for the whole GNP, was set at 3%, an "ambitious but attainable" target according to Administration officials. The figure, which was predicated on a decline in the Consumer Price Index to 2.5% by the end of 1973, could fall below 3% if food prices diminished.

An unemployment goal in the "neighborhood" of 4.5% was cited. The Administration reiterated its position that the longstanding 4% jobless target was a "less reliable guide to policy for the 1970s."

Business inventories were expected to more than double, registering gains of $12.5 billion.

Homebuilding would drop off from the record 1972 pace, the report said, to total 2.2 million in 1973.

State and local governments would increase spending levels by 12% although federal purchases would remain nearly constant and thereby show a decline in terms of inflationary effects on the spending level.

Capital spending on fixed investments would show a 14% gain.

Consumer spending would increase by 9.5%, propelled by a 10% gain in disposable income as a result of tax overwithholding.

The foreign trade deficit was expected to decrease by more than $2 billion, as the demand for imports waned, but the trade imbalance would remain at an estimated $4 billion level by the end of 1973.

The report also suggested that consideration be given "temporary, limited changes" in tax structure, including a "one-year, positive or negative surcharge rate on personal and corporate income taxes" and a "one-year shift in the rate of the investment tax credit."

A brief section on monetary policy, conducted by the independent Federal Reserve System, suggested that as in fiscal policy, action taken to slow the expected economic expansion, such as a "slower increase in the supply of money and credit," would be an "appropriate goal."

The CEA report summarized the thrust of 1973 fiscal and monetary policies, saying "the dollar value of the GNP . . . rose by 11% from the fourth quarter of 1971 to the fourth quarter of 1972. The aim of policy is to cut back growth of demand so as to make this figure 9% from the fourth quarter of 1972 to the final quarter of 1973."

State of Union message. President Nixon sent Congress his State of the Union message Feb. 2 saying the basic state of the union was "sound and full of promise." The President departed from precedent by dividing the missive into a series of messages.

This first message, he said, would present an "overview of where we stand as a people" and "outline some of the general goals" to be pursued. Other messages would follow on economic affairs, natural resources, human resources, community development and foreign and defense policy.

"We enter 1973 economically strong, militarily secure and . . . at peace after a long and trying war," Nixon said in his 1,-800-word initial message. The nation had survived one of "the most difficult periods" in its history "without surrendering to despair and without dishonoring our ideals," he said. "By working together with the leaders of other nations, we have been able to build a new hope for lasting peace" and "at home, we have learned that by working together we can create prosperity without fanning inflation, we can restore order without weakening freedom."

As for the challenges facing the nation, Nixon looked forward to "the best four years in American history" if everyone continued to work together.

"At home," Nixon continued, "we must reject the mistaken notion . . . that ever bigger government is the answer to every problem." There was "a critical choice in 1973," he said, "between holding the line in government spending and adopting expensive programs which will surely force up taxes and refuel inflation. . . . It is vital at this time that we restore a greater sense of responsibility at the state and local level, and among individual Americans."

"The time has come for us to draw the line," he stressed, to "take a stand against overgrown government and for the American taxpayer."

The President said:

We have learned only too well that heavy taxation and excessive government spending are not a cure-all. In too many cases, instead of solving the problems they were aimed at, they have merely placed an ever heavier burden on the shoulders of the American taxpayer, in the form of higher taxes and a higher cost of living. At the same time they have deceived our people because many of the intended beneficiaries received far less than was promised, thus undermining public faith in the effectiveness of government as a whole. . . .

The answer to many of the domestic problems we face is not higher taxes and more spending. It is less waste, more results and greater freedom for the individual American to earn a rightful place in his own community—and for states and localities to address their own needs in their own ways, in the light of their own priorities. By giving the people and their locally elected leaders a greater voice through changes such as revenue sharing, and by saying "no" to excessive federal spending and higher taxes,· we can help achieve this goal. . . .

In the field of economic affairs, our objectives will be to hold down taxes, to continue controlling inflation, to promote economic growth, to increase productivity, to encourage foreign trade, to keep farm income ·high, to bolster small business, and to promote better labor-management relations. . . .

State-of-economy message. President Nixon's state of the union message dealing with economic matters, submitted to Congress Feb. 22, contained no changes in previously stated Administration economic plans.

The report concentrated heavily on a defense of fiscal restraint, proposed White House cutbacks in social assistance programs and general promises of tax relief.

Nixon defended his planned budget cuts: "We are budgeting 66% more to help the poor next year than was the case four years ago; 67% more to help the sick; 71% more to help the older Americans, and 242% to help the hungry and malnourished."

Nixon also emphasized his determination to enforce Phase 3 regulations. "We will regard any flouting of our anti-inflationary rules and standards as nothing less than attempted economic arson threatening our national economic stability—and we shall act accordingly," he stated.

Nixon had previewed the message Feb. 21 in a 15-minute nationwide radio address. The speech offered no specific indications of Administration policies but the President promised a slowdown in the food price rise spiral during the "second half of the year" that would "bring relief to the American housewife without damaging the prosperity of our farmers."

"We will probably see increases in food prices for some months to come," Nixon predicted. "But we must not accept rising food prices as a permanent feature of American life."

He promised further increases in food supply to meet greater demand and pointed to recent Administration measures to boost acreage, increase food imports and end stockpiles and subsidies as actions that would eventually halt inflationary food prices.

Democratic reply—In a Democratic Party rebuttal to Nixon's message, Sen. William Proxmire (D, Wis.) charged Feb. 28 that the Administration's "mistaken and weak economic policies" had encouraged inflation, permitted excessive unemployment and resulted in a dollar devaluation costly to the consumer.

"Our answer is to cut inflationary military and foreign aid spending and channel some, but not all of these funds, into programs that will not only make for a more humane America, but a stronger country and one in which housing will be built, the unskilled labor trained and the food produced to hold down the prices you pay," Proxmire said.

News conference. Several items concerned with inflation were discussed by Nixon at an impromptu news conference March 2. Among his remarks:

Stability of the dollar—The dollar was "a good bet in the world markets today" because the U.S. had "the lowest rate of inflation of any major industrial country," the "strongest economy of the major industrial countries," "a program, which we believe is going to work, for continuing to control inflation" and "a very tight budget."

The U.S., Nixon said, would "survive" the "international attack" upon the dollar by speculators and "there will not be another [dollar] devaluation." The U.S. would continue its efforts to get the other major countries to participate more in the goal "of getting an international monetary system which is flexible enough to take care of" what he believed were "temporary attacks on one currency or another."

Rent control—The Administration was not giving any thought to revival of the Rent Control Board because a rent-control ceiling that was not "economically viable" led to a housing shortage and inadequate upkeep of rental units by landlords. Rent control was not "the right answer" to the problem of high rents. The answer, he said, was "production of housing."

Wage guideline—The 5.5% wage guideline was not as important as "the bottom line," the 2.5% figure set by the Administration as a goal for the inflation rate. What the Administration was concerned about was to see that the wage negotiations in 1973 were "undertaken with enough flexibility" to avoid a wage-price push that would destroy that goal.

Public eyes Nixon business ties. A poll conducted by the Louis Harris Survey and published Feb. 4 indicated that 77% of the public surveyed thought the White House should adopt tougher federal policies toward the business sector. An estimated 57% of those questioned thought the Nixon Administration was "too close to big business."

Congressional report. The Democratic majority of the Congressional Joint Economic Committee reported its concern March 25 that the current economic upswing could degenerate by year's end into less output and more unemployment if the government restricted the availability of credit to counteract the persistent inflation. "Any abrupt move toward overly restrictive monetary policy could have disastrous effects on the growth of real output," the majority warned.

Furthermore, the Democrats warned, a decreasing fiscal stimulus from the federal budget combined with "unusually large surpluses" in state and local budgets would have "a dampening effect on the economy." There was a possibility that "the investment boom may build to an insurmountable pace and then fade abruptly."

The Democrats endorsed a proposal by Rep. Wright Patman (D, Tex.) for creation of a "national development bank" to provide funds at reasonable rates of interest "for all priority areas of the economy which cannot obtain funds through the usual lending channels."

The committee's Democrats were concerned that "a large share of the burden of fighting inflation will be left to monetary policy" because of lack of direct wage-price restraint. The "relaxation of price and wage controls implied" by the move to Phase 3 of the Administration's economic stabilization program was called by the Democrats "a totally inappropriate step." Legislation imposing stricter wage-price controls on large firms and unions was recommended. Most of the Democrats agreed that the 5.5% wage guideline should be retained, with a cost of living adjustment built in, and that businesses should not be permitted to pass on as higher prices any part of a wage settlement that exceeded the 5.5% guideline.

Phase 3's "self-administering, nonmandatory controls" were generally endorsed by the committee's Republican minority, which conceded there were problems the stabilization program "hasn't fully solved" but lauded the Administration's economic programs.

The GOP members, however, took exception to the handling of the 1972 Soviet wheat deal, expressing doubt whether the sales "had the beneficial effects on the economy which the Administration claims" and "considerable dismay" over the subsidies paid. "These costs to the American taxpayer to benefit grain exporters and foreign purchasers," they said, "don't accord with our view of the nation's priorities."

Although the Democrats and Republicans wrote separate reports in the committee's annual evaluation of President Nixon's economic report, both said that total government spending should be held to Nixon's recommended ceiling of $268 billion for fiscal 1974. While the Republicans did not comment on spending priorities, the Democrats recommended that Congress "make major reallocations" within the spending ceiling. "Expenditures can be significantly reduced in areas the Administration has failed to cut such as defense and foreign military aid," they said, and "funds should be restored to meet pressing domestic needs for housing, health, manpower and antipoverty programs."

The Democrats also recommended delaying enactment of the President's proposed special revenue sharing plan and continued funding of categorical programs until more data was available on the efficacy of the general revenue sharing plan already enacted.

The Democrats also favored continuation of the emergency public employment program until the unemployment rate, currently at 5% of the national work force, was reduced to 4%.

Another major Democratic recommendation was for "revenue-raising tax reform," especially in the areas of capital gains taxes, mineral depletion allowances and foreign tax preferences for businesses. Immediate elimination of the oil import quota system also was urged.

Democrats seek wage-price controls— A return to Phase 2 controls was advocated March 27 by Democratic Congressional leaders. A statement issued after a meeting of the leaders said that the shift from Phase 2 was "premature" and anything short of Phase 2 controls would be "inadequate."

The leaders endorsed a House bill calling for a 60-day freeze on all prices and interest rates at their March 16 levels and on rents at their Jan. 10 level.

Price indexes soar. The consumer price index, registering the sharpest gains in 22 years, rose to 127.7% of the 1967 average in January, to 128.6% in February and to 129.8% in March. The wholesale price index rose to 124.5% of the 1967 average in January, to 126.9% in February and to 129.7% in March.

The purchasing power of the dollar, as measured by consumer prices, declined to 78.3¢ in January, 77.8¢ in February and 77¢ in March (using 100¢ as the dollar's purchasing power in 1967). As measured by wholesale prices, the purchasing power of the dollar was 80.3¢ in January, 78.8¢ in February and 77.1¢ in March.

Unit labor costs soar. Higher Social Security taxes paid during the first quarter of 1973 contributed to a quarterly increase in the unit labor cost rate that was more than triple the gain recorded during 1972. The Labor Department released the figures April 27.

Despite a strong rise in productivity and unusually small wage increases negotiated during the period, unit labor costs rose 6.7% at an annual rate during January–March (compared with a 2% increase for all of 1972). The quarterly figure was based on a 4.7% annual rate gain in productivity for the private sector (compared with a 4.2% advance during 1972); a 5.3% annual rate increase in 138 major first year wage contracts (compared with a 7% increase in 1972); and an 11.7% annual rate increase in compensation paid by employers for each man hour (compared with a rate rise of 6.2% in 1972).

According to the department April 6, the nation's labor costs per unit of output increased at a slower rate during 1972 than for other major industrial countries. (The figure was considered a basic measure of inflationary pressures caused by higher costs rather than by excessive demand.)

The 2.1% annual gain calculated for the U.S. compared with a 20.3% increase in Japan, a 6.4% increase in Great Britain and a 5.4% increase in Canada.

Corporate profits soar. During the first quarter of 1973, U.S. corporations showed a 28% gain in pretax profits, which totaled $113.1 billion at a seasonally adjusted annual rate, according to the Commerce Department May 17. Aftertax profits were up 26% to $62.3 billion.

The nation's 500 largest industrial corporations showed a combined sales increase of 10.9% during 1972, according to the May issue of Fortune magazine. It was the largest yearly gain since 1968.

The sales increases were broad-based: four-fifths of the group showed growth while more than two-thirds had median sales increases of 10% or better.

Black income, jobs cited. Andrew F. Brimmer, a member of the Federal Reserve Board, said in a March 2 lecture at the University of California at Los Angeles that while black income continued to rise in 1972, unemployment remained a major problem, especially among youths.

Brimmer said total income for blacks had increased to a record $51 billion in 1972, up from $46 billion in 1971, increasing the black proportion of total income from 6.6% to 6.7%. Blacks were 11.3% of the total population.

Blacks suffered disproportionately from the 1969–70 recession, Brimmer said, with sharply increased joblessness among women and youths, so that "blacks suffered all of the recession-induced decline in jobs, while whites made further net job gains." Unemployment among black youths had actually increased in the 1971–72 expansion, rising to 35.9% of the work force in the fourth quarter of 1972.

Among other points, Brimmer cited evidence that blacks earned as large a percentage of their income through jobs as whites, to refute charges of "excessive" dependence on welfare.

Home ownership costs soar. Labor Department statistics, reported by the New York Times June 10, indicated that the costs of home ownership rose 91.7% between 1952 and 1972. The increase was greater than any other measure of consumer costs, except service increases, which rose 145.5% in the 20-year period.

During the same period, food costs were up 61.2%, consumer finished goods gained 37.5% and the entire Consumer Price Index advanced 73.5%.

Home costs, including purchase price, mortgage interest, maintenance and property taxes, were adjusted to reflect changes in quality.

The inability of the home building industry to meet the increased demand for houses, despite two record breaking years of construction, was cited as the principal factor in inflating prices.

Population pressures also caused land costs, measured as a portion of sales prices of single family homes, to increase from 11.6% in 1946 to over 22% in 1972.

Other factors in the housing price increases were the rising cost of lumber; higher construction workers' wages (by 1972, labor's share in the cost of single family homes was 32%, according to construction industry economists); and Administration policy establishing a moratorium on subsidized housing construction.

Government Spending Debated

Controversy raged over the effect government expenditures have on inflation and over an old Presidential custom of refusing to spend money that Congress had voted but which the President considered unnecessary or excessive.

Dispute over impounded funds. The Nixon Administration reported 3 to Congress Feb. 5 that its impoundment of federal funds (funds it was holding in reserve from mandated programs) totaled $8.7 billion. The report, required by Congress in legislation completed Jan. 17, was signed by Roy L. Ash, director of the Office of Management and Budget.

The total was substantially less than the $12 billion–$15 billion total of such funds that had been estimated by Congressional authorities. But the Administration omitted pollution funds from its list, on the ground impoundments related only to funds actually appropriated. The pollution funds had been authorized but not appropriated.

The Ash report largely justified the impoundments under the President's "constitutional duty to 'take care that the laws be faithfully executed.'"

Among the items it listed as in reserve were $2.9 billion for the Transportation Department, including $2.5 billion in highway construction funds; $1.9 billion for Defense Department; and $1.5 billion for the Agriculture Department, such as for rural electrification loans ($456 million), rural water and waste disposal grants ($120 million), rural environmental assistance ($210 million), forest roads and trails ($280 million) and food stamps ($159 million).

In testimony Feb. 1 before the Senate Judiciary Subcommittee on Separation of Powers, Ash supported the Administration's impoundment action as necessary when legislated appropriations conflicted with other laws the President must obey, such as the legal limit on the national debt. The subcommittee was considering a bill, co-sponsored by 51 of the 100 senators, to curb the President's impoundment proceedings by permitting a Presidential hold on Congressionally mandated spending for only 60 days unless specifically endorsed by Congress. Sen. Sam Ervin (D, N.C.), main sponsor of the bill, told Ash the President must abide by appropriations laws and that, by picking and choosing which funds to spend or withhold, "You're choosing between programs the Congress likes and programs the President likes."

Ervin also had a confrontation with the new deputy attorney general, Joseph T. Sneed, who told the subcommittee Feb. 6 the President had an implied constitutional right to refuse to spend money as Congress directed since he was sworn to uphold "all" the laws. This right could be applied, he said, whenever appropriations bills conflicted with other legislation, for example, to limit the national debt, curb inflation or improve employment. Sneed even upheld the President's authority in such cases to abolish programs through withholding funds.

In reply to a query from Ervin concerning the constitutional grounds for such alleged authority, Sneed declared, "We rest on Articles I, II and III."

"I can't reconcile that conclusion with what the words say" in the Constitution, Ervin said.

At a joint hearing on the Ervin bill with a Senate Government Operations Committee panel, consumer spokesman Ralph Nader urged Congress Jan. 30 to go beyond the Ervin bill and declare the impoundment process "illegal per se." Nader was a party to several taxpayer suits challenging the Administration's impoundment of legislated highway, health and environmental funds.

At a Senate Agriculture Committee hearing Feb. 1, where the impoundment subject also arose, Agriculture Secretary Earl Butz defended the agricultural fund impoundments as necessary to restrain inflation, avoid higher taxes and remain within the national debt ceiling. His views were contested by Sen. Hubert H. Humphrey (D, Minn.), who told him, "I don't believe the President, or some GS-12 in the OMB or the secretary of agriculture has a right to end a law."

The impoundment subject also led to clashes between Ash and Sen. Edmund S. Muskie (D, Me.). In defending the Administration's authority to make unilateral decisions in the budget area, and in opposing Muskie's proposed bill to require federal departments to submit their budget requests to Congress at the same time they were submitted to the Office of Management and Budget, Ash drew Muskie's ire. "Congress creates these departments," Muskie shouted at him Feb. 1 at the Ervin committee hearing. "It provides their money. Are you saying . . . that we don't have the right to the information they generate?"

HEW curbs social services. The Department of Health, Education and Welfare (HEW) Feb. 15 disclosed a series of proposed rule changes in the social services program for welfare recipients and other poor people that would cut off federal funds for a variety of state and private programs. The changes would curb spending beyond the $2.5 billion limit set by Congress in 1972.

Under the program, the federal government provided 75% of funding for programs including day care, job training, meals for the aged, and services for the blind and mentally retarded, with the other 25% supplied by local governments or private agencies. The fiscal 1972 federal share came to $1.7 billion, but mushrooming costs and a lack of program or eligibility limits led to the $2.5 billion Congressional ceiling.

HEW Secretary Caspar Weinberger said the curbs were intended to "permit available resources to be used most effectively for those who need them most," in view of the ceiling, although observers believed the rules would limit spending to about $1.8 billion a year. Weinberger said the "unfocused nature" of the programs led to doubts about who they "were really benefitting" and to suspicions of major abuses. The new rules would tend to limit benefits to welfare recipients.

The most important change would bar matching funds to private programs. The proposal was criticized in a letter sent to Weinberger Feb. 15 by a bipartisan group of 46 senators, led by Sen. Walter F. Mondale (D, Minn.), who said the change "would seriously undermine the excellent private-public partnership approach to human problems that now exists."

A number of services for welfare families, the aged and the blind which had been mandatory for states would become optional. Weinberger claimed the old rules provided "a very broad opening for states to provide services to people who may not have been in need at all." Block certification, under which residence in designated areas established eligibility for certain programs would be eliminated

Federal day care standards would be revised to allow double the number of children per adult. Since many day care programs were operated by private groups, such services would be especially hard hit by the new rules.

Funds would be distributed only to expanded state activities, and states could not reorganize existing programs to qualify. HEW spokesmen said a large part of the recent rise in social services costs resulted from HEW paying for programs formerly financed by the states.

Veto warning. The White House made it clear March 9 that President Nixon would veto some 15 funding bills before Congress and if necessary impound the funds if the veto were overridden. The warning was relayed by John D. Ehrlichman, the President's special assistant on domestic affairs, who spoke of the 15 bills as a "$9

billion dagger aimed at the heart of the American taxpayer."

If they became law, he warned, they would produce a 9% tax increase for individuals. He said the President would try to avoid a tax increase by "non-spending" if necessary.

On the ABC "Issues and Answers" broadcast March 11, Ehrlichman rejected contentions that revenue to offset such spending programs could be realized through tax reform. "You can't raise $9 billion by simply readjusting corporate income tax exemptions," he said. He said tax reform revision to gain such amounts of revenue would have to be extended to individuals by ending mortgage interest deductions for homeowners and exemptions for dependents.

Meanwhile Congress continued its consideration of the fund bills to which Ehrlichman referred. A program already approved by the Senate to extend social service and employment programs for the elderly was passed by the House March 13 by a 329–69 vote.

Both houses March 15 approved the final version of a bill pocket-vetoed in 1972 to extend and enlarge the job-training program for the mentally and physically handicapped. The program level was set at $2.6 billion over the next three years, $800 million less than the vetoed version but about $300 million more than the amount acceptable to the Administration. This was the first of the 15 bills in controversy to be cleared by Congress and sent to the President for signature.

Handicapped aid veto sustained. A $2.6 billion vocational rehabilitation bill was vetoed by President Nixon March 27 in his continuing battle against the "big spenders" in Congress. A vote in the Senate April 3 to override the veto failed 60–36, four less than the two-thirds necessary to carry the program into the House for another test on the veto.

In his veto message, Nixon said "this bill is one of several now before the Congress which mask bad legislation beneath alluring labels." They were "fiscally irresponsible, badly constructed bills," he said, which would mandate an increase of more than $50 billion a year in federal spending before June 30, 1975 and "force upon us the unacceptable choice of either raising taxes substantially—perhaps as much as 15% in personal income taxes—or inviting a hefty boost in consumer prices and interest rates."

Hailing the vote to sustain the veto in the Senate April 3, Nixon said, "Because enough senators had enough courage to stand up against the big spenders in defense of the average American's pocketbook, the tide in this battle of the budget is running in the people's favor."

The outcome of the Senate vote came about in large part because of the defection of five Southern Democrats who voted with 31 Republicans to sustain the veto. Ten Republicans joined 50 Democrats to override.

Second fund bill vetoed—The President vetoed another controversial fund bill April 5. This one—directing the Administration to release $120 million appropriated by Congress for rural water and sewer system grants—had been cleared by the Senate March 22.

The program had been established eight years ago to provide financing in rural areas where property values were too low to obtain financing through regular channels. The Administration had impounded funds for the program Jan. 1.

In his veto message April 5, Nixon said the funds had been stopped because the program "failed" to meet "one simple question: Would this program justify an increase in taxes in order to pay for it?" If he allowed the program, he said, its $300 million annually in grants for the 1973–75 fiscal years "would represent a dangerous crack in the fiscal dam."

Spending ceiling & impoundment curb. The Senate April 4 voted 88–6 to impose a $268 billion spending ceiling on the 1974 federal budget. The bill set a limit $700 million less than the amount requested by the White House. The amendment, proposed by Sen. Edmund S. Muskie (D, Me.) was intended to counter Administration charges that the Democratic controlled Congress had been guilty of reckless spending which threatened Nixon's anti-inflation program.

Approved at the same time was a parallel amendment aimed at curbing the President's power to impound funds already voted by Congress.

The attempt to reassert Congress' authority over its constitutionally mandated power of the purse was proposed by Sen. Sam J. Ervin Jr. (D, N.C.).

Muskie's proposal would permit only proportional, across-the-board spending cutbacks in the budget and specifically forbade the withholding of funds for veterans' and Social Security benefits, Medicare and Medicaid, welfare, food stamps, judges' salaries, interest on the national debt and military retirement pay.

Ervin's proposal, passed 70–24, forbade other efforts by the executive to withhold allocated funds beyond a 60 day period, unless the President obtained the approval of both houses of Congress.

Gold ownership OK'd—Another proposal opposed by the Administration was the amendment approved April 4 on a 68–23 vote. The measure permitted private U.S. citizens to own gold after Jan. 1, 1974. Sen. James McClure (R, Ida.) proposed the amendment, which Western states contended would stimulate mining activity. The Nixon Administration maintained that the proposal, overturning a 1934 prohibition against private ownership of gold, would have an unsettling effect upon an already disturbed international monetary system and ongoing currency reform talks.

Prices & Wages

Chrysler boosts prices. Chrysler Corp. became the first U.S. auto maker to raise car prices after the lifting of Phase 2 controls when it raised the price of its Japanese-built Colt model by $15–$26, effective Feb. 15.

Chrysler also won Price Commission approval Jan. 8 to raise 1973 car and truck prices by an average $7.25 a vehicle to cover the cost of side door impact protection required by federal safety standards.

The price hike was in addition to an earlier gain won in October 1972.

Chrysler announced March 19 that it planned a 1.25% price increase, averaging $42 a vehicle, on 1973 model cars.

The corporation said that it had absorbed costs totaling $190 a vehicle for labor, material and freight increases since January 1972, when its last price hike to recover "economic" costs had been allowed by the Price Commission.

Townsend got record '72 pay—Lynn Townsend, Chrysler's chairman, received an annual salary of $225,000 and bonuses of $413,600 in 1972, according to the Wall Street Journal March 12.

Townsend's record total was more than triple his 1971 pay, which consisted only of salary, when Chrysler's earnings were depressed. But the 1972 figures were 1.3% above 1968 levels, when Chrysler also reported record net income.

Ford & GM roll-backs. The Cost of Living Council April 14 ordered Ford Motor Co. and General Motors Corp. to roll back price increases for automobile parts and accessories. Nearly 9,000 of 25,-000 car dealers surveyed were not in compliance with federal regulations, the CLC said. The agency ordered Ford dealers to return $5.1 million in overcharges; GM dealers owed $4.5 million in excessive markups.

Oil companies raise prices. Mobil Oil Co. and Atlantic Richfield Co. raised bulk prices for gasoline sold to distributors by as much as 10%, the Wall Street Journal reported March 28. Cities Service Co. also boosted prices, effective May 1.

The Cost of Living Council (CLC) May 11 denied the first application by a large oil company for a price increase. Ashland Oil, Inc.'s request for a 2.4% price hike was rejected.

The Wall Street Journal reported May 14 that the CLC had eased restrictions on the oil industry in an effort to provide an incentive for major companies to resell crude oil and gasoline to independent refiners and jobbers. According to the new rule, price increases paid by the major companies for crude oil could be passed on in the resale and would not be included in their 1.5% ceiling for price increases set by the CLC.

U.S. Steel, auto price hikes planned. Two major price increases were announced May 10 following annual stockholder meetings.

U.S. Steel Corp. announced it was ending a 17-month freeze on prices with a 4.8% average increase on the prices of sheet and strip products, effective with shipments June 15. Overall steel mill prices would be 1.3% higher as a result. The Cost of Living Council announced it would review the cost justification for the increase.

Henry Ford II, president of Ford Motor Co., predicted there would be a "substantial" price increase for 1974 model vehicles "to cover the cost of safety, damagability and emission improvements required by government standards and because we have had no general price increase to cover rising costs of labor and materials since January 1972."

American Motors Corp. announced June 1 that the price of 1973 model cars and jeeps would be increased an average $59, effective June 30. The company claimed the 1.5% boost was authorized under a Price Commission decision in October 1972.

Dress workers' pact. A new contract for dress workers was reached Jan. 30 and signed in New York Feb. 6. The new three-year pact, covering 30,000 dressmakers in the city and 30,000 others in other areas of the Northeast, called for a 20% wage increase over the three years—8% the first year, and 6% the second and third years. The previous contract had expired Jan. 31.

The union involved was the AFL-CIO International Ladies' Garment Workers' Union.

Early rail settlement reached. Negotiators for the nation's major railroads and rail unions reached tentative agreement March 13 on a new 18-month contract with a 10.7% package increase in wages and benefits. Labor Secretary Peter J. Brennan March 16 described the settlement as "well within reasonable guidelines," and CLC Director John T. Dunlop indicated that the government would not contest it.

The settlement covered 15 unions, each of which would take a ratification vote, and all of the nation's major rail lines except the Penn Central Railroad. The 4% wage boost set for Jan. 1, 1974 under the new tentative pact would apply to all rail employes except those of the Penn Central and some other Northeast lines also undergoing reorganization.

PATH strike ends. A 63-day strike against the Port Authority Trans-Hudson Railroad (PATH) linking New York City and suburban New Jersey ended May 2 as members of the AFL-CIO Brotherhood of Railway Carmen ratified a 27½-month contract tentatively reached two days earlier.

The new contract called for a compounded wage increase of 19.3%, with the first 6.6% raise retroactive to Feb. 1, 1972. The agreement also provided improvements in fringe benefits and productivity.

Shell accords reached. Strikes that began Jan. 25 against oil and chemical plants of Shell Oil Co. ended May 31 at West Coast locations and May 18 at a Texas plant.

Members of the Oil, Chemical and Atomic Workers union accepted terms providing wage increases of 30¢ an hour (6%) in 1973 and 27¢ an hour in 1974.

The Shell settlement was generally similar to agreements reached with other major oil companies shortly after contract expirations in January.

(Mobil Oil Corp. and Phillips Petroleum Co. pacts were reported Jan. 22; American Oil Co. settled Jan. 1).

Rubber pacts reached. The United Rubber Workers union ended a strike against B. F. Goodrich Co. May 31, accepting a three-year pact providing wage increases of 80.8¢ an hour over the life of the contract in most company plants. The strike had begun May 7.

The wage agreement paralleled an accord reached April 25, without a strike, with the Goodyear Tire & Rubber Co. On the pension issue, however, the Goodrich pact provided $10 a month per year of service by the third year of the contract; Goodyear had agreed to $8.50 a month. A

contract almost identical to the Goodrich pact was reached with Uniroyal Inc., also without a strike, the Wall Street Journal reported June 11. The Uniroyal contract also provided better job security guarantees than the Goodyear pact, the Journal said, and union president Peter Bommarito began formal moves to reopen negotiations with Goodyear to amend the earlier agreement.

GE, Westinghouse settle. Strikes were averted at General Electric Co. and Westinghouse Electric Corp. as short contract extensions led to similar three-year union agreements with both companies. General Electric settled June 6 and Westinghouse June 16.

In addition to pension and fringe benefit improvements, the agreements provided wage increases of 47¢ an hour over the life of the contracts, plus cost-of-living escalators which could add 41¢ an hour.

The major unions involved were the International Union of Electrical Workers (AFL-CIO) and the United Electrical Workers (independent).

Teamsters pact negotiated. Negotiators for the International Brotherhood of Teamsters and the nation's trucking industry agreed June 28 on a new 33-month master freight contract calling for wage and benefit increases totaling about 21%.

The contract, covering 400,000 truck drivers and 1,200 companies, would replace one expiring June 30.

The wage provision would provide a 35¢ increase July 1 and 30¢ boosts in each of the next two years of the pact for drivers paid on an hourly basis. Their current wage averaged $6 an hour. Drivers paid by the mile would receive three-quarters of a cent more per mile in the first and second years, a half a cent in the third year. Their current rate was 12.5¢ a mile.

A cost-of-living clause in the contract called for an increase of at least 8¢ an hour and no more than 11¢ an hour in the first and third years of the pact.

Fringe benefits included additional holidays, vacation time and funeral leave.

The wage-benefit increases totaled 7.2% in the first two years of the contract, 6.6% in the third year.

Labor Secretary Peter J. Brennan hailed the new pact later June 28 as "good news for the American public and for the nation's economy."

Cigarette prices boosted. The first increase in wholesale cigarette prices in three years was announced Feb. 2 by Philip Morris Inc. Similar increases of less than 2% were undertaken Feb. 5 by the Lorillard division of the Loews Corp., Feb. 7 by American Brands Inc. and Liggett & Myers Inc. and Feb. 28 by the largest cigarette manufacturer, R. J. Reynolds Industries Inc.

Despite the Price Commission's rejection in June 1972 of Philip Morris's application to raise prices 2%, the company defended the increase as "within the 1.5% weighted average standard of Phase 3."

The price hike was expected to cost smokers 1¢ a pack and 5¢–10¢ a carton.

Cost of Living Council action. In its first challenge to a Phase 3 price increase, the Cost of Living Council (CLC) June 12 suspended a 7.1% boost in zinc prices announced by National Zinc Co. Zinc industry increases had totaled 13% in the past six months, CLC spokesmen said.

Its first test of a wage increase—an 8.9% raise won by airline mechanics—was withdrawn May 14 by the CLC.

The CLC issued tightened Phase 3 reporting requirements for hospitals and nursing homes June 4 in an effort to stem health care cost hikes.

Policy & Action

Economic controls bill signed. President Nixon April 30 signed a compromise bill extending the Economic Stabilization Act until April 30, 1974 despite inclusion of several measures the Administration had opposed in the bill's final version.

Congress had returned from a 12-day Easter recess that day facing the necessity for immediate action on a conference committee report, voted April 18, which gave the President wide discretionary authority to impose wage and price controls. The current law expired at midnight April 30.

The Senate quickly passed the compromise controls measure on a voice vote after supporters of mandatory rent controls failed in their effort to return the bill to conference.

Adoption of the final bill had been considered doubtful in the House because proponents of stiffer food and rent restrictions had appealed to supporters of weaker economic controls for defeat of the compromise legislation. Despite their efforts, the House voted 267–115 (153 D & 114 R vs 58 D & 57 R) to approve a continuation of the Economic Stabilization Act, sending the bill to the White House.

Proposals in the bill which were accepted reluctantly by the President increased the number of workers exempt from wage regulations from 16.3 million to 25.2 million jobholders by raising the maximum wage for such exemption from $2.75 an hour to $3.50 an hour; required public disclosure of cost and profit information by companies raising prices by more than 1.5% during the year; stated the bill could not be used by Nixon to justify his impoundment of funds appropriated by Congress; required the Cost of Living Council to hold public hearings when considering reductions of negotiated wage increases; and authorized the President to ration crude oil and petroleum products in the event of regional shortages.

Despite mounting public and Congressional pressure for a return to stringent federal guidelines, Administration economic advisers, led by Treasury Secretary George P. Shultz, voiced support April 5 for a continuation of Phase 3, contending that a renewed wage-price freeze could not deal with the inflationary consequences of short supply and high demand. According to Herbert Stein, chairman of the President's Council of Economic Advisers, "the controls system will be adapted to play its most useful role in restraining inflation," but, he added, the "fundamental fact [is] that the controls system can only be effective in an environment where demand is not generally excessive."

In an attempt to shift the political focus of the battle against inflation, Stein declared, "The key to success in this and therefore in the whole anti-inflation program is to hold the federal budget under prudent restraint, as proposed by the President."

Wage control actions. In its first challenge to wage increases negotiated during Phase 3 that exceeded the 5.5% ceiling, the Cost of Living Council (CLC) April 3 blocked part of a tentative wage pact between the International Association of Machinists (IAM) and North Central Airlines.

The CLC approved an increase retroactive to April 1, 1972, but refused to permit an 8.9% boost, which would be spread over 12 months, to take effect April 1.

The government's action indicated a change in Phase 3 enforcement policy. During Phase 2, the Pay Board had not challenged wage settlements until the total increases had exceeded the 5.5% limit. In the IAM settlement, affecting 600 airline mechanics, the contract would not violate the federal guideline until Jan. 1, 1973 when the third of three increases would take effect.

CLC Director John T. Dunlop indicated the government would not contest the 10.7% wage and benefit increase won by the railroad industry's 15 unions, according to the Wall Street Journal April 3. Labor Secretary Peter J. Brennan March 16 had described the 18-month pact as "well within reasonable [wage control] guidelines."

The CLC reported April 2 that the increases won by corporate executives and salaried employes during 1972 had averaged 5.1%, although the figures were not broken down by category. The survey was based on 67 companies employing 1,-136 executives and 452,967 salaried personnel.

The formation of a health industry wage and salary committee similar to Phase 3's food industry panel was announced April 21 by the CLC.

Minimum wage proposals. Labor Secretary Peter J. Brennan presented the Administration's proposals April 10 to raise the federal minimum wage and to set a lower minimum for youth. The latter proposal drew immediate fire from or-

ganized labor, whose spokesman, AFL-CIO President George Meany, said Brennan had "completely abandoned the trade union principles he espoused for all of his life before coming to Washington." Brennan had been president of the New York Building and Construction Trades Council before assuming the Cabinet post.

Their forum was a hearing of a House Education and Labor subcommittee. Brennan testified that the Administration recommended: a federal minimum wage of $1.90 in 1973 since 1966, and rising to $2.10 in 1974, to $2.20 in 1975 and to $2.30 in 1976. For the youth minimum wage, because of "a persistent and perplexing problem" or unemployment among the group, he proposed a minimum wage of 80% of the general minimum scale, or $1.60 an hour, whichever was higher, for youths under 18 years of age in non-farm jobs, and a minimum wage of at least 85% of the regular minimum for youths 18 and 19.

As safeguards against the possible practice of replacing older workers with the less-expensive youthful workers, Brennan suggested several strategies. The subminimum for youth could be applied only for the first 13 weeks of employment, he said, or an employer could be prohibited from hiring more than 12% of his work force at the lower rate, or his department could be given special authority to investigate and correct abuses.

Brennan also stated the Administration's opposition to extending minimum wage coverage to domestic workers or to employes of state and local governments.

Meany, in a prepared statement presented to the panel later April 10, cited Brennan's previous testimony at his confirmation hearings that if youth performed the same work as adults there should not be any difference in the wage rate.

Brennan was coolly received later April 10 during an appearance before the AFL-CIO Amalgamated Meat Cutters and Butcher Workmen Union, where he indicated his position on the youth wage was against his personal opinion. "You don't quit the team the first time you have a disagreement," he said. Union Vice President Leon Schachter commented to him later, "You negotiated for the workers with the highest wages in the country when you were in New York. Now let someone else have a piece of the pie."

Nixon defends Brennan—President Nixon joined the debate on Brennan's proposals before a legislative conference of the building and construction trades unions in Washington April 16. Brennan had argued unsuccessfully within the Administration against a subminimum wage for youth, Nixon told the conference, but he had won in arguing for a ceiling on meat prices against Agriculture Secretary Earl L. Butz.

In his Cabinet, Nixon said, "you win some and you lose some." "Peter Brennan is a team player and he knows that you can't win them all."

Meany condemned Phases 1, 2 and 3 of the Administration's economic stabilization program as "complete and miserable failures."

"Without equity, any phase is doomed to failure," he said, and charged that throughout the program wages had been held down but not prices or profits. He said organized labor was "still in there pitching" on Phase 3 but "how long we will stay," he added, "I don't know."

House Republican Leader Gerald R. Ford's (Mich.) assessment of the economy—"jobs are up and unemployment down" and the economy was "in good shape generally"—evoked boos.

Meany April 26 accused Nixon aides of using "the big lie technique" and embarking "on a new propaganda campaign designed to hide the facts of soaring inflation, continued high unemployment, mounting budget deficits and a shocking drop in public confidence. It is trying to convince the American public that 'You're all right, Jack.'"

In the speech, Meany cited a column in the New York Times April 25 by Roy L. Ash, director of the Office of Management and Budget. Ash had declared that the "second Nixon Administration is off to an excellent start," but Meany offered a point-by-point refutation of the statistics and claims in the Ash column.

Meany was also critical of the Administration policy granting economic and trade concessions to the Soviet Union.

Meany, addressing the group after the President April 16, commented: "If Pete is on the team, and that is a team, then I submit he will have to admit that he cannot be on two competing teams at the same time."

Phase 3 rules tightened. President Nixon announced May 2 that he was tightening Phase 3 price controls for an estimated 600 major companies with annual sales in excess of $250 million. They would be required to provide the government' with 30 days notice of any price hikes having the effect of raising average prices 1.5% above the level set Jan. 10.

Nixon rejected public and congressional pressures to make broader changes in the largely voluntary Phase 3 regulations. He acknowledged that "price increases will probably be higher than we would like for some months," but concluded, "we should be mature enough to recognize that there is no instant remedy for this problem."

Pressure mounted in Congress for executive action dealing with the inflation crisis. Sen. William Proxmire (D, Wis.), chairman of the Joint Economic Committee, said June 7 the Administration's "paralysis" regarding economic decision-making "is impossible to understand, justify or defend."

In a unanimous resolution adopted June 4, the Senate Democratic Caucus had termed the President's Phase 3 voluntary economic guidelines "an unmitigated failure" and pledged to attach a mandatory 90-day freeze on wages, salaries, prices, profits, rents and consumer interest rates "to the first appropriate bill coming before the Senate."

Dow rebounds from record low—The Nixon announcement occurred after the close of the New York Stock Exchange, but the Dow Jones industrial average showed its best advance in three weeks, gaining 11.13 points May 2 to close at 932.34 in anticipation of the President's actions.

Trading had hit a new low for the year April 27 as the index fell 15.57 points, closing at 922.19. During the week of April 23–27, the Dow lost 14.01 points, its largest decline since May 1970.

Martin scores economic policies. William McC. Martin Jr., former chairman of the Federal Reserve Board, told a subcommittee of the Senate Finance Committee June 1 that a "flood of business froth . . . is now cresting and will, I think, result in at least a moderate recession by the end of this year or the middle of the next."

In other comments on the economic situation, Martin said the current business boom was "unbalanced and dangerous." He labeled the Administration's efforts at achieving economic expansion by engaging in fiscal stimulus "in excess of any reasonable requirement that, in my judgment, borders on the irresponsible."

He also urged the government to intervene in foreign money exchanges in support of the dollar "whenever [it was] threatened." Martin termed the dollar devaluation undertaken in February unnecessary and said the dollar currently was "undervalued."

CLC broadens reporting rules. The Cost of Living Council (CLC) announced June 18 that companies with annual sales of $50 million–$250 million would be required to submit quarterly reports on profits, prices and costs. Previously, only companies with annual revenues exceeding $250 million were required to file financial statements. The action increased the number of reporting companies from 800 to 3,100.

According to the Wall Street Journal June 18, the CLC broadened its public disclosure rules, requiring companies with annual sales above $250 million to make public the percentage increases in costs they had used to justify price increases for their products. The firms would also be asked to reveal the dollar amount by which profits either fell below or exceeded base period profit margins during Phase 3.

The new rules affected companies boosting prices more than 1.5% during Phase 3 on any products that represented at least 5% of annual sales.

Dual rate plan detailed. The Administration's Committee on Interest and Dividends April 16 announced two new policies designed to bring banks within voluntary regulations established under Phase 3 of the economic stabilization program.

The committee announced that,

effective immediately, banks would be subject to profit margin restrictions required of other businesses. At the same time, it issued guidelines to establish "dual" prime interest rates for business loans.

Under the split rate plan, a "small business prime rate" would apply to commercial, industrial or agricultural borrowers "whose total borrowings outstanding at any time over the preceding 12 months (exclusive of long-term real estate mortgage debt) did not exceed $350,000 and whose assets do not exceed $1 million."

Small business interest charges (as well as those for consumer loans and home mortgage loans) "should remain at levels no higher than those prevailing on the date these criteria are issued unless an increase can be fully justified by increases in costs."

The new "large business prime rate" was not fixed by such a cost rule but would be permitted to "respond flexibly to changes in open market interest rates"; however, banks were cautioned to keep large business rate increases moderate in order to avoid disrupting credit flow. (Banks were free to apply the small business interest formula to other firms regardless of size. According to the committee, the regulated rate for small borrowers could "vary from bank to bank.")

The "cost rule" limiting interest charges for small firms would be based on banks' Phase 3 profit margins, defined as "the ratio of net operating income, on a fully taxable equivalent basis, before income taxes and securities gains or losses, to gross operating income on a fully taxable equivalent basis."

Profit margin restrictions were set at the average of the best two years within the last four calendar years.

Included in the enforcement plan was a new reporting system providing a breakdown for large and small business loans.

The two-tier rate plan, which resulted from a series of confrontations between the Administration and major banks, represented an attempt to provide small business borrowers with government protection against "burdensome" rate increases while maintaining a flexible structure of fluctuating credit rates for large firms.

Arthur F. Burns of the Federal Reserve

Board, committee chairman, conceded that past "jawboning" efforts to hold down prime rate increases had established artificially low interest rates resulting in a run on bank loans at the expense of commercial paper financing.

Other bank developments—Reacting to increases in private market rates, the Federal Reserve Board (FRB) announced Jan. 12 that the discount rate for the nation's 12 FRB banks would increase by .5% to 5%, effective Jan. 15.

In taking the anti-inflation measure, the FRB noted that the discount rate had been at 5% when Phase 1 had been implemented.

Three of four major banks that had raised prime rates to 6.25% Feb. 2 rescinded the increase Feb. 6 under Administration pressure.

The Bank of New York, Franklin National Bank of New York, and Girard Trust Bank of Philadelphia set the new rate at its former level of 6%. Philadelphia's First Pensylvania Banking and Trust Co. refused to lower its minimum rate for corporate customers. In a statement issued Feb. 7, the bank claimed that a "frozen prime" could lead to cutbacks in loans to consumers and small businessmen. But First Pennsylvania ended its holdout Feb. 13 and also reduced its prime rate to 6%.

The Administration's Committee on Interest and Dividends, in a telegram delivered to the four banks Feb. 4, had demanded "full information on recent changes in costs and earnings" that could "justify" the rate increase.

A copy of the message, which expressed regret at the rate hike, was sent to all commercial banks throughout the country in an effort to head off other planned increases.

The committee request was the first such action taken under the Economic Stabilization Act, which empowered the group to monitor interest rates on a voluntary basis.

Burns told the Senate Banking Committee Feb. 7 that the committee "is now expanding its monitoring activity to include full attention to the costs and profits of banks and other financial institutions."

The First National City Bank of New York (Citibank), the nation's second

largest bank, also crumpled under Administration pressure Feb. 8.

The effect of the Citibank decision, taken after consultation with Burns, was to hold the interest rate on basic commercial loans to 6% instead of allowing it to float to 6.25%.

"This action is the direct result of government pressure," the bank declared. "The base rate, which previously was determined by the free market is now being administered by the federal authorities."

Citibank charged that the decision could hurt rather than help the battle against inflation and linked the government's prime rate policy to the dollar crisis abroad.

"The weakness of the dollar abroad is partly due to the fact that the world perceives that, in asking banks to hold down the price of credit to large borrowers, the United States government is asking commercial banks to assume the burden which in the end must be borne by monetary policy," the bank maintained.

But rates quickly headed up again. The Federal Reserve Board Feb. 23 unanimously approved a .5% increase in the discount rate to 5.5% for four of its 12 regional member banks in New York, Philadelphia, St. Louis and Kansas City effective Feb. 26. The remaining FRB banks won approval for similar increases Feb. 27–28 and March 2.

At the same time, the Committee on Interest and Dividends made public a letter to the Girard Trust Bank of Philadelphia permitting an increase in the prime rate to 6.25%. Other major banks made similar raises Feb. 26.

In allowing the prime rate increase, the committee also issued guidelines for banks in establishing business loan rates:

■ Future prime rate increase "should be decidedly less than for related open market interest rate" because "institutions operate with certain relatively stable costs that can be spread over a rising volume of business."

■ "Such adjustments should be delayed until it has become clear that the increase in open market rates is not a temporary phenomenon."

■ "Special moderation should be observed" by banks in raising rates charged consumers and small businessmen.

Following the lead of Manufacturers Hanover Trust Co. of New York, seven major banks raised their prime interest rate March 19 from 6.25% to 6.75%. Three other banks took similar action March 24 in boosting the minimum interest charges for corporate customers; however, the credit crisis subsided by March 26 as most of the nation's major banks posted a 6.5% prime rate following discussions March 22 and March 24 with

Burns had demanded that bank representatives appear before his committee to justify the rate increases.

Agreement was reached on the 6.5% figure after the Administration had rejected the higher lending rate but offered a compromise plan for setting "split" rates.

The proposal emerged from the March 22 meeting when the committee concluded that, although the "cost of interest-sensitive funds to banks has risen considerably," a 6.75% interest rate was "not justified at this time."

The FRB raised the discount rate for the third time in 1973 when it approved an increase in the interest rate from 5.5% to 5.75%, effective April 24, for seven of its 12 district banks, those in Philadelphia, Cleveland, Minneapolis, Kansas City, San Francisco, Richmond, Va. and Atlanta. Similar action was authorized for the remaining banks April 26–May 3.

The action, taken in response to "developments in the money markets that have occurred since the discount rate was raised to 5.5%, effective Feb. 26," indicated a further tightening of credit as the Administration continued to issue reports of an overstimulated economy.

Citibank and other major banks raised their prime rates to 7% May 4.

The Administration, which had abandoned efforts to control rising prime rates when it promulgated rules for a dual, or two-tier, prime rate system, had no comment on the latest increase.

Analysts concluded that the Committee on Interest and Dividends was signaling its tacit approval for quarter point hikes over three-week intervals.

(In apparent confirmation of this conclusion, Chase Manhattan Bank of New York and other major banks raised their prime rates to 7.25% May 24, and a 7.5% rate was posted by major banks June 6.)

The FRB authorized a new .25-point increase in the discount rate for 11 regional FRB banks May 10 and for the 12th May 17.

The board said the action was "in recognition of increases that have already taken place in other short-term interest rates and is intended to bring the discount rate into better alignment with short term rates generally."

There was further evidence of a tightening of monetary policy:

In a six-month period ending May 2, the nation's money supply, representing the total of private demand deposits plus cash in the public hands grew at an annual rate of 5.2%. The growth rate was short of the annual rate of 7.5% established from January 1971 to October 1972.

The Federal Reserve Board announced a series of complex changes May 16 designed to slow the growth of bank loans to large businesses and "help moderate inflationary pressures." Key measures:

■ Banks were required to keep on deposit with the FRB 8% of any additional funds raised by issuing large certificates of deposits that were in excess of certificates outstanding during the week of May 16. (Large certificates of deposits were issued in order to relend them at a profit to corporate customers. According to the New York Times May 16, banks had raised about $15 billion by issuing these certificates during the first four months of 1973. There had been a corresponding increase of about $15 billion in bank loans to business.)

■ The same marginal 8% reserve requirement was also imposed on commercial paper issued by affiliates of banks.

■ Reserve requirement on certain foreign borrowings of U.S. banks, primarily in Eurodollars, was reduced to 8% from 20%.

■ The ceiling on interest rates paid on certificates of deposit of $100,000 or larger that mature within 90 days or more was removed.

The FRB June 8 increased the discount rate to 6.5%, its highest level since 1921 (when it was 7%).

For the first time, the Federal Reserve cited inflation as a factor in its decision to raise the interest rate, its fifth increase of 1973.

Federal Reserve efforts to place further checks on the nation's money supply followed an announcement June 7 that there had been a 12% annual rate of monetary expansion during May. The rate of acceleration was up sharply from the 7% increase during April and a 1.7% rate of growth during the first quarter of 1973 (measured at an adjusted annual rate).

Strategic stockpiles to be sold. President Nixon announced at a news conference March 15 that "it will be safe for the U.S. to very substantially reduce our [strategic] stockpiles, and we are going to go forward and do that."

He justified his decision "on the basis of national security," saying that the "stockpiles were really irrelevant to the kind of a world situation we presently confront."

"Squeals" and "complaints," Nixon warned, could be anticipated from "those who produce and sell some of the materials in which we are going to sell the stockpiles. But ... we need to take every action we possibly can to drive down prices, or at least to drive down those particular elements that force prices up."

Stockpiles had been sold in the past to raise revenues, but massive sales had never before been undertaken as an anti-inflationary measure, according to the New York Times March 14.

Copper, lead, zinc, nickel, chromium, aluminum, silver, tin, rubber and other items among the 80 strategic commodities held by the government would be affected. Total value of the reserves was put at $6.5 billion.

Nixon announced April 16 that he had submitted to Congress a proposal that would permit him to sell $4.1 billion worth of strategic materials.

In his statement, Nixon reasoned that release of the materials would help ease pressures in a world economy whose short-term demand had outstripped short-term supply. "By disposing of unneeded items in the strategic stockpile, we can strike a critical blow for the American consumer," he said.

Nixon also noted that increasing technological abilities lessened the need for long term stockpiling. A 12-month stockpile would give the U.S. sufficient time to mobilize resources, so as not to place an intolerable burden on the economy or the people, he said.

The materials would be sold so as to avoid displacement in world markets. Items such as silver and platinum could be marketed quickly, but disposal of commodities like tungsten and manganese might take a number of years.

Increased timber harvest sought. Cost of Living Council (CLC) Director John T. Dunlop told a subcommittee of the Senate Banking, Housing and Urban Affairs Committee March 26 that the Administration had authorized the increased cutting of trees from national forest to raise 1973 supplies by 1.8 billion board feet. Agriculture Secretary Earl L. Butz, acting as the President's special adviser on natural resources, would formulate plans to bring national forest timber production to 11.8 billion board feet by the end of 1973, Dunlop said.

Other action taken to deal with rising lumber costs included negotiations with Japan to seek its voluntary compliance in reducing purchases of U.S. timber. Japan, experiencing a housing boom, had bought 85% of the three billion board feet exported during 1972.

Hearings on rising lumber prices to consider reimposition of mandatory price controls were scheduled for April, Dunlop told the subcommittee. Softwood lumber and plywood prices had climbed 56% since January 1971 and had gained 8% during February.

Sen. Robert W. Packwood (R, Ore.) argued that the President could also demonstrate his regard for the timber cost problem by releasing $18 million in appropriated Forest Service funds used to build access roads to forested areas. He also pointed out that the Forest Service's fiscal 1974 budget had been cut in half.

Food stamp rise set. The Agriculture Department reported March 26 that the 12 million recipients of food stamps would receive a 3.6% cost-of-living increase in allocations beginning July 1 to $116 per month for a family of four. The stamps were sold at varying rates to poor families depending on size and income.

Pentagon closes bases. The Defense Department informed members of Congress April 16 it intended to either close or cut back 274 military bases as part of an economy move expected to save $350 million a year.

By mid-1974, 26,172 civilian and 16,640 military jobs were to be eliminated. Affected were 199 Navy, 40 Air Force, and 35 Army installations in 30 states, the District of Columbia and Puerto Rico.

60-Day Price Freeze

Tighter standards promised. President Nixon announced June 13 that he was ordering a freeze (based on prices during the week of June 1-8) on all "prices paid by consumers," except those on "unprocessed agricultural products at the farm levels, and rents" for up to 60 days in an effort to check rampant inflation.

In his nationally televised address, Nixon said Treasury Secretary George P. Shultz and Cost of Living Council Director John T. Dunlop would prepare new wage-price policies for Phase 4, which would impose "tighter standards and more mandatory compliance procedures" than under the present Phase 3.

Concurrent with the 60-day freeze, Nixon ordered the Internal Revenue Service to begin immediate audits of companies that raised prices above the 1.5% ceiling allowed under Phase 3.

Congressional approval was required for other aspects of the President's plan to deal with rising costs:

■ A new system of export controls on agricultural products. (Exporters were ordered to notify the government of future export contracts. "We will not let foreign sales price meat and eggs off the American table," Nixon said.)

■ Authority to reduce tariffs where necessary to replenish American supplies of scarce products.

■ Power to make further reductions in the nation's commodities stockpile.

■ Quick approval of the Alaska pipeline project to "combat the shortage of oil and gasoline."

■ A farm bill that encouraged production and discouraged price increases. Nixon promised to veto any other kind of legislation.

Nixon rejected Congressional pressure for a more extensive economic controls package—wages, salaries, profits, interests and dividends were not included in the freeze but remained subject to the minimal restrictions of Phase 3.

Nixon blamed "rising food prices" for "unacceptably high rates" of general price hikes. "Wage settlements reached under Phase 3 have not been a significant cause of the increases in prices," Nixon said, and therefore were not subject to the 60-day freeze. "As long as wage settlements continue to be responsible and non-inflationary, a wage freeze will not be imposed," he added.

Nixon's decision to undertake a limited policy of tightened controls reflected political considerations as well as economic imperatives.

High Administration officials had conceded that the President was preoccupied by the Watergate affair and that government was at a standstill.

Some economists, however, contended that the economic boom was subsiding and that new price controls could promote a recession.

Nixon's address mirrored these mixed considerations. While adopting a 60-day "shock treatment" for the inflation problem, the President warned, "We must not let controls become a narcotic and we must not become addicted."

In an attempt to deflect attention from the crises of the Administration, Nixon's speech emphasized what was "right about our economy," including "one of the biggest, strongest booms in our history." He pledged not to "control the boom in a way that would lead to a bust."

Sen. William Proxmire (D, Wis.), sponsor of the bill, said June 13 he was withdrawing the freeze legislation.

Despite these policy dilemmas, there was some consensus about the economic situation. Shultz told reporters, "Everyone thinks that Phase 3 was a failure, so let's not argue about that."

Congressional reaction to Nixon's proposals generally was favorable, although Rep. Wilbur D. Mills (D, Ark.), chairman of the House Ways and Means Committee, predicted, "It's probably too late, probably too little."

Senate Republicans June 12 had voted 22-8 in favor of tightened Phase 3 controls, but they were able to delay a vote on a Democratic-sponsored bill calling for a 90-day across-the-board freeze in an effort to give Nixon the opportunity to act first.

Freeze-related price cutbacks—Postponements or rollbacks were announced June 15 for industries and commodities affected by the 60-day price freeze ordered June 13 by President Nixon:

Text of President's June 13 Price Freeze Order

On Jan. 11, 1973, I issued Executive Order 11695, which provided for establishment of Phase 3 of the economic stabilization program. On April 30, 1973, the Congress enacted, and I signed into law, amendments to the Economic Stabilization Act of 1970, which extended for one year, until April 30, 1974, the legislative authority for carrying out the economic stabilization program.

During Phase 3, labor and management have contributed to our stabilization efforts through responsible collective bargaining. The American people look to labor and management to continue their constructive and cooperative contributions. Price behavior under Phase 3 has not been satisfactory, however. I have therefore determined to impose a comprehensive freeze for a maximum period of 60 days on the prices of all commodities and services offered for sale except the prices charged for raw agricultural products. I have determined that this action is necessary to stabilize the economy, reduce inflation, minimize unemployment, improve the nation's competitive position in world trade and protect the purchasing power of the dollar, all in the context of sound fiscal management and effective monetary policies.

Now, therefore, by virtue of the authority vested in me by the Constitution and statutes of the United States particularly the Economic Stabilization Act of 1970, as amended, it is hereby ordered as follows:

Section 1
Effective 9 p.m., EST, June 13, 1973, no seller may charge to any class of purchaser and no purchaser may pay a price for any commodity or service which exceeds the freeze price charged for the same or a similar commodity or service in transactions with the same class of purchaser during the freeze base period. This order shall be effective for a maximum period of 60 days from the date hereof, until 11:59 p.m., EST, Aug. 12, 1973. It is not unlawful to charge or pay a price less than the freeze price and lower prices are encouraged.

Section 2
Each seller shall prepare a list of freeze prices for all commodities and services which he sells and shall maintain a copy of that list available for public inspection, during normal business hours, at each place of business where such commodities or services are offered for sale. In addition, the calculations and supporting data upon which the list is based shall be maintained by the seller at the location where the pricing decisions reflected on the list are ordinarily made and shall be made available on request to representatives of the economic stabilization program.

Section 3
The provisions of this order shall not extend to the prices charged for raw agricultural products. The prices of processed agricultural products, however, are subject to the provisions of this order. For those agricultural products which are sold for ultimate consumption in their original unprocessed form, this provision applies after the first sale.

Section 4
The provisions of this order do not extend to (A) wages and salaries, which continue to be subject to the program established pursuant to Executive Order 11695; (B) interest and dividends, which continue to be subject to the program established by the Committee on Interest and Dividends and (C) rents, which continue to be subject to controls only to the limited extent provided in Executive Order 11695.

Section 5
The Cost of Living Council shall develop and recommend to the President policies, mechanisms and procedures to achieve and maintain stability of prices and costs in a growing economy after the expiration of this freeze. To this end, it shall consult with representatives of agriculture, industry, labor, consumers and the public.

Section 6
A. Executive Order 11695 continues to remain in full force and effect and the authority conferred by or pursuant to Executive Order 11695 including authority to grant exceptions and exemptions under appropriate standards issued pursuant to regulations.

B. All powers and duties delegated to the chairman of the Cost of Living Council by Executive Order 11695 for the purpose of carrying out the provisions of that order are hereby delegated to the chairman of the Cost of Living Council for the purpose of carrying out the provisions of this order.

Section 7
Whoever willfully violates this order or any order or regulation continued or issued under authority of this order shall be subject to a fine of not more than $5,000 for each such violation. Whoever violates this order or any order or regulation continued or issued under authority of this order shall be subject to a civil penalty of not more than $2,500 for each such violation.

Section 8
For purposes of this Executive order, the following definitions apply:

"Freeze price" means the highest price at or above which at least 10% of the commodities or services concerned were priced by the seller in transactions with the class of purchaser concerned during the freeze base period. In computing the freeze price, a seller may not exclude any temporary special sale, deal or allowance in effect during the freeze base period.

"Class of purchaser" means all those purchasers to whom a seller has charged a comparable price for comparable commodities or services during the freeze base period pursuant to customary price differentials between those purchasers and other purchasers.

"Freeze base period" means (A) The period of June 1 to June 8, 1973; or (B) in the case of a seller who had no transactions during that period, the nearest preceding seven-day period in which he had a transaction.

"Transaction" means an arm's length sale between unrelated persons and is considered to occur at the time of shipment in the case of commodities and the time of performance in the case of services.

Postal rate increases planned for second, third and fourth rate mail; natural gas prices at the wellhead; telephone and telegraph companies; airlines; railroads; bus companies; steel; automobiles; and rubber.

The CLC June 19 suspended pay raises of 16%–70% for Georgia state officials, scheduled to take effect July 1, while it determined if the increases were justified.

Dividends rule eased. The Committee on Interest and Dividends announced revised guidelines June 21 that would permit companies to base 1973 dividend payments either on the present 4% increase allowed over the amount paid in 1972, or on an amount equal to the company's ratio of dividends to profits for the years 1968–1972.

Easing the dividends payments rule, according to committee chairman Arthur F. Burns, who was also chairman of the Federal Reserve Board, would "make it possible for many corporations to increase their dividends payments significantly this year, and to a greater extent next year. This should be of particular help to elderly individuals and widows dependent on dividend income. At the same time, increased dividend payments will raise tax revenues and thereby improve the conditions of the federal budget," Burns said.

Nixon economy message. In a brief radio broadcast July 1, President Nixon gave the nation a progress report on his recently implemented 60-day price freeze.

He listed enforcement actions that were being taken to insure compliance and promised that the freeze would be "only temporary."

The forthcoming Phase 4, Nixon said, would be "comprehensive and realistic," providing a "basis for returning to free markets" because a long term program of economic controls would "destroy the economy and demolish our prosperity."

Nixon referred to several actions taken by the Administration during the previous week to curb inflation. Export controls on agricultural products would be "only temporary," according to Nixon. He endorsed the Federal Reserve Board's imposition of higher interest rates and reiterated an Administration theme that

"the battle against higher prices begins with the battle of the federal budget."

Wholesale Price Index declines. The Wholesale Price Index (WPI) dropped dramatically in July as a result of the 60-day price freeze imposed June 13, the Labor Department announced Aug. 2. The 1.4% seasonal decline was the sharpest since February 1948. But with the index at 134.9, based on a 1967 level of 100, the WPI remained 12.7% higher than the previous year.

Farm product, processed foods and feed prices at the wholesale level fell a record 4.6%, reflecting government restrictions on feed gain exports; however, wholesale prices for farm and food products were 26.5% above July 1972 levels. Industrial commodities were less affected by the price freeze, gaining an adjusted .1%.

Herbert Stein, chairman of the President's Council of Economic Advisers, cautioned that the wholesale price decline was "temporary," and would be offset by sharp increases when the price freeze was lifted.

Social Security hike OKd. The House by a 327–9 vote and the Senate by a voice vote June 30 approved a 5.6% cost of living increase in Social Security benefits, effective with checks to be received July 3, 1974. The increase, which came out of a House-Senate conference committee, was a rider to a bill extending for one year the Renegotiation Act enabling the government to recapture excess profits on federal contracts.

The conferees had agreed June 28 to postpone the original April 1, 1974 effective date of the increase to offset Administration complaints (and the threat of a veto) because of the estimated $1.4 billion impact on budget deficit projections for fiscal 1974. Under the final version, the impact would be delayed until fiscal 1975.

Among the major provisions:

■ Average monthly benefits for retirees would rise to $293 from the current $277, and the minimum monthly payment would rise to $89.30 from the current $84.50.

■ The maximum annual wage base for

Social Security taxes would rise to $12,-600, effective Jan. 1, 1974, providing a maximum tax of $737.10, instead of the $631.80 on the current maximum base of $10,800.

■ The amount a recipient under the age of 72 could earn without loss of benefits would rise to $2,400 a year from $2,100, effective Jan. 1, 1974.

■ Benefits paid to the aged, blind and disabled would rise $10 a month to $140 for individuals and $15 to $210 for couples, effective July 1, 1974.

Debt limit extended. Rushing to complete action before the end of fiscal 1973, Congress June 30 approved a bill extending the national debt limit of $465 billion to Nov. 30. Without the action, the limit would have dropped to $400 billion at midnight June 30, while current actual debt was estimated at $455 billion. The vote was 294–54 in the House and 63–2 in the Senate.

The bill also contained a provision permitting states with unemployment rates over 4.5% to extend unemployment compensation payments through Dec. 31. President Nixon signed the bill July 1.

Interest ceilings rise. In an effort to stem a flow of funds away from their banks, the Federal Reserve Board and the Federal Deposit Insurance Corporation (FDIC) agreed July 5 to allow their member institutions to pay higher interest rates for savings accounts.

The Federal Reserve and the FDIC raised from 4.5% to 5% the maximum interest rate commercial banks could pay on passbook savings accounts.

Similarly the FDIC, acting for mutual banks, and the Federal Home Loan Bank Board, acting for savings and loan institutions, allowed maximum passbook rates to rise from 5% to 5.25%.

In a related development, the maximum interest rate permitted on home mortgages backed by the Federal Housing Administration and the Veterans Administration was permitted to rise from 7% to 7 3/4%.

The three agencies said the rise in rates would enable their members to better compete for consumer dollars. In the case of savings and loan banks, net inflow was $13 billion for the first six months

of 1973, compared with $18 billion in 1972. The 28% drop constituted a threat to home building, which relied heavily on savings and loan banks for financing.

The FRB had acted June 29 to slow the growing increase in interest rates.

The discount rate for district Federal Reserve banks was raised from 6.5% to 7%. In a parallel action, bank reserve requirements were raised an estimated $800 million, in an effort to reduce banks' lending capacities.

The measures were "designed to restrain continuing excessive expansion in money and credit," according to the Federal Reserve. First National Bank of Chicago had raised its prime rate charged on loans to large businesses from 7.5% to 7.75% June 18, with other major banks joining in the action by June 22. The increase represented a sharp escalation in the schedule of commercial interest rate increases to which the Federal Reserve had given its tacit approval.

The Federal Reserve announcement also precipitated another round of rapid prime rate increases. The nation's largest banks raised the prime rate for large businesses to 8% July 2, following Girard Trust Bank's decision June 29 to issue the quarter point increase.

First National City Bank of New York, the nation's second largest commercial bank, reinstated its "floating" prime rate system June 29, tying interest charges to conditions on the open market.

The pace of rate increases went on accelerating: on July 2, the prime rate moved to 8%; by July 6, most banks were charging 8.25%; First National City Bank of New York said July 13 it was bowing to government pressure in not raising its floating rate to 8.5%; but by July 16, the 8.5% rate became acceptable. Further rate increases were expected.

Jobless rate drops. The Labor Department reported July 6 that unemployment in June dropped to 4.8% from 5% during May. The figure, which represented the lowest jobless rate since May 1970, was a real improvement and not a statistical fluke, department officials said.

Industrial output gains .3%. The Federal Reserve Board announced July 16 that the nation's industrial production during June advanced .3%, the smallest monthly increase registered since July 1972. The report was widely assumed to indicate a slowdown in the booming U.S. economy.

The index was at 123.9, based on a 1967 level of 100, after upward revision in the May figures. At an annual rate, output rose 8.8% during the first quarter of 1973 and 7.9% in the April–June period.

Productivity decline reported. The Labor Department reported July 27 that nonfarm worker productivity, or output per manhour, declined at a seasonally adjusted annual rate of .3% in the second quarter of 1973. The decline was the first since 1970. In the first quarter, nonfarm productivity had risen at a 5% annual rate.

Wage and benefit increases won during the first half of 1973 averaged 5.8% for first year contracts, compared with a 7.3% rate of increase for first year pay raises signed during 1972.

Productivity Commission expires. The House, by a 238–174 vote July 17, defeated a bill to extend the life of the National Commission on Productivity for one year. The commission's authorization expired June 30. The commission was established by President Nixon in 1970.

During House consideration, Rep. H. R. Gross (R, Iowa) noted that national productivity had dropped "despite the expenditure of $2.5 million on this commission in the past year."

FTC charges oil industry monopoly. The Federal Trade Commission (FTC) filed a complaint in Washington July 17 charging that the nation's eight largest oil companies, "individually and with each other, have maintained and reinforced a noncompetitive market structure in the refining of crude oil into petroleum products" in the eastern and middle portions of the nation.

Named, according to rank, were: Exxon Corp., Texaco, Inc., Gulf Oil Corp., Mobil Oil Corp., Standard Oil Co. of Calif., Standard Oil Co. (Indiana), Shell Oil Co., and Atlantic Richfield Co.

The complaint, which was aimed at the "noncompetitive structure" of the entire petroleum industry, cited violations in the Federal Trade Commission Act arising out of the vertical integration of the eight companies. Each firm combined crude oil exploration, production, pipe-line transportation and refining operations as well as transportation and marketing of refined petroleum products.

Monopolistic practices among the eight companies had been ongoing at least since 1950 in 11 areas, the FTC alleged. Illegal activities charged were: conspiracy to maintain artificially high profits from the sale of crude oil and artificially low profits from refining operations in order to deter independent companies from entering the refining business; refusal to sell gasoline and other refined products to independent marketers; conspiracy to "abuse and exploit" their ownership and control of the production and transportation of crude oil; and conspiracy to avoid competition in the pricing of their own products.

Alleged collusion among the eight major companies "hindered, lessened, eliminated or foreclosed" actual or potential competition at all levels of the oil industry, the complaint charged.

The FTC also charged that although independent oil refiners and marketers were the principal targets of these efforts to control the supply and distribution of oil and fuel, consumers were forced to pay "substantially higher prices" under distorted market conditions "than they would have in a competitively structured market."

Treasury study defends oil firms—A Treasury Department study, prepared for Deputy Treasury Secretary William E. Simon, who was also chairman of the President's Oil Policy Committee, urged the Federal Trade Commission (FTC) to withdraw its antitrust suit.

According to the report, released Sept. 5, the FTC's charges of monopolistic practices were based on "many inaccurate facts" and misinterpretations of "many actions and motives of the petroleum industry." "As a result of this bias, the FTC's final conclusions are incorrect or misleading at best," the report declared.

The Treasury Department disputed several FTC allegations, claiming that the eight major oil companies' "concentration in the refinery industry had lessened [since 1960], not increased." In contrast to FTC charges that independents were being "squeezed out of the market," the Treasury Department claimed that their share of the retail gasoline market had increased from 19.8% in 1968 to 25.4% in 1972. The report also defended industry profits, stating that "refining has been one of the least profitable manufacturing industries in the U.S."

The current shortages of oil and gas were unrelated to "anticompetitive" practices, but could be traced instead to a variety of other factors, "mostly governmental laws and policies," according to the report.

Corporate profits soar. The Commerce Department announced Aug. 17 that pretax corporate profits in the second quarter increased $10.5 billion to reach a seasonally adjusted annual rate of $130.1 billion. Profits were 37% above 1972 levels. Profits for durable goods manufacturers accounted for 40% of the increase.

After-tax earnings totaled $72.6 billion at an annual rate, a gain of 8.5% from the upwardly revised first quarter figures and 35% higher than 1972 levels.

Phase 4 Explained

Controls to replace freeze. The Administration's Phase 4 economic control program was outlined by President Nixon in a statement issued July 18. The Phase 4 plan, which would end the current price freeze, was based on mandatory compliance with a system of price controls similar to the controls in effect under Phase 2 and abandoned in January. Nixon said the program would be both tough and selective.

The price freeze would remain in effect until Aug. 12 for the industrial and service sectors; however, price restrictions on food (with the exception of beef) and health care were lifted immediately. Price limits on beef, imposed March 29, would continue until Sept. 12. Raw farm products remained exempt from price controls.

Price increases under the new system would be permitted only on a dollar-for-dollar basis, to reflect cost increases since the end of 1972. Profit margin restrictions, governing any price increase, would continue.

Firms with annual sales exceeding $100 million would be required to provide the Cost of Living Council (CLC) with prenotification for any proposed price hikes. The flexible 5.5% wage increase guideline followed in the past would continue in force, and large companies would be required to give advance notice to the CLC of planned wage boosts.

At a briefing for reporters following the President's announcement, Treasury Secretary George P. Shultz provided details for the special regulations imposed on the petroleum industry. New guidelines, to be issued July 19, would provide separate price ceilings for two categories: crude oil; and gasoline, heating oil and diesel fuel. Exemptions in increased crude oil production, it was hoped, would provide the industry with incentives to increase petroleum supplies.

Shultz indicated that the Administration expected an economic slowdown during the next six months, permitting the economy to absorb the anticipated bulge of price increases latent during the freeze period. By 1974, the Nixon statement said, "the good feed crops in prospect for this year should have produced a much larger supply of food, and total demand should be rising less rapidly than in 1973."

Shultz said he hoped the annual rate of inflation for 1973 would be less than 3%, but declined to give a specific growth target.

As in the past, Nixon tied the success of his anti-inflation program to fiscal restraint in Congress. Shultz said the President was determined to balance the budget by holding Congressional spending at $268.7 billion for fiscal 1974, which began July 1.

Nixon also reiterated his belief that the system of economic controls should be "selective." The Phase 2 rule exempting firms with fewer than 60 employes from wage restrictions was reinstituted. Public utilities, the lumber industry and the price of coal sold under long-term contract were also decontrolled.

Nixon's oft-stated distaste for economic

controls and his desire to return to conditions of a free market were repeated in his Phase 4 message; but Nixon urged "patience" with the current policy and refused to commit the Administration to a specific termination date for Phase 4.

Nixon conceded in his statement that the price freeze "is holding down production and creating shortages which threaten to get worse, and cause higher prices, as the freeze and controls continue.... Confidence in our fiscal affairs is low, at home and abroad," he continued.

Text of the Nixon statement:

The American people now face a profoundly important decision. We have a freeze on prices which is holding back a surge of inflation that would break out if the controls were removed. At the same time the freeze is holding down production and creating shortages which threaten to get worse, and cause still higher prices, as the freeze and controls continue.

In this situation we are offered two extreme kinds of advice.

One suggestion is that we should accept price and wage controls as a permanent feature of the American economy. We are told to forget the idea of regaining a free economy and set about developing the regulations and bureaucracy for a permanent system of controls.

The other suggestion is to make the move for freedom now, abolishing all controls immediately.

While these suggestions are well meant, and in many cases reflect deep conviction, neither can be accepted. Our wise course today is not to choose one of these extremes but to seek the best possible reconciliation of our interests in slowing down the rate of inflation on the one hand, and preserving American production and efficiency on the other.

The main elements in the policy we need are these:

First, the control system must be *tough*. It has to hold back and phase in gradually a large part of the built-in pressure for higher prices which already exists in the economy.

Second, the system must be *selective*. It must permit relaxation of those restraints which interfere most with production, and it must not waste effort on sectors of the economy where stability of prices exists. The control system should also be designed to accommodate the special problems of various sectors of the economy under the strains of high use of capacity.

Third, the system must contain sufficient assurance of its *termination* at an appropriate time to preserve incentives for investment and production and guard against tendencies for controls to be perpetuated.

Fourth, the control system must be backed up by firm steps to *balance the budget*, so that excess demand does not regenerate inflationary pressures which make it difficult either to live with the controls or to live without them.

We have had in 1973 an extraordinary combination of circumstances making for rapid inflation. There was a decline of domestic food supplies. The domestic economy boomed at an exceptional pace, generating powerful demand for goods and services. The boom in other countries and the devaluation of the dollar, while desirable from most points of view, raised prices of things we export or import.

These forces caused a sharp rise of prices in early 1973. The index of consumer prices rose at an annual rate of about 8% from December 1972, to May 1973. The freeze imposed on June 13 put a halt to this rapid rise of prices. But many of the cost increases and demand pressures working to raise prices in the early part of the year had not yet resulted in higher prices by the time the freeze was imposed. Thus a certain built-in pressure for a bulge of price increases awaits the end of the freeze. Moreover, aside from this undigested bulge left over by the freeze, the circumstances causing the sharp price increase in early 1973 will still be present, although not on so large a scale. The demand for goods and services will be rising less rapidly than in the first half of the year. Our position in international trade is improving and this will lend strength to the dollar.

All in all, the tendency for prices to rise in the remainder of 1973, a tendency which will either come out in higher prices or be repressed by controls, will be less than in the first half of the year but greater than anyone would like. Particularly, there is no way, with or without controls, to prevent a substantial rise of food prices. However, by 1974, we should be able to achieve a much more moderate rate of inflation. By that time, the good feed crops in prospect for this year should have produced a much larger supply of food, and total demand should be rising less rapidly than in 1973.

This more satisfactory situation on the inflation front will be reached if three conditions are met:

First, we do not allow the temporary inflationary forces now confronting us to generate a new wage-price spiral which will continue to run after these temporary forces have passed. To do this we must hold down the expression of those forces in prices and wages.

Second, we do not allow the present controls to damp down 1974 production excessively, a problem that is most obvious in the case of meats and poultry.

Third, we do not permit a continuation or revival of excess demand that will generate new inflationary forces. That is why control of the federal budget is an essential part of the whole effort.

The steps I am announcing or recommending today are designed to create these conditions.

Our decisions about the new control program have been reached after consulting with all sectors of the American society in over 30 meetings and after studying hundreds of written communications. The advice we received was most helpful and I want to thank all those who provided it.

The Cost of Living Council will describe the Phase 4 controls program in detail in statements and regulations. These will take effect at various times between now and Sept. 12. They will include special regulations dealing with the petroleum industry, published for comment. Here I will only review the general features of the program, to indicate its basic firmness and the efforts that have been made to assure that production continues and shortages are avoided.

The controls will be mandatory. The success of the program, however, will depend upon a high degree of voluntary compliance. We have had that in the past. Study of the reports on business behavior during Phase 3 shows that voluntary compliance was almost universal. Nevertheless, the rules we are now proposing are stricter, and it is only fair to those who will comply voluntarily to assure that there is compulsion for the others.

Except for foods, the freeze on prices will remain in effect until Aug. 12. However, modifications of the freeze rules will be made to relieve its most serious inequities.

The fundamental pricing rule of Phase 4 is that prices are permitted to rise as much as costs rise, in dollars per unit of output, without any profit margin on the additional costs. Cost increases will be counted from the end of 1972; cost increases which occurred earlier but had not been reflected in prices may not be passed on. In addition to the cost rule, there remains the previous limitation on profit margins.

Large firms, those with annual sales in excess of $100-million, will be required to notify the Cost of Living Council of intended price increases and may not put them into effect for 30 days. During that period, the council may deny or suspend the proposed increase.

The wage standards of Phase 2 and Phase 3 will remain in force. Notification of wage increases will continue to be required for large employment units.

These are, we recognize, tough rules, in some respects tougher than during Phase 2. But the situation is also in many ways more difficult than during Phase 2. So long as the system is regarded as temporary, however, we believe that business can continue to prosper, industrial peace can be maintained, and production continue to expand under these rules. Machinery will be established in the Cost of Living Council to consider the need for exceptions from these rules where they may be causing serious injury to the economy. And we will be prepared to consider modification of the rules themselves when that seems necessary or possible.

Nowhere have the dilemmas of price control been clearer than in the case of food. In the early part of this year, rising food prices were the largest part of the inflation problem, statistically and psychologically. If price restraint was needed anywhere, it was needed for food. But since the ceilings were placed on meat prices on March 29, and especially since the freeze was imposed on June 13, food has given the clearest evidence of the harm that controls do to supplies.

We have seen baby chicks drowned, pregnant sows and cows, bearing next year's food, slaughtered, and packing plants closed down. This dilemma is no coincidence. It is because food prices were rising most rapidly that the freeze held prices most below their natural level and therefore had the worst effect on supplies.

We must pick our way carefully between a food price policy so rigid as to cut production sharply and to make shortages inevitable within a few months and a food price policy so loose as to give us an unnecessary and intolerable bulge. On this basis we have decided on the following special rules for food:

1. Effective immediately, processors and distributors of food, except beef, may increase their prices, on a cents-per-unit basis, to the extent of the increase of costs of raw agricultural products since the freeze base period (June 1-8).

2. Beef prices remain under present ceilings.

3. The foregoing special rules expire on Sept. 12, after which time the same rules that apply to other products will apply to foods.

4. Raw agricultural products remain exempt from price control.

To relieve the extreme high prices of feeds, which have an important effect on prices of meat, poultry, eggs, and dairy products, we have placed limitations on the export of soybeans and related products until the new crop comes into the market. These limitations will remain in effect for that period.

But permanent control of exports is not the policy of this government, and we do not intend at this time to broaden the controls beyond those now in force. To a considerable degree, export controls are self-defeating as an anti-inflation measure. Limiting our exports reduces our foreign earnings, depresses the value of the dollar, and increases the cost of things we import, which also enter into the cost of living of the American family.

Moreover, limiting our agricultural exports runs counter to our basic policy of building up our agricultural markets abroad. Unless present crop expectations are seriously disappointed, or foreign demands are extremely large, export controls will not be needed. However, reports of export orders for agricultural commodities will continue to be required. Our policy must always be guided by the fundamental importance of maintaining adequate supplies of food at home.

The stability of the American economy in the months and years ahead demands maximum farm output. I call upon the American farmer to produce as much as he can.

There have been reports that farmers have been reluctant to raise livestock because they are uncertain whether government regulations will permit them a fair return on their investment, and perhaps also because they resent the imposition of ceilings on food prices. I hope that these reports are untrue. In the past year real net income per farm increased 14%, a truly remarkable rise.

I can assure the American farmer that there is no intention of the government to discriminate against him. The rules we are setting forth today should give the farmer confidence that the government will not keep him from earning a fair return on his investment in providing food.

The Secretary of Agriculture will be offering more specific advice on increasing food production and will be taking several steps to assist, in particular he has decided that there will be no government set-aside of land in 1974 for feed grains, wheat and cotton.

I am today initiating steps to increase the import of dried skim milk.

When I announced the freeze, I said that special attention would be given, in the post-freeze period, to stabilizing the price of food. That remains a primary objective. But stabilizing the price of food would not be accomplished by low price ceilings and empty shelves, even if the ceilings could be enforced when the shelves are empty.

Neither can stabilization be concerned only with a week or a month. The evidence is becoming overwhelming that only if a rise of food prices is permitted now can we avoid shortages and still higher prices later. I hope that the American people will understand this and not be deluded by the idea that we can produce low-priced food out of acts of Congress or executive orders.

The American people will continue to be well-fed, at prices which are reasonable relative to their incomes. But they cannot now escape a period in which food prices are higher relative to incomes that we have been accustomed to.

There is no need for me to reiterate my desire to end controls and return to the free market. I believe that a large proportion of the American people, when faced with a rounded picture of the options, share that desire. Our experience with the freeze has dramatized the essential difficulties of a controlled system—its interference with production, its inequities, its distortions, its evasions, and the obstacles it places in the way of good international relations.

And yet, I must urge a policy of patience. The move to freedom now would most likely turn into a detour, back into a swamp of even more lasting controls. I am impressed by the unanimous recommendations of the leaders of labor and business who constitute the Labor-Management Advisory Committee that the controls should be terminated by the end of 1973. I hope it will be possible to do so and will do everything in my power to achieve that goal. However, I do not consider it wise to commit ourselves to a specific date for ending all controls at this time.

We shall have to work our way and feel our way out of controls. That is, we shall have to create conditions in which the controls can be terminated without disrupting the economy, and we shall have to move in successive stages to withdraw the controls in parts of the economy where that can be safely done or where the controls are most harmful.

To work our way out of controls means basically to eliminate the excessive growth of total demand which pulls prices up faster and faster. The main lesson of that is to control the budget, and I shall return to that critical subject below.

But while we are working our way to that ultimate condition in which controls are no longer, we must be alert to identify those part of the economy that can be safely decontrolled. Removing the controls in those sectors will not only be a step towards efficiency and freedom there. It will also reduce the burden of administration, permit administrative resources to be concentrated where most needed, and provide an incentive for other firms and industries to reach a similar condition.

During Phase 2 firms with 60 employes or fewer were exempt from controls. That exemption is now repeated. We are today exempting most regulated public utilities, the lumber industry (where prices are falling), and the price of coal sold under long-term contract. The Cost of Living Council will be studying other sectors for possible de-control. It will also receive applications from firms or industries that can give assurance of reasonable noninflationary behavior without controls. In all cases, of course, the Cost of Living Council will retain authority to reimpose controls.

The key to success of our anti-inflation effort is the budget. If federal spending soars and the deficit mounts, the control system will not be able to resist the pressure of demand. The most common cause of the breakdown of control systems has been failure to keep fiscal and monetary policy under restraint. We must not let that happen to us.

I am assured that the Federal Reserve will cooperate in the anti-inflation effort by slowing down the expansion of money and credit. But monetary policy should not, and cannot, be expected to exercise the needed restraint alone. A further contribution from the budget is needed.

I propose that we should now take a balanced budget as our goal for the present fiscal year, in the past I have suggested as a standard for the federal budget that expenditures should not exceed the revenues that would be collected at full employment. We are meeting that standard. But in today's circumstances, that is only a minimum standard of fiscal prudence.

When inflationary pressure is strong, when we are forced to emergency controls to resist that pressure, when confidence in our management of our fiscal affairs is low, at home and abroad, we cannot afford to live by that minimum standard. We must take as our goal the more ambitious one of balancing the actual budget.

Achieving that goal will be difficult, more difficult than it seems at first. My original expenditure budget for fiscal 1974 was $268.7-billion. Since that budget

was submitted economic expansion, inflation and other factors have raised the estimated revenues to about the level of the original expenditure estimate.

However, while that was happening the probable expenditures have also been rising as a result of higher interest rates, new legislation enacted, failure of Congress to act on some of my recommendations, and Congressional action already far advanced but not completed.

It is clear that several billion dollars will have to be cut from the expenditures that are already probable if we are to balance the budget. That will be hard, because my original budget was tight. However, I regard it as essential and pledge myself to work for it.

We should remember that a little over a year ago I set as a goal for fiscal year 1973 to hold expenditures within a total of $250-billion. There was much skepticism about that at the time, and suggestions that the number was for political consumption only, to be forgotten after the election. But I meant it, the people endorsed it and the Congress cooperated. I am able to report today that the goal was achieved, and total expenditures for fiscal year 1973 were below $249-billion.

I will take those steps that I can take administratively to reach the goal of a balanced budget for fiscal year 1974. I shall start by ordering that the number of federal civilian personnel at the end of fiscal year 1974 total below the number now budgeted. The Office of Management and Budget will work with the agencies on this and other reductions. I urge the Congress to assist in this effort. Without its cooperation achievement of the goal cannot be realistically expected.

Despite the difficult conditions and choices we now confront, the American economy is strong. Total production is about 6.5% above a year ago, employment has risen by 3 million, real incomes are higher than ever. There is every prospect for further increases of output, employment and incomes. Even in the field of inflation our performance is better than in most of the world. So we should not despair of our plight. But we have problems, and they are serious in part because we and the rest of the world expect the highest performance from the American economy. We can do better. And we will, with mutual understanding and the support of the American people.

The White House issued this "fact sheet summary" of Phase 4 of the Economic Stabilization Program:

Objective

To moderate the rate of inflation existing during first six months of 1973 with minimum adverse effect on supply.

Design

Phase 4 is mandatory, covers most sectors of the economy, requires pre-notification and restricts price increases to dollar-for-dollar pass-through costs.

Freeze prices remain in effect until Aug. 12 in all sectors, except food and health, which have special rules effective immediately.

Proposed rules for non-food sectors will be effective Aug. 12 and are being issued for comment. Comments required by July 31.

Continues wage and benefit guidelines in effect during Phase II and III.

Exempts on Aug. 12 small businesses (60 employes or fewer), public utility rates, interest rates and rents, wages and prices in lumber and plywood.

Establishes procedures to consider de-control industry by industry.

Food Sector

Phase IV price regulations on food are divided into two stages, Stage A and Stage B.

Stage A (effective immediately)

Ceiling prices on beef continued.

All other food prices may be increased only to reflect raw agricultural cost increases since June 8 on dollar-for-dollar basis.

Stage B (effective Sept. 12)

Ceiling prices on beef terminated.

Manufacturers and processors allowed to pass through all cost increases on a dollar-for-dollar basis.

Other aspects of food regulations to be similar to controls for industrial, service, wholesale and retail sectors.

Industrial and Service Sector

Prices remain frozen until Aug. 12 at which time Phase IV regulations become effective.

Regulations to be issued July 19 for public comment. These regulations will:

Require companies with annual sales of more than $100-million to give the Cost of Living Council 30 days pre-notification before price increases may go into effect.

Require companies with sales over $50-million to file quarterly reports.

Require companies with sales less than $50-million but over 60 employes to file an annual report.

Establish a new base period of price increases and cost justification—the last fiscal quarter ending before Jan. 11, 1973. Costs incurred prior to the new Phase 4 base period are not allowed as justification for higher prices.

Permit costs to be passed through only on a dollar-for-dollar basis.

Continue the profit margin limitations.

Nonfood Retail and Wholesale Sector

Prices remain frozen until Aug. 12 at which time Phase IV regulations become effective.

Regulations to be issued July 19 for public comment. These regulations will require:

Pre-approval by the Cost of Living Council of pricing plans based on merchandise categories for companies with sales over $50-million.

Gross margin controls on these categories.

Continuation of profit margin limitation.

Petroleum Sector

Prices remain frozen until Aug. 12 at which time Phase 4 regulations become effective.

Regulations to be issued July 19 for public comment. These regulations will provide:

Price ceilings for gasoline heating oil and diesel fuel. The ceiling price is computed as the seller's actual cost of the product plus the dollar and cents markup applied to a retail sale of the same product on Jan. 10, 1973.

A ceiling price for crude oil.

Increased crude production and equivalent amount of old oil to be exempted.

Ceiling prices and octane ratings to be posted on each gasoline pump.

Regulations for Special Sectors

The health service industry is to be removed from the freeze immediately and returned to the mandatory Phase 3 controls.

Proposed regulations for the insurance industry to be issued on July 19 for public comment. The new regulations will go into effect Aug. 12. Until then the freeze remains in effect.

Wages

The general wage and benefit standards of Phase 2 and Phase 3 will be retained. More detailed information for reporting wage and benefit increases will be required.

Notification of wage and benefit increases by the largest bargaining units will be continued to be required. Pre-notification will be required in individual cases.

A new organizational component of the Cost of Living Council has been established to review wage and salary and benefit increases in the state and local government sector.

Reaction to new program. Opponents and proponents of economic controls rejected Phase 4 as either excessively restrictive or ineffective in curbing inflation, according to newspaper reports July 19–20.

Sen. James Buckley (Conservative-N.Y.) termed the plan "odious." Arch Booth, chief executive officer of the U.S. Chamber of Commerce, said Phase 4 was "another in a series of charades," although he conceded it was an improvement on the 60-day freeze.

I. W. Abel, president of the United Steelworkers of America, declared "there has been special consideration given to some and no consideration given to others." The oil and cattle industries also rejected the stabilization program as "discriminatory." The president of the Grocery Manufacturers of America, George W. Koch, predicted "food prices will go up, possibly even higher than they would have without controls, and shortages and dislocations will continue. Under Phase 4 nothing really has changed for the consumer."

Economists' reactions were more mixed. Walter W. Heller, a former Kennedy Administration official, labeled the program "reasonable," but said, "everything depends on implementation. . . . If they really approach this with some resoluteness and conviction, this thing could work." Milton Friedman of the University of Chicago, however, termed Phase 4 "a disaster."

The confusion and skepticism voiced by Senate Democratic Whip Robert C. Byrd (W. Va.) appeared to be shared by many. Byrd remarked: "Controlling and decontrolling, freezing and unfreezing, and the perpetuation of instability and uncertainty can never become a satisfactory substitute for sound economic policy."

The Executive Council of the AFL-CIO released a statement Aug. 1 contending that Phase 4 represented a continuation of "inequitable policies" and would create a "framework of recession-breeding and job-destroying tight money, soaring interest rates and additional cuts in essential federal programs."

At a press conference, AFL-CIO President George Meany said he believed that a recession was imminent, possibly before the end of 1973. Meany called for a rapid end to the controls system, claiming that it had failed to deal with inflation while generating a sharp economic slowdown.

CLC's guidelines. The Cost of Living Council June 19 issued supplemental guidelines for Phase 4. These rules covered nonfood sectors of the economy.

Despite Nixon's pledge that the rules would be "tough," CLC director John T. Dunlop told reporters that more exemptions from Phase 4 pricing rules would be issued because the new system was more stringent than that of Phase 3. The CLC would establish a special exceptions committee to devise liberalized criteria for price increases, Dunlop said.

In order to administer the complex system, he announced that the total staff of the CLC and its enforcement agency, the Internal Revenue Service, would be increased by 1,200 persons, bringing the number of Phase 4 officials to 5,000.

Details of the proposed stabilization program, which was subject to amendment following the close of public comment July 31:

Petroleum industry: Some crude oil supplies would be decontrolled as an incentive to spur domestic production. Price rollbacks to the May 15 level were proposed for each grade of domestic oil from individual oil-producing fields; however, supplies produced by each field exceeding the 1972 total, and an equal amount of current crude oil production, would be exempt. Increased costs of imported oil could be passed to consumers. The crude oil ceiling would be raised "periodically" to bring domestic prices in line with higher world prices.

Manufacturing and service sectors: Phase 4 rules, effective Aug. 12, would be more stringent than those of Phase 2. Price rises could not include profit markups, which had been permitted under Phase 2. Base prices could be computed only from actual prices in effect during the last quarter of 1972. In contrast, under Phase 2 computation was based on prices which had been authorized but not put in effect.

Retailers and Wholesalers: Rules would be similar to Phase 2.

Insurance: The new system would be similar to Phase 2. Insurers seeking a rate boost of more than 5% on $1 million or more of annual premiums must prenotify state insurance commissions and the CLC.

Exemptions: U.S. tanker rates on all "coastwide trade"; prices for custom products and services; royalties; dues to nonprofit organizations; antiques and art objects; handicraft objects; collectors' coins and stamps; university tuition fees; brokerage fees; real estate and rent. Postal rates were not exempted, thereby delaying implementation of a 10¢ first class postage rate.

Final rules—The CLC announced final changes in Phase 4 regulations Aug. 7. CLC Director John T. Dunlop said the revisions, which largely represented technical modifications in guidelines released July 18, "do not change the policy of Phase 4." The new rules were based on comments received from 700 individuals, companies and trade associations.

Changes in rules governing the industrial and service sectors at the wholesale and retail levels:

Companies would be released from profit margin restrictions if no price increases were implemented; new products would not be subject to prenotification; companies with annual sales below $50 million would not be required to file reports with the CLC; companies could charge an "adjusted freeze price" during Phase 4 even if that price was higher than the legal base price; a "110% rule" would permit companies to charge more than a 10% increase on an individual product price provided price increases for the rest of the product line were below the average price hike allowed by the CLC.

Copper scrap controls lifted—In a separate action, the CLC announced Aug. 6 that all price controls would be removed from copper scrap in order to alleviate the current domestic shortage. Dunlop said that during the 60-day price freeze, deliveries of copper scrap to U.S. users had "virtually ceased." The CLC hoped its action would reduce incentives for exporters to sell scrap on the world market where the price was considerably higher.

Petroleum industry gets Phase 4 rules. Final Phase 4 regulations for the petroleum industry were released Aug. 17. The Cost of Living Council's rules, which took effect Aug. 20, replaced a price freeze which had been extended one week, although the freeze on gasoline and diesel fuel prices would not be lifted until Aug. 31.

Price ceilings were ordered for all petroleum products but increased costs of imported home heating oil could be passed along to consumers and wholesalers could pass through higher costs on imported crude oil. Despite this flexibility, CLC officials predicted that price rollbacks for crude and heating oil could result from the price ceilings.

In an effort to mitigate the impact of the recent oil shortage, retailers' markups were restricted to their minimum on Jan. 10, before the shortage became widespread. (Ceiling prices were based on retailers' costs of buying gasoline on Aug. 1 plus their markup.)

Gasoline and diesel fuel retailers also were required to post the ceiling prices as well as octane ratings for each grade of gasoline.

Early end seen for Phase 4. There were growing indications from Administration sources that President Nixon hoped to end wage-price controls as quickly as possible, perhaps by the end of 1973, according to United Press International Aug. 8.

Herbert Stein, chairman of the President's Council of Economic Advisers, told a meeting of the American Bar Association Aug. 8 that current economic conditions "aren't likely to be helped by controls." Under Phase 4, Stein said, "we are going to be continually confronted

with choices between higher prices and shortages." The economic controls program's inability to provide a remedy for these problems had caused public "disillusionment," Stein said.

(Stein denied July 26 that Administration strategy was to enforce Phase 4 so strictly as to turn the public against the program in order to create support for an end to controls.)

Secretary of Commerce Frederick B. Dent told businessmen Aug. 8 that Phase 4 would be a "phase-out" period leading to a quick return to free market conditions.

New minimum wage approved. Final Congressional approval of a bill to increase the minimum wage came on a 62–28 Senate vote Aug. 2 and a 253–152 House vote Aug. 3.

The minimum wage would be increased for most workers from the current $1.60 an hour to $2.20 July 1, 1974. Minimum wage coverage would be extended to approximately 6.7 million more workers, in addition to the 47 million already covered by federal minimum wage legislation. The new coverage would be extended to about 5 million federal, state and local government employes, one million domestic workers and 700,000 retail and service establishment employes, the latter over a four-year period.

For most nonagricultural workers covered by the federal legislation prior to 1966, the minimum wage would rise to $2 an hour two months after enactment and to $2.20 July 1, 1974.

For nonagricultural workers first covered in 1966, the minimum rate would go to $1.80 in two months, to $2 on July 1, 1974 and to $2.20 a year beyond that.

The minimum for agricultural workers would rise from the current $1.30 to $1.60 in two months, to $1.80 in July 1974, to $2 in July 1975 and to $2.20 in July 1976.

The Administration had preferred a more gradual rise in the rate and also objected to extension of coverage to workers currently not covered and to the refusal of both houses of Congress to permit a subminimum wage for young persons.

Farm bill passed. Prior to adjourning for a month-long recess Aug. 3, both houses of Congress concluded an extended debate over a farm bill and sent it to the President. Much of the controversy centered around an amendment to bar food stamps for most strikers and their families.

The House had passed an amended farm bill July 19 by a 226–182 vote. It would extend the basic support programs for wheat, feed grains, cotton, and dairy products for four years.

The bill also provided an "escalator clause," effective the last two years of the bill, to push price supports up with any rise in production costs.

The dairy price support loan rate was to be raised from the current level of 75% of parity to 80% during the four years of the bill.

Floor amendments included a $20,000 subsidy limitation per farmer, with a prohibition against lease or sale of cotton allotments, and a ban on food stamps to strikers and their families.

Nixon proposes banking overhaul. President Nixon sent a message to Congress Aug. 3 outlined proposals for major changes in the nation's banking system.

His proposals were predicated on "one basic assumption," Nixon declared: "The public interest is generally better served by the free play of competitive forces than by the imposition of rigid and unnecessary regulations."

Five recommendations were designed to increase competition among banks and thrift institutions, eliminate inequities imposed on large and small borrowers, reduce the cost of financial services to the consumer and sufficiently strengthen thrift institutions to warrant a withdrawal of government support.

The proposals would phase out interest ceilings on time and savings deposits over a 5½ year period; expand deposit services, including checking accounts and credit cards to federally chartered savings and loan institutions; broaden savings and loan institutions' abilities to offer consumer loans and invest in corporate bonds and commercial paper; provide federal charters to stock savings and loan institutions and mutual savings banks; and provide credit unions with greater access to funds.

Two proposals were designed to ease the tight credit situation currently experienced by consumers: interest ceilings on Federal Housing Administration (FHA) and Veterans Administration (VA) loans would be removed; and far-reaching tax changes would be implemented for banks and thirft institutions.

"The inflexibility of our financial system can be directly attributed to the methods used by the government to direct credit flows," Nixon said, methods which were applicable in the 1930s but which were "poorly suited to cope with the expansionary conditions of the past decade."

Recent Federal Reserve Board actions were cited as particularly ineffective because the "consumer-saver was denied a fair market return on his savings, while the consumer and small businessman, as borrowers, often could not obtain adequate funds to meet their requirements."

The "credit crunch" was particularly severe in the home mortgage area because thrift institutions were unable to compete with higher market interest rates in attracting depositors, whose funds formed the basis of the mortgage lending system. But interest rate ceilings, imposed as a "protective shield for the housing market," had had the opposite effect of causing depositors to invest in higher yielding securities, Nixon said. Consequently, funds available for mortgage loans had dropped off sharply.

The Administration position was based partially on recommendations issued in December 1971 by the 21-member Commission on Financial Structure and Regulation. The group became known as the Hunt Commission, after its chairman Reed O. Hunt, retired chief executive of Crown Zellerbach Corp.

Burns differs on Administration policies—Federal Reserve Board Chairman Arthur F. Burns appeared before the Joint Economic Committee of Congress Aug. 3. He urged legislators to cut $5 billion–$10 billion from the federal spending limit of $268.7 billion set by President Nixon for fiscal 1974. Burns also warned that if serious inflation persisted, he would advocate increased federal taxes.

Treasury Secretary George P. Shultz had told the committee Aug. 2 that the Administration remained opposed to any tax hikes. Shultz and Burns agreed, however, that worsening inflation, rather than fears of an imminent recession, was the primary economic danger in 1973.

In other areas of conflict with the Administration, Burns said he supported an immediate end to the beef price freeze. He also favored a "continuing role" for wage-price policies, especially in large industries where competition was "inadequate."

Federal Reserve policies were not aimed at a zero growth rate for the money supply resulting in a credit crunch situation, Burns said. Government policies sought to "keep the monetary aggregates expanding, but at more moderate rates," he declared. Burns warned, however, that the Federal Reserve would take "further restrictive measures" to halt the money supply growth rate if no slowdown were indicated "in the very near future."

Prime rate rises. Franklin National Bank of New York Aug. 3 initiated another quarter point increase in the prime, or minimum, interest rate charged to large corporate borrowers. It was the 12th rate hike of the year, bringing the prime to 9%. Other major commercial banks joined the move by Aug. 6. The prime rate had been set at 8.75% July 28.

Bank spokesmen attributed the increase to cost pressures from the continued heavy demand for credit and the rising money market rates on funds obtained by banks to finance their lending operations. The Wall Street Journal reported Aug. 7 that major New York banks were paying 10% interest on negotiable one-year certificates of deposits (CDs). The rate of three-month CDs also was at a record level—10.62%.

In an effort to curb the rise in short term money rates, the Federal Reserve Board imposed a limit July 26 on the amount of new high-interest, four-year certificates which could be issued to depositors by commercial banks.

Effective immediately, banks were permitted to issue up to 5% of their total time and savings deposits. A recent federal ruling had removed interest ceilings from the four-year certificates with minimum deposits of $1,000, prompting a flood of deposits to commercial banks.

First National City Bank of New York announced Aug. 10 that it was raising its prime rate to 9.25%, effective Aug. 13.

Other major banks moved to the new level when remarks delivered Aug. 10 by Treasury Secretary George P. Shultz appeared to indicate Administration approval of the new record-setting rate. Shultz told reporters that higher interest rates were "desirable" short-term developments in bringing about an economic slowdown.

The Federal Reserve Board raised the discount rate from 7% to 7.5% Aug. 13 in a similar effort to curb the demand for money and credit.

The action, taken to bring the discount rate "into better alignment with short-term rates generally," set the discount at a record level.

Three-month Treasury bills were auctioned Aug. 13 at a record rate of 8.976%. In May, three-month bills had been sold at an average rate of 6.136%.

The Federal Reserve reported Aug. 9 that its efforts to restrain the growth of money and credit appeared to be showing results. During the four weeks ending Aug. 1, the money supply grew at an average annual rate of 9.5%. In the five preceding weeks, the rate of expansion had reached 10.5%. For the first six months of 1973, the annual growth rate was set at 6.6%.

The FHA also announced Aug. 10 that it had raised the interest ceilings on its low interest loans from 7% to 7.75%.

Current market rates for home mortgages were near 8.5%.

Phase 4 in Effect

Phase 4 of Nixon's anti-inflation program went into effect Aug. 13.

Major price hikes planned. Phase 4's first week of operation was marked by announcements of planned price increases by several of the nation's industrial giants. The Cost of Living Council (CLC) had 30 days to respond to the requests. If unchallenged, the price increases would then take effect automatically.

Chrysler Corp. notified the CLC Aug. 13 that it planned to raise prices by an average $71 on 1974 model cars and trucks. American Motors Corp. also asked CLC approval for a proposed price increase, averaging $55 or 1.4%, to cover the costs of federally mandated safety and pollution control equipment.

General Motors Corp. (GM) and Ford Motor Co. announced larger price hikes Aug. 14. GM sought a 2.1% price increase, averaging $102—of which $85 would cover safety equipment costs and $17 would cover the costs of product improvements. Ford planned a 2.4% increase, averaging $106, to compensate for the costs of safety and emission control features.

Price increases affecting consumers also were planned by the steel industry, which petitioned the CLC for a "reinstatement" of a previously announced 4.8% price increase. Steel prices had not been raised June 15 as planned because of the 60-day price freeze. Armco Steel Corp. and four other major steel companies notified the CLC Aug. 13 of their intention to raise prices on sheet steel products, a basic commodity used in home appliances and cars. U.S. Steel Corp. joined the move Aug. 14.

Three major airlines sought permission from the Civil Aeronautics Board (CAB) to raise prices on domestic flights. (Regulated industries were not subject to CLC restrictions.) Trans World Airlines announced July 26 that it planned to implement a 7% price increase Sept. 15. American Airlines sought approval Aug. 14 for an 8% rate increase, effective Sept. 15 and United Air Lines said it would file a 5% price increase request with the CAB, to take effect Oct. 15.

American Telephone and Telegraph Co. announced Aug. 13 that rate increases, already approved by six state regulatory agencies but delayed by the price freeze, would be implemented immediately. States affected were Massachusetts, Rhode Island, Oregon, Florida, Ohio and Texas.

Auto raises OKed—The CLC announced Sept. 7 it would permit the four major car manufacturers to institute 70%–90% of their proposed price increases.

The approved price hikes covered only dollar for dollar pass-throughs of costs incurred by manufacturers' attempts to comply with strict federal pollution and safety standards.

The price increases were estimated at $73 for General Motors Corp., a 28% reduction in its proposed price; $74 for Ford Motor Co., a 30% cutback; $51 for Chrysler Corp., a 27% reduction; and $55 for American Motors Corp., a 10% reduction.

In issuing its ruling, CLC officials emphasized their efforts to scale down price requests from the car makers. The proposed full increases were "of such magnitude ... as to be unreasonably inconsistent" with the Administration's efforts to slow inflation, CLC Director John T. Dunlop said.

The government action followed public hearings Aug. 28 on the issue of the price requests.

In addition to the price increase won to recoup the cost of federally mandated equipment, Ford revealed that it had also obtained CLC approval for base price revisions which would raise the cost of 1974 cars and trucks another 3%, or an average $62 a unit.

Ford had not previously made a public disclosure of its request for the 3% hike and the CLC did not publicize its approval. According to the Wall Street Journal Sept. 10, the council took action on the 3% increase, which covered the costs of making standard certain equipment previously sold as optional, at the same time it was ruling on the safety and pollution price issue. The total per unit price increase planned by Ford would reach $136 for 1974 models as a result of the two decisions.

Ford's pricing strategy involved passing on the entire cost of safety and pollution features to the small car market, where sales were booming. Average increases of 7.1% were announced. Buyers of the next line of cars, intermediate sized Torinos and others, would absorb most of the equipment price increases in price hikes estimated at 2.3% a unit. The larger cars, which were not experiencing increased sales as a result of tight money conditions and the emphasis on fuel economy, would show the smallest price increases.

General Motors Corp. announced Sept. 12 that the cost of 1974 models would be

$97 or 2.5% higher than 1973 levels. In addition to the $73 price hike allowed by the CLC to cover the cost of federally mandated pollution and safety features, GM also would charge an average $24 per unit (.6%) to cover the cost of making certain optional equipment standard. Most of the price increases would be passed on to small car buyers where the average price hike would be 6.7% per unit (up $150 per unit).

Chrysler Corp. announced Sept. 13 that the cost of 1974 model cars and trucks would be 2.4% above 1973 levels. The $87 average per unit increase included a $51 increase authorized by the CLC to cover safety and pollution features as well as a $36 average per unit increase (.8%) for standard equipment changes. Chrysler also passed on the bulk of its higher prices to the small car market, where 1974 prices were 5.3% higher than the previous year (an average $135 per unit boost).

Chrysler appealed to the CLC Sept. 18 for another 1974 model price increase of an estimated $73 at the wholesale level, but the request was quickly rejected. The CLC replied Sept. 19 that no proposal would be considered until the current round of wage negotiations was completed.

Steel price rises approved—The CLC ruled Sept. 10 that steelmakers could raise prices on flat rolled products the full amount they had requested, but the steel companies were ordered to spread the increases over a 3½-month period. Flat rolled product prices could be raised an estimated $4.50 a ton Oct. 1 and another $4.50 a ton Jan. 1, 1974.

The total allowable increases varied between 4.4% and 8% because 36 companies sought different price hikes based on individual cost justifications.

While approving these increases as "fully cost justified," the CLC notified steel makers that the government would not consider any proposed increases on other steel products before Dec. 1.

The CLC had held public hearings on the issue Aug. 30–31. Steel company officials reminded the council that prices on flat rolled products had been frozen since January 1972 because of competitive market conditions and the recent price freeze.

Despite strong 1973 profits, officials said the industry "required substantially greater profits" than it had earned recently if it were to implement capital spending plans and expand U.S. steel production. The increases on the flat rolled products line, which accounted for about 40% of all steel sales, were expected to return $400 million annually to the industry.

Sen. William Proxmire, chairman of the Joint Economic Committee of Congress, appeared before the hearing Aug. 30 to urge the CLC to deny the proposed increases. "The eyes of the nation so directly focus on steel that a price increase would signal to millions of investors that the inflation they face is not a temporary aberration" in selected areas of the economy, but rather was a part of the "bedrock, bellweather, fundamental American industry of steel," he said.

Other CLC decisions—Companies were required to establish an "executive control group" including all officers and employes who were company directors, according to a CLC ruling Aug. 30. The group's annual salary increases could not exceed the 5.5% wage stabilization guideline binding on other workers. Bonus payments for executives also were restricted.

Under former rules, officials had been included in the larger category of company workers. Legally, officials could have adhered to the 5.5% restriction by authorizing a 20% wage increase for themselves and holding wage hikes to 3% for the larger number of lower paid workers.

The new rules were subject to public comment until Sept. 17, when they would take effect retroactively to Aug. 30.

The Postal Service won permission from the CLC Aug. 31 to raise rates for second, third and fourth class mail in an effort to boost annual revenues $52 million. The increases, which had been deferred since July 6 by the recent price freeze, took effect Sept. 9.

Magazines, newspapers and bulk mail were the items most directly affected. First class postal rates were not increased.

The CLC also announced it would not challenge a two-year, $1 billion pay increase won by 700,000 postal employes. The two-stage wage boosts of 6.8% during the first year and 3.9% during the second year fell within the standards of a 5.5% wage increase ceiling and a .7% annual increase in fringe benefits, the council said.

The CLC Aug. 31 also ordered a rollback in the salaries of Georgia Gov. Jimmy Carter (D) and 400 state legislators. Carter's salary was reduced from $50,000 to $47,500. (It had been raised from $42,000.) The disallowed portions of the salary increase could take effect July 1, 1974, according to the CLC.

The CLC ruled Oct. 2 that paper manufacturers could implement 4%–17% price increases on an estimated 10% of their products. The additional revenue would be spent on meeting pollution abatement standards and expanding plant production.

Makers of soap and detergents were permitted an average 9.32% increase. Tire and tube manufacturers won hikes of 2.6%–4.9%, half the size requested. CLC spokesmen said additional increases would be permitted after the beginning of 1974. The current hikes would raise rubber industry revenues 3.38%.

The council said all the proposed increases had been justified by higher costs, but that the tire makers' request had been reduced because sharp price hikes would have had an inflationary effect on the economy.

Health bill veto upheld. President Nixon's veto of a bill to provide emergency health services was upheld by a 273–144 House vote Sept. 12.

The House vote to override the veto was five short of the two-thirds majority necessary to override.

Nixon had vetoed the bill Aug. 1, and the Senate voted the next day, before Congress went into its summer recess, to override it. The margin was 77–16, 15 more than the two-thirds needed.

Nixon said the bill, which authorized spending of $185 million over a three-year period, "represents a promise of federal financial assistance that cannot be kept" since the funding was "far in excess of the amounts that can be prudently spent." He said the federal role in this area should be limited to such programs as a current demonstration program costing about $15 million in the year ending June 30, 1974.

Stein on inflation psychology. Rapidly rising food costs prompted most consumers to disregard recent gains in after-tax spendable earnings, according to Herbert Stein, chairman of the President's Council of Economic Advisers.

He contended that the highly visible and dramatic increases in food prices drew attention from the more moderate rates of inflation for the rest of the economy.

This fear of a general runaway inflation, Stein said, had tended to overshadow a 5% gain in real income over a one year period from the second quarter of 1972 to the second quarter of 1973. It gave rise to a pardoxical situation in which "people will be unhappier with an income increase of 10% and a price increase of 7% than with an income increase of 3% and no price increase, especially if the more rapid price increase is fairly recent and people are not used to it," he said. "All money income increases are commonly regarded as barely suficent to keep pace with the recipient's just desserts, whereas price increases tend to be regarded as extortions which make a person worse off than he ought to be," Stein declared.

Stein's remarks were delivered Aug. 23 at his regular monthly press briefing. Under questioning from reporters, Stein conceded that statistics indicating an aggregate gain in spendable earnings did not necessarily mean that all persons were better off in 1973. (The data were largely a reflection of a 2.9 million rise in the number of employed persons and a reduction in unemployment, causing total personal income to rise.)

(For persons with nonfarm jobs, weekly earnings adjusted to delete the effects of inflation showed a .9% gain over the previous year, and declined during the first half of 1973, according to the Wall Street Journal Aug. 24.)

Meany assails Administration. AFL-CIO President George Meany condemned the Nixon Administration's economic policies Sept. 3, in a Labor Day radio address, as having "caused havoc in every area of American life" except in the area of corporate profits.

Since Nixon became President, Meany continued, the inflation rate had almost doubled, "the greatest food-producing nation on earth is experiencing food shortages," the housing shortage "has grown to crisis proportions" and federal budget deficits had totaled $66.8 billion.

Meany attacked the Administration's economic controls program for inequity. "Wages, and wages alone, have been rigidly controlled," he said.

The same themes dominated Meany's traditional pre-Labor Day meeting with labor reporters Aug. 30 (reports released Sept. 1).

Meany also spoke of the changing labor situation with regard to strikes. While there was pressure on wages from the soaring cost of living, he said, unions did not want to strike because what could be gained beyond the wage guidelines was not worth the cost of the strike.

Abel, Woodcock join attack—Meany continued the attack upon Administration economic policies Sept. 2 and was joined by union presidents I. W. Abel of the AFL-CIO United Steelworkers of America and Leonard Woodcock of the United Automobile Workers.

On ABC's "Issues and Answers" broadcast, Meany said "the President refuses to face up to the problems of inflation and higher unemployment" and "just keeps going from one improvisation to another."

Woodcock, on NBC's "Meet the Press" program, said "the business of the people has fallen on hard times while the business of the great corporations prospers as never before."

Abel referred in a Labor Day statement to the economic plight of workers facing wage curbs and rising living costs. "There is no end in sight," he said. "The Nixon Administration has offered no workable program."

Nixon on policy. At his press conference Sept. 5, Nixon was questioned about his anti-inflation policy.

Nixon said he could not "be any more perceptive than my economic advisers have been and their guesses" with regard to the inflation "numbers" in 1973 "have not been very good." He did not blame them, however, because of the weather problems in the U.S. and abroad, the unprecedented demand abroad, also unforseen, "that gave the impetus to food prices," and "other factors which led to

the inflationary pressures which our economic advisers did not foresee."

He said "we are doing everything that we think should be done and that can be done to stop the inflation without bringing on a recession."

He referred to the controls program, "tightening up on the Federal Reserve" and "increasing supplies on the food front."

Asked if the tax structure could be "altered in any way to help strengthen the economy," Nixon said a number of his advisers, including Federal Reserve Board Chairman Arthur F. Burns, had "strongly recommended that the answer to this whole problem of inflation is the tax structure . . . that there's this gimmick and that one." As an example, he cited the suggestion to give the President power to move the investment credit from 3% to 15%, which he considered "an excellent idea" but added that "there isn't a chance the Congress is ever going to give the President that power."

A number of suggestions had been made on the tax front that might be helpful in controlling inflation, he said, "but there isn't a chance that a responsible tax bill would be passed by this Congress in time to deal with that problem."

Radio appeal to nation—In a radio address to the nation on his legislative program Sept. 9, President Nixon said "the spotlight of public attention and public debate" should be held "on those issues that directly and personally affect your lives." Congress, he said, "should join the executive in making up for the precious time lost this year in failing to act on those measures which vitally affect every American, by going into extra session, if necessary, to complete the people's business before the year ends."

The goal, Nixon said, was "to achieve what America has not enjoyed since the days of President Eisenhower—full prosperity without inflation and without war."

"We must recognize that the American system requires both a strong Congress and a strong executive," Nixon said. He warned against curbing presidential power. "We therefore must not place limits on presidential powers that would jeopardize the capacity of the President in this and in future administrations to carry out his responsibilities to the American people."

He also cautioned that Congress could be responsible for "higher prices for every American family." "We still face the prospect of strong new inflationary pressures," Nixon said, "as a result of overspending by the federal government" because of Congressional action on measures exceeding his budget and Congressional inaction on his proposals to cut spending.

Spirit of bipartisanship sought. President Nixon sent Congress Sept. 10 his seventh State of the Union message in 1973 to "refocus attention" on more than 50 legislative measures he had proposed previously in the year. The President put major emphasis on national defense, the fight against inflation and bipartisan cooperation between his Administration and the Congress to enact his proposals.

While bidding for "a spirit of constructive partnership" with Congress, Nixon stated his intention to veto any measures that substantially reduced his defense budget or substantially increased his budgets for domestic social programs.

The President allotted "first priority" in his message to the battle against inflation, where "the single most important weapon," he said, was "control of the federal budget. Every dollar we cut from the federal deficit is another blow against higher prices."

Nixon ruled out a tax increase now, renewing his "strong opposition" to such a measure. But he said the "important task" of making the current system "fairer and simpler" should be "undertaken now rather than during an election year when political pressures invariably make such reform more difficult."

He specifically recommended anti-inflation action to give him "more flexible authority to establish certain controls on food and other exports" and authority for selling part of the national strategic stockpile.

Federal raise delay barred. President Nixon Aug. 31 ordered a two-month delay in a pay raise for 3.5 million federal em-

ployes who had been scheduled to receive the raise Oct. 1. But the Senate, by 72–16 vote Sept. 28, nullified the delay.

Nixon said government employes had a "special obligation" to display an "element of self-denial" by avoiding "any action that would needlessly fan the flames of inflation."

The deferral of the raise would have been the third since Congress had passed legislation in 1970 with the aim of making government wages comparable to those in the private sector by an automatic adjustment process. According to Nixon, Roy Ash, director of the Office of Management and Budget, and Robert E. Hampton, chairman of the Civil Service Commission, the presidential advisers who were empowered to determine the extent of wage increases due federal workers, had recommended award of a 4.77% increase for the Oct. 1 period.

UAW & auto firms settle. Negotiators for the United Auto Workers (UAW) and the Chrysler Corp. reached agreement Sept. 17 on a new three-year labor contract calling for a 5.5% wage increase in the first year of the pact. The union had begun a strike against Chrysler when the old contract expired at midnight Sept. 14.

The pact would cover 117,000 blue collar workers at 56 plants in the U.S. and Canada.

The Chrysler Corp. had been named by the UAW Aug. 21 as the "target" company in its Big Three negotiations, which had opened July 16.

The tentative Chrysler settlement, reached after a bargaining session of almost 24 hours, called for a wage increase of 3% in each year of the three-year pact, plus an additional 12¢ an hour in the first year. The 5.5% first-year wage increase would increase the basic wage of $4.48 an hour to $4.73.

Union members ratified the Chrysler contract Sept. 23.

Agreements on similar three-year contracts were reached by the UAW with the Ford Motor Co. Oct. 26 and General Motors Nov. 19.

Other pacts—Four other new contracts following the auto pattern also were achieved. A new three-year contract between the United Auto Workers (UAW) and Deere & Co. was resolved by negotiators Sept. 30 and ratified by union members later that day. The pact, covering 23,000 workers in Illinois and Iowa, was expected to set a pattern for the farm equipment industry. The wage settlement was similar to one recently negotiated by the UAW in the auto industry.

A settlement between the UAW and International Harvester Co. was reached Nov. 1 and, after ratification by the union membership was announced Nov. 4, ended a 15-day strike idling 40,500 employes at 25 plants in 11 states.

An 11-day strike by the UAW against the Caterpillar Tractor Co. ended Nov. 26 after negotiators reached an accord Nov. 21. Some 33,000 workers in five states were involved.

A strike threatened at five GM electrical parts plants was averted by a settlement Nov. 26 with the AFL-CIO International Union of Electrical Workers, bargaining for 32,000 workers.

Reserve requirements tightened. The Federal Reserve Board acted Sept. 7 to slow the recent dramatic rise in bank lending operations. In a move toward tighter money, the board voted to increase the amount of paper money reserves that banks were required to hold from 8% to 11%, effective Sept. 20. The 11% marginal reserve requirement applied to increases in the level of large certificates of deposit since May 16. The 3% boost would force banks to withhold an estimated $450 million from their credit operations, according to the board.

Total bank loans had increased at an annual rate of more than 20% since midyear and loans to business borrowers had risen more sharply, the Federal Reserve reported. Increased lending operations, which reflected expansion in the nation's economy and also contributed to continued inflation, were financed by the sale of large denomination certificates of deposit.

'Wild card' certificates limited. President Nixon signed a bill Oct. 15 requiring federal agencies to set interest rate ceilings on special long-term certificates of deposits known as "wild

card" certificates issued by banks and savings and loan institutions. The Senate had passed the measure Oct. 1 and House action followed Oct. 2.

The Federal Reserve Board Oct. 17 limited interest rates to 7.25% on certificates with four-year maturity dates, minimum deposits of $1,000 and maximum deposits of $100,000, effective Nov. 1. However, banks no longer would be required to limit the number of wild card certificates to 5% of their deposits.

The Federal Deposit Insurance Corp. issued similar guidelines but the Federal Home Loan Bank Board set a 7.5% rate for certificates issued by savings and loan banks under their jurisdiction.

Prime rate at 10%. Wells Fargo Bank of California Sept. 13 raised the prime interest rate on loans to large business borrowers from 9.75% to 10%, effective Sept. 14. The action spread slowly throughout the banking industry because of the Committee on Interest and Dividend's immediate request for proof of Wells Fargo's compliance with cost justification guidelines. It was the 16th increase of 1973. (The First National Bank of Chicago had started a move to 9.5% Aug. 20, and the Chase Manhattan Bank had initiated a raise to 9.75% Aug. 27. The FHA and Veterans Administration meantime had raised interest rates on home mortgage loans Aug. 24 to 8.5%, at a time when private lenders were reported to be charging as much as 9.25%.)

A decline to a prime rate of 9.75% was started by the small Southwest Bank of St. Louis Sept. 27, but initially only small- and medium-sized banks followed this change. The larger banks waited until the First National City Bank of New York (Citibank) cut its prime rate to 9.75% Oct. 19 and then to 9.5% Oct. 26.

But Citibank then led a move back to 9.75% Nov. 30 and to 10% Dec. 7.

CAB reapproves 6% fare hike. The Civil Aeronautics Board (CAB) Oct. 16 reaffirmed its earlier decision to permit a 6% increase in airlines fares for transatlantic routes to compensate for the February dollar devaluation.

The federal appeals court in Washington had rejected the CAB's first action on the 1973 fare package and re-manded the issue to the CAB for re-consideration. The agency said, however, that disapproval of the 6% increase "would provoke, not new and different fares, but fruitless dispute with the major European nations." Failure to reapprove the rate structure would have resulted in competitive open rates for the duration of 1973.

The Civil Aeronautics Board Nov. 28 28 rejected an average 2%-3% increase in transatlantic economy fare boosts proposed by the International Air Transport Association (IATA).

The increase, part of a package of in-creases averaging more than 6%, had been scheduled to take effect Jan. 1, 1974.

The CAB withheld action on a proposed 10% increase for 22-45 day excursion fares, suggesting instead that the IATA renegotiate a larger increase or eliminate the special bargain rate. It had been the CAB's recent position that the inexpensive excursion fare, utilized by 60% of non-first class travelers on the North Atlantic routes, had caused airlines to lose money and make up the losses on other fares.

Output rises, real compensation declines. Third quarter reports showed an increase in workers' productivity but a decline in "real" compensation, according to the Labor Department Oct. 25.

Output per manhour in the nation's nonfarm work force rose at a seasonally adjusted annual rate of 1.9%, paced by a "significant increase" in manufacturing productivity. During the second quarter, nonfarm productivity had declined .8% (revised).

For the entire private sector, the in-crease in output per manhour was 1.6% at an adjusted annual rate, compared with a .7% decline in the previous quarter. In the past 12 months, nonfarm productivity in-creased 2.7%, and 2.5% for the entire private sector.

"Real" compensation per manhour de-clined at an annual rate of .7%, meaning that inflationary prices exceeded workers' pay. It was the second consecutive quarterly drop. Real compensation was only 1.1% higher than in September 1972.

Stein sees inflation subsiding—Herbert Stein, chairman of the President's Council of Economic Advisers, said Oct. 5 that the "worst of the economic fever of 1973" had passed. But he predicted further increases in the prices of retail food and wholesale industrial commodities.

Stein said food costs would continue their "fairly rapid rise" and show a 10% annual rate of increase during the next six months. (Prices currently were rising at an annual rate of about 30%). Grocery prices would not begin to decline until the end of 1974, he added.

Controls for health care industry. The Cost of Living Council issued new price regulations for the health care industry Nov. 6. The proposals would take effect Jan. 1, 1974 after the council considered public comment.

The program's general aim was to reduce the 9% average annual increase in hospitals costs to 7.5% by limiting the overall annual increase in each patient's total bill. The current regulations had controlled price increases on individual hospital services, but there had been in-creases in the use of patient tests and in the use of more expensive equipment, the council said.

(Despite the 7.5% ceiling, Adminis-tration officials said exemptions to the regulations could bring the total increase to 9% and raise consumers' health care costs $5 billion annually.)

If the overutilization of hospital care were reduced, the Administration argued, the total cost of health care would also de-cline as unnecessary hospital admissions and the average patient's length of stay were cut back.

According to the plan: if a hospital had 1,000 patients with an average cost per stay of $1,000 in 1972, it could charge an average of $1,075 per stay and it could change its charges in order to earn $1,075,-000 in revenues in 1973, compared with $1 million in 1972. If admissions declined, average charges per patient could rise more than 7.5%; if there were increases in hospital admissions, the average charges would be less than 7.5%.

The American Hospital Association, which represented most of the nation's 7,-000 acute care facilities, criticized the plan, contending that economic incentives built into the program put a premium on short uncomplicated medical cases while causing an overall decline in the quality of services offered. Health care for patients requiring long term, intensive and expensive treatment would be impaired, the association charged.

Physicians and dentists would be permitted to increase their prices an average 4%, although no fee over $10 could be raised more than 10% in a single year and no fee under $10 could be raised more than $1. The medical lobby had sought a 5.5% increase. Previous controls had allowed a 2.5% increase in medical costs. During 1972, physicians had raised prices 2.4% and dentists 2.8%.

A 6.5% limit was imposed on nursing homes' per diem costs. The outpatient departments in hospitals were allowed a 6% increase.

Auto industry controls lifted. The Cost of Living Council (CLC) eliminated wage and price controls for the auto industry Dec. 10 in exchange for promises from General Motors Corp. (GM), Ford Motor Co. and American Motors Corp. not to increase 1974 car and truck prices by more than $150 a unit. Chrysler Corp. refused to give the price limit pledge but was included in the government's ruling.

American agreed to limit its increase to an average wholesale price of $100 per big car. Like Ford and GM, whose wholesale price increase for big cars was limited to $150, American agreed to the ceiling barring "unforeseen major economic events."

Increases in the retail prices of small cars were limited to $150 a unit for the three automakers. In the past, car manufacturers had been adding a disproportionate share of the CLC-permitted price hikes to the cost of small cars.

CLC officials justified the decision, saying privately that the agreement corresponded roughly to increases that would have been permitted under Phase 4 rules. According to CLC Director John T. Dunlop, the pact also gave auto makers "flexibility" in planning production schedules for 1975 and beyond, especially in the small car market. Dunlop also said that decontrolling the price of small cars would offer car manufacturers the incentive to shift their production priorities from gasoline-consuming big cars to the

smaller models. The move was expected to lessen the impact of the energy crisis on two fronts by aiding fuel conservation efforts and reducing industry layoffs related to the scarcity of petroleum products, Dunlop said.

The wage ruling applied only to the industry's estimated 500,000 assembly line workers. Wages and prices in the automotive parts operations were not decontrolled.

Chrysler President Lynn Townsend said the firm had declined to participate in the price restraint pact because of its imprecise definition of "major economic events." The CLC included Chrysler in its ruling, government spokesmen said, because competitive market conditions would act to inhibit any unreasonable price increases planned by Chrysler.

By Nov. 20, when the CLC held hearings on pending price hikes, the automakers had requested approval for major price increases that totaled $114 a unit at American, $136 at Chrysler, $188 at Ford and $208 at GM (later revised downward to $150).

The CLC temporarily suspended the planned increases Nov. 30 in order to prepare the broader ruling issued Dec. 10.

Although the auto makers' ruling represented a major step toward dismantling wage-price controls, Dunlop emphasized that there would be no headlong rush to abandon Phase 4.

CLC delays action on steel price hike. The Cost of Living Council (CLC) Dec. 21 delayed action on a steel industry request to raise prices on about half its product lines by more than 5% on Jan. 1, 1974. The CLC suspended its rule requiring federal consideration of the proposed increases within 30 days and promised a decision by the end of January.

However, the CLC permitted steel companies to institute dollar for dollar pass throughs of the costs incurred for scrap iron. The ruling, which primarily benefitted smaller companies, would allow increases for products prices not raised during Phase 4.

Other CLC action—Wage and price controls were lifted for the cement industry and most of its 33,000 employes

Nov. 27 in an effort to expand production capacity. CLC Director John T. Dunlop said he had been assured that cement prices would not be increased before Jan. 1, 1974 and that the "new levels of prices will remain essentially stable during the first half of 1974." Fifty-three producers also promised to expand output "as rapidly as possible," according to Dunlop, to meet key construction and industrial needs. If more factories could be built during 1974, inflationary pressures could be reduced in the economy during future years, Dunlop added.

In the same announcement, the CLC said processors of honey and dehydrated alfalfa, an important ingredient in cattle feed, were granted exemptions from price controls.

A subsequent decision to withdraw the economy gradually from wage-price controls on a "sector by sector" basis was announced Dec. 6 when the CLC lifted price controls for the makers of 40 nonferrous metals, including lead, zinc, tin and platinum. Price restraints were also removed from most nonferrous scrap metals. Dunlop said low domestic prices had caused many nonferrous metal producers to increase their exports. Domestic supplies had dwindled, prompting the CLC decision.

Aluminum prices were allowed to increase 16% and the base price of copper was allowed to rise 13.3%. Although price ceilings were largely removed as a result of the CLC action, Dunlop said price controls were not lifted entirely because "unacceptably" large price increases would have resulted.

Increases in nonferrous metal workers' wages remained under government control.

The CLC announced Dec. 21 that the Postal Service's proposal to raise its total 1974 mail revenues by $1.5 billion, or 18.7%, had been reduced by $236 million.

Other cutbacks in requested price increases were announced by the CLC Dec. 18: Mattel Inc. was allowed a 12.5% increase instead of a 13.4% raise; Spartan Mills Inc. was granted a 21.9% price hike instead of the requested 31.3% increase; Square D Co.'s proposed 4.85% increase was reduced to 4.73%.

The CLC Dec. 13 ordered five aerospace companies to pay 108,000 workers increases of 17¢ an hour. The award for back pay could cost the industry $85 million, officials said. The raise had been challenged in 1971 by the Administration's Pay Board but a special appeals court in Washington had ruled in favor of the employes.

The CLC Dec. 30 lifted price controls from animal feed products. Wage and price controls were ended at the same time for makers of brooms, and for recreational and educational camps.

Debt limit raised. The temporary national debt limit of $465 billion expired Nov. 30 and the ceiling automatically reverted to its permanent statutory level of $400 billion, $64.9 billion less than the government's outstanding debt. After the expiration, the Treasury Department announced plans to halt the sale of savings bonds and Treasury bills and issuance of special obligations to federal trust funds, since the legal borrowing authority had already been exceeded.

The Senate Dec. 3 finally approved a bill, passed by 263–147 House vote Nov. 7, to raise the ceiling to $475.75 billion through June 30, 1974. President Nixon signed the measure Dec. 3.

Joint panel probes arms costs. The Joint Economic Committee's Subcommittee on Priorities and Economy in Government held hearings Nov. 14–16 to investigate rising costs in weapons acquisition.

Prior to the opening of the hearings, subcommittee chairman Sen. William Proxmire (D, Wis.) released a study Nov. 11 which said the cost of military hardware fell by 50% or more when defense contractors were forced to compete. (Proxmire said Oct. 25 that 90% of all defense contracts were let without bids).

The study, prepared by Larry Yuspeh of the Center for Defense Information, found that the average price reduction achieved when competition replaced sole-source procurement was 51.9%.

Testifying before the subcommittee Nov. 15, Air Force cost expert A. Ernest Fitzgerald cited a study by the Army in 1972, which showed, for example, that if a $400 color television set were manufactured by some electronic firms used by the Pentagon, the price of the same set would be $8,000.

Brandeis University political scientist Robert J. Art told the subcommittee Nov. 15 there was a "direct correlation between inefficiency and profit" for contractors. The computation of profits on the basis of costs encouraged contractors to inflate prices, Art testified.

Jack L. Bowers, an assistant secretary of the Navy, and Arthur I. Mendolia, an assistant secretary of defense, both appearing before the panel Nov. 16, criticized the report by Yuspeh. They called the analysis "grossly misleading," and contended that Yuspeh had overstated the benefits of competition, which the Pentagon sought whenever possible.

Dow closes at 850.86. The Dow Jones industrial average closed Dec. 31 at 850.86, a sharp contrast to the 1972 closing of 1,020.02. The index had reached a record high in early January of 1,051.70 but had fallen gradually, finally staging a strong recovery in October when the index rallied at 987.06.

The last months of 1973 had been marked by steep declines and technical rallies. The Dec. 10–31 period gave further evidence of the market's characteristically erratic pattern in a time of worsening political and economic uncertainties. Among the closing figures:

Dec. 10—851.14, up 13.09 points.
Dec. 11—834.18, down 16.96 points.
Dec. 12—810.73, down 23.45 points.
Dec. 13—800.43, down 10.30 points.
Dec. 14—815.65, up 15.22 points.
Dec. 18—829.49, up 18.37 points.
Dec. 21—818.73, down 9.38 points.
Dec. 26—837.56, up 22.75 points.
Dec. 27—851.01, up 13.45 points.

Rising Food Prices

Food Costs Increase Steadily

The overall cost of food for consumers continued to rise with only slight pause in 1973. The increase in food prices during most of the year exceeded the gain in the consumer and wholesale prices of all items.

Food prices lead CPI surges. Sharply rising food prices caused the Consumer Price Index (CPI) to rise by .5% during January, the Labor Department reported Feb. 22.

Food prices rose a seasonally adjusted 1.9% during the month for an adjusted annual rate increase of 22.8%, the highest figure since March 1958. Supermarket prices, which constituted the most important component of the food index, rose an adjusted 2.3% during January. The increase represented the largest one-month gain since statistics were first published in 1952.

Consumer food prices rose to a level of 128.6% of the 1967 average in January, 131.1% in February, 134.5% in March, 136.5% in April, 137.9% in May, 139.8% in June and 140.9% in July and spurted to 149.4% in August before declining slightly to 148.3% in September and 148.4% in October. The consumer food price index set record highs of 150% in November and 151.3% in December.

Meat, dairy and fresh fruit and vegetable prices showed a "particularly sharp" increase, according to a department spokesman.

Ezra Solomon of the President's Council of Economic Advisers denied that the food price increases were caused by price "bulges" resulting from a switch to quasi-voluntary wage-price guidelines under Phase 3 after a period of strict controls during Phase 2. He attributed the price hikes to bad weather and to heavy exports of food commodities, including the sale of grain to the Soviet Union.

The increase in the CPI during Phase 2 was 3.7% compared with 3.8% in the prefreeze period; however, the food index rose 6.3% during Phase 2 in contrast with a 5% growth rate before the freeze.

The Agriculture Department had reported Feb. 28 that its "market basket" index, which indicated the cost of feeding a typical family of 3.2 people for a year, had risen to a record $1,374.98 in the month ended Feb. 15. It rose 2.7% during the 30-day period, its largest increase on record since statistics were first collected in 1947. Prices were $102 higher than the same period in 1972, and $37 above the annual rate of grocery price increases registered in December 1972.

The "market basket" index rose to $1,409.47 in the month ended March 15, to $1,458.11 in the March–April period, to $1,481.32 in the 30 days ended May 15, to $1,493.78 in the period ended June 15, to $1,517.55 in the June–July period, to $1,529.28 in the month ended Aug. 15 and to $1,653.76 in the August–September period. The index then dropped to $1,626.73 in the 30 days ended Oct. 15 and to $1,620.20 in the following month before rising again to $1,634.07 in the period ended Dec. 15 and to $1,650 in the period ended Jan. 15, 1974.

Butz anticipates food price rise—Agriculture Secretary Earl L. Butz Feb. 20 had attempted to prepare the public for the Labor Department's price report when he told a news conference that the January increase in food costs would show the largest monthly gain in "20 to 25 years."

Butz also criticized "big city newspapers and the urban press" for sensationalizing the price jumps by reporting "grossly unfair and phoney" statistics of annual rate increases. Computation of annual rates, which roughly represent the monthly increase multiplied by 12, often failed to reflect seasonal variations, Butz charged.

"Use of such statistics is like saying that if you have a cold this week, it is at the annual rate of 52 colds a year. This kind of arithmetic is preposterous," Butz declared.

Sen. William Proxmire (D, Wis.), chairman of the Joint Economic Committee of Congress, also was critical of the Butz remarks.

"When the price has been good for a month, they [the government] don't ever hesitate to translate that into an annual rate," Proxmire declared.

Butz expanded his defense of rising food costs Feb. 20. He claimed that the press had underplayed the fact that food expenses constituted only 16% of spendable earnings; however, the New York Times reported Feb. 22 that the department's research bureau computed several widely differing "market basket" budgets for families of four based on income variations. Spending on food in "economy," "low," "moderate" and "liberal" budgets ranged from 25% when yearly take-home pay was $6,000 to 16% for families with annual after-tax incomes of $17,125.

Meany criticizes price increases—George Meany, president of the AFL-CIO, Feb. 22 called for imposition of direct federal controls on food and agricultural products and an "adjustment of the whole farm policy."

Meany charged that the "Administration's attack on food prices so far is just a series of statements of what they are going to do and what they expect." He warned that it was "quite obvious" that a continuation of rising food costs would require an upward adjustment in the 5.5% wage guideline.

Administration reaction—In a second effort to prepare the public for reports of worsening economic conditions, Herbert Stein, chairman of the Council of Economic Advisers, and James W. McLane, deputy director of the Cost of Living Council (CLC), March 20 predicted a slowdown in the food cost spiral.

Stein said lower farm prices at year end "would at least slow down markedly the rise in food prices at retail."

At a press conference called to present a CLC "white paper" on food prices, McLane asserted orally and in a prepared statement that within six months, food prices would be lower than their present levels.

Under questioning, however, he retracted that statement and limited his forecase to a "much slower" rate of increase in food costs by the end of 1973.

Stein and McLane cited Administration efforts to increase food supplies, but the CLC report cautioned, "Much of the price restraining benefits of bumper crops this year will not be felt by consumers until early 1974."

10% food price rise predicted. The Congressional Joint Economic Committee released a staff study April 4 that predicted a 10% increase in food costs during 1973 "even if the Administration's best hopes for farm price stability are realized."

According to the study, compiled in association with a Washington consulting firm headed by John Schnittker, undersecretary of agriculture in the Johnson Administration, "the overriding single cause of the recent sharp rise in the prices of agricultural commodities was a decline of 42 million tons in world grain production in 1972."

Because of declining grain and potato production in the Soviet Union, short grain crops throughout the world and a falloff in rice production in Southern Asia, "internal stocks have been drawn down to rock bottom levels in virtually all importing and exporting countries."

The report cited several instances of "chaotic decision making" within the USDA that had contributed to the recent price spiral:

■ By continuing wheat subsidies at "buyer's market" levels until Sept. 22, 1972, the USDA wasted "some $300 million in public funds."

■ Two weeks after the Soviet Union began to purchase U.S. wheat, the USDA announced a "maximum acreage set-aside for the 1973 crop" and continued restrictions on barley acreage, which remained in effect until it was too late to expand the fall, 1972 planting of wheat.

■ On Dec. 11, 1972, the USDA announced a "feed grain program designed to divert some 25 million acres from production and to produce a 1973 corn crop of only 5.7 billion bushels." Modifications in the allotment system were not made until Jan. 31 and March 27.

■ Because the USDA allowed farmers to substitute corn for soybeans under a 1970 acreage allotment program, soybean production in 1971 and 1972 was reduced. The shortage contributed to the high prices of oil seed and protein meals, such as soybean meal used as feed for livestock and poultry.

Farmer defended. Many Congress members from farm states defended farmers against charges of price gouging and insisted that the farmer was a victim rather than a villaian of the inflationary spiral.

Sen. James B. Pearson (R, Kan.) told the Senate April 3: "Since 1952 the cost of food to the consumers has increased 43% while the cost of medical care has increased 150%, the cost of housing 80%, and the overall consumer price index by 80%. But even more revealing is the fact that farm prices have increased only 6% over the past 20 years. Thus most of the

increase in the cost of food is attributable to increased processing and marketing costs.... The farmer also suffers the burden of inflation. Thus, farm parity, the relationship between prices received by the farmer and prices paid by the farmer, was actually lower in 1972—74%—than in 1963—80%. The farmer is not getting rich at the expense of the housewife."

Rep. Neal Smith (D, Ia.) published in the Congressional Record April 16 the following table "showing the rate of increase—or decrease—" in the prices of various items since 1952 (in per cent):

	Increase over 1952	
Item	1962	1972
Overall cost of living	13.8	57.6
U.S. per capita income before taxes	36.6	158.2
U.S. per capita income after taxes	36.0	150.8
Corporate profits, after taxes	59.2	168.4
Price of common stocks	154.6	345.7
Wages, private selected, nonagricultural industries	41.6	124.0
Welfare payments, family of 4 in Detroit[1]	30.5	111.1
Price paid by farmers for tractors	21.4	59.8
Price paid by farmers for all motor vehicles	20.8	76.4
Price paid by farmers for all types machinery, except tractors	22.1	98.5
Meat:		
Price received by farmer for beef	−12.4	30.7
Retail price for round steak	19.2	63.2
Retail price for chuck roast	16.4	63.5
Price received by farmer for hogs	−8.3	45.0
Retail price for pork chops	9.7	53.3
Grain:		
Price received by farmer for corn	−26.3	−15.1
Price received by farmer for wheat	−2.4	−20.1
Retail price for white bread	28.4	64.7
Retail food prices (average)	5.6	41.2
Furniture and bedding	1.0	31.6
Floor coverings	10.4	19.7
Apparel and upkeep	6.6	43.3
Women's shoes	31.5	90.5
Drycleaning	19.9	67.8
Transportation costs	19.7	55.1
New cars	9.7	17.0
Auto insurance rates	41.7	156.9
General physician office calls	35.1	127.7
Semiprivate hospital room daily rate	78.4	375.1
Movie admissions	57.1	211.7
Cigarettes	28.2	114.6
Beer	9.5	32.3
Buying and renting of housing	16.5	64.2

[1] Increases based on 1955 and 1961, as compared to 1972.

Government Action

Butz backs farm cuts. In the face of rising Congressional opposition, Agriculture Secretary Earl L. Butz told a Jan. 4 news conference that he would oppose restoration of a $1.2 billion cutback in federal agriculture assistance programs in the current, 1973 fiscal year (ending June 30).

PRICES PAID BY FARMERS
[1950=100]

Year	Feed	Livestock	Motor supplies	Motor vehicles	Farm machinery	Farm supplies	Building and fencing materials	Fertilizer	Seed	Autos and auto supplies	Interest payable per acre	Taxes payable per acre	Wage rates for hired farm labor
1947	112.4	77.6	86.6	81.3	74.9	89.9	88.8	93.1	99.1	83.9	85.4	74.1	98.6
1948	119.0	96.3	96.6	90.9	87.3	95.5	98.7	101.4	115.4	92.9	87.6	86.2	104.0
1949	98.1	85.6	98.0	100.0	98.2	99.6	97.4	104.2	104.4	98.8	92.1	93.1	101.2
1950	100.0	100.0	100.0	100.0	100.0	100.0	100.0	100.0	100.0	100.0	100.0	100.0	100.0
1951	112.4	121.9	104.7	106.9	108.0	106.9	110.9	105.6	102.2	105.1	110.1	104.7	110.6
1952	119.5	102.2	105.4	111.9	112.0	113.4	111.5	108.5	115.4	111.0	121.3	109.4	118.4
1953	108.1	73.6	107.4	110.9	113.5	110.5	112.5	109.0	105.3	113.0	131.5	114.1	120.7
1954	107.6	75.1	108.7	110.9	113.5	106.9	111.5	109.7	98.2	115.0	140.4	120.0	120.0
1955	100.5	73.9	110.1	111.9	113.5	104.9	114.1	107.6	103.1	116.9	152.8	125.0	121.4
1956	98.1	68.7	112.1	114.7	117.8	105.3	118.9	105.6	91.2	118.5	169.7	135.0	126.1
1957	95.7	77.1	116.1	123.4	123.6	106.1	122.8	106.3	94.3	124.4	187.6	144.4	131.3
1958	94.3	94.5	115.4	128.7	128.7	106.9	123.4	105.6	93.0	126.4	204.5	154.4	135.1
1959	94.8	94.5	116.1	132.8	134.5	106.1	126.0	105.6	88.6	129.9	224.7	166.2	144.0
1960	92.4	89.1	117.4	131.1	138.5	106.1	126.0	106.3	92.5	128.3	248.3	183.4	148.5
1961	93.3	88.8	118.1	130.0	142.2	107.3	125.3	106.9	91.7	125.6	271.0	193.1	150.8
1962	94.3	92.3	116.8	135.3	144.7	107.7	125.0	106.9	95.2	127.6	301.1	205.0	155.3
1963	98.6	87.3	117.4	139.7	147.3	107.7	124.7	105.6	101.3	129.5	337.1	212.8	159.3
1964	97.6	77.6	118.1	141.9	150.5	108.5	124.4	104.9	101.4	130.3	380.9	221.9	163.1
1965	98.6	85.6	118.8	145.0	154.9	109.3	125.3	105.6	103.9	131.1	430.3	236.2	171.3
1966	103.3	95.3	121.5	150.0	160.7	109.7	127.9	105.6	101.8	132.7	482.0	255.9	184.7
1967	101.0	92.5	123.5	155.6	168.0	110.9	130.4	106.3	103.9	136.2	537.1	277.5	199.3
1968	97.6	96.8	127.5	164.1	176.0	113.0	138.1	102.8	109.6	143.3	589.9	308.4	215.8
1969	102.9	108.5	130.2	170.3	185.1	115.8	148.7	98.6	111.4	148.0	639.9	342.8	237.6
1970	105.7	111.9	137.6	177.2	195.3	118.2	150.3	102.8	116.2	154.3	686.5	372.2	254.8
1971	106.2	116.9	138.3	192.2	214.5	123.5	166.3	107.6	124.1	166.1	739.2	400.3	272.0
1972	141.0	136.3	138.3	198.1	224.4	127.5	174.4	109.0	131.1	169.7	811.2	420.6	283.1
1973		165.4		198.1	234.2	127.5	174.4	109.0	138.6		887.6	447.2	291.1

Note: Compiled from Federal and State official data.

Source: Economics Department, South Dakota State University.

INCREASES IN HOURLY EARNINGS & FOOD PRICES*
[In percent]

	Railroad workers	Transportation equipment workers	Contract construction workers	Auto workers	Rubber workers	Food and kindred workers	Prices for all food	Prices for food at home
1952-57	23	23	27	20	23	28	1	-1
1957-62	20	22	22	22	16	21	6	4
1962-67	19	18	24	19	12	18	11	10
1967-72	52	38	47	44	31	36	24	22
1952-72	169	143	185	149	111	150	47	38

*From Agriculture Department April 1973

The administration had announced changes in crop subsidy programs that would result in a cutback of $800 million in corn and livestock subsidies and $110 million in cotton subsidies. In addition, the Agriculture Department had eliminated two farm conservation programs totaling $235 million and a program of emergency disaster loans.

Butz said higher farm prices and increased exports would keep farm income in 1973 at the 1972 record of $19 billion despite the subsidy cut.

Food price control action. The Agriculture Department (USDA) took further steps Jan. 10-11 to increase food supplies in order to hold down retail food prices.

Actions taken included the rapid disposal of Commodity Credit Corp. grain stocks; termination of additional loans to farmers for grain crops harvested before 1972 and for 1972 wheat crops; expansion of grain and meat supplies by allowing production and grazing on 15 million acres set aside for conservation under the wheat program; and termination of remaining export subsidies.

Despite these anti-inflation measures, Secretary of Agriculture Earl L. Butz warned Jan. 11 that the actions would have little immediate effect on the food cost spiral.

The New York Times reported Jan. 13 that the new Phase 3 guidelines for food processors and distributors had been "softened." Rule changes included exemption of some companies from record-keeping requirements; modification of markup rules according to supermarkets' wishes; price addition of "government-mandated operating cost increase," such as taxes, Social Security payments and health and safety improvements.

Several top USDA officials met at the White House March 12 with Herbert Stein, chairman of the Council of Economic Advisers, Cost of Living Council Director John T. Dunlop and presidential assistant John D. Ehrlichman in an effort "to convey the sense of urgency that is being felt by the White House" regarding rising food costs.

"We are having to turn the Department of Agriculture around to work in the other direction" after many years when it "had as its task keeping food prices up for the benefit of the farmer," Ehrlichman had said March 11.

In other USDA developments, the federal support price for milk was raised 36¢ to $5.29 a hundredweight, the Wall Street Journal reported March 9. Butter prices were cut, but the support levels for nonfat dry milk and cheese were increased.

CLC acts on food prices—The Cost of Living Council (CLC) issued its first Phase 3 wage-price rulings for the food industry March 9. American Brands Inc. was denied a 5.71% increase for the price of snack foods; price hike requests from six major companies—General Mills Inc., Nabisco Inc., Kellogg Co., Consolidated Foods Corp., Carnation Co. and Campbell Taggart Inc.—were rolled back; increases from 23 companies were cleared.

In a related development, the Cost of Living Council announced Feb. 28 that price restrictions imposed in August 1972 had been lifted from coffee producers because the price of imported beans had been rising.

Food price controls rejected. President Nixon reiterated his opposition to mandatory price controls on raw agricultural products at his press conference March 15. Strict price limits would "discourage supply, lead to black market, and we would eventually have to come to rigid price controls, wage controls and rationing," he warned.

A "better way" to control rising food costs, Nixon said, was "to open our imports to the greatest extent that we possibly can." He said he had asked the Agriculture Department (USDA) to provide him with a legal opinion regarding his authority to remove a 3% tariff on imported beef. (The tariff was actually 3¢ a pound, according to the USDA.)

If executive action were not possible, the President said he would ask Congress to lift the tariff.

The President also referred to a reporter's question about housewives' strikes against stores and products featuring high costs. Without directly supporting food boycotts, the President declared that the "greatest and most powerful weapon in this country is the American housewife.... Her decisions ... have a far greater effect on price control than anything we do here."

He acknowledged "that some of the pressure on prices may be lessening now, as a result of housewives buying more carefully."

Meat Prices Curbed

Meat prices set records. Livestock prices in the 30-day period ending March 15 advanced 9% and were 43% higher than the 1972 level, the Agriculture Department reported March 30.

Meat prices set records for cattle (per hundredweight) at $43.60, hogs at $38.30 and lamb at $39.50 (a 22-year high).

Meat packers under controls. The Cost of Living Council (CLC) March 22 extended price control regulations to most meat packers, warning them that any cost increases could be passed along to consumers only on a dollar for dollar basis. That directive barred packers from setting a higher markup than the actual price increase paid for livestock. The packers were also instructed to pass along any decline in the costs of meat to consumers.

The CLC acted because, it said, "it is very possible" that the growing price spread between packers' costs and charges were unwarranted.

Previously, only 21 packing companies (50% of the industry) had been subject to the restrictions. Only packers employing fewer than 61 workers and having annual revenues less than $50 million remained exempt from the new regulations.

CEA Chairman Herbert Stein told a news conference March 22 that meat boycotts were having an impact on prices. He cited a drop in the wholesale carcass price of beef from $70.25 a hundredweight March 16 to $67 a hundredweight March 21 in Chicago despite continued short supplies.

Meat price ceiling set. President Nixon March 29 ordered a ceiling on the prices of beef, lamb and pork "for as long as necessary to do the job."

The limit, which was effective immediately, would bar processors, wholesalers and retailers from selling meat at prices above their average highest prices charged in the 30 days prior to March 28. Livestock prices were not directly affected.

Enforcement procedures would be similar to those utilized during Phase 2.

The President made the announcement in a nationally broadcast radio and television address.

Treasury Secretary George P. Shultz supplied further details at a White House briefing. He said the President would also ask Congress "for immediate action" to authorize the reduction or suspension of tariffs and import quotas on commodities whose supplies were "inadequate to meet domestic demand at reasonable prices."

The White House also announced that wage increases for all food industry workers would require prior approval of the Cost of Living Council (CLC).

Both the President and Shultz gave restrained backing to a widespread consumer boycott of meat planned for April 1–7. Shultz admitted that the timing of the meat price ceiling may have been wrong. "Perhaps it should have been done two months ago," he said, but he defended the decision not to include livestock in the meat price limit, saying shortages of supply would result if controls were imposed on farm products.

According to Shultz, the Administration had acted after labor leaders exerted pressure on him in private conversations March 23. Major wage contracts were scheduled to be negotiated during the year and unions had warned they would not comply with Phase 3 voluntary guidelines if the food price spiral were not halted.

AFL-CIO President George Meany had told the House Banking Committee March 28 that "if food prices aren't brought down, there is no way union members are going to let their unions settle for wage increases that won't even pay for their increased food bill. That's not a threat. That's just merely a fact of life."

(Meany set six other labor demands for cooperation with the Administration in the anti-inflation battle: prices should be rolled back to December 1972 levels; increases won by workers earning less than $3.50 an hour must be exempt from controls; interest rates must be rolled back and a ceiling set while credit must be allocated; rent controls should be reimposed; excess profits should be taxed and tax loopholes should be plugged; there must be "a continuing Congressional oversight review of Phase 2 to assure that fairness and equity will prevail.")

The Cost of Living Council (CLC) announced April 3 that only meat retailers with annual revenues less than $100,000 would be exempt from the federal price ceiling. All food industry outlets remained subject to CLC regulations concerning wage increases.

By April 2, the Internal Revenue Service (IRS), which was charged with enforcing Phase 3 guidelines, had made a 10% increase in its 2,500 staff in preparation for the April 9 deadline when wholesalers and retailers were required to post new meat prices.

An IRS spokesman said the agency would "concentrate on the big supermarket chains on the theory that if we get them to follow the rules, the ability of the small fellow to jack up the price is strictly limited."

Meat boycott ends. A nationwide consumers' boycott of meat ended April 7 with meat prices holding firm at their previous high levels despite an estimated 50%–80% drop in retail meat sales during the week beginning April 1.

Led by Rep. Benjamin S. Rosenthal (D, N.Y.), consumer representatives from 19 cities announced plans March 16 to launch the protest. Following the boycott, which had won widespread grass roots participation, leaders met in Washington April 11 to plan further demonstrations against inflated food prices.

The group announced the formation of a National Consumers Congress to organize a national day of protest May 5, as well as the continued abstinence from meat on Tuesdays and Thursdays. Protesters also sought a rollback in food prices and the resignation of Agriculture Secretary Earl L. Butz.

Spokesmen emphasized that their protest was aimed at public policy changes and noted that a prolonged boycott of meat could drive small farmers out of business, leaving consumers "at the mercy of agribusiness."

Results of the April 1–7 boycott had been mixed. The Grand Union Co., the nation's 10th largest supermarket chain with 500 stores in 11 Eastern states, announced a cut in retail meat prices, April 5, an action spokesmen said had been "triggered" by the boycott. The company vowed to set meat prices at least 10¢ a pound below the federal ceiling, effective immediately and extending through April.

But supplies of beef were sharply reduced during the boycott period as farmers withheld livestock from market, causing wholesale prices to remain at high levels, it was reported April 7. Patrick E. Gorman, an official of the Amalgamated Meat Cutters and Butcher Workmen's union, estimated April 5 that 20,000 meat industry employes had been laid off as a result of the militant consumer action.

Butz commented April 9 on the boycott's effectiveness. "I give her [the housewife] credit for it, but, having given her credit for that, I immediately ask who it was that drove the prices up two months before. It was identically the same forces in the marketplace."

Nixon raises cheese quota. President Nixon April 25 authorized a 50% increase in cheese imports through July 1973 in an effort to lift supplies and lower prices for consumers who had been substituting cheese for higher priced meat. Per capita consumption of cheese had risen 9% in 1972 while its price had increased 5%–10% since June 1972.

An additional 64 million pounds of cheese could be imported above the 128 million pounds permitted to enter the country annually.

Meat prices and supply. Rising prices and growing shortages of meat had prompted widespread consumer anger. Herrell Degraff, president of the American Meat Institute, Aug. 1 predicted price increases of 20% when the ceiling on beef was lifted Sept. 12. The steep rise would be followed by a small decline, Degraff said, "but not to freeze levels."

Representatives of the beef industry met with Agriculture Secretary Earl Butz Aug. 1 urging the Administration to end the freeze. (Butz indicated his support but other Administration spokesmen flatly rejected the proposal.) Degraff said that across the nation, 46 beef packing houses had closed, 37 were cutting back operations and 6,000 packers had been laid off because cattle men were refusing to sell livestock while prices were frozen.

As fears of shortages mounted and consumers began to hoard meat supplies, large beef retailers were buying cattle directly, contracting to have it slaughtered and absorbing the price increases. Degraff contended that a "gray market" in beef already existed in the form of short weight sales and packaging of excess fat.

The Agriculture Department reported Aug. 1 that cattle slaughter was 80% lower than during the previous week, and was at its lowest level since the consumer boycott of April.

Institutional buyers were among the first to notice diminishing meat supplies. Pentagon spokesmen reported purchasing problems July 28 and New York City was unable to obtain a two-week supply of meat for the Aug. 6-17 period, spokesmen said. It was reported Aug. 9 that New York City received only one bid from meat suppliers for the second half of August and that those prices were up to 40% higher than in mid-July.

Fears of shortages were causing some consumers to buy meat in Canada and Mexico where supplies were both cheaper and plentiful. U.S. customs officials at the California-Mexico border termed the shopping trips "nothing less than a stampede" and refused to allow travelers to import more than $100 worth of meat (at Mexican retail prices), the New York Times reported Aug. 13.

U.S. shoppers in Canada were purchasing poultry and grocery products in addition to meat, according to the Times. Canadian merchants claimed that U.S. demand for their meat had not been equaled since World War II.

Canada curbs exports. Prime Minister Pierre Trudeau announced Aug. 13, at the end of a Canadian Cabinet meeting on soaring food prices, that controls would be placed on the export of beef and pork

for an indefinite period because of market distortions resulting from the beef price freeze in the U.S.

Industry, Trade and Commerce Minister Alastair Gillespie said controls would not affect "traditional" customers, who could continue purchases "provided they don't exceed last year's level." He said export licenses would be denied in cases of "raids" by U.S. buyers, and licenses would be revoked on profiteering companies.

The U.S. price freeze did not apply to imported beef, and increased exports to the U.S. had helped drive up prices for steer in Toronto to over $60 a hundredweight by Aug. 8.

Courts rule on beef supply issue. A special U.S. appeals court panel in California upheld the beef price freeze Aug. 18, rejecting meat industry claims that the Cost of Living (CLC) had acted illegally, arbitrarily and capriciously in ordering the freeze.

The decision, announced in Washington, affirmed a U.S. court ruling in San Francisco refusing an injunction against the CLC. Another California appellate court had upheld a similar ruling by a Seattle, Wash. court, the Associated Press reported Aug. 18.

Beef price freeze lifted early. The freeze on beef prices ended at midnight Sept. 9 as a result of a CLC decision to implement Stage B of the Phase 4 regulations for the entire food industry three days earlier than planned.

Stage B guidelines would allow all segments of the food industry, including beef processors and retailers, to reflect costs increases—such as labor, transportation and overhead—in addition to the higher costs of farm products.

According to the CLC, the scheduled termination date for the beef price freeze had been revised to offset any beef shortages caused by withholding cattle, and to ease industry accounting procedures under the complex Phase 4 program.

CLC Director Dunlop predicted that a "fairly sharp" bulge in beef prices would occur when the freeze ended, but he emphasized that beef prices were not decontrolled since they were subject to the same price regulations covering other food products.

Cattle prices dropped dramatically from $55.20 to $38.50 per 100 pounds in mid-August in Midwest markets Sept. 28.

Food prices decline—The Agriculture Department reported Nov. 30 that prices paid to farmers dropped 1.5% in the 30-day period from mid-October to mid-November. It was the third consecutive monthly decline in farm prices, but consumers' cost for farm products remained 38% above mid-November 1972 levels.

A sharp drop in wholesale beef prices accounted for a large part of the drop in food prices, but, according to the Labor Department, that decrease was not being passed on to consumers. During October, wholesale beef prices dropped 12.9% while retail beef prices fell only 3.6%,

Grain Developments

Feed grain export controls ordered. The U.S. imposed export controls on soybeans, cottonseed and their oil and meal byproducts June 27 in an effort to avert a livestock feed grain shortage. An embargo on all shipments was in effect from June 27–July 2, when rules for the export program were announced. (Soybean and cottonseed oil controls were lifted at that time.)

The action, announced jointly by Commerce Secretary Frederick B. Dent and Agriculture Secretary Earl L. Butz, was taken to supplement the Administration's 60-day price freeze announced June 13. Dairy farmers and poultry and cattle producers had been warning the Cost of Living Council (CLC) and the public that the nation faced an imminent food supply crisis because costs for feed grains, already skyrocketing, were not limited by price restrictions; food processors, however, were subject to price ceilings.

The limit on food grain shipments abroad would remain in effect until new crops were harvested in September. The brief embargo was replaced by a system of export licenses allowing exporters to ship

50% of soybean orders on hand by June 15 and 40% of their orders for soybean meal.

Cottonseed and cottonseed oil exports were also subject to licensing restrictions, but all orders on hand before June 13 were permitted to be shipped.

The export level was selected to provide the U.S. grain processing industry with sufficient stocks to keep production at full capacity, according to Carroll G. Brunthaver, assistant secretary of agriculture.

U.S. export controls were expected to have international repercussions. Japan relied heavily on U.S. soybean, importing 98% of its supplies from the U.S. European livestock producers were also dependent on U.S. supplies of feed grains.

Trading in commodities futures at the Chicago Board of Trade had been explosive in recent weeks. After it had been reported June 26 that the CLC would administer the 60-day price freeze "in a fairly tight manner" allowing few exceptions to the price ceilings, the price of soybeans dropped up to 49¢ a bushel at the Chicago commodities market.

Soybean trading had been resumed June 22 after a one-day suspension requested by the Agriculture Department, but the suspension was reactivated June 28 in the wake of the government's embargo announcement.

Trading resumed June 29 with soybean prices closing down 25¢ a bushel.

The extraordinary price increase resulted from poor spring weather which ruined the crop in Illinois, where most of the nation's supply of soybeans was produced. Other factors were: depleted stockpiles caused by large grain sales in a controversial Soviet deal in 1972; severe shortage of railroad cars to distribute the grain, also caused by the strain imposed on the nation's transportation system by the Soviet purchases; and a sharp decline in the anchovy catch off Peruvian waters.

Anchovy meal and soybeans comprised the principal source of protein in livestock feed.

More farm export controls ordered. The U.S. imposed export controls on 41 more farm commodities in the categories of livestock feeds, edible oils and animal fats

July 5 in an attempt to prevent a shortage of domestic supplies.

Commerce Secretary Frederick B. Dent said the added controls were necessary because foreign demand for feed supplements had increased after controls were imposed on soybean and cottonseed exports. The expanded list included peanuts, sunflower, alfalfa and feed meals, all sources of high-protein feed supplements.

Agriculture Secretary Earl L. Butz said the controls were expected to continue until this year's soybean crop was harvested in the fall. He said that the controls could be extended after the harvest, but that would depend on the amount of the harvest, export demand and the level of domestic prices.

Butz then called on farmers July 19 to "begin planting now for all-out production in 1974" because the Administration planned to end production controls during Phase 4 on basic food commodities, such as wheat, cotton and feed grains.

The action, last undertaken during the Korean War period, would free 19 million acres, Butz said. (Acreage restrictions would continue on other commodities, such as tobacco, peanuts and rice.)

If projected record harvests of grain were realized for 1973 crops, Butz said the Administration also would terminate export controls.

Butz Aug. 16 lifted all planting restrictions on wheat.

The Agriculture Department announced Aug. 29 that it was establishing a "target price" program to facilitate a 6% increase in the 1974 harvest of livestock feed grains. Despite predictions of a record 1973 crop, production was expected to fall short of demand.

The target price mechanism, authorized under the recently passed farm bill, allowed farmers to cultivate 89 million acres of corn, sorghum and barley with the assurance that if target prices on the crops were not matched or exceeded by market prices, government payments would make up the difference.

Grain prices soar. Grain prices on the Chicago Board of Trade were at record levels as a result of President Nixon's decision to end the food price freeze July 18.

Trading was chaotic at the commodities market Aug. 9 as wheat buyers sent futures prices soaring to daily high limits for the ninth consecutive day. The price of a 60-pound bushel of wheat for delivery in September closed at $4.04 Aug. 6, topping the $3.50 record set in late 1919. (Exporters, negotiating secret sales to the Soviet Union, had paid farmers as little as $1.32 for a bushel of wheat in July 1972.)

The price of corn soared Aug. 7 to $3.01 for a 56-pound bushel for September delivery. The previous record had been $2.98 in 1948. Soybean futures also showed continued advances Aug. 9.

High grain prices caused three major bakers to raise prices Aug. 8, actions that would result in 1¢–4¢ increases for consumers in the price of bread. (Meat and poultry prices paid by livestock feeders also would be affected by the rise in grain prices.)

Near-panic buying in the commodities market was attributed partially to a world shortage of grain, observers reported Aug. 6–9.

The Agriculture Department announced July 25 that more than half the expected U.S. wheat crop had been booked for export by July 6, the first week of the 1973–1974 crop year.

Assistant Agriculture Secretary Carroll G. Brunthaver told the American Soybean Association Aug. 21 that controls on grain exports would not be extended because the restrictions could damage the U.S. dollar value and balance of payments position. The Commerce Department then announced Sept. 7 that exporters would be able to fulfill all of their soybean and other grain contracts, effective Sept. 8. Although the action effectively lifted export controls, license procedures and reporting requirements were retained, allowing reimposition of export controls at any time.

1972 Soviet grain deal probed. A Government Accounting Office (GAO) investigation of the massive U.S. sale of grain to the Soviet Union during the summer of 1972 indicated that the Department of Agriculture had subsidized the effort "much beyond what appeared necessary or desirable" and had provided the Soviets with wheat at "bargain prices."

Comptroller General Elmer B. Staats presented the GAO report to the House Agriculture Committee March 8. Although there was "no indication of law violations," Staats noted that "farmers were not generally provided timely information with appropriate interpretive comments. Agriculture reports presented a distorted picture of market conditions."

The GAO reported to Congress July 9 that USDA mismanagement of the deal had resulted in excessive export subsidies and an inflationary effect on U.S. food prices.

The GAO report charged the USDA with failing to keep informed of the size of the sales while making commitments to private grain dealers to pay enough subsidies to keep wheat export prices at $1.63-$1.65 a bushel. As a result, the report said, more than $300 million was paid out unnecessarily by the time the subsidies were suspended Sept. 22, 1972.

The GAO alleged that the USDA knew early in 1972 the world wheat situation would have allowed export prices higher than the $1.65 target, but set the price without "a detailed analysis to support such a major policy decision." Subsequently, departmental regulations permitted dealers to speculate in the subsidies by delaying registration of sales until rising domestic prices forced government payments upward.

Domestic food prices were affected, the report said, by removal of a significant portion of wheat production from the domestic market, pressure on livestock feed prices and severe disruption of transportation facilities. The report noted that the domestic price of wheat had risen from $1.68 to $3 a bushel between July 1972 and May 1973.

There were, however, benefits to the U.S. economy, the GAO said, including an improvement in the balance of payments, a reduction in surplus stocks, increases in farm income and a return of idle acreage to production.

The Justice Department said July 11 that it had refused to give Senate investigators access to FBI files on the grain deals with the U.S.S.R., but it reported in a summary that the FBI had found no criminal fraud or conflict of interest in its investigation of alleged price manipulation by grain companies.

The summary was released in response to a request by Sen. Henry M. Jackson (D, Wash.), whose Permanent Investigations Subcommittee had scheduled hearings on the allegations for July 20.

Deputy Attorney General Joseph T. Sneed said in a letter to Jackson accompanying the summary that the FBI had to respect a pledge of confidentiality of information voluntarily provided by Continental Grain Co., the largest participant in the sales to the Soviet Union.

The summary said Continental had during the summer of 1972 submitted weekly position reports to the USDA's Commodity Exchange Authority which failed to reflect the company's sales to the Soviet Union. But the FBI concluded that the "inaccurate reports in no way adversely affected the government."

The FBI position was challenged by Rep. John Melcher (D, Mont.), who contended that the false reports and the possible delay in registering the sales to take advantage of rising domestic prices could have constituted fraud.

Treasury Secretary George P. Shultz conceded at a White House press conference Sept. 7 that the U.S. had been "burned" in the controversial sale.

Other Administration officials had refused to admit that the massive sales of wheat and other grains to the Soviet Union had contributed to recent U.S. price increases in grain, flour and bread.

Sen. Walter D. Huddleston (D, Ky.) had charged earlier Sept. 7 that the Soviet Union had profited doubly from the U.S. grain deal. In addition to obtaining U.S. supplies at very low prices, Huddleston said, the Soviet Union had resold some of its U.S. wheat to Italian dealers at inflated prices.

The U.S. Commerce Department had announced June 5 that a new shipping agreement with the U.S.S.R. called for higher Soviet payments to U.S. ships carrying grain to the Soviet Union after June 30.

Under the old agreement the Soviet Union paid a fixed rate of $10.34 per ton, supplemented by U.S. government subsidies of an additional $11 per ton. The new rate would fluctuate according to world market conditions, and would be $16.94 in the first week of the agreement. Most of the 19.5 million tons of grain sold by the U.S. to the Soviet Union in 1972 was covered by the earlier shipping contract.

Controls & Legislation

Butz vs. freeze. Agriculture Secretary Butz July 19 repeated his criticism of the food price freeze, ordered June 13 and abandoned July 18. He contended that the price ceiling had discouraged farm production; however, Butz defended the continued freeze on beef prices, insisting that cattlemen were not cutting back production and scoffing at predictions of beef shortages.

Butz referred to the food price freeze July 22 in a televised interview. "I think our people have learned a great lesson. You don't get more by paying less," he said.

Surveys of food prices taken after the President's announcement that the freeze had been lifted July 18, indicated sharp increases in eggs, pork, poultry and grains, especially feed grains, throughout the country.

Farm bill. President Nixon Aug. 10 signed a basic farm bill that he described as "a realistic compromise" between Congressional and Administration proposals.

While the legislation "falls short of the high standards I have set for reforming farm legislation and eventually moving the government out of agriculture," Nixon said in his statement, it did "provide a constructive framework for encouraging the expansion of farm production."

Under the bill's new price guarantees, he said, farmers could expand production "during the current period of world-wide food and fiber shortages without fear of a serious drop in farm income." "Thus," he continued, "it will encourage full production and dampen inflationary pressures without risking a market disaster."

The President noted with approval the anticipated decline in federal expenditures for farm support payments—from about $4 billion in 1972 to discourage farmers from producing—to an estimated $2 billion in 1973 and less than a half billion after the new law took effect.

Proposed controls for food industry. The Cost of Living Council issued proposed regulations for the food industry Aug. 22. The new Phase 4 rules, scheduled to take effect Sept. 12 when the freeze on beef prices was lifted, would cause "some price increases at the consumer level," according to John T. Dunlop, CLC director.

The proposed regulations were designed to spread out the bulge of price increases resulting from the recent price freeze, Dunlop said.

Current controls, imposed as an interim measure, permitted the food industry to raise prices only on a dollar for dollar basis to reflect increases in raw agricultural commodity costs. The new rules resembled Phase 4 restrictions on other areas of the economy: dollar for dollar increases on overall costs generally could be passed on to the consumer. Additional profit markups were not allowed.

The food sector was divided into three categories with varying restrictions. Food manufacturers would be subject to two different types of price rules. Raw material costs could be passed through as price increases not requiring prenotification, but nonfood costs, such as labor and overhead, could be passed through only on a cost-justification basis and would require prenotification. There also would be a dual base period, with meat processors subject to a separate timetable.

Wholesale and retail firms could choose between gross margin restrictions or the customary initial percentage markup test. They would be expected to absorb nonmerchandise costs, such as labor, transportation and rent. Because retail firms had experienced an "exceptionally low level of profitability" in 1972, they were permitted to select as a base period either one of the first two fiscal years ended before Feb. 5. The base period for food wholesalers was limited to the last fiscal year ended before Feb. 5.

Restaurants and other food service businesses could pass through "all net allowable cost increases," including those for raw agricultural prices and indirect costs such as labor and utilities. They also would be able to compute an adjusted freeze price.

Further milk price increases opposed. The Cost of Living Council announced Oct. 17 that the Agriculture Department would oppose further increases in the federal price support for fluid milk. Three increases in the prices paid to dairy farmers had occurred since August.

A 60¢ per hundredweight increase, scheduled to take effect Oct. 1, was made effective Sept. 9 because of a reported rise in milk production costs and a drop in milk production. The 13% increase came only three weeks after the federal government had raised prices 6% to bring the subsidy into line with minimum provisions of the newly enacted farm bill.

An additional 53¢ per hundredweight increase was allowed to take effect Nov. 1.

According to the council, dairy farmers had sought a federal floor price that was "above the record levels" set Nov. 1. Federal milk support prices had become a matter of political dispute with charges growing out of a lawsuit and Watergate-related investigations that the White House had reversed an Agriculture Department decision in 1971. Critics charged that the White House had permitted increases in the federal supports because dairy farmers pledged large campaign contributions to President Nixon's reelection effort.

Fertilizers decontrolled. The CLC Oct. 25 lifted price controls on the fertilizer industry. CLC Director John T. Dunlop conceded there would be substantial increases in the cost of fertilizers, but he said they would be offset by higher crop production needed to stabilize food costs in 1974.

Other steps were being taken to increase fertilizer supplies according to Dunlop. Nearly 40 fertilizer companies had promised to divert exports to the domestic market, a move that was expected to raise supplies by 10%.

Dunlop cautioned that the action, which also decontrolled the price of nutrients used in the manufacture of explosives, was not part of a program to lift all price controls. Economic conditions were not "suitable" for an across-the-board end to Phase 4 by the end of 1973, he said.

International Trade, Payments & Monetary Problems

U.S. Seeks Better Trade Terms

Domestic inflation in the U.S. had an injurious effect on the country's balances of trade and international payments and on the value of the dollar in international exchanges. The trade, payments and monetary setbacks then heightened the effects of inflation in the U.S. As part of the struggle against inflation, the U.S. made a major effort to improve its foreign trade position.

The Senate Foreign Relations Committee noted in a 1974 report: "Endemic inflation led to extraordinary balance of trade and payments deficits between 1970 and 1972 which in turn created a massive run against the dollar.... [T]he fixed exchange rate structure collapsed on Aug. 15, 1971. Several dollar devaluations have occurred since that date. By making imports more expensive and exports relatively less expensive, the dollar devaluations contributed significantly to ... inflationary pressures ..., creating shortages of raw materials and leading to ... export controls on these products for which the U.S. enjoys its largest comparative advantage (e.g., soybeans).... [D]uring the 1960s and early 1970s, the U.S. economic preeminence in the world economy declined relative to western Europe and Japan...."

"*The value of world exports increased from $129.6 billion in 1960 to $575 billion in 1973,*" *according to the Senate report.*

"*Unfortunately, however, much of the increasing volume of trade was attributable to inflation and occurred within preferential and discriminatory trading arrangements.... One result of discriminatory trade practices has been a decline in the U.S. share of world trade.... [T]he U.S. share underwent a steady decline from 15.9% in 1960 to 14.6% in 1965 and to 12.4% in 1973...."

In 1973, however, the U.S. balance of trade improved. Exports (excluding Defense Department shipments) rose from a value of $49,218,600,000 in 1972 to $70,-798,400,000 in 1973. Imports also rose, from $55,582,800,000 to $69,121,200,000. A trade surplus of $1,677,200,000 was recorded in 1973 as compared with a $6,364,200,000 deficit in 1972.

The deficit in the balance of payments, on the "official reserves" basis, declined from $10.354 billion in 1972 to $5.304 billion. On a "net liquicity bais," the deficit dropped from $13.856 billion to $7.796 billion. The deficit in the "basic" balance on current account and long-term capital flow declined from $11.235 billion in 1972 to $744 million in 1973.

U.S. triples exports to Soviet. According to figures released Jan. 16 by the U.S. embassy in Moscow, American exports to the Soviet Union rose to $449 million for the first 11 months of 1972, compared with $134 million for the same period in

177

1971. Soviet exports to the U.S. rose from $54 million to $83 million. The increased U.S.-Soviet trade was described as indicating success in Nixon Administration efforts to improve the U.S.' international economic position.

In a related development, the New York Times Jan. 17 quoted a recent article by Evgeny C. Shershnev, a specialist on Soviet-U.S. trade, who said the U.S.S.R. would not be able "systematically to finance its purchases from the U.S. from hard currency earnings from exports to other countries."

Shershnev said a "balanced, mutually profitable and most efficient trade structure" could be established if the U.S. were to offer the Soviet Union equal tariff treatment and Export-Import Bank credits. Both nations could engage in "various forms of cooperation" such as joint ventures to exploit and ship large quantities of liquefied natural gas from the Soviet Union to the U.S.

Soviet trade deficit—The Soviet Union experienced an overall trade deficit in 1972 for the first time since World War II, according to the May issue of the Soviet journal Foreign Trade, it was reported May 29.

Soaring imports of grain and industrial equipment caused an imbalance of 1.1 billion rubles in Soviet trade with advanced Western nations ($1.47 billion at the official exchange rate) more than canceling out a Soviet surplus in trade with other Communist countries and with the underdeveloped world. The overall deficit was 600 milion rubles ($780 million), with imports of 13.3 billion rubles ($17.8 billion) and exports of 12.7 billion rubles ($17 billion).

Since the ruble was not a convertible currency, the deficit would have to be financed out of foreign currency or gold reserves, or with Western credits.

U.S.-Japanese trade. In the first official estimate of Japan's fiscal 1972 surplus in trade with the U.S., the Ministry of International Trade and Industry predicted Jan. 22 that the U.S. deficit would total $4 billion by March 31.

In an effort to relieve that trade imbalance, the Japanese Export-Import Bank, instead of the U.S. Export-Import

Bank, would finance Japan's purchase of 10 large U.S. commercial airlines valued at $237 million. The effect of the action, which was announced Jan. 17, was to insure payment immediately upon delivery rather than having payments stretched over 10 years.

U.S. Ambassador Robert Ingersoll warned Japan Jan. 18 that unless it reduced its growing trade surplus with the U.S. within the next two or three months, the American Congress might retaliate by adopting protectionist measures against Japan and other trading nations. Ingersoll expressed his views at a Tokyo news conference.

Eximbank policies criticized. The General Accounting Office (GAO) charged Feb. 15 that the U.S. Export-Import Bank had been making unnecessary loans abroad. Although the bank "sees its role as a lender of last resort . . . borrowers tend to seek Eximbank financing as a first resort," the report said.

Eximbank loans contained a "grant element" because the long term, low interest financing included a "permanent transfer of real income to the borrower and/or exporter" and could contribute to a worsening of the U.S. balance of payments problem by reducing or delaying cash inflows from abroad.

The GAO based its report on an examination of $386 million in credits to Japan during fiscal 1969–71, when Japan accumulated a large payments surplus.

Trade deficit cut. The Commerce Department reported April 26 that the trade deficit dropped to $52.6 million (seasonally adjusted) in March from $476 million in February. The improvement was attributed to a $315 million gain in exports and a $109 million drop in imports.

During the first three months of 1973, the trade deficit dropped from $1.584 billion in the preceding quarter to $832,6 million, its smallest level since the July-September period of 1971. The 1973 first quarter deficit was $3.7 billion at an adjusted annual rate, compared with $6.8 billion for all of 1972.

Total exports for March were at a record level of $5.38 billion (up 6.2%); imports were down slightly to $5.43 billion (down 2%). First quarter exports totaled

$15.34 billion (up $2.11 billion); imports were $16.26 billion (up $1.33 billion).

Measured on a balance of payments basis, the trade gap narrowed to an adjusted $920 million in the first quarter from $1.685 billion recorded in the last three months of 1972.

The first trade surplus since September 1971 was recorded in April, according to the Commerce Department May 24. At an annual rate, the 1973 trade deficit was reduced to $1.9 billion.

Exports exceeded imports by $196.3 million, compared with a trade deficit of $595 million registered in April 1972. A dollar devaluation undertaken in February was a major factor in the improvement.

During the first four months of 1973, exports were up 19% from the preceding four months. In the same period, imports grew by 11%.

Commerce Secretary Frederick B. Dent attributed the strengthened January–April trade position to a "significant reduction in the trade deficit with Japan." He cautioned, however, that rising oil imports, expected to rise by $1 billion during fiscal 1974, could cause a reversal in the improving trade figures.

The favorable balance in the April trade figures was attributed to a decline in imports from Canada.

But a $157.9 billion trade deficit was recorded in May.

The U.S.' foreign trade balance then improved sharply in June, with a surplus recorded in the second quarter, the first time since the first quarter of 1971.

Imports exceeded exports by only $15.5 million in June, but exports exceeded imports by a seasonally adjusted $22.9 million in the second quarter.

The foreign trade deficit for the first six months of 1973 narrowed sharply, with imports exceeding exports by $809.7 million, compared with a deficit more than four times as large as for the same period in 1972.

Big trade surpluses in the final months of 1973 ($792.4 million in September, $615.4 million in October, $243.1 million in November and $869.6 in December) finally cancelled the trade deficit and produced the year's trade surplus of $1,677,-200,000.

Payments deficit widens. The Commerce Department reported May 15 that two measures of the nation's balance of payments worsened during the first quarter of 1973.

The deficit reflected massive dollar outflows during the period of speculative assaults on the dollar in February and March.

On an "official reserves" basis, the payments gap was $10.2 billion, compared with $1.61 billion in the final quarter of 1972 and $5.93 billion in the final quarter of 1971. For all of 1972, the official reserves deficit totaled $10.35 billion (revised). The first quarter figure, which combined changes in foreign official dollar holdings with changes in U.S. monetary reserves, was the second largest on record, exceeded only by the third quarter report for 1971.

On a "net liquidity" basis, the first three months of 1973 posted a $6.8 billion deficit, up from $3.7 billion in the fourth quarter of 1972 and $4.19 billion in the fourth quarter of 1971. That figure reflected net outflows of short term capital to foreigners in private and governmental dealings.

A $5.91 billion outflow in liquid private capital during January-March, prompting a $3.44 billion deficit, contributed to the worsening official reserves deficit.

But the "basic" deficit on current account and long-term capital declined by $1,038,000 in the first quarter to $1.006 billion, its lowest level since the final quarter of 1970, the Commerce Department reported June 20.

Improvement in the "basic" balance, which measured the internal flow of trade, services, government loans and long term private capital, reflected a gain in the U.S. foreign trade position.

Surplus in 2nd quarter—The Commerce Department announced Aug. 15 that the nation registered its first balance of payments surplus since 1969 during the second quarter of 1973.

Measured on the "official reserve transactions basis," the U.S. showed a surplus of $287 million.

The $11 billion turnaround was not as dramatic as it appeared, department spokesmen cautioned, because the figure represented the changes in dollar holdings of foreign central banks. Since most currency systems had been placed on a floating basis in March, fewer governments were holding dollar reserves and supporting the dollar's value.

The "net liquidity" balance registered a $1.7 billion deficit for the second quarter.

The "basic" balance of payments during 1973's second quarter amounted to $1.158 billion.

On a "current account" basis, the deficit was $937 million.

On an "official reserves" basis, the payments surplus climbed to $1.942 billion in the third quarter and to $2.661 billion in the fourth. There was a $1.626 billion surplus in the "net liquidity" balance in the third quarter but a $959 million deficit in the fourth. The "basic" balance showed a $1.917 billion balance in the third quarter and a $498 million deficit in the fourth.

First quarter dollar outflow analyzed. Preliminary results of a Treasury Department study showed that net capital outflows of major U.S. corporations during the first quarter of 1973 were $1.1 billion greater than during the first three months of 1972, it was reported Aug. 14.

Contending that the increase in dollar outflows was relatively small, Treasury Department officials concluded that transactions by U.S. firms did not constitute the "major component" in the dollar drain occurring during speculative assaults on the U.S. currency.

Some of the corporate outflow, which totaled $2.8 billion, was "caused by or accelerated by the widespread expectation of exchange rate changes at times during the [first] quarter," but was not a principal factor in the worsening of U.S. balance of payments figures, according to the department.

The Administration identified other more significant sources of dollar outflows: U.S. banks and U.S. branches of foreign banks accounted for withdrawals estimated at $2.3 billion each during the first quarter.

Broad trade authority requested. President Nixon asked Congress April 10 for

new basic trade legislation that would give him unprecedented authority to raise, lower or eliminate tariffs or other trade barriers. In a special message, Nixon said the new authority was necessary to expand trade and "prosperity" for the U.S. and its trading partners and to allow the U.S. to enter into forthcoming international trade negotiations with bargaining power equal to that of the other countries.

His proposed Trade Reform Act of 1973 would be the first major revision of trade legislation since the Kennedy Administration's Trade Expansion Act of 1962. Nixon said that in addition to equipping the Administration to negotiate for "a more open and equitable world trading system," it would provide the President with authority to handle the problem of rising imports that brought domestic market and employment imbalance. The President sought authority to "strengthen our ability to meet unfair competitive practices," to explore the "new trade opportunities" with Communist countries, to open the U.S. market to less-developed countries on a tariff-free basis and to revise in a limited way tax provisions on income earned by U.S. corporations abroad.

It contained both "free trade" and protectionist provisions.

For the first time, it would permit retaliation by the U.S. against countries the President deemed to be employing unfair competitive practices. He could also raise tariffs to improve the U.S. balance of payments or lower them to curb domestic inflation. He would have five-year authority to negotiate increases, reductions or elimination of tariffs in the multilateral trade talks scheduled for September.

On nontariff trade barriers, he would have a variety of techniques to gain reciprocal adjustments. In cases requiring revision of domestic law—such as quotas on imports of agricultural products, or health regulations—the President said he would submit the proposals to Congress subject to veto by either house.

The President also proposed to subject to the Congressional veto any trade agreement negotiated with the Soviet Union or other Communist nation.

On the tax laws applying to U.S. companies with overseas operations, the President urged caution. "There is no reason that our tax credit and deferral provisions relating to overseas investment should be subjected to drastic surgery," he said. The basic provisions were "fundamentally sound," Nixon said, and U.S. business should not be penalized "by placing it at a disadvantage with respect to its foreign competitors."

In the U.S., he continued, "some people have feared that American investment abroad will result in a loss of American jobs. Our studies show, however, that such investment on balance has meant more and better jobs for American workers, has improved our balance of trade and our overall balance of payments, and has generally strengthened our economy."

Nixon message on State of the World. President Nixon submitted his annual State of the World message to Congress May 3. The message, subtitled "Shaping a Durable Peace," was summarized by Nixon in a national radio broadcast the same day.

The theme of his written report was the primacy of world economic problems— the need for finding economic solutions within a political context.

Calling 1973 "the year of Europe," Nixon stressed the need for reconciliation of the larger goal of Atlantic unity in defense and security with the increasingly more regionalistic economic policies of the European Economic Community.

Turning to Japan, Nixon warned that "persistent disputes over . . . economic issues threaten to disrupt the political relations that hold our alliance together." He said the "imbalance is a threat to a stable international system in which Japan itself has a major stake."

The message behind these references indicated that Europe and Japan should assume responsibilities commensurate with their improved economic positions.

Brezhnev asks more U.S. trade; exit tax reported suspended. Soviet Communist party Chairman Leonid I. Brezhnev told a group of seven U.S. senators, during a lengthy unscheduled conversation in Moscow April 23, that the Soviet Union

looked forward to a major expansion of its trade with the United States, and would not let the issue of Jewish emigration interfere with trade growth.

Brezhnev assured the senators that the education tax on prospective emigrants from the U.S.S.R. had been suspended.

Sen. Vance Hartke (D, Ind.) said in Moscow April 23 that Brezhnev had expressed interest in long-term trade arrangements of up to 30 or 40 years, and at levels higher than any thus far between the U.S.S.R. and a Western nation. He said Soviet officials talked of exchanging their raw materials and energy resources for technology and equipment, and predicted a long-term need for American grain.

President Nixon, in meetings with a group of senators April 18 and a delegation of Jewish leaders April 19, had reported receiving oral assurances March 30 and April 10, relayed through the Soviet Embassy in Washington, that the U.S.S.R. would exercise a waiver included in the August 1972 education tax decree, to suspend the tax except in a limited number of cases involving state security. The second message said there would be no time limit on the waiver, but did not say whether the waiver was equivalent to repeal of the tax.

Brezhnev visited the U.S. June 16–25 and held protracted talks with Nixon. A joint communique issued June 25 said the U.S. and U.S.S.R. "should aim at a total of $2–$3 billion of trade over the next three years."

U.S. exports climb. U.S. Commerce Department statistics showed that U.S. exports to the Soviet Union during the first half of 1973 exceeded two-way trade between the two countries for the entire 1972 year, the Journal of Commerce reported July 31.

Trade data showed that U.S. exports to the U.S.S.R. totaled $696.4 million for the January–June period. Imports from the Soviet Union to the U.S. totaled $6.5 million for the period.

U.S. Devalues Dollar

Continued attacks on the U.S. dollar by currency speculators brought about the second devaluation of the dollar in 14 months.

Bonn defends weakening dollar. In the wake of speculative assaults on the U.S. dollar in Europe and Japan, the West German government imposed capital controls on the dollar Feb. 3. A Nixon Administration spokesman warned Feb. 6 that unilateral protective actions by the U.S. could become necessary.

The New York Times Feb. 8 attributed the dollar crisis to a chain reaction triggered by Italy's recent decision to adopt a two-tier exchange system for the lira. This Italian action caused an influx of dollars from speculators to appear in Switzerland, where the Swiss refused to buy up the U.S. currency, in effect allowing the Swiss franc to float at speculative levels.

After reports of a large 1972 trade surplus accumulated by West Germany, surplus dollars appeared during the week of Jan. 29 in West Germany and in Japan, which had also announced a huge trade surplus.

Inflationary fears generated by President Nixon's fiscal 1974 budget, the massive U.S. trade deficit and fragile cease-fire arrangements in Vietnam were blamed for the initial lack of confidence in the dollar, the Wall Street Journal reported Jan. 30.

Faced with hectic trading, European central banks acted to support the dollar Jan. 29 for the first time since July 1972. The New York Federal Reserve Bank also sold "substantial" quantities of West German marks, the Times reported Jan. 30. The European banks bought up nearly $700 million Feb. 1 to prevent the dollar from falling below its minimum level established in December 1971. In Frankfurt, the central bank Feb. 2 bought $1 billion to maintain the currency floor of 3.15 marks to the dollar.

Following an emergency Cabinet meeting late Feb. 2, the Bonn government Feb. 3 established foreign exchange controls, effective Feb. 5, to stem the influx of dollars and halt speculation.

Despite the Bonn government's actions, West Germany was forced to defend the dollar parity level Feb. 6

with a $1.3 billion purchase, bringing its total dollar support to $2.5 billion since Feb. 1. By Feb. 7, additional support for the dollar was required from the Japanese yen, which like the West German mark, had been under strong U.S. pressure for upward revaluation.

Bonn officials indicated Feb. 7 that the government no longer opposed a joint European effort at establishing a two-tier foreign exchange market, which would uphold the commercial values of currencies while permitting a currency float under conditions of certain speculative and other financial transactions. (France, Belgium and Italy already maintained a two-tier system.) West German Chancellor Willy Brandt made the announcement in Brussels before European Economic Community representatives.

U.S. reaction—In response to a charge Feb. 6 by Rep. Henry Reuss (D, Wis.) that the Nixon Administration had been "much too languid and lackadaisical" regarding the problems of a payments deficit and international monetary reform, Herbert Stein, chairman of the President's Council of Economic Advisers, indicated that actions under consideration in the White House to deal with the dollar crisis included an import surcharge.

Stein, testifying before the Congressional Joint Economic Committee, warned that "we recognize we will have to take our own action" if a currency agreement could not be negotiated with U.S. trading partners.

Rep. Wilbur D. Mills (D, Ark.) Feb. 7 called for another currency realignment exceeding the scope of the Smithsonian Agreement. The action would require a further devaluation of the dollar.

U.S. monetary reform plan—The Nixon Administration had revealed the details of its proposals for international monetary reform Jan. 30 in a report attached as an appendix to the President's economic report to Congress.

The currency proposals included:

■ A "base" reserves rate set for each

nation, with rate movements up or down providing the signal for adjustments in the country's balance of payments.

■ Sanctions, such as a universal surcharge or a tax on excess reserves to be paid underdeveloped nations, could be imposed on a nation refusing to restore equilibrium after it passed an upper or lower "warning point."

■ Distinctions would be made between "primary" reserves (gold and Special Drawing Rights) and IMF (International Monetary Fund) reserves (foreign exchange credits).

The aim of the reform plan was a return to "convertibility," requiring that nations relinquish their primary reserves which, in the past, had been used to offset payments deficits.

Under the U.S. plan, nations with deficits and declining reserves would be allowed to undertake "small" currency devaluations without international approval; however, "large" devaluations would require IMF authorization and "would ordinarily be looked on with disfavor unless a country's reserves had fallen below its 'lower warning point'." Currency floats, used as an instrument of payments adjustment, would be relatively unrestricted.

U.S. dollar devalued 10%. Treasury Secretary George P. Shultz announced Feb. 12 that the U.S. would devalue the dollar by 10%, effective "immediately." He said "Japanese authorities have indicated that the yen would be permitted to float." Canada, Britain and Switzerland would continue to float their currencies, Shultz added.

According to exchange rates set by the International Monetary Fund (IMF), the par value of the dollar in relation to gold would decrease from $38 an ounce to $42.22; in terms of paper gold or "Special Drawing Rights" (SDRs), the dollar's value would decrease from .921053 SDRs to .828948 SDRs.

The decision to devalue the dollar was the second such action taken by the Administration in 14 months. International exchange rates had undergone a major revision in December 1971 at the Smithsonian meeting in Washington.

The currency change, necessitated by more than 10 days of speculative assaults on the U.S. currency and efforts by U.S. trading partners to bolster the weakening U.S. dollar, was undertaken only after consultations with European and Japanese officials.

In addition to devaluing the dollar, Shultz said, President Nixon would send to Congress "comprehensive trade legislation."

As a third element, Shultz said, the U.S. would phase out three controls on investment and lending abroad by the end of 1974. The restrictions, which had been in effect since 1963, covered purchase of foreign stocks and bonds, bank lending to foreigners and direct investments abroad by U.S. corporations.

The purpose of the Administration's sudden monetary and trade moves, Shultz said, was to speed the work of the IMF's Committee of 20 toward reaching an agreement on currency reform, to improve the U.S. balance of payments position, to "lay the legislative groundwork for broad and outward looking trade negotiations paralleling our efforts to strengthen the monetary system," and "to assure that American workers and American businessmen are treated equitably in our trading relationships."

Commenting on the "serious deficit" in U.S. trade abroad which had been a major contributor to the recent monetary instability, Shultz claimed that "too often, we have been shut out [of foreign markets] by a web of administrative barriers and controls. . . . We cannot be faced with insuperable barriers to our exports and yet simultaneously be expected to end our deficit."

Shultz singled out the Japanese trade problem, saying "In particular, they [the President's actions] are designed . . . to correct the major payments imbalance between Japan and the U.S. which has persisted in the past year."

Acknowledging the "heartening" cooperation of the U.S.'s trading and financial partners, Shultz also called on Congress to provide domestic assistance by exercising budgetary discipline in order to "avoid a revival of inflationary pressure in the U.S."

Citing the dollar devaluation as "only a

temporary solution of the problem," President Nixon Feb. 13 emphasized that under his proposed trade legislation the U.S. must have the power to raise trade barriers as well as to lower them. "Other nations must get away from their discriminatory policies and we must be in a position to bargain harder."

The President outlined his trade policy at a meeting with Treasury Secretary Shultz to which reporters were admitted.

Nixon said the devaluation would raise the cost of some imports to the U.S. and of tourism but added, "as far as the great majority of the American people is concerned, it does not affect their dollars."

(Compromise legislation ratifying the devaluation received final Congressional action Sept. 7 and was signed by Nixon Sept. 21.

(An earlier Senate version had contained a provision giving private citizens the right to own gold after Dec. 31. Private possession had been prohibited since 1933 when the U.S. went off the gold standard. The final version of the bill gave President Nixon discretion to lift the prohibition when he determined that private ownership of gold would not impair the U.S. monetary position during the current period of currency instability.)

Volcker lays groundwork abroad—Paul A. Volcker, U.S. undersecretary of the Treasury for monetary affairs, had conferred with government leaders in Japan and European capitals Feb. 5–12 on a joint solution to the worsening dollar crisis.

Volcker's talks were supplemented Feb. 8–12 by Paris conferences between French Finance Minister Valery Giscard d'Estaing, British Chancellor of the Exchequer Anthony Barber, and West German Finance Minister Helmut Schmidt, who sought a "common European position."

As the finance ministers were meeting, the West German Bundesbank Feb. 8, made its largest single daily purchase of dollars—$1.7 billion, a record exceeded the next day by a $2 billion purchase. In Japan Feb. 8, $105 million was purchased, bringing that country's total support for the U.S. currency to more than $1 billion since the crisis began. At the close of trading Feb. 9, West Germany had bought

up $6.1 billion since Feb. 1 and Chancellor Willy Brandt appealed to the U.S. to permit the New York Federal Reserve Bank to buy dollars from its own supply of foreign currencies.

Brandt conferred by telephone Feb. 8 with President Nixon, French President Georges Pompidou and British Prime Minister Edward Heath. (The combined efforts of European and Japanese central banks absorbed a record $2.3 billion Feb. 9.)

Japan floats yen—Japanese Finance Minister Kiichi Aichi had negotiated the yen float at meetings with Nixon's envoy, Paul A. Volcker. Aichi made the decision to float the yen Feb. 13 (Feb. 12, EST).

Premier Kakuei Tanaka did not publicly comment on his government's action until Feb. 14 when members of the four opposition parties in the Diet demanded his resignation and that of his Cabinet because of the precipitous exchange measures.

Tanaka denied responsibility for the float, saying, "This time it was not Japan that broke the ice. The U.S. itself decided on the 10% devaluation of the dollar and other nations had to take appropriate measures."

Other government officials were also critical of the U.S. devaluation. "The timing [of President Nixon's actions] was very bad. This was done without any consideration for a friendly government, the only friendly government of the U.S. in Asia," a spokesman said Feb. 13.

The Japanese foreign exchange market, closed since Feb. 10 to prevent speculative trading, reopened Feb. 14 with the dollar dropping quickly in value.

The price of the dollar fell Feb. 15 at the close to 265 yen from its prior trading level of 301 yen, an effective devaluation of the dollar of 16%. (The official parity before the float had been 308 yen to the dollar.) The Bank of Japan was forced to intervene during the first day of trading to prevent too rapid a rise in the yen's value and was expected to continue its support of the dollar until trading slowed.

Italy floats lira—Italy announced Feb. 13 that the "commercial lira," which previously had been supported by the Bank of Italy under the newly adopted two-tier currency system, would be allowed to float in an effort to achieve a moderate devaluation.

(The financial lira, traded by speculators and other investors on the money market, had already been suspended from fixed exchange rates.)

Despite the announcement, Italian officials said the dual currency system would remain operative.

Swiss franc floats—The government of Switzerland announced Feb. 19 that the franc would temporarily float on a "controlled" basis, supported by the Swiss National Bank at 3.38 francs to the dollar. That figure represented a 13.5% revaluation against a prefloat parity with the dollar and a 2% upward adjustment with gold and Special Drawing Rights, or paper gold.

The measure marked a halfway step between the previous "free" float and reestablishment of a fixed exchange rate.

International reaction — Uncertain money conditions marked the reopening of foreign exchange markets in London and Zurich Feb. 13.

Despite heavy selling of U.S. currency Feb. 14, trading was uneven as other money markets opened. The price of gold set records Feb. 14 and Feb. 15 on the London bullion market, closing at $72.30 and $73.75 an ounce.

Britain's Anthony Barber, chancellor of the exchequer, Feb. 13 hailed the devaluation as a "bold and constructive action," approval which was echoed the same day by Chancellor Willy Brandt of West Germany.

Bonn's Finance Minister Helmut Schmidt termed the U.S. action a "vindication" of West Germany's determined support of the dollar. (The Wall Street Journal reported Feb. 14 that speculators made an estimated $330 million in profit from the parity changes between the dollar and mark.)

Schmidt stressed that the actions represented no "victory or defeat" for any nation, but rather were undertaken in an unusually conciliatory atmosphere of negotiation, especially among European Economic Community member nations.

The West German central bank Feb. 20 sold $400 million–$500 million, its first significant sale of the U.S. currency since

its absorption of $6 billion during the recent monetary instability.

The action was taken as the dollar held firm at its new ceiling of 2.96 marks to the dollar, indicating declining speculative pressures.

The Soviet Union, which profited from the dollar devaluation, pegging its currency at 74.61 kopeks to the dollar as versus a previous 82.6, was critical of the U.S. action.

"The devaluation of the dollar, which increases exports of the United States, does not remove the reasons for the currency crisis, because the dollar continues to be the reserve currency of the capitalist system," the government newspaper Izvestia commented Feb. 13.

U.S. reaction—There was widespread approval in Congress for the President's new monetary and trade policies although the White House was criticized for allowing the dollar crisis to develop. "We have had too many easy pat answers from the Administration for every economic catastrophe," Rep. Wright Patman (D, Tex.), chairman of the House Banking and Currency Committee, said Feb. 13. The recent monetary upheaval represented "an international vote of no confidence in the Nixon economic program," Patman added.

Other lawmakers, anticipating future devaluations, termed the President's action "merely a breathing spell," and called for a complete overhaul of the international monetary system, according to the Washington Post Feb. 14.

Leading economists of both parties reacted with approval to the President's announcement, the New York Times reported Feb. 12. Walter W. Heller, chairman of the Council of Economic Advisers under the Kennedy and Johnson Administrations, said Feb. 12, "I am really pleased that at last we are getting some common sense about currency parities, and are willing to devalue when we really need to devalue."

Business indicated solid support for the Administration decision, according to the Wall Street Journal Feb. 14. The auto and steel industries were expected to gain the most from the devaluation while the oil industry, a major importer, expected adverse results from the parity changes.

In a reflection of the uncertainty that

marked trading on international money markets, the Dow Jones industrial average plunged to its lowest level in nearly 20 months Feb. 13 as the index closed at 979.91, a drop of 16.85 points, on the New York Stock Exchange.

In another development related to the recent turmoil in international currencies, the FRB intervened in the domestic money market Feb. 15 to alleviate the tightest reserve position on record experienced by banks. Borrowings from the FRB Feb. 15 averaged $2 billion, the highest level since the early 1920s, according to the Wall Street Journal Feb. 16.

Burns testifies—Arthur F. Burns, chairman of the Federal Reserve Board (FRB), testified before the Joint Economic Committee of Congress Feb. 20 and said he opposed further devaluations of the dollar. "If we travel this route [of devaluations], what little discipline exists in the world with respect to currency parities will erode," Burns declared.

"If the potential benefits of the new exchange rate realignment are to be realized, the rate of inflation in the U.S. must be reduced further," Burns added. "For monetary policy, these considerations indicate a need to practice greater moderation during 1973 in the provision of new supplies of money and credit. . . . If excessive extensions of credit are averted through the exercise of prudence by lenders and borrowers, the need for strong monetary restraints won't arise."

Burns reiterated his belief that domestic inflationary pressures were directly linked to trade deficits and monetary chaos abroad. He called on Congress to restrict spending and urged passage of the Administration's trade bill which would permit the U.S. to impose restrictions unilaterally. Burns also directed an admonition to the consumer asking families to observe a meatless day during the week in order to bring down the price of meat.

Monetary Crisis Continues

Gold prices soar. The price of gold climbed to $95 an ounce in London Feb. 23 after hovering near $90 an ounce at most foreign bullion markets Feb. 22.

When the dollar was devalued Feb. 22, the free market price of gold had been $68 an ounce.

(There had been no official link between the internationally established price of gold, set at $42.22 an ounce by the International Monetary Fund Feb. 12, and the bullion market prices, since members of the London Gold Pool agreed in March 1968 to establish a two-tier system with a free floating price subject to speculation and a governmentally supported price level.)

Authorities attributed the price increases and the extraordinary volume of gold transactions (estimated at $50 million–$100 million throughout Europe Feb. 22 in contrast with the usual trading of $5 million–$10 million) to a general instability in paper currencies, despite the recent dollar devaluation and yen float.

Gold purchases were being financed by the sale of dollars, which caused its value to weaken further against stronger European currencies.

Dollar crisis worsens. Foreign exchange markets in London, Brussels, Frankfurt, Amsterdam, Vienna and Tokyo were ordered closed March 2 as the third monetary crisis in three weeks erupted in Europe and Japan.

Six European national banks in West Germany, France, Belgium, the Netherlands, Sweden and Switzerland had intervened Feb. 23 to halt frantic trading as the price of gold peaked. Gold closed at $85 as a result of the banks' actions, but in West Germany the dollar had fallen below its minimum level of 2.835 marks to the dollar. (Bundesbank purchases caused the dollar to close higher at 2.86 marks.)

By March 1, nine central banks in Europe had absorbed more than $3 billion as speculation renewed. West Germany bought $2.5 billion, the Netherlands purchased a record $600 million, Belgium $100 million, France $100 million–$150 million. Banks in Sweden, Norway, Denmark, Austria and Spain were also forced to intervene to maintain the new dollar parity rates; however, the gold price remained steady at $86 an ounce.

EEC sets temporary float. European Economic Community (EEC) finance ministers meeting in Brussels announced March 4 that until a solution to the current monetary crisis was reached at a meeting of major industrial nations March 9, its member nations would permit a temporary and uncoordinated float of their currencies against the dollar.

Their foreign exchange markets would remain closed from March 5–9, preventing central banks from intervening in support of the dollar while unofficial currency trading took place.

EEC representatives were unable to agree on a formal joint float involving an upward revaluation of their currencies against the dollar. That plan had the backing of West Germany, which threatened a unilateral revaluation if no solution were reached. Denmark and the Netherlands also supported the Bonn proposal.

The principal opponent of the West German plan was French Finance Minister Valery Giscard d'Estaing, who said March 4, "We see no reason to undermine our competitiveness for purely monetary considerations."

Giscard d'Estaing termed the crisis an American problem requiring an American solution, such as U.S. intervention in foreign exchange markets in support of the dollar.

(EEC ministers Jan. 24 had approved an artificial fixed parity rate for the British pound to be used in the calculation of compensatory farm payments that bridged the gap between the generally lower prices of the new members and the higher prices of the six older members.

(The agreement, reached in Brussels after nearly 30 hours of talks that began Jan. 22, would devalue sterling by 9.2% against the dollar. The new system took effect Feb. 1.)

U.S. reaction—President Nixon met March 3 with his financial advisers, Treasury Secretary George P. Shultz, Federal Reserve Board Chairman Arthur F. Burns, Undersecretary of the Treasury Paul A. Volcker and Herbert Stein, chairman of the Council of Economic Advisers.

Shultz appeared before a subcommittee of the House Appropriations Committee March 5 and ruled out further devaluation of the dollar. He characterized the current monetary turmoil as a "speculative phenomenon indicative of a "transition period" from an "increasingly obsolete" monetary system to new arrangements.

In testimony March 7 to the International Finance subcommittee of the House Banking Committee, Burns also called for prompt agreement in reaching a monetary solution.

"There are some problems we can fiddle with for years," Burns said. "I want to do the job now in three months. . . . I want the dillydallying to stop." Burns was refering to ongoing talks by the International Monetary Fund's Committee of 20.

Burns admitted that "we have to convince others of the urgency of the task." In Bonn March 2, a West German government official declared, "It is not a currency crisis, but a dollar crisis." French officials echoed those remarks March 4.

Appearing before the same subcommittee March 5, Undersecretary of Treasury Volcker refused to rule out eventual U.S. intervention in foreign exchange markets in order to support the dollar parity, a policy favored by European governments.

"It is not the intention of the U.S. to try to maintain an artificial value" for the dollar by intervening in currency trading, Volcker remarked, but he added that he did not consider the 10% dollar devaluation to be an artificial rate and cited the need for "operating flexibility" in the matter of a dollar defense policy.

Rep. Henry Reuss (D, Wis.) expressed the general view of the subcommittee which welcomed the temporary European float. Reuss said he feared that the U.S. "could be conned into massive intervention" in support of the dollar abroad which would bring heavy pressure to bear on scarce U.S. gold reserves and could force the U.S. to accept loans from other nations with stronger currencies.

Joint EEC float—Six EEC nations— France, West Germany, the Netherlands, Denmark, Belgium and Luxembourg— agreed March 12 to establish a joint float against the U.S. dollar when international money markets reopened March 19. Britain, Ireland and Italy decided to maintain their individual currency floats.

(Sweden and Norway notified the EEC March 15 that they would join the joint float.)

France and Belgium announced that their two-tier currency systems would remain in effect during the joint float. Under the agreement, West Germany also revalued the mark upward by 3% against the currencies of the joint float participants. (The New York Times reported March 12 that the compromise figure had been reached after France had sought a 5% realignment.)

French Finance Minister Valery Giscard d'Estaing explained his government's new policy of support for a joint float:

"The system of fixed parities broke up without our being able to do anything about it. It made no sense to hold on to a fixed parity alone. The objective being the growth of the French economy, our interest was to maintain the parity of our currency in relation to European currencies rather than in relation to the dollar."

A communique issued by the EEC in Brussels March 12 established the parameters of the joint float:

■ "The maximum margin between the Deutschemark, the Danish crown, the [Dutch] florin, the Belgian franc, the Luxembourg franc and the French franc will be maintained at 2.25% in the case of member states operating a two-tier exchange market. This undertaking will only apply to the regulated market."

■ "The central banks will no longer intervene in the fluctuation margins of the United States dollar."

■ "In order to protect the system against disruptive capital movements, the directive of March 21, 1972, will be more effectively implemented, and additional controls will be put into operation as far as is necessary."

■ "The British, Irish and Italian members of the council [of Finance Ministers of the EEC] stated that their governments intended to associate themselves as soon as possible with the decision, which had been taken to maintain the community exchange margins."

■ "The representative of the Federal German Government gave notice of the intention of his government to make a minor adjustment of the central rate of the Deutschemark before the exchange markets were reopened in order to make a contribution toward the orderly development of the operation of the exchange markets."

The EEC decision, which ratified an informal agreement undertaken March 4, was reached following a meeting of the representatives of 14 countries and one observer nation March 9 in Paris. In addition to the nine EEC members and the U.S., Canada, Japan, Sweden, and Switzerland participated in the financial discussions. Indonesia, which chaired the

International Monetary Fund's (IMF) Committee of 20, joined the meeting as an observer. The Committee of 20 had been conducting lower level negotiations toward far-reaching monetary reforms.

A communique issued March 9 in Paris expressed the group's "spirit of cooperation" but revealed a continuing lack of agreement on a solution to the dollar crisis:

"The ministers and central bank governors . . . agreed that the crisis was due to speculative movements of funds. They also agreed that the existing relationships between parities and central rates, following the recent realignment, correspond . . . to the economic requirements and that these relationships will make an effective monetary contribution to a better balance of international payments. In these circumstances, they unanimously expressed their determination to insure jointly an orderly exchange-rate system."

The West German revaluation, which took effect March 12, would peg the deutschemark to Special Drawing Rights (SDRs) issued by the IMF instead of to the dollar. One mark would equal .294389 SDRs. In money markets, the mark would continue to be quoted in terms of the dollar until another benchmark could be agreed on to replace the system established in 1944 at the Bretton Woods conference.

Austria announced March 13 that it would follow Bonn's lead and revalue the schilling by 2.25%.

Japanese officials announced March 13 that Tokyo would support the EEC's joint float while maintaining its "dirty float" of the yen by continuing to intervene to keep the upward float level at about 16%.

Federal Reserve sold marks, guilders. Charles A. Coombs, senior vice president of the Federal Reserve Bank of New York, revealed March 11 that the U.S. had sold $318.6 million worth of West German currency, beginning Jan. 24 and continuing throughout February, and had sold $20.4 million in Dutch guilders, beginning Feb. 1.

The sales were made public in the bank's semiannual report of foreign exchange transactions.

The West German figure included a $104.6 million repayment made under a swap arrangement with the Bundesbank. (Swaps involved reciprocal currency transactions permitting a standby line of credit worth $11.7 billion between the New York Federal Reserve Bank, acting for the U.S., 14 foreign central banks and the Bank for International Settlements.)

By Feb. 2, the New York bank had exhausted its supply of deutschemarks, valued at $167.4 million, and was forced to sell $46.6 million from Treasury Department reserves. The swap agreement was concluded soon after the announcement Feb. 12 that the U.S. would devalue the dollar.

The highly unusual action was undertaken during January and February to deal with "deteriorating market conditions," the "massive rush out of dollars" and the "profound shock" caused by the 10% devaluation of the dollar. Coombs cited the impact of Italy's decision to operate a two-tier exchange market as a trigger for the U.S. action.

Monetary accord signed. Representatives of the U.S., the European Economic Community (EEC), Canada, Sweden, Switzerland and Japan met in Paris March 16 and reached agreement on a package settlement for the recent monetary crises.

According to the communique, the accord was based on renewed support for two rules of international monetary relations:

"Attachment for the basic principles which have governed international economic relations since the last war—the greatest possible freedom for international trade and investment and the avoidance of competitive changes of exchange rates."

"The conviction that international monetary stability rests, in the last analysis, on the success of national efforts to contain inflation. They [the delegates] are resolved to pursue fully appropriate policies to this end."

The pact included specific actions agreed upon to deal with speculative pressures on international money markets:

■ The delegates "agreed in principle that official intervention in exchange markets may be useful at appropriate times to facilitate the maintenance of orderly con-

ditions, keeping in mind also the desirability of encouraging reflows of speculative movements of funds. Each nation stated that it will be prepared to intervene at its initiative in its own market, when necessary and desirable, acting in a flexible manner in the light of market conditions and in close consultation with the authorities of the nation whose currency may be bought or sold. The countries which have decided to maintain 2.25% margins between their currencies have made known their intention of concerting among themselves the application of these provisions. Such intervention will be financed when necessary through use of mutual credit facilities. . . ."

■ "The U.S. authorities emphasized that the phasing out of their controls of longer-term capital outflows by the end of 1974 was intended to coincide with strong improvement in the U.S. balance of payments position. Any step taken during the interim period toward the elimination of these controls would take due account of exchange market conditions and the balance of payments trends. The U.S. authorities are also reviewing actions that may be appropriate to remove inhibitions on the inflow of. capital into the U.S. Countries in a strong payments position will review the possibility of removing or relaxing any restrictions on capital outflows, particularly long-term."

■ Delegates "stated their intentions to seek more complete understanding of the sources and nature of the large capital flows which have recently taken place. With respect to Eurocurrency markets, they agreed that methods of reducing the volatility of these markets will be studied intensively, taking into account the implications for the longer-run operation of the international monetary system. These studies will address themselves, among other factors, to limitations on placement of official reserves in that market by member nations of the International Monetary Fund and to the possible need for reserve requirements comparable to those in national banking markets. With respect to the former, the ministers and governors [attending the Paris meeting] confirmed that their authorities would be prepared to take the lead by implementing certain undertakings [so] that their own placements would be gradually and prudently withdrawn. The U.S. will review possible action to encourage a flow of Eurocurrency funds to the U.S. as market conditions permit."

Broad agreement in Committee of 20.

Finance ministers negotiating international monetary reform concluded a two-day Washington meeting of the International Monetary Fund's (IMF) Committee of 20 March 27.

A communique, hailed as a "major step toward reform" by the group's chairman, Ali Wardhana of Indonesia, indicated broad agreement that the world money system should "remain based on stable but adjustable" currency values with floating rates permitted in "particular situations."

The group called for "better international management of global liquidity" through reduction of reserve currencies and increased use of the IMF's Special Drawing Rights (SDRs) as the "principal reserve asset of the reformed system."

Other points of agreement:

■ "There should be a better working of the adjustment process, in which adequate methods to assure timely and effective balance of payments adjustments by both surplus and deficit countries would be assisted by improved international consultation in the fund, including the use of objective indicators. The importance of effective domestic policies for balance of payments adjustment was underlined."

■ Deputies of the Committee of 20 "were asked to study further the conditions for a resumption of general convertibility, including questions relating to consolidation of excess reserve currency balances and to methods of settlement."

■ "An intensive study should be made of effective means to deal with the problem of disequilibrating capital flows by a variety of measures, including controls, to influence them and by arrangements to finance and offset them."

■ "There should be a strong presumption against the use of trade controls for balance of payments purposes."

U.S. Undersecretary of the Treasury Paul A. Volcker termed the outcome "quite satisfactory," noting that the meeting had given a "procedural push that was needed" to the urgent reform

issue. Experts observed that the principles accepted at the Washington talks were similar to those detailed by the U.S. at the IMF's annual meeting in September 1972.

Dollar plunges, gold soars. As the price of gold was reaching record levels in European bullion markets and the dollar was hitting new lows, French President Georges Pompidou and Olivier Wormser, governor of the Bank of France, told an American Bankers Association (ABA) meeting in Paris June 5 that the U.S. should intervene in support of the dollar.

Pompidou, referring to the continued instability of the dollar, which had been widely attributed to the Watergate scandal, said, "We are witnessing the third devaluation of the dollar." Wormser added that the international monetary system was "on the reefs" as a result of the dollar's de facto depreciation of 7%–8% against the West German mark and French franc.

The dollar closed at a record low of 2.5935 marks in Frankfurt June 5 but staged a moderate recovery against other currencies. Gold was traded at $127.25 an ounce in London June 5 before closing at $126.

Bonn revalues mark—In an attempt to curb the influx of foreign currency, West Germany June 29 raised the value of the mark 5.5% against the currencies participating in the joint European Economic Community float.

The move pegged the mark at .310580 Special Drawing Rights.

In announcing the revaluation, Finance Minister Helmut Schmidt said West Germany had been forced to absorb foreign currencies worth more than 4 billion marks in the last 12 trading days to maintain the EEC float.

West Germany acted as the dollar's value had continued to plummet, hitting a low of 2.4710 marks June 28. The dollar had declined 12% in value in relation to the mark over the previous month.

The revaluation came the same day that West Germany reported a widening of its trade surplus in May, to 2.82 billion marks, more than twice the comparable 1972 figure.

Other currency changes—New Zealand revalued its dollar upward by 3% and severed its link with the U.S. dollar July 9. The Austrian government had revalued the schilling by 4.8%.

Cyprus announced July 9 it would float the Cyprus pound.

China was reported July 10 to have revalued the renminbi, formerly called the yuan, by 5.23% in terms of the Hong Kong dollar.

A 5% revaluation of the Australian dollar, raising its value from 1.4167 U.S. dollars to 1.4875, was announced Sept. 9.

Volcker assesses currency system. Paul A. Volcker, U.S. undersecretary of the Treasury for monetary affairs, June 28 gave his assessment of the three-month-old system of floating currency rates to a subcommittee of the Congressional Joint Economic Committee June 28.

Volcker said that by allowing market forces, rather than government decisions, to set the value of currencies, the recent monetary crisis had subsided.

As a result, "economic policies at home and abroad have not been distorted by the need to deal with massive flows of speculative capital in an atmosphere of crisis. International business has not been impaired," Volcker declared, adding that the volume of trade and long term investment also had not been seriously affected by the floating rate system.

Volcker warned that "an attempt to fix a rigid structure of exchange rates would risk a return to massive capital flows, increased restrictions and intermittent closing of markets—precisely the conditions we want to avoid, and have avoided."

Despite his belief that the system "seems to be working for the present," Volcker admitted that he was not "at all happy about . . . an unnecessary depreciation of the dollar in recent weeks or about the size of some of the fluctuations in exchange rates from day to day."

Central banks ready to back dollar. Representatives of the central banks of the U.S., Western Europe, Canada and Japan announced July 8 that the "necessary technical arrangements are in place" for central bank intervention to support currencies in foreign exchanges. The declaration was made at a meeting of central bank governors, or their deputies, at the Bank for International Settlements in Basel, Switzerland.

The bank representatives reaffirmed their decision, reached in Paris March 16, endorsing central bank intervention in the exchanges at "appropriate times."

In line with the Basel and Paris accords, the U.S. Federal Reserve Board announced July 10 a $6.25 billion increase to $17.98 billion in its standby "swap" credit lines with other central banks under which foreign currencies could be borrowed toward the dollar's support. The Federal Reserve disclosed the following day that the "swap" credit lines of Canada, France, West Germany and Japan had each been increased by $1 billion, with smaller increases by nine other countries and the Bank for International Settlements. The nine were Austria, Belgium, Denmark, Italy, Mexico, Netherlands, Norway, Sweden and Switzerland.

The dollar rallied July 9–11 in the wake of the Basel announcement.

The rally followed previous weeks of generally declining dollar values in which record lows were hit and gold increased in value. Turmoil had broken out on European foreign exchanges July 6 as the dollar fell to new lows for the ninth consecutive day. It closed at 2.26 West German marks.

Gold prices soared to $128 an ounce in London and Zurich July 6, a $4 increase in 24 hours. Gold sold in Paris July 6 at $132 an ounce.

U.S. reveals dollar support. The U.S. Federal Reserve Board had intervened since July 10 in New York foreign exchange markets to support the value of the dollar, Treasury Secretary George P. Shultz and Federal Reserve Board Chairman Arthur Burns disclosed in a joint statement issued July 18.

The statement said that "active intervention" would continue "at whatever time and in whatever amounts are appropriate for maintaining orderly market conditions." The announcement, however, did not disclose a specific support level for the dollar.

Despite the Federal Reserve intervention, the dollar's value dropped in most foreign exchange markets July 12, ending a three-day rally.

The dollar fell to 2.3710 West German marks July 12 and closed trading at 2.3840. It also declined against the French and Swiss francs. The price of gold rose in London by $2 to $121 an ounce.

The drop in the dollar's value, particularly against the German mark, continued even after the U.S. confirmed intervention in the exchange markets. The dollar fell 1.03% July 20 to close at 2.31 marks, down from the previous day's close of 2.334. It closed at 4.0625 French financial francs, down from 4.0888 francs, although the dollar rose against the commercial franc, from 4.04 francs to 4.0725.

The price of gold declined in London July 19 by $4.50 to $115 an ounce, its lowest point in six weeks. In Zurich gold sold for $114.25 an ounce, a drop of $5.50. However, gold prices quickly increased again, closing at $117.75 an ounce in London July 22 and $118.75 the following day.

Dollar climbs, gold drops in price. Earlier trends on the foreign exchange market were reversed Aug. 14 as the dollar reached a six-week peak and the price of gold hit a three-month low of $94 an ounce in London.

The dollar closed at 2.46 marks in Frankfurt Aug. 15 but the pound sterling continued to weaken against most European currencies, closing at $2.46. Observers cited a lack of investor confidence in British efforts to deal with inflation as the principal reason for the downward trend of spot sterling since July.

The decline in gold prices was attributed to increased short-term investment in high interest paying currencies.

World money reform delayed. The International Monetary Fund's (IMF) annual meeting, which was to have climaxed a year of negotiations in a three-year timetable for reform of the world monetary system, was preceded Sept. 22 by an announcement that there would be at least a one-year delay in reaching agreement on currency exchange rate issues and related problems.

Representatives from 126 member nations were meeting in Nairobi, Kenya for preliminary discussion and formal sessions, which began Sept. 24.

H. Johannes Witteveen, IMF managing director, told reporters Sept. 22 that no "Nairobi Declaration" would be forthcoming to signify an end to a tempestuous period of monetary troubles that had plagued the major industrial nations for several years.

The Committee of 20, which had been established at the 1972 annual meeting to conduct negotiations for all members, met Sept. 23 and decided not to pursue its talks at the Nairobi meeting. Instead the committee set a deadline of July 31, 1974 for reaching agreement on the principal objectives of a restructured money system.

IMF, World Bank meetings. The International Monetary Fund (IMF) and the World Bank, which held joint annual meetings Sept. 24–28 in Nairobi, Kenya, grappled with issues related to developing nations.

Poorer nations, whose bargaining power in the IMF had been enhanced by their veto power over forthcoming rule changes in the world monetary structure and by rising prices for commodities traded to the richer industrial countries, sought larger shares of Special Drawing Rights (SDRs) issued by the IMF.

Although there appeared to be growing support for the linkage of SDRs and aid, the U.S. remained opposed to the concept. Economists feared that the excessive liquidity which could result from large allocations of SDRs would undermine world confidence in the asset, which was without intrinsic value and useful as a yardstick of monetary relationships only while governments retained confidence in SDRs.

Others feared that large SDR holdings by developing nations would exacerbate international inflationary trends because new money would be printed without a corresponding rise in the output of goods and services.

Proponents of the SDR-aid link argued that reckless outlays of SDRs were not possible since payments schedules would require the approval of 85% of the IMF.

U.S. Treasury Secretary George P. Shultz was harsh in his criticism of the SDR-aid proposal. In a speech delivered Sept. 27 Shultz accused developing nations of asking the monetary system to provide a "printing press" for new money, an action which could only distort the international monetary situation.

"Experience strongly demonstrates the wisdom of keeping separate the function of money creation—which is what the SDR is all about—and the essentially political decision of resource transfer and redistribution," Shultz said.

Robert S. McNamara, president of the World Bank, announced Sept. 24 that the bank would lend $22 billion over a five-year period. The money, which represented a 40% increase over outlays of the previous five years, would be directed toward "soft loans" in which funds were earmarked for projects such as agriculture that were directly related to the daily life of the poor, rather than to large civil engineering projects.

Agreement was reached Sept. 25 on the amount of contributions to the International Development Bank, which was the soft loan arm of the World Bank group. Twenty-five nations promised a total of $4.5 billion in donations over a three-year period beginning July 1, 1974. The U.S. share was reduced from 40% to about 30%, with total payments of $1.5 billion spread over four years. The annual contribution would be $375,000.

U.S. Congressional opposition to foreign aid had been evident in recent years and already had caused a delay of more than a year in the current IDA contribution.

Two-tier gold system ended. Arthur Burns, chairman of the U.S. Federal Reserve Board, announced Nov. 13 that the U.S. and six European nations had agreed to end the two-tier gold accord of March 1968. The decision, taken at a meeting of central bankers in Basel, Switzerland, allowed the U.S., Italy, Belgium, Switzerland, Great Britain, the Netherlands and West Germany to buy and sell gold on the open market.

The action was expected to lower the free market price of gold, which had reached a record level of $132 an ounce July 6 as central banks became free to sell their stockpiled supplies. (The London bullion market price was $97 an ounce Nov. 12.) The U.S. did not plan to buy gold, Burns said, but "we consider ourselves free to sell gold."

The 1968 agreement had been intended to halt pressures on the dollar by speculators who had bought gold in hopes that heavy trading would so weaken the dollar that a devaluation would occur and raise the price of gold.

Burns said the agreement had been signed when there was "great uncertainty" about the deteriorating U.S. balance of payments and central bankers were concerned about a depletion of their gold reserves. Those circumstances "no longer had any relevance to the actual world," Burns explained, especially since President Nixon had, in effect, suspended one tier of the two-tier system by ending the convertibility of the dollar into gold in August 1971.

The decision to end a prohibition on government gold transaction in the free market gave nations "a certain flexibility, which is of some importance, particularly at a time of floating [currency] exchange rates," Burns said. Another effect of the decision, also related to the international monetary system, was its official recognition of the diminishing role of gold as a currency standard.

As the bankers were meeting in Switzerland, the dollar was staging one of its strongest rallies in months. The dollar traded at 2.635 German marks Nov. 12, but closed at 2.6305.

Secret talks held. Key finance officials of the U.S., Great Britain, France, West Germany and Japan met secretly Nov. 24–26 near Tours, France to discuss a reordering of the world monetary system.

French Finance Minister Valery Giscard d'Estaing termed the talks "frank and very deep," but no decisions were reported to have resulted. Other matters under discussion included "inflation and the international financial considerations of the oil situation," according to Anthony Barber, Britain's chancellor of the exchequer.

The dollar had risen to record highs recently against European currencies, a factor which both pleased and displeased U.S. officials because it indicated the increasing strength of the dollar but also threatened to remove the competitive edge given U.S. trade by two recent devaluations.

Gold, dollar strengthen. Gold prices hit a four-month high Dec. 31 on the London bullion market, closing at $112.50 an ounce. The dollar on Dec. 28 was at its highest level since February.

According to the Morgan Guaranty Trust Co., the dollar had been devalued only 4.78% from central rates set in

December 1971. In comparison, the British pound had declined 20.65% since December 1971.

The dollar's rally was related to improving U.S. trade figures and the Arab oil embargo. As the oil crisis worsened, European currencies weakened and the dollar rallied, largely as a reflection of investors' fears that Europe, which was more dependent on Middle East supplies of fuel than the U.S., faced correspondingly more severe economic consequences as a result of the embargo.

The French franc closed at just over 20¢ Dec. 27, a decline of 5¢ in six months. In Tokyo, the government was forced to intervene by selling millions of dollars to support the yen at its unofficial level of 280 to the dollar. In contrast, the dollar broke through a major psychological barrier that day in Frankfurt, closing at 2.695 West German marks. By Dec. 31, the dollar was at 2.7015 marks.

Energy Developments

The price of oil had been rising during the recent inflationary period under pressure from OPEC (Organization of Petroleum Exporting Countries) members, who argued that industrialized nations had been draining their energy resources for years at unfairly low prices. After the outbreak of the Arab-Israeli war of October 1973, Arab producing nations used oil as a "weapon" by first curtailing production and shipments and then completely embargoing shipments to Israel's supporters. The embargo was accompanied and followed by price increases that quickly quadrupled the cost of oil. Non-Arab members of OPEC participated fully in the planning and imposition of the price increases. The OPEC action merely intensified a trend toward higher prices for non-renewable energy sources.

In early 1973, however, domestically produced U.S. oil was still more costly than non-U.S. oil, and the market for the U.S. product was protected by quotas on petroleum imports. But U.S. oil production was declining, and American oil and natural gas interests were urging the authorization of higher prices as an induce-ment for oil and gas exploration and for production from secondary sources.

Oil import quotas relaxed. President Nixon Jan. 17 authorized the unlimited purchase of home heating oil and diesel oil from foreign sources for the next four months. Quotas were also relaxed for the import of crude oil during 1973 with states east of the Rockies to receive 2.7 million barrels a day (the 1972 level was 1.78 million barrels a day) and with the West Coast area to receive 800,000 barrels a day (up from 717,000 in 1972).

Legislation introduced in the House and Senate Jan. 18 by a coalition of Northeastern and Midwestern lawmakers called for a 90-day suspension of oil import quotas. A bipartisan group of senators had proposed Jan. 16 that the government end its regulation of the wellhead price of natural gas. Deliveries of natural gas had been cut back one-third, the Federal Power Commission reported Jan. 16.

Despite the Administration action, White House spokesman George A. Lincoln, director of the Office of Emergency Preparedness (OEP), warned, "We're going to have a tight fuel situation all winter."

Lincoln said oil refineries had increased production by 5% in the last two months under government pressure, but that another 5% gain of "about a million barrels a day" was still needed.

Higher prices for home heating oil, permitted under Phase 3 regulations, could provide a likely inducement for increased production, according to Lincoln.

Interior Secretary Rogers C. B. Morton had told the Senate Interior Committee Jan. 10 that "it is no longer feasible to set [oil] quota levels in a fixed relationship to domestic production or demand."

Morton predicted that the nation's "energy trade deficit," currently $4 billion a year, would reach $20 billion by 1985 when imported oil would total 50% of use. "We're in a bind until we get in hand the economic and technologic techniques to fully exploit our own coal and oil resources," Morton said.

In testimony before the committee

Jan. 10, Lincoln attributed the fuel oil shortage to federal price restrictions and manufacturing practices. "We froze the price of gasoline too high and of heating oil too low. The result is the refineries have been on a gasoline binge since last summer."

The FPC Feb. 21 agreed to allow a natural gas producer, George Mitchell and Associates Inc. of Texas, to raise interstate rates above FPC ceilings on the condition that the firm invest $16.5 million in a five-year gas exploration program.

Oil industry controls reimposed. The Administration acted March 6 to reimpose mandatory price controls on the nation's 23 largest manufacturers of crude oil, gasoline, heating oil and other refinery products. The Cost of Living Council (CLC) set a 1% limit for the first year of Phase 3 on average price increases which could be undertaken without government approval. Price hikes of 1.5% on a weighted annual average basis would be permitted if justified by higher costs.

Natural gas producers were not covered by the action but 95% of the petroleum industry, or those companies with sales in excess of $250 million annually, were included in the controls program.

The CLC decision resulted from its hearings held Feb. 7-9 to investigate price increases in home heating oil.

Venezuelan oil raise. Venezuela announced it would increase oil prices by as much as 10% to compensate for the U.S. dollar devaluation, it was reported Feb. 21. It also revalued the bolivar by 2.2%, bringing its exchange rate to 4.30 to the dollar.

Oil import limit lifted. President Nixon March 23 removed the ceiling on the volume of oil imports available as "hardship" allocations by the Oil Import Appeals Board to small, independent distributors. Previously the board had limited imports to no more than 60,000 barrels a day.

Large refiners, allowed to import 2.7 million barrels a day, were not affected by the executive order.

The Administration also appealed to domestic refiners to increase gasoline pro-duction. In the five weeks ending March 16, gasoline production "averaged only 42.5 million barrels a week," which was only 1 million barrels greater than during 1972, according to Darrell M. Trent, acting director of the Office of Emergency Preparedness.

"Consumption of gasoline is up 7% over last year and gasoline stocks of 215 million barrels are down 25 million barrels from last year," Trent said. (There are 42 gallons in a barrel.)

Wholesale fuel price hike OKd. A Cost of Living Council (CLC) decision, announced Sept. 14, permitted Atlantic Richfield Co. to institute a planned 1¢ a gallon increase in gasoline prices. A scheduled 2¢ a gallon increase for distillate fuel was rolled back to 1¢ a gallon. The oil company had announced its price hikes Aug. 20, but had "voluntarily suspended" them Sept. 7, pending a CLC investigation.

Director John T. Dunlop promised that the CLC would consider requests by gasoline dealers to raise ceiling prices after Sept. 25 when retailers were scheduled to supply cost justification data to the council. Dunlop was critical, however, of earlier "inflationary" price increases undertaken "during the period of the feared gasoline shortage this spring" when retailers "substantially hiked their prices and obtained significantly increased markups."

Gas price deregulation extended. The Federal Power Commission (FPC) ruled Sept. 15 that natural gas pipelines could purchase gas on an emergency basis for 180 days without submitting the purchase price to the FPC for approval. The action, which observers interpreted as another step toward deregulation of interstate natural gas prices, was intended to alleviate temporary winter shortages, FPC spokesmen said.

Gasoline, heating oil prices raised. Gasoline prices were permitted to rise 1¢-2.5¢ a gallon Oct. 1 as a result of a Cost of Living Council (CLC) ruling Sept. 28. President Nixon Sept. 24 had asked the council to expedite processing of price and cost information received from gasoline dealers.

At the same time, the CLC permitted increases of 1¢–2¢ a gallon in heating oil under new rules that would allow distributors to pass through higher costs for domestic fuel.

Gasoline price increases (as well as higher prices for diesel fuel) took effect as part of new, streamlined rules for setting ceiling prices. According to the new markup formula, retailers based their ceiling prices on a May 15 selling price plus any cost increases since then. Prices were higher in May than in January, which was the former markup date.

Gasoline dealers across the country had launched widespread shutdowns to protest ceiling price restrictions, which, they said, required them to absorb price increases when refiners were permitted to pass through higher costs for imported fuel. CLC Director John T. Dunlop warned retailers to use the larger markup allowance as a "cushion" against expected cost increases between Oct. 1 and the next periodic review of gasoline prices by the CLC. According to the council, every penny per gallon increase in gasoline brought $1 billion in revenues to gasoline dealers.

(Chief Justice Warren E. Burger Sept. 6 denied a request by 165,000 brand name gasoline dealers to block imposition of price controls.)

Refiners lift wholesale prices. Three major oil companies Oct. 1 announced increases in the price of gasoline sold to retailers. Shell Oil Co. planned .2¢ a gallon hikes; Atlantic Richfield Co. sought 1.5¢ a gallon increases; Phillips Petroleum Co. would raise prices .5¢ a gallon.

Gulf Oil Corp. announced its second increase in eight days Sept. 27 and warned that other price hikes "must be anticipated." Another .5¢ a gallon increase would be added to the .9¢ increase already planned.

Two more major firms acted Oct. 9. Standard Oil (Ohio) announced a 1¢ a gallon increase in the price of gasoline sold to company-owned stations and a 1.2¢ a gallon increase for gasoline purchased by independent dealers. It was Sohio's second

major increase in three weeks—wholesale and retail gasoline prices had been raised 1¢ a gallon Sept. 21.

Exxon also announced price increases Oct. 9. Heating oil and kerosene prices would be .3¢ a gallon higher, diesel fuel was up 1.15¢ a gallon and propane was raised 2¢ a gallon. Exxon had announced previous increases Sept. 6.

John T. Dunlop, director of the Cost of Living Council, said Oct. 3 that if gasoline dealers passed on every price increase from their suppliers, the system of price controls would be unenforceable.

Despite the warning, gasoline dealers across the country continued to curtail service in sporadic, but effective, protests against the Administration's policy of price controls.

Gasoline prices allowed to rise. The Cost of Living Council (CLC) permitted an immediate 1.5¢ per gallon increase in the price of retail gasoline Oct. 15. (Home heating oil and diesel fuel prices also were allowed to increase.)

Gasoline price controls had been a controversial issue for the council since its first ceiling price regulations had gone into effect. The Temporary Emergency Court of Appeals upheld the Administration's Phase 4 gasoline rules Oct. 10 in a case that had been brought by independent gasoline dealers to protest CLC guidelines.

Retailers had objected to government rules requiring them to absorb higher costs while permitting refiners to raise wholesale gasoline prices because of higher importing costs.

Under new regulations proposed Oct. 15, retailers would be permitted automatic pass-throughs for prices that were increased by their wholesale distributors. In an effort to slow the accelerating rise in gasoline prices, the council said refiners would be allowed to raise wholesale prices only in full penny increments.

Retail gasoline prices were frozen until Nov. 1 when the proposed Phase 4 rules would become final, pending public comment.

Saudis want price increase. Saudi Arabian Petroleum Minister Ahmed Zaki

Yamani called Sept. 7 for a revision of the 1971 Teheran Agreement to permit higher prices for the oil-producing countries.

The Teheran accord, aimed at regulating oil prices, expired in 1975. Yamani said the pact was "dead" and proposed that oil producers and major Western companies hold new talks in October to consider an increase in posted prices for oil exports, which determined the governments' revenue. Yamani also demanded an increase in the annual 2.5% price rise allowed to compensate for inflation.

The minister warned that unless the oil companies cooperated in amending the Teheran agreement, "we would have to exercise our rights on our own."

Oil imports soar—The U.S. was importing a record 1.2 billion barrels of oil daily from the Middle East, according to Deputy Treasury Secretary William E. Simon, who also was chairman of the Oil Policy Committee, Sept. 21.

Overall imports of oil had risen 32% in one year to six million barrels a day, Simon said. In 1972, the Middle East had exported 800,000 barrels a day to the U.S. Price increases by Middle East suppliers, combined with increased demand, would result in record 1973 costs of $7.5 billion for oil imports. Higher tanker rates and a shortage of supertankers also contributed to the higher costs.

OPEC to ask for higher rates. Following a meeting in Vienna Sept. 15–16, the 11-nation Organization of Petroleum Exporting Countries (OPEC) announced it would demand higher prices from Western oil companies in forthcoming negotiations.

A communique issued after the two-day parley set Oct. 8 as the date for meeting with petroleum representatives in Vienna to revise the industry's basic pricing agreements signed in Teheran in 1971. The statement said the current agreements "are no longer compatible with prevailing market conditions as well as the galloping world inflation."

Arab-Israeli war, Arabs cut oil output. War started in the Middle East Oct. 6 with a coordinated Arab attack on Israel. The Soviet Union, the Arabs' principal

weapons supplier, began an early resupply airlift to the Arabs to replace arms the Arabs were losing in combat. A U.S. airlift to Israel was started Oct. 14 to redress what the U.S. called the imbalance caused by the Soviet airlift.

Ministers of 11 members of OAPEC (Organization of Arab Petroleum Exporting Countries) met in Kuwait and agreed Oct. 17 on a program of cuts in oil production and export in an attempt to force a change in the U.S.' policy.

The largest producer, Saudi Arabia, announced Oct. 18 it was immediately slashing oil production by 10%, and would cut off all shipments to the U.S. if it continued to supply arms to Israel and refused to "modify" its pro-Israel policy.

The Persian Gulf state of Abu Dhabi announced Oct. 18 it was stopping all oil shipments to the U.S.

The Kuwait meeting had announced that each country would reduce production by 5% each month over the previous month until Israel withdrew from the territories occupied during the 1967 war and agreed to respect the rights of Palestinian refugees, which were not defined.

The ministers' statement said the cutback was not intended to "harm the Arabs' friends," although they acknowledged some hardships would result in Europe, which they hoped would bring pressures on the U.S. to change its pro-Israel policy.

Oil prices increased. The six largest Persian Gulf oil-producing countries announced in Kuwait Oct. 17 a 17% increase in the price of their crude oil, and a 70% increase in taxes to be paid by oil companies on oil produced and sold by the companies.

Talks begun Oct. 8 between the producers and the companies in Vienna had broken down Oct. 12 after the companies refused demands for substantial revision of the 1971 Teheran agreement, which had called for limited annual price increases through 1975. The exporting nations had argued that world inflation had been exceeding the price increases in the agreement, and charged that the companies had benefited from the increase in market prices.

The six nations—Iran, Saudi Arabia,

Iraq, Abu Dhabi, Kuwait and Qatar—accounted for over one half of non-Communist countries' oil exports. They said the "action was unrelated to the Middle East war."

The countries set a market price on their own oil of $3.65 per barrel for light crude, up from $3.12. Their own oil constituted about 25% of production. The tax reference price, on which the companies paid taxes at a 60% rate on the oil they produced and sold themselves, was raised to 1.4 times the actual market price, resulting in a tax increase of $1.25 a barrel.

(Ecuador announced Oct. 17 it would increase its tax reference price from $3.60 to $5.33 a barrel.)

Arabs impose total ban against U.S. Arab oil-producing states carried out their threat to embargo all petroleum exports to the U.S. for its support of Israel.

Libya Oct. 19 ordered a complete halt in shipments of crude oil and petroleum products to the U.S. At the same time Tripoli raised the price of its oil for other importers from $4.90 to $8.25 a barrel.

Riyadh radio announced Oct. 20 that Saudi Arabia had decided to halt all oil exports to the U.S. in view of Washington's aid to Israel.

Algeria had announced it would reduce by 10% its annual oil production, it was reported Oct. 20.

The Arab boycott of U.S. markets became total when Kuwait, Bahrain, Qatar and Dubai announced a cutoff of their supplies Oct. 21.

Canada raises oil price. The Canadian government Nov. 1 ordered immediate price increases for domestic sales of gasoline and heating oil. A recently imposed tax on oil exports to the U.S. was increased from 40¢ to $1.90 a barrel.

The moves were caused by the recent increases in the price of Arab and Venezuelan oil, and by the threat of a cutoff of Arab oil imports.

The oil export tax hike was explained as an effort to benefit from the increase in world market prices while maintaining the old price level for Alberta oil sold domestically, and to prevent U.S. consumers from buying more of Alberta's

production at the expense of Ontario and West Canada consumers.

The government said Nov. 1 that the export quota to the U.S. would be reduced to 1,005,280 barrels a day, the lowest since export controls were introduced in February, and down more than 25% from the peak in April.

Oil price spiral continues. Prices for gasoline and distillate fuels were at record levels after the Cost of Living Council lifted its freeze on the price of petroleum products Nov. 1. Oil companies raised prices to reflect the rise in imported oil prices.

Phillips Petroleum Co.'s 3¢ a gallon hike of gasoline and distillate prices announced Nov. 1 was the largest single increase for either product ever recorded, according to industry spokesmen, but Standard Oil Co. (Ohio) announced a 4¢ a gallon increase in the price of gasoline Nov. 2. Gulf Oil Co. announced its fourth increase in two months Nov. 7 when prices were raised 1¢ a gallon.

Oil company profits soar. British Petroleum Co. Ltd.'s third quarter earnings were 483% higher than in the previous year, reaching $204 million.

According to the Nov. 29 report, earnings in the first nine months of 1973 were at a record $462 million, up 413% from the same period in 1972.

Royal Dutch-Shell Group announced third quarter earnings of $413.7 million, up 274% from the previous year's figure of $110.5 million. For the first nine months of 1973, Royal Dutch's earnings were $1.03 billion, up 147% from the same period in 1972.

Reports of sharply rising profits were compiled by the New York Times Oct. 25. Figures show net earnings for the July–September period and the percentage gain over the third quarter of 1972: Exxon—$638 million, 80%; Texaco—$307 million, 48%; Mobil—$231 million, 64%; Gulf—$210 million, 91%; Standard Oil (Indiana)—$147 million, 37%; Shell—$82 million, 23%; Atlantic Richfield—$60 million, 16%; Phillips—$54 million, 43%; Continental—$54 million, 38%; Getty—$32 million, 71%; Marathon—$31 million, 35%; Cities Service Co.—$27 million,

61%; Ashland—$24 million, 17%; Standard Oil (Ohio)—$18 million, 14%.

OPEC membership expanded. The Organization of Petroleum Exporting Countries (OPEC) accepted Ecuador as its fifth non-Arab member and Gabon as an associate member at a meeting in Vienna Nov. 19.

The OPEC announced it had established a committee that would link oil prices more closely to the soaring costs of other international commodities such as wheat, soybeans and oil.

Venezuela again raises oil prices. Venezuela Nov. 30 raised its posted prices for crude oil and oil products by an average 50¢ a barrel, to a record $7.74 a barrel. Residual fuel shipped to the U.S. East Coast was increased by 98¢ a barrel to $8.46 a barrel.

The increase would boost the government's income from oil to an average $4.57 a barrel, compared with $1.62 a barrel at the beginning of 1973.

Mines Minister Hugo Perez La Salvia had announced Nov. 15 that foreign oil companies operating in Venezuela had signed an agreement with the government, effective Nov. 1, raising royalty payments on oil production by about one-third.

Ecuador also raised prices—Ecuador Nov. 10 raised posted prices for crude oil by an average of $2.05 a barrel, to $7.30 a barrel for a key grade. It was the seventh time posted prices were raised since Ecuadorean petroleum production began.

Airline fares rise to cover fuel. Domestic and international airline fares were allowed to rise as a result of higher fuel costs. The Civil Aeronautics Board (CAB) Nov. 21 approved a 5% increase in domestic fares, effective Dec. 1, that was based on surging airlines costs.

The CAB also said it would monitor the carriers' financial records "to insure the continued provision of vital services at fair prices and to measure the effect of the [new] fare increase on traffic." Critics had charged that airlines, which had overextended their flight capacity during 1973 and had reported a subsequent decline in

revenues, would profit from the forced reduction in scheduled flights by filling more seats on the planes and laying off personnel.

The CAB-approved fare increase was the fifth in a series since 1969.

Airlines flying international routes announced Nov. 23 that an average 6% fare increase was needed "to meet the recent drastic increase in fuel costs."

New York sues 7 oil firms. New York Attorney General Louis Lefkowitz announced Dec. 2 that an antitrust action had been initiated against seven major oil companies—Exxon Corp.'s USA division, Shell Oil Co., Gulf Oil Corp., Sun Oil Co., Texaco, Inc., Mobil Oil Corp. and Amoco Oil Co., a subsidiary of Standard Oil Co. of Indiana.

The defendants were charged with "engaging in a common course of conduct" and making an "illegal understanding and arrangement" to fix gasoline prices for the purpose of driving rival independent gasoline dealers out of business.

Unlike antitrust suits brought against a number of major companies by Florida and Connecticut which sought to break up the firms' allegedly monopolistic structure, the New York suit emphasized price behavior exhibited by the companies, particularly in regard to rebates (for high "official" wholesale prices) granted on an allegedly discriminatory basis to selected gasoline dealers.

In another aspect of the suit, Lefkowitz noted, "The major companies do not compete with each other on the basis of price, but instead make advertising claims stressing the alleged unique qualities of their products. Nevertheless, gasoline of any given octane rating is an essentially standard product, as evidenced by the fact that the companies exchange products with each other."

Oil firms again raise price. Seven major oil companies and subsidiaries announced another in a series of fuel price increases. Exxon Corp.'s USA division, Standard Oil Co. (Ohio) and BP Oil Corp., a Sohio unit, announced the price boosts Dec. 4.

Exxon raised retail and wholesale gasoline prices 1.1¢ a gallon; wholesale heating, kerosene and diesel fuel were boosted .8¢–2.5¢ a gallon (but home heating oil sold directly to the consumer was cut .5¢).

Sohio raised retail and wholesale gasoline prices 1.5¢ and 1.1¢ a gallon; home heating oil 4.3¢ a gallon. New prices for home heating oil were 28.6¢ a gallon. Per gallon pump prices for gasoline at company-owned stations were 45.4¢ for regular and 49.4¢ for premium.

BP upped gasoline prices 3¢ a gallon, but reduced wholesale home heating oil prices .5¢ a gallon.

Shell Oil Co., Atlantic Richfield Corp. (Arco), Sun Oil Co. and Union Oil Co. announced immediate increases in gasoline prices Nov. 30.

Shell raised gasoline prices 3.2¢ a gallon; Arco increased prices 2¢ a gallon and Sun instituted a 2.9¢ a gallon increase for the entire Eastern Seaboard and a 2¢ a gallon hike for the rest of the country. Union raised prices 2¢ a gallon.

The increases caused middle range gasoline prices to top 50¢ a gallon in the Washington area.

Arco spokesmen added that because domestic supplies of home heating oil were so short, imports at sharply higher prices had risen to meet demand. According to the company, imported home heating oil had cost 14.5¢ a gallon in May, but in November was costing 41.2¢ a gallon.

Distillate fuel price hike OKd. The Cost of Living Council (CLC) said Dec. 5 that refiners of middle distillate fuel would be allowed a 2¢ a gallon increase as an incentive to increase production of home heating oil.

It was estimated that by January 1974, consumers would be paying 7% more for fuel to heat their homes as a result of the CLC decision. The 15.4% price increase also affected users of diesel and jet fuel and kerosene.

Further price increases designed with the double purpose of encouraging greater output of certain fuels and discouraging fuel consumption in other areas could be expected, CLC officials warned.

In a parallel move, the CLC announced a 1¢ a gallon rollback in gasoline prices paid to refiners. (Motorists were not expected to benefit from the wholesale price adjustment because increases in crude oil

prices passed along to consumers would offset any drop in gasoline costs.)

John T. Dunlop, director of the CLC, said the dual aim of the price reduction was to prevent refiners from earning "very substantial windfall profits" and to remove their incentives for producing large supplies of gasoline. It was hoped that crude oil supplies and manpower used to refine gasoline would be diverted to increase production of home heating oil, Dunlop said, because the nation's 250 refineries currently were operating "substantially below the physical limits of their capacity to produce distillate fuels.

According to the CLC, the adjustments in its price control mechanism would bring about a 14% reduction in gasoline output and expand distillate fuel supplies 9% to nearly 1.5 million barrels a day. Current gasoline production represented 45% of the total refinery output. Production of distillate fuels represented 25% of total refinery operations.

Economic dislocations feared. Herbert Stein, chairman of the President's Council of Economic Advisers, told the Joint Economic Committee of Congress Dec. 11 that the energy shortage would raise the 1974 inflation rate 3% above the expected increase of 4.5%–5% in the cost of living. Stein's figures were based on an estimated 50% boost in fuel prices during 1974.

Despite his warning, Stein continued to support the Administration position that price increases for petroleum products were needed to stimulate exploration that could result in a long-term solution to the nation's declining supplies of domestic fuel.

'Windfall' profits tax proposed. President Nixon made a brief appearance before reporters Dec. 19 to announce that the White House would propose legislation to levy an "emergency windfall profits tax" on the oil industry. The measure was actually a misnomer because profits—revenues minus costs—would not be taxed. Instead, an excise-type levy would be placed on crude oil prices that rose above a certain base.

The proposal was designed to offset excess profits accruing to producers as a result of the scarcity of crude oil and the recent enormous increases in the price of petroleum products without diminishing the industry's incentive to spend money on exploration for new oil reserves.

In a parallel announcement Dec. 19, the Cost of Living Council (CLC) authorized an immediate $1 a barrel increase in the price of crude, a 23% boost over the current price of $4.25 a barrel. Retail prices were expected to rise by 2.3¢ a gallon for both gasoline, whose average national price was 44.6¢ a gallon, and home heating oil, which cost 30.7¢ a gallon on the national average, CLC spokesmen said.

The full effect of the increase would not be felt until February 1974. Under current CLC rules, producers could institute one-third on the increase Jan. 1, 1974 and the remainder Feb. 1.

Treasury Secretary George P. Shultz conducted the White House news briefing after President Nixon left without answering any questions. According to Shultz, the windfall profits tax would take effect when oil prices topped $4.75 a barrel. The tax would rise progressively, reaching a maximum 85%.

Schultz estimated that producers eventually would have to charge $7 a barrel to balance supply and demand, but he warned that while new supplies of petroleum were being sought in the interim, prices could reach $9 a barrel before conditions stabilized.

The CLC action would apply only to "old" oil—equal to the volume the producer pumped in 1972. (Old oil represented about 75% of current production.) The price of "new" oil, or the additional output, was not regulated by government price control. New oil was selling for $6.17 a barrel ($7.17 with the CLC-approved increase). The price of imported crude was about $6 at the end of November.

EEC agrees to unity in crisis. The leaders of the nine member nations of the European Economic Community (EEC) agreed at their summit conference in Copenhagen Dec. 14–15 to develop a common energy policy to deal with the oil crisis.

The conference began Dec. 14 with the unexpected arrival in Copenhagen of the foreign ministers of Algeria, Tunisia, the

Sudan and the Union of Arab Emirates, who later met with EEC foreign ministers. The Arabs reportedly stressed that the EEC nations would have to take a stronger pro-Arab position if they wanted an end to the oil squeeze.

The final summit communique reaffirmed the EEC's Nov. 6 Middle East declaration calling for Israel to withdraw from Arab territories occupied since the 1967 war.

In an accompanying energy statement, the leaders said the oil crisis was "a threat to the world economy as a whole" and warned it would hurt developing as well as developed nations.

Arabs double price, ease embargo. Oil producers of six Persian Gulf states announced after a two-day meeting in Teheran Dec. 23 that they would double the price of a barrel of oil effective Jan. 1, 1974. The decision was followed by an announcement by Arab petroleum producers in Kuwait Dec. 25 that starting Jan. 1 they would ease their embargo, but would continue the total ban against the U.S. and the Netherlands.

The gulf states of Iraq, Iran, Saudi Arabia, Kuwait, Abdu Dhabi and Qatar raised their posted price for crude oil to $11.65 a barrel from the current price of $5.11. The oil ministers' communique said the government income under the new price system would be $7 a barrel, compared with the present price of $3.09.

The six states were meeting under the aegis of the Organization of Petroleum Exporting Countries with five other OPEC members—Algeria, Indonesia, Libya, Nigeria and Venezuela—attending as observers.

Shah Mohammed Riza Pahlevi of Iran said after the meeting, "The industrial world will have to realize that the era of their terrific progress and even more terrific income and wealth based on cheap fuel is finished. They will have to find new sources of energy and tighten their belts."

Following a two-day meeting in Kuwait, the nine members of the 10-member Organization of Arab Petroleum Exporting Countries (OAPEC) announced Dec. 25 that starting Jan. 1 they would cancel a scheduled further 5% cut in production and would increase their output by 10%

instead. Production, however, would remain 15% below what it had been in September when the oil countries began their cutbacks.

The move was announced by Saudi Arabian Oil Minister Sheik Ahmed Zaki al-Yamani. He said the OAPEC had acted to ease their oil ban because Arab pressure had brought about favorable shifts in some countries' positions in the Arab-Israeli conflict. Yamani cited the change in the neutral policies adopted by Japan and Belgium, both of whom had called on Israel to withdraw from occupied Arab territory.

The countries that took action in Kuwait were Saudi Arabia, Kuwait, Abu Dhabi, Algeria, Libya, Bahrain, Qatar, Syria and Egypt. The 10th OAPEC member, Iraq, had expressed opposition to cutting back oil production.

The shah of Iran had called on the Arabs Dec. 20 to end their oil embargo. He warned, "Playing with the oil weapon is extremely dangerous. What's the use of all that money in the bank if the whole system crumbles?"

Five more nations raise prices—Five more oil-producing nations adjusted to the pattern of the Persian Gulf states and sharply increased their prices.

Venezuela announced Dec. 28 that it was raising the posted price of a barrel of oil from the December level of $7.74 to $14.08. The new price became effective Dec. 31.

Libya, Nigeria, Bolivia and Indonesia announced Dec. 31 a 60%–80% increase in the price of their crude oil. New prices (former prices in parentheses): Indonesia—$10.80 a barrel ($6); Nigeria—$14.60 ($8.31); Libya—$18.77 ($13.40); and Bolivia—$16 ($7.44).

Inflation Hits Most Countries

Increasingly strong action was taken in many countries to counteract inflation.

The rate of inflation in most countries far exceeded the rate in the U.S., which, according to figures from the Organization of Economic Cooperation & Development (OECD), had the second lowest

inflation rate in the non-Communist world. Citing OECD statistics, a United Press International report listed these inflation rates for 23 non-Communist countries for the 12 months ended in June and for the 12 months ended in May (Australia's figure applied only to May):

	June	May
Iceland	18.2	18.2
Greece	13.2	10
Ireland	11.7	11.7
Portugal	11.7	9.2
Turkey	11.3	11.3
Italy	11	5.1
Japan	11.1	10.9
Spain	10.8	10.8
Finland	9.9	10
Britain	9.5	9.5
Denmark	8.8	8.4
Netherlands	8.3	8.3
Canada	8.1	7.3
Switzerland	8.0	8.0
Germany	7.9	7.8
Norway	7.8	7.8
France	7.2	7.2
Austria	7.2	8.1
Belgium	6.9	7.5
Sweden	6.9	6.5
Luxembourg	6.7	7.8
United States	5.9	5.5
Australia	5.7	5.7

Worldwide wage gains reported. The International Labor Organisation (ILO), a United Nations agency, reported Feb. 17 that Japanese workers received wage increases during 1972 that were 10% higher than comparable gains in consumer prices.

In the next 11 countries, which included the U.S., Austria, Czechoslovakia, France, Britain, and Italy, purchasing power rose from 5% to 10%. Workers in nine countries, including Canada, the Netherlands and West Germany, experienced relative wage hikes of 2% to 5%.

In Argentina, wage increases were 10% less than increases in living costs. The drop was 5.5% in the Philippines.

Britain announces 'Stage 2' plan. In a nationally televised press conference Jan. 17, Prime Minister Edward Heath announced the broad outline of "Stage two" of Britain's anti-inflation program to follow expiration of the current 90-day wage-price freeze, or "standstill."

Details of Britain's most comprehensive anti-inflation program since World War II were presented in two White Papers issued the same day, one of which embodied a draft bill.

In announcing the program, Heath pledged to pursue "a continuing vigorous fight . . . to get on top of inflationary pressures." The government's adoption of Stage 2 followed the failure Jan. 11 of labor, management and the government to agree on a program of voluntary restraints.

The anti-inflation bill called for creation of a Pay Board and Prices Commission to regulate prices, pay, dividends and rents for up to three years. Pending parliamentary approval, the government extended the current freeze on wages through the end of March, when the new mandatory curbs were expected to become effective, and on prices through April.

The bill also provided for a maximum pay increase of £1 (about $2.35) a week per worker in any bargaining labor group, plus 4% of the current earnings of that group. Employers and unions would be free to determine by themselves how to distribute the allowable wage fund as long as no raise exceeded £250 annually.

The program would permit manufacturers to raise prices only to meet unavoidable cost increases. Manufacturing profit margins would be limited to the average two best of the previous five years.

Heath acknowledged his government drew heavily on the experience of the Nixon Administration's anti-inflation program.

The opposition Labor party called the government's program unfair and unworkable Jan. 17 and singled out the absence of controls on food prices for particular criticism.

Victor Feather, general secretary of the Trades Union Congress, also complained Jan. 17 of inadequate restraints on price increases and too low a limit on wage raises.

Stage 2 went into effect April 2, when the Pay Board, empowered to rule on wage claims, officially came into existence. The price standstill continued until April 29, when the Price Commission began its operations.

The implementation of Stage 2 followed the government's publication March 26 of a White Paper presenting detailed proposals to control wages and prices.

Tacitly admitting the failure of recent strikes to budge the government from its anti-inflation program, the General Council of the Trades Union Congress (TUC) announced its "resentful and reluctant acquiescence" in the Stage 2 guidelines April 25.

Action taken in France. France's guaranteed hourly minimum wage was increased by 2% to 4.64 francs Feb. 1. The raise, which reflected the cost of living rise, would raise the guaranteed monthly pay to 805 francs a month for a 40-hour week and to 895 francs for a 44½ hour week ($175).

France modified its anti-inflation price program May 3, restricting price increases of manufactured goods to an average 3.6% rather than the 3% in effect previously. However, within the new price structure, to be in force through March 31, 1974, high output industries would be restricted to lower increases, while less productive industries could exceed the ceiling.

Business profit margins would have to remain stable in real money terms under the new program. Increases in payments for services would vary according to expenses incurred in each profession. Rises in public sector rates would be subject to annual review, but the government stipulated they should not set off overall price increases.

The program provided for sanctions against companies that persisted in ignoring the government's price guidelines.

Finance Minister Valery Giscard d'Estaing, expressed concern, at the Cabinet meeting May 3 at which the program was approved, that salaries were increasing at a rate of more than 12% annually, a factor he thought was one of the main causes of France's current inflation.

Japanese anti-inflation plan. A seven-point plan aimed at curbing inflation was adopted by the Japanese government April 13.

The program stressed tight credit, expanded imports, controls over government spending and improved administrative surveillance of price trends. The two principal items in the project were an increase in the import quota of beef, wheat flour and 22 other agricultural products by more than 30% from the 1972 figures and the tightening of existing easy-money policies. The other measures included: postponement of some low-priority public works projects; price reductions on such items as air fares, imported tobacco products and international cable and telephone fees; and improved price information for consumers.

Private economists criticized the program for vagueness and not providing for price and wage controls.

In other emergency actions aimed at curbing inflation, the government June 29 ordered a further cut in public works outlays, carrying part of budgeted expenditures to 1974, imposed credit restraints and froze the price of rice.

The government adopted another series of anti-inflation measures Aug. 31, including an 8% deferment of fiscal expenditures for public works until the next fiscal year, starting April 1, 1974. It also tightened consumer credit terms for car purchases.

Export controls on about 20 major items were allowed to expire on schedule at the end of August. The Cabinet, which decided on the action Aug. 24, said the curbs, imposed in September 1972, were no longer necessary to help reduce Japan's surplus in its balance of trade with other nations. The items released from controls included radios, stereo sets, home electric appliances, trucks, automobiles and lenses.

EEC backs anti-inflation measures. A series of anti-inflation measures was approved by the nine EEC ministers in Luxembourg June 28.

They agreed to try to moderate the rate of expansion of overall demand, substantially reduce the rate of money expansion by 1974, restrict credit and implement tight budgetary policies.

The ministers also decided to postpone implementation of the second phase of their economic and monetary union, planned for January 1974, which was to entail the creation of common institutions to manage an embryonic currency bloc. The postponement was attributed to the high rate of inflation in Europe, international monetary turbulence and the

continuing refusal of Italy and Britain to join the joint EEC float.

Britain readies 'Stage 3.' Great Britain's "Stage 3" anti-inflation plan, issued Oct. 8, called for more flexibility in wage increases but tighter curbs on prices. The proposals were published in a government Green Paper, or consultative document, and explained to the nation by Prime Minister Edward Heath in a television broadcast.

Heath said he hoped Stage 3 would "keep prices within the limits of what people will be able to afford," adding that prices had risen by 9% in the year since Stage 1 was introduced. He indicated that deadlocked talks with the Trades Union Congress (TUC) precluded a return to a voluntary wage-price control system.

Stage 3 called for a 7% ceiling on pay increases for any group of workers, or if negotiators preferred, up to an average £2.25 (about $5.40) a week, with the maximum to be 350 a year. Workers could also be granted extra payments for efficiency, and new wage accords could contain cost-of-living "threshold safeguards" that would provide additional pay boosts if the retail price index reached 7%.

The new program would maintain current controls on manufacturing prices and profits. It would extend to medium-size firms, with sales of $12 million–$120 million annually, the requirement to obtain government permission for price rises, rather than simply notify the Prices Commission of increases. It would also eliminate "artificial subdivision of enterprises," a tactic used to get around profit margin control. As an investment incentive, the government would allow depreciation costs to be taken into account in requests for price increases.

Heath continued to reject price curbs on food despite the fact that food prices had increased nearly 13% in a year.

The TUC criticized the proposals and called again for price controls on certain food staples. The Confederation of British Industry, representing the nation's major firms, criticized the program as "too inflationary."

France adds to price curbs. Facing soaring inflation, the French government imposed price restraints on a number of basic foods and consumer items Nov. 2. The action sparked widespread strikes by greengrocers and other independent shopkeepers.

The government froze profit margins between wholesale and retail levels on basic foodstuffs such as beef, bread, and certain fruits, vegetables and cheeses, and on some consumer goods, including shoes. Price controls were reintroduced Nov. 3 on some industrial sectors that had been exempted in June 1972 because of foreign competition; only industrial firms with fewer than 20 workers were still exempt from government surveillance.

Official figures released Oct. 29 had shown a .9% increase in the inflation rate for September, following a .7% in August. Food prices had risen 1.3% during September.

Retailers hit by the new price restraints immediately protested the measures. The nation's butchers association said it would not accept the decisions and ignored them. The greengrocers struck in Paris Nov. 8–16, reopening their stores after talks with Agriculture Minister Jacques Chirac Nov. 16 produced an agreement for a meeting with Finance Minister Valery Giscard d'Estaing and hints that the price margin restraints on fruit and vegetables would be made more flexible. The greengrocers' strike had also spread to the provinces.

All small shopkeepers staged a one-day strike Nov. 15 to protest the inflation measures. Cafes, food shops, barbers and other independent merchants closed, while union action shut down supermarkets, department stores, restaurants and independent gas stations.

Giscard d'Estaing announced new anti-inflationary measures Dec. 5.

The steps included sharp restrictions on bank credit to curb consumer spending, reduced government expenditures, increased advance payments of income and company taxes, a rent freeze until June 1974, a 5% ceiling on corporate dividend increases, higher savings deposit interest and closer surveillance of prices.

The new anti-inflation action followed release Nov. 26 of official figures showing that retail prices had increased 1.1% in October, the highest in four years. Prices had been rising at an annual rate of more than 11.2% over the past three months. Food prices had increased by 1.4% in October despite imposition of price controls. (It was announced Nov. 23 that Giscard d'Estaing had agreed to "adjustments" of taxes on some fruits and vegetables, following talks between him and a delegation of greengrocers.)

The guaranteed minimum hourly wage, geared to the inflation rate, was increased from 5.32 francs an hour to 5.43 francs Dec. 1.

General strike staged—A 24-hour general strike called by Socialist and Communist trade unions and parties to protest the government's anti-inflation policies disrupted the nation Dec. 6. The stoppage halted the steel, chemical and other industries, the stock market, docks and ports, and most newspapers and Paris subway trains.

Fresh EEC anti-inflation. action. Finance ministers of the European Economic Community (EEC), at the end of a two-day meeting in Brussels Dec. 4, approved a modest new voluntary anti-inflation program.

Among the recommendations: government curbs on current public spending, postponement of increased civil service hiring and tax changes that would stimulate consumer spending, control of money and credit supplies, harmonization of interest rates to encourage savings, prior notification of price increases, start of an information campaign on price rises and strict application of antitrust regulations.

Dutch Finance Minister Willem Duisenberg agreed to the plan after expressing reservations that any anti-inflation plan that ignored the energy crisis would be useless. He warned that his government would give priority to preserving jobs over fighting inflation as the oil shortages cut industrial activity. His warning came as the nine EEC foreign ministers, also meeting in Brussels, failed to adopt joint energy measures to meet the Arab oil squeeze.

1974

Richard M. Nixon resigned as U.S. President in August 1974. His Administration had failed to halt the price-wage spiral, and he had seen the U.S. economy sink toward recession by the time scandal had forced him out of office. Inflation was increasing during 1974 at rates in excess of 11%, and the nation's "real" Gross National Product was falling. Despite his demands for reduced government spending, Nixon submitted a budget proposing federal expenditures that, for the first time, would exceed $300 billion in a single year. Congress allowed the Economic Stabilization Act to expire as scheduled April 30 without approving proposed legislation to authorize standby wage-price controls. The Nixon Administration had already decontrolled most of the economy, and Nixon used fiscal and monetary policy as his main anti-inflation weapons. Congressional investigators produced additional testimony indicating that the U.S.-Soviet wheat deals of 1972 had helped push up the prices of food in the U.S. and abroad. An even more potent factor in worldwide inflation was the action of the world's oil producing countries. The Arab oil embargo against the U.S. was largely ended March 18 but was followed by further increases in royalties that added to world fuel costs—and ultimately to food prices. Exacerbating the situation was a resumption of deficits in the U.S. trade and payments balances and continued instability of the world monetary system.

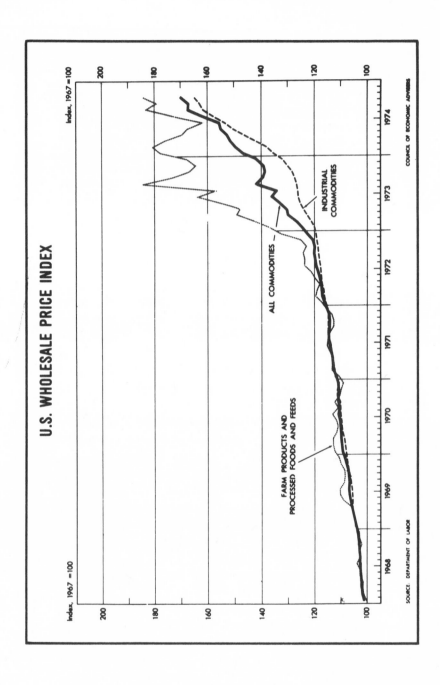

U.S. WHOLESALE PRICE INDEX

Index, 1967 = 100

FARM PRODUCTS AND
PROCESSED FOODS AND FEEDS

ALL COMMODITIES

INDUSTRIAL
COMMODITIES

1968   1969   1970   1971   1972   1973   1974

SOURCE: DEPARTMENT OF LABOR

COUNCIL OF ECONOMIC ADVISERS

Government Policy

Economy Deteriorates

The Nixon Administration came to an end Aug. 9, 1974 as Richard M. Nixon resigned the Presidency at the height of the Watergate scandal. Inflation had grown worse during his final months in office, and the economic situation was widely described as a recession.

As measured by the GNP (Gross National Product) implicit price deflator, inflation increased at an 11.5% annual rate during 1974's first quarter, at an 8.8% rate in the April-June period and at an 11.8% rate in the third quarter. The "real" GNP (adjusted to reflect inflation) declined at a seasonally adjusted annual rate of 6.3% in the first quarter, 1.6% in the second and 2.1% in the third.

GNP slump sparks dispute. The second-quarter slump produced the first period of two consecutive quarters of economic decline since the recession of 1969–70. According to most economists, a recession was generally evidenced by at least two straight quarters of a decline in real GNP.

Commerce Secretary Frederick B. Dent refused to accept that definition, contending that the current downturn lacked the depth, duration and pervasiveness of a recession. Instead, Dent declared, the report "indicates that the downtrend in production is being arrested and that there was also substantial improvement in the rate of inflation." The June quarter represented a "period of adjustment," Dent said, to what he called an ongoing "energy crisis spasm."

Dent's assessments were contradicted July 22 in a report prepared by First National City Bank of New York, the nation's second largest commercial bank. The second quarter GNP figures showed that the economy was "being gripped by a pervasive recession" rather than a temporary slowdown, the report stated. Although the oil embargo caused the first quarter GNP to decline more than otherwise would have been expected, the report said, "there is no escaping the extent of the decline in output" during the first half of 1974. "The U.S. economy has not experienced anything like it [the GNP decline] since the recession of 1957–58," the report stated.

Price indexes rise steadily. The consumer price index, rising steadily to new monthly record heights, reached 139.7% of the 1967 average in January, 141.5% in February, 143.1% in March, 144% in April, 145.6% in May, 147.1% in June, 145.6% in May, 147.1% in June, 148.3% in July and 150.2% in August.

The wholesale price index rose to 146.6% of the 1967 average in January, 149.5% in February, 151.4% in March,

209

152.7% in April, 155% in May, 155.7% in June, 161.7% in July and 157.4% in August.

According to the Commerce Department report, a deterioration in the foreign trade balance, caused largely by increased volume of high-price oil imports, had the single most negative influence on second quarter figures.

Income gain exceeded inflation in '73. A Census Bureau report published July 3 indicated that there had been a 2.2% gain in real purchasing power for families at the 1973 median income level. Gains in income over the year for the typical family totaled 8.4% while prices they paid rose an estimated 6.2%. The median family income increased from $11,116 in 1972 to $12,051 in 1973—nearly double its 1963 level of $6,249.

The report, which was based on a survey conducted in March, also showed that the number of persons with income below the officially defined poverty level ($4,540 in 1973) fell by 1.5 million to about 23 million persons during the year. (However, the statistics did not take into account the effect that soaring food prices had on the poor, indicating that the inflation adjustment for poor families was too small.)

'72, '73 money supply data revised. The Federal Reserve Board announced Jan. 31 that according to revised data, the nation's money supply in 1973 grew at a 5.7% rate.

Growth rate in the money supply, which was equal to the total of private demand, or checking, deposits plus cash in public circulation, also was revised upward for 1972 from an 8.3% expansion rate to 8.7%, which was the highest yearly rate since World War II.

Record drops for productivity, pay value. Worker productivity fell at an annual rate of 5.5% during the first quarter of 1974, according to the Labor Department April 25. It was the biggest decline since 1947 when records were first compiled and much steeper than the .8% drop registered in the fourth quarter of 1973.

The value of workers' paychecks, adjusted to reflect inflation, fell at an annual rate of 5.6% during the first three months of 1974. That figure also set records—it was the fourth consecutive quarterly drop and the biggest decline in two years. At the same time, employers' unit labor costs rose 14.6% despite the fact that hourly compensation, which was not adjusted for inflation, rose only 5.2% (its smallest increase since late 1972).

With the drop in output per worker hour, productivity was 1.8% lower than the figure for 1973's first period; workers' real pay was off 2.8% and unit labor costs were 8.7% higher over the 12-month period.

Productivity, real pay rise—The nation's productivity, measured as output per manhour, registered a 1.4% annual rate gain during the second quarter of 1974 after four consecutive quarters of decline or no growth. The value of workers' paychecks adjusted for inflation also rose during the three-month period, gaining 1.2% at a yearly pace.

In the key manufacturing sector, productivity increased at an annual rate of 4%, but there was a 2.5% decline in productivity in the private nonfarm sector during the second quarter. A real factor in the steep rise in labor costs was the 14.2% rise in workers' compensation.

Despite the gains in productivity, unit labor costs soared by 13% during the second quarter.

Union drive on wages predicted. Labor Secretary Peter J. Brennan predicted Jan. 8 that organized labor "will be looking for its pound of flesh" in its 1974 contract negotiations. "And I'm not saying they are wrong," he added. "If inflation continues," he said, "it will be normal for working people to demand their share of the spoils, and they will be entitled to, as matters are going." Brennan said the government "should not interfere with free collective bargaining."

Brennan said he considered 1973 "a good year for working people." "It's a good year," he said, when "everybody can still be running their automobile as they did in 1973, when the ball parks are full, when people have their television sets and all." He cited the record employment total reached in 1973 and the drop in the jobless rate near the end of the year to 4.5%.

Brennan's views drew fire from others in the Administration and from the ranks of organized labor.

Herbert Stein, chairman of the Council of Economic Advisers, later Jan. 8 contradicted Brennan's contention that workers were entitled to higher wages because of inflation. "We cannot pay workers for food that was not produced and oil we didn't get from the Arabs," Stein said, "Price increases from those sources cannot be compensated by giving more money to workers." The answer, according to Stein, was "to generate additional supplies on the food side and to obtain more energy. Nobody can be insulated if the whole world is going to pay $10 a barrel more for oil."

The United Steelworkers of America would seek a "very substantial improvement" in wages, according to its president, I. W. Abel, Jan. 10. Abel spoke after a meeting of union leaders in Washington to draft demands for a new three-year pact. The current basic steel contract would expire Aug. 1.

Calling the Cost of Living Council's 5.5% wage-price guideline "obsolete," Abel said the union would demand an increase of 10¢ an hour just to catch up with price rises. An additional cost-of-living increment also would be demanded, he said.

USW gets boost in pensions. The AFL-CIO United Steelworkers of America and three major aluminum companies reached agreement Feb. 1 on new contracts that would add cost of living (COL) increments to the pensions paid retired workers. The feature was a breakthrough in contract terms with potential precedent for other industries.

The new pension plan would become effective Feb. 1, 1975 and apply to employes retiring from the date of the agreement. The full-pension retirement age was lowered from 65 to 62 years. The COL escalator, figured at 65% of the annual rise in the Consumer Price Index, would be applied to pensions Feb. 1, 1976 and again a year later.

The new contracts, with the Aluminum Company of America (covering 9,700 workers), Kaiser Aluminum and Chemical Corp. (10,100 workers) and Reynolds Metals Co. (9,700 workers), also made other changes in the pension program. The benefit rate was raised from $9 a month for each year of service to $11–$15, depending on the level of earnings. Pensions of previous retirees were increased $15–$60 per month. Full pensions, with the COL clause and $230 extra a month until they became 62, were authorized for employes retiring because of displacement by permanent shutdown or unable to work because of prolonged layoffs.

Other provisions of the new pacts included wage increases totaling 69.7¢ an hour, or about 15%, over the 40-month term of the agreements. The basic COL clause also was adjusted, effective June 1, to provide for a 1¢ an hour increase in wages for each .3 (was .4) of a point rise in the Consumer Price Index.

Similar pacts set with can companies— The USW reached accord with the major can manufacturers Feb. 14 prior to the strike deadline that midnight. The new three-year contracts followed the pattern of the aluminum pacts. They would cover 37,700 employes at Continental Can Co., American Can Co., National Can Corp. and Crown Cork & Seal Co.

The contracts included the pension improvements with the built-in escalator increases, increases for retired pensioners, the improvement in the original COL clause. The wage provision was worth 61¢ more an hour—28¢ the first year, 16¢ the second and 17¢ the third year.

'Indexation' system debated. University of Chicago economist Milton Friedman stimulated a lively debate within political and academic circles when he suggested that the U.S. adopt a system of wage-price escalators tied to economic indexes to combat inflation. (Some economists referred to the system as "indexing" and "indexation.")

Friedman's proposal was first published in the Jan. 11 issue of Newsweek. He cited Brazil's successful use of the method in gradually reducing inflation from about 30% in 1967 to its current level of about 15% without inhibiting rapid economic growth.

Prior to its adoption of what it called

"monetary correction," Friedman said, Brazil had attempted to suppress inflation rates of more than 100% a year by fixing wages and prices, controlling foreign exchange transactions and using multiple exchange rates. These measures were followed by several years of "tight" money policies. Although inflation was reduced to the level of about 30% a year by 1967, the reduction was accompanied by economic waste, black markets, recession and increased unemployment, Friedman said.

In 1967, however, Brazil "introduced purchasing power escalator clauses into a wide range of contracts" on a voluntary and statutory basis having broad public acceptance. Under the adjustment program, "monetary correction" equal to the amount of inflation was applied to wage rates, bank loans, government securities, personal tax exemptions, the exchange rate, the value of fixed business assets and a variety of other items.

The system proved a remedy for inflation, the conservative economist declared, because it allowed the price system to operate freely while offering protection from wide fluctuations in general prices.

Critics of the Brazilian model charged that the system was designed to protect capital investment rather than wages. They also noted that inflation levels tolerated as politically acceptable by the government and calculated at monetary correction rates did not reflect actual levels of price increases. The continued existence of black markets in Brazil belied the government's claims that inflation had been contained, opponents of the plan declared.

Other critics opposed to the use of escalator clauses in the U.S. rejected the idea as an acceptance of the inevitability of inflation. Indexing would legitimate and build further price increases into the economic system, they said. William J. Fellner of the President's Council of Economic Advisers termed Friedman's proposal a "surrender to inflation." Its use, Fellner warned, would weaken the government's will to impose more orthodox, and often politically unpopular, anti-inflation measures, such as tight money policies and curbs on federal spending.

Supporters of the proposal claimed the new method would eliminate inequities resulting from an inflationary redistribution of income and wealth. The poor and those on fixed incomes were the usual victims of soaring price increases, adjustment proponents noted, while government, which took a larger proportion of taxes out of inflated incomes, and some corporations tended to benefit from the inflationary spiral.

The incomes of an estimated 50 million persons in the U.S. already were pegged by escalator clauses to the Consumer Price Index (CPI)—5.1 million workers with newly negotiated wages rates tied to CPI rises, 13 million food stamp recipients and 31.4 million Social Security and government pensioners.

According to Business Week May 25, the system was utilized in different forms in Israel, Belgium and France. Finland, which had adopted a similar system after World War II, abandoned it in 1968 because of a fear that rising import costs and an increased demand in exports would distort inflation adjustments, according to the magazine.

Waste treatment funds impounded. President Nixon ordered the impoundment of $3 billion of the $7 billion authorized by Congress for the construction of sewage treatment plants in fiscal 1975 beginning July 1. The order was contained in a letter to Environmental Protection Administration (EPA) head Russell E. Train dated Jan. 1 and made public by the EPA Jan. 10.

Nixon explained his action as an effort "to control spending in order to avoid renewed inflation or a requirement for increased taxes." The remaining $4 billion, Nixon said, would allow the states to build the "high priority projects which are most critical for improving water quality."

Congress had anticipated Nixon's action with a bill to ease the effect of possible impoundments of $3 billion or $4 billion. The measure, cleared by voice votes Dec. 21, 1973, set an allocation formula under which no state would receive less sewage treatment aid than in fiscal 1972. Nixon signed the bill Jan. 4.

Pay raise delay ruled illegal. The U.S. Court of Appeals for the District of Columbia held illegal Jan. 25 President Nixon's failure to grant a legislated pay increase to federal workers in 1972. The President had delayed the increase from October 1972 to January 1973 in light of the 1972 wage guidelines.

Nixon pledges economic improvements. President Nixon delivered a State of the Union Message in person before a joint session of Congress Jan. 30. In his nationally televised prime-time address, he pledged there would be no recession, inflation would be checked and the back of the energy crisis broken. He declared major new initiatives for a national health-care insurance plan, welfare reform and mass transit.

Before he began his address, Nixon handed a longer 22,000 word message to Congressional officials.

Among goals Nixon outlined for 1974:

■ "We will break the back of the energy crisis. We will lay the foundation for our future capacity to meet America's energy needs from America's own resources."

■ "We will check the rise in prices without administering the harsh medicine of recession, and we will move the economy into a steady period of growth at a sustainable level."

■ "We will establish a new system that makes high quality health care available to every American in a dignified manner and at a price he can afford."

■ "And we will start on a new road toward reform of a welfare system that bleeds the taxpayer, corrodes the community and demeans those it is intended to assist."

■ "And together with the other nations of the world, we will establish the economic framework within which Americans will share more fully in an expanding world-wide trade and prosperity in the years ahead, with more open access to both markets and supplies."

Nixon said in his message:

In the past five years the average American's real spendable income—that is what you really can buy with your income, even after allowing for taxes and inflation—has increased by 16%.

Despite this record of achievement, as we turn to the year ahead, we hear once again the familiar voice of the perennial prophets of gloom telling us now that because of the need to fight inflation, because of the energy shortage, America may be headed for a recession.

Well, let me speak to that issue head on. There will be no recession in the United States of America.

Primarily due to our energy crisis our economy is passing through a difficult period, but I pledge to you tonight that the full powers of this government will be used to keep America's economy producing and to protect the jobs of America's workers.

We are engaged in a long and hard fight against inflation. There have been and there will be in the future ups and downs in that fight. But if the Congress cooperates in our efforts to hold down the cost of government, we shall win our fight to hold down the cost of living for the American people.

The Budget

Anti-recession moves readied. President Nixon submitted a new budget to Congress Feb. 4 with total federal outlays of $304.4 billion in fiscal 1975*, $29.8 billion more than in fiscal 1974. It was the nation's first $300 billion budget.

Fiscal 1975 receipts were estimated at $295 billion, a $25 billion increase over the previous year. The $9.4 billion deficit was pegged primarily to an anticipated economic slowdown cutting into the normal revenue. The increase in outlays was more fixed, with approximately 90% of the increase in mandatory spending areas, such as interest on the national debt and maintenance of the Social Security system.

On a "full-employment" basis (budget totals calculated on a basis of full employment—"conventionally defined as a 4% unemployment rate," the President said), receipts would rise and spending drop compared with the published figures for an $8 billion surplus in fiscal 1975 ($4 billion in fiscal 1974).

The new estimates for fiscal 1974 were $274.7 billion in expenditures and $270 billion for receipts, a deficit of $4.7 billion.

To better gauge the scope of the budget totals and direction of trends, the President forecast that spending totals, under current programs and proposals only and calculated on a full-employment basis, would rise to $329.4 billion by fiscal 1976 for a $10 billion surplus and to $390.8 billion by fiscal 1979 for a $37 billion surplus.

The President defined his budget as one

*Begins July 1 and ends June 30, 1975

of "moderate restraint" and said special emphasis was put on "the proper fiscal balance to keep the economy on the track to sustain high employment and more stable prices." The budget continued, he said, "a policy of fiscal responsibility as part of a continuing anti-inflation program."

"In the face of economic uncertainty," Nixon added, the budget also "would maintain the flexibility to take further action, if needed, to offset the effects of energy shortages." "My Administration is developing and will be prepared to use," he said, "a range of measures to support the economy if that should be necessary— measures tailored to the special conditions of the energy shortage."

He said the economic slowdown "shouldn't be permitted to go too far."

The new budget contained few new initiatives and, unlike its controversial predecessor, few cutbacks of existing programs.

The only cutbacks targeted by the President in fiscal 1975 were in ending the Hill-Burton grant program for construction of hospitals, phasing out special education aid for federally-impacted areas and ending the antipoverty domain of the Office of Economic Opportunity, which would be replaced by the Administration's own "economic adjustment assistance" effort.

The budget did not suggest any increase in basic tax rates, aside from the already proposed plan to tax "windfall" profits of oil companies.

Total corporate income tax revenue was estimated at $48 billion. The total income tax from individuals was expected to be $129 billion.

The largest increases in the new budget were alloted to defense, pollution control and payments to individuals. The latter area, directed to retired persons, veterans, the poor and the unemployed, was noted by the President. Federal money, as a result of his New Federalism philosophy, he said, "is being channeled into payments to individuals and into broader, more flexible assistance to state and local governments." And "the federal government is having and will continue to have an increasingly indirect budgetary impact on the marketplace."

The President also noted that "defense costs have been a decreasing share of our national budget, falling from 44% of federal spending in [fiscal] 1969 to an estimated 29% in 1975. . . . The form that Federal spending takes has shifted dramatically away from support for direct federal operations and toward benefit payments to individuals and grants to state and local governments."

However, defense spending remained massive. Its $86 billion, if added to one other huge item, the $63 billion in outlays for Social Security, comprised about half the total budget. Two-thirds of the total was attained by addition of three other items—$29 billion for interest on the national debt, $14 billion for Medicare and $12.6 billion for retirement payments for former federal employes ($7 billion for civilians, $5.6 billion for military personnel).

Aides affirm anti-recession intent—At a briefing on the new budget Feb. 4, Frederic Malek, deputy director of the Office of Management and Budget, said the President was not going "to tolerate a recession" and "if we have to bust the budget to prevent it, we'll bust the budget."

Treasury Secretary George P. Shultz, at the same briefing, offered a list of steps the Administration recommended to counter a recession. He stressed that tax reduction was "at the end of the list" because of the necessity to maintain federal revenue.

Shultz's anti-recession steps included: unemployment compensation improvements, requiring legislation; accelerated federal projects in high unemployment areas; accelerated federal payments to the public; expanded public housing and

---

The Budget Dollar

Where it comes from:

Individual income taxes	42¢
Social insurance receipts	28¢
Corporation income taxes	16¢
Excise taxes	6¢
Borrowing	3¢
Other	5¢

Where it goes:

Benefit payments to individuals	37¢
National defense	29¢
Grants to states and localities	17¢
Other federal operations	10¢
Net interest	7¢

defense spending; "classic" expansionist monetary policy; prompt action by Congress on appropriations; and less tax-withholding on individuals.

Defense. Fiscal 1975 spending for defense was budgeted to rise $6.3 billion from the previous year to $85.8 billion, the biggest defense budget in the nation's history. The President also requested a supplemental defense appropriation for fiscal 1974 of $6.2 billion, of which $2.8 billion was to improve the military readiness posture and $3.4 billion was for pay increases.

Personnel costs accounted for 55% of the fiscal 1975 budget, and a $5.5 billion rise in total obligational authority (including commitment to appropriate funds

in future years) sought by the Pentagon, to the $92.6 billion level, was attributed entirely to pay and price increases, the pay share being $3.5 billion.

The budget was posed to maintain strength at current levels—no major expansion of combat forces was planned in the immediate future—and increase "readiness" by modernizing arms and substantially increasing research and development, particularly of strategic weapons.

Pentagon officials pointed out that fiscal 1975 defense spending was a continuation of a decline both as a percentage of the total federal budget, to 27.2%, and of the gross national product, to 5.9%, the lowest proportions since 1950.

Strategic forces were to receive a $700

Budget Receipts

(In billions of dollars for the fiscal year)

	1973 actual	1974 estimate	1975 estimate
Individual income taxes	103.2	118.0	129.0
Corporation income taxes	36.2	43.0	48.0
Social insurance taxes and contributions (trust funds)	64.5	77.9	85.6
Excise taxes	16.3	17.1	17.4
Estate and gift taxes	4.9	5.4	6.0
Customs duties	3.2	3.5	3.8
Miscellaneous receipts	3.9	5.0	5.2
Total receipts	**232.2**	**270.0**	**295.0**

Budget Outlays

(In billions of dollars for the fiscal year)

	1973 actual	1974 estimate	1975 estimate
National defense	76.0	80.6	87.7
International affairs and finance	3.0	3.9	4.1
Education and manpower	10.2	10.8	11.5
Health	18.4	23.3	26.3
Income security	73.1	85.0	100.1
Veterans benefits and services	12.0	13.3	13.6
Agriculture and rural development	6.2	4.0	2.7
Natural resources and environment	.6	.6	3.1
Commerce and transportation	13.1	13.5	13.4
Community development and housing	4.1	5.4	5.7
General revenue sharing	6.6	6.1	6.2
General government	5.5	6.8	6.8
Space research and technology	3.3	3.2	3.3
Special allowance for acceleration of energy research and development			.5
Allowances*		.3	1.1
Interest	22.8	27.8	29.1
Interest received by trust funds	−5.4	−6.4	−7.1
Employer share, employe retirement	−2.9	−3.5	−3.6
Total outlays	**246.5**	**274.7**	**304.4**
Budget Deficit	**14.3**	**4.7**	**9.4**

*For pay raises and contingencies   Source: Office of Management and Budget million increase from fiscal 1974 to $7.6 billion. The funds covered continued development of the Trident submarine and its missile, the B1 long-range bomber and $248 million for the new nuclear warheads.

General purpose forces were allotted $29.2 billion, a $1.3 billion increase from fiscal 1974.

Service force levels were set at a total of 2,152,000 by June 30, 1975, a decrease of 22,000 from the fiscal 1974 budget level.

The only major shifts in conventional forces would be adding one-third of an Army division to the current 13 and an additional aircraft carrier for a total of 15, six nuclear attack submarines and five other warships.

The service fund breakdown: Navy $29.6 billion; Air Force $28 billion; Army $23.6 billion.

The new budget directed $1.9 billion to the Southeast Asia theater of operations—$450 million to maintain U.S. forces in Thailand and the remainder to support South Vietnamese forces.

Space. The space program budget was $3.3 billion, up $95 million from fiscal 1974. A major share, $800 million, went to the space shuttle project. While this was a $325 million increase from the previous year's funding, it was below the space agency planning level and would necessitate a six-month stretch-out for the project's timetable to the second quarter of 1979.

Energy. Federal spending on energy research and development was projected at $1.6 billion, an increase from an estimated $942 million in fiscal 1974. In addition to focusing on coal and nuclear fission and fusion, $48 million was sought for development of geothermal energy and $50 million for solar energy projects. Large sums—$179 million—were allotted to environmental control, with emphasis on increasing supplies of low-pollution coal, and research on energy conservation, $129 million.

Development of a coal liquefaction plant on a cost-sharing basis with industry was being planned. Projects also were being funded for augmenting coal production.

The Atomic Energy Commission budget reflected the energy crisis. For the first time in its history, the agency would spend more (58%) on civilian activities than on its military aspect. Funding for nuclear weapons testing, for the first time in 10 years, fell below $100 million, to $97.5 million.

The energy situation also affected the National Science Foundation, whose budget rose $32 million to $630 million, not all of the increase devoted to special energy projects. Work on a new radioastronomy facility was to be accelerated, as well as the agency's special project to find practical applications for science and technology, known as Research Applied to National Needs.

Health. Nixon mentioned his plan for "basic reform in the financing of medical care," to bring "comprehensive insurance protection against medical expenses within reach of all Americans." But the proposed date was January 1976 so there were no funds for it in the fiscal 1975 budget.

The budget was dominated by the Medicare and Medicaid programs providing health care for the aged and poor, which absorbed 60¢ of every health dollar. The increase alone in Medicare spending was massive—$2 billion—which took the program to the $14.2 billion level. Medicaid spending followed with a $736 million increase to $6.6 billion.

The Administration made several proposals to try to hold down these costs. It suggested eliminating payments under Medicaid for dental care, and it planned tighter admission procedure for Medicaid patients proposed for elective surgery and an attempt to shorten hospital stays.

A $149 million increase was proposed for medical research spending at the National Institutes of Health, whose total budget would 'e $2 billion. But authorizations for all of the member institutes except those studying cancer and heart disease were decreased.

The health budget contained a new proposal for a $75 million program to finance regional health planning. The funds would provide for 200 regional health systems boards to plan facility sites and assist the states in regulation of rates and capital expenditures of hospitals and other health care units.

Welfare. The new Supplemental Security Income (SSI) program for the aged poor, disabled and blind was allotted $3.9 billion for fiscal 1975 for 5.6 million beneficiaries. The total of beneficiaries for the previous year was put at 3.4 million.

A $3.9 billion figure for fiscal 1975 also was attached to the program of Aid to Families with Dependent Children (AFDC). But this total was a $14 million drop from the previous year's anticipated total, which was a drastic reversal from the customary increases—up to 15%—of recent years. Little or no growth was forecast by officials for the next year and a closer watch for payments to ineligible recipients was given credit for the decline.

The Health, Education and Welfare Department (HEW), whose entire budget was up $14 billion to $111 billion, was currently campaigning against payments to ineligible recipients and overpayments. The ineligibility factor was said to consist of 10% of persons receiving welfare; overpayments were said to encompass 23% of the eligible recipients. The department wanted to reduce the ineligible factor to 3% and overpayments to 5% and set a deadline of June 30, 1975 for the states to reach these marks, using loss of federal welfare funds as inducement.

On the food programs, the Administration advocated HEW administration of $5.9 billion worth of welfare programs currently lodged in the Agriculture Department. These included the food stamp program, budgeted at $3.9 billion, up $900 million, and school lunch subsidies and nutrition education.

Agriculture. The fiscal 1975 budget for the Agriculture Department was $9.3 billion, but this would be drastically reduced to $3.3 billion if Congress sanctioned the Administration's proposal to transfer the food-welfare programs to HEW.

Drastic reductions also were built into other areas of the department's budget. Direct payments to farmers, pegged to crop prices or failures, running at the $2.5 billion level for fiscal 1974, were expected to drop to $461 million in fiscal 1975, reflecting record exports and the price escalation.

The loan level for rural housing was set at $2.1 billion, but the department anticipated recouping $200 million more than that from selling off its inventory of commercial paper.

Transportation. The budget contained considerable thrust for transportation spending and commitment to spend in the future. Much of the impetus was directed at mass transit, reflecting the energy crisis. The commitment in new spending authority under a new urban transportation program would begin in fiscal 1975 at the $2.3 billion level, earmarked either for transit-system capital projects, city streets and roads or for transit system operating losses. The commitment was a 28% boost from the $1.8 billion funding level of fiscal 1974. $1.4 billion of the authority would come from the Transportation Department, a 54% increase; the remainder would be taken from the Highway Trust Fund, which was estimated to suffer a 2.7% drop in fiscal 1975 revenue from its gasoline tax income because of the fuel shortage.

Half the $1.4 billion for transit aid would be apportioned to states by a formula based on population, with the cities opting for capital projects or operating losses. The other half, or $700 million, would be in grants for specific rail-transit projects.

A new six-year program, based on the 1973 opening of the Highway Trust Fund to mass transit funding, was planned to rise to a $2.7 billion authorization by fiscal 1977 before becoming funded entirely from general revenues, when the Highway Fund could revert to completion of the interstate highway program.

The $700 million spending in fiscal 1975 for transit buses and subways contrasted with the $488.5 million in fiscal 1974. Comparable highway spending was $4.88 billion, up from $4.7 billion.

The budget also envisioned a new rural bus program starting with $10 million in fiscal 1975 and rising to $20 million in fiscal 1976 and to $45 million in fiscal 1977. It would be a demonstration project in aid to rural areas for buying and operating buses.

While obligation for highway aid would decline 3% in fiscal 1975 to $4.8 billion, increases were set for some safety projects, such as bridge replacement. The authority level also was augmented to allow inducement to the states to act to reduce traffic fatalities, such as enacting seatbuckling legislation.

Amtrak funding was raised in the fiscal 1974 budget year to $155 million, an extra $52 million to be requested from Congress. The loan guaranty for fiscal 1974, for purchase of locomotives and passenger cars, was to rise to $217 million, up from $100 million.

The restructured Northeast railway system was to receive $68.5 million in fiscal 1975.

Spending for aviation was projected at $2.1 billion (up from $1.9 billion), for merchant shipbuilding at $282.8 million (up from $200 million), for the Coast Guard at $908.6 million (up from $847.6 million).

The share for airport improvement would rise 23% to $290 million, for airway systems 27% to $320 million. An increase in user fees for private planes was projected, without details.

Spending for a civil supersonic transport (SST), a project killed in Congress, was continued in the budget, but on a greatly reduced scale; $3.6 million was allocated for a study of an SST's effect on the environment ($6 million in fiscal 1974); $8.5 million ($12.5 million currently) was proposed for a study of SST wing design and engine noise.

Transportation research and development work was boosted $27 million to $417 million in fiscal 1975. It was focusing on safer, more efficient automobiles, more efficient use of freight cars by railroads, bigger buses and better mass transit.

Education. As outlined in the President's special message to Congress, the focus in aid to education was on consolidating grants to elementary and secondary schools. The effort was to reach $2.9 billion by fiscal 1975 from an additional $179 million requested for fiscal 1974 and a $23 million request the next year.

The program to provide emergency school aid for districts coping with desegregation problems was to be shrunk to one-third its size at conception, which had been $1 billion in the original plan. Because of existing authority, spending would rise $40 million to $233 million in fiscal 1975. The Administration asked an additional $75 million.

The budget also scaled down the "impacted aid" program, channeled into school districts with abnormal numbers of federal employes. It proposed a $65 million cut in spending to $482 million by denying eligibility for children whose parents worked but did not live on federal property.

The budget provided a new $15 million program of aid to public libraries, mainly for instruction in library service but it proposed to cut current support for public libraries and to eliminate support for college libraries. It also sought to reduce land-grant college aid by $15 million.

A funding increase of $17 million to the $113 million level was requested for the new National Institute of Education.

Environment. Aside from grants for construction of sewage plants, which was an area under litigation, the Environmental Protection Agency (EPA) budget for operating programs was $731 million, up $215 million from fiscal 1974. Of the increase, $169 million was allotted for energy research, which comprised $191 million of the agency's budget.

The research areas were improved technology for the electric utility and auto industries, health effects of pollutants and environmental impact of new sources of energy.

The sewage plant funding was in the courts from local challenge to impoundment. Congress had authorized commitment on a $7 billion scale for fiscal 1975, a scale endorsed by the EPA, but Nixon, calling the total "excessive," directed the EPA to spend only $4 billion.

Economic development. The Administration planned to seek $330 million for economic development in fiscal 1975. The fiscal 1974 total was $282.5 million. But the budget proposed a redrafting of the operation to decentralize it with block grants to the states, along Nixon's "New

Federalism" philosophy featuring special revenue sharing, with the funding split between the older programs and the new ones.

The older Economic Development Administration (EDA) and its regional commissions were budgeted at $170 million for EDA, down $70.6 million, and $35 million for the regional commissions, down $7 million. The reduced levels were set for "an orderly transition" period to the new program, an Economic Adjustment Assistance agency which would replace the EDA to operate its "New Federalism" concept. The Administration intended to ask for initial funding for a supplemental fiscal 1975 appropriation of $100 million after Congress established it.

Filling out the $330 million total to be sought by the Administration for economic development, $25 million was requested for economic aid to Indians, now under purview of the EDA. The request, however, would come from the Interior Department, which was putting the program into its Bureau of Indian Affairs.

The EDA budget for public works grants and loans to stimulate development of economically depressed areas was set at $135 million, down $39 million from fiscal 1974. In addition to the change in Indian aid, the deduction reflected the Administration's plan to end EDA's Public Works Impact Program providing relief for the construction industry when necessary through temporary employment.

Urban development. Spending by the Housing and Urban Development Department was projected at $5.6 billion for fiscal 1975, up from $5 billion. Payments to subsidize low- and moderate-income housing were allotted $2.3 billion, up from $1.9 billion. The Administration's proposal for a reshaped community development program was budgeted at $560 million, although this was dependent upon Congressional sanction of the new program. The urban renewal program, which the Administration terminated in 1973 because of the uncertain status of the new legislation, was budgeted at $1.1 billion.

Further uncertainty existed in projections for the subsidized housing area.

Subsidized starts in fiscal 1975 were estimated at 285,000 units, with leased units accounting for about half the total. The previous year figure was 187,000.

Manpower. Manpower programs were funded at about the same level as in fiscal 1974, receiving $23 million more for a total of $4.8 billion in fiscal 1975. The programs included operation of state employment services, vocational rehabilitation, job training and child care related to jobs and veterans' programs.

The Comprehensive Manpower Assistance program, slated to begin July 1, was funded at $1.6 billion. Under it, state and local agencies would assume administration of many federal job aid and training programs funded with $1.4 billion in fiscal 1974. The total did not include the public service jobs program, which was put under the new setup after separate budgeting in previous years.

In reference to the switch to state and local administration, the budget said that "there are significant limitations to the impact that manpower programs can exert on national economic conditions," that the effect of the programs on total employment "cannot be adequately measured or controlled."

The Work Incentive Program to provide job training to recipients of Aid to Families with Dependent Children was maintained at the $300 million level, the same as in fiscal 1974.

Foreign aid. The President requested $4.1 billion for foreign economic and other nonmilitary assistance. The largest amount, $1.6 billion, was targeted for the poorer nations.

The Food for Peace program was budgeted at $742 million, a $54 million cut "because of commodity shortages and increased food prices," according to the budget. Requests for Indochina rehabilitation, including South Vietnam, Laos and Cambodia, totaled $648 million. North Vietnam was not included.

Pay raise for Congress. The President proposed a pay raise for Congress members, Cabinet officers and federal judges. The totals proposed (current salary in parentheses): senators and representatives ($42,500) $45,700 in March, $49,100 in 1975, $52,800 in 1976; Cabinet ($60,-

000) $64,500 in 1975; top federal civilian executives ($36,000) $38,700 in March, $41,600 in 1975, $44,700 in 1976; Supreme Court chief justice ($62,500) $67,200 in 1975, associate justices ($60,000) $64,500 in 1975.

(The pay-raise proposal was vetoed by 72–26 Senate vote March 6.)

Defense budget boost to aid economy. James R. Schlesinger, secretary of defense, told the House Appropriations Committee Feb. 26 that the White House at the last minute had added more than $1 billion to its proposed fiscal 1975 military budget to help "stimulate the economy." Schlesinger said the late addition was justified on military grounds and represented funds that originally had been trimmed from the Pentagon's budget request by the White House Office of Management and Budget.

Committee Chairman George H. Mahon (D, Tex.) said he had it on "good authority" that overall defense spending was to be increased by $5 billion to stimulate the economy. Mahon questioned why this stimulation had to take place in the military sector of the economy and not the civilian sector.

An ancillary matter before the panel was a supplemental budget request of $2.8 billion by the Pentagon for fiscal 1974. The request, made, the Pentagon said, to increase the readiness of U.S. forces in light of lessons learned in the 1973 Middle East War, included items providing for the start of a $500 million program to stretch the fuselage of the C-141 military transport produced by Lockheed Aircraft Corp., and $700 million to be given to U.S. airlines to modify their Boeing 747 transports, grounded for lack of jet fuel and passenger traffic, to carry military cargo and troops in an emergency.

These additions, Mahon charged, were made at the last minute to "take up the slack" in the aerospace industry and to help "bail out" the airlines. Schlesinger denied the charge and insisted the additions were for military purposes.

The $2.8 billion supplemental request also came under fire from Sen. William Proxmire (D, Wis.), chairman of the Subcommittee on Priorities and Economy in Government of the Joint Economic Committee, who accused the Pentagon of juggling expenses from one year to another to give the appearance that the defense budget was leveling off.

Proxmire also challenged the Administration's contention that the 1975 spending request "means no more than holding our own as compared to 1974." A study by the subcommittee indicated that the budget included a real 8% increase, after allowing for inflation, he said.

Proxmire warned May 1 that "if Congress approves the record-high defense budget . . . , the chances of bringing inflation under control in 1974 will be reduced to zero." He quoted the April monthly economic letter of the First National City Bank of New York as asserting that "if defense spending swings up as planned . . . , the result could be inflationary stimulus to an economy that has already started on the road to recovery."

Government Plans & Actions

Economic report to Congress. In his annual economic message to Congress and a companion report prepared by the Council of Economic Advisers (CEA), President Nixon revealed the Administration's strategies for dealing with a "highly uncertain" outlook for 1974 when inflation and recession both threatened to overtake the economy.

The forecasts, which were submitted to Congress Feb. 1, stressed the need for policy flexibility in dealing with the possibility of economic stagnation, prolonged inflation and the domestic consequences of international economic upheavals.

CEA Chairman Herbert Stein and Treasury Secretary George P. Shultz both reaffirmed Nixon's flat assertion that a recession could be avoided. Their remarks, however, were qualified by an attempt to redefine the term recession. Stein said Feb. 1 that the standard definition—two quarters of declining economic output—was a "simplistic and mechanistic" guide having "no standing in the economic profession."

Under Stein's new definition, a recession was a "departure of the economy from its normal growth path of considerable intensity, durability and breadth."

At a briefing on the budget Feb. 4, Shultz also supported Nixon's statement. "I'm sure the President will be proved right," he said, "especially as we define it [a recession]." "This classification process is to a considerable extent a political exercise," he added.

(A Harris poll released Feb. 2 showed that 54% of those surveyed believed the nation already was undergoing a recession. A larger proportion, 61%, felt the country would experience a recession within one year.)

1974 forecasts—Gross National Product would reach $1.39 trillion, up by 8% in one year. However, only 1% of that would be "real" growth, since inflation was expected to advance by 7%. In a briefing for reporters Feb. 1, Stein said he expected output to shrink over an unspecified "interval," but that by the second half of 1974, inflation would gain at a rate of less than 5% as food and fuel price increases were put "behind us."

Stein predicted that consumer prices would rise by 6% in 1974, compared with 8.2% in 1973. Unemployment, he said, would "average a little above 5.5%" but would not reach 6%.

On wage-price controls, the council said "the nation may now be running into a problem which is new, at least in magnitude, and potentially very serious: the uncertainty created for private investment, and all private long-term commitments, by government economic controls that are unprecedented in scope and unpredictable in operation.

"Taken together, the controls connected with the energy shortage and the environmental regulations add up to a massive entry of government into the affairs of almost every business in the country." Nixon added, "We will continue our policy of progressive removal of price and wage controls in order to restore the flexibility needed for efficiency and expansion in a time of economic strain."

Regarding anti-recession measures, Nixon said, "It is extremely important to be prepared with fiscal measures to support or restrain the economy if it is clearly running outside the general track

described here for 1974. We will be prepared to support economic activity and employment by additional budgetary measures, if necessary."

On the oil crisis, the council said the situation "does not require any decline in the level of economic activity in the industrialized world," but added there was a danger of a world recession if nations reacted to the high oil prices by "squeezing down the economy at home or by checking imports and spurring exports."

Nixon concluded his message with the observation that "the American people generally prospered despite the inflation of 1973." "As I see it," he said, 1974 "will be a good year for the economy" as a whole.

Administration wants controls ended. Administration spokesmen Feb. 6 urged Congress not to renew legal authority for the Economic Stabilization Act, which was due to expire April 30, and thereby end wage-price controls for all but two industries—health care and petroleum products.

Treasury Secretary George P. Shultz and John T. Dunlop, director of the Cost of Living Council (CLC), also told a subcommittee of the Senate Banking Committee that Congress need not legislate standby authority for President Nixon to control the economy; however, they suggested that Congress give the CLC new authority to function as an inflation-watchdog agency after April 30 with the power to hold public hearings, gather information and monitor industries' decontrol commitments to restrain prices and expand production.

The recommendations reflected the Administration's belief that broad economic controls had outlived their usefulness and could "become an inflationary force in and of themselves." According to Shultz, Nixon preferred to rely on monetary and budgetary policies to check inflation.

Shultz and Dunlop said the gradual process of decontrol would continue through April as Phase 4 restraints were lifted in return for pledges from industries that prices would be held down. To avoid eroding the CLC's bargaining position in the interval, they said, those companies not cooperating in the decontrol negotiations could be included with the petroleum and health care industries in the post-April 30 program of mandatory controls.

Dunlop told Congress Feb. 6 that costs of Phase 4 to the government in federal salaries and other expenses would total nearly $80 million by April 30. Previous phases of the economic stabilization program, including freezes, had cost about $118 million. According to various estimates, Dunlop said, the nation's industries had spent $721 million–$2 billion in complying with the Administration's wage and price regulations.

Controls eased. The CLC lifted price controls from most nonferrous metal alloys, the Wall Street Journal reported Jan. 7. The CLC Feb. 15 exempted ferrous and nonferrous scrap metal from Phase 4 limits.

The CLC Jan. 7 allowed manufacturers of rubber tires to raise prices an average 3.3%, their second such increase in three months.

In other action on price requests reported by the Journal Jan. 6, the CLC permitted six major firms to raise prices 2.9%–31.5% after the requested increases were trimmed slightly. Three other firms won approval for price boosts ranging from 3.3%–33.1% after small cutbacks were made in their proposals Jan. 10. Kellogg Co. was allowed a 2.6% increase instead of the requested 3.3% and Nabisco Inc. was permitted to lift prices 5.4% instead of 6.6%, in action reported Jan. 15.

Final price regulations limiting the increase in hospital costs to 7.5% annually and physicians' fees to 4% a year were issued Jan. 16. The final rules, effective retroactive to Jan. 1, were eased slightly to allow hospitals to decide whether to shift to Phase 4 for this fiscal year or to remain under Phase 3 limits for the rest of the fiscal year. Other rule changes permitted the hospitals to calculate free care, capital improvements and changes in their mix of patients against cost guidelines.

In a decision announced Jan. 24, health care facilities also were allowed to pass through increases in fuel costs on dollar for dollar basis.

A federal district court in Washington barred the CLC Feb. 7 from enforcing its price control guidelines for nursing homes. The ruling jeopardized the Administration's plans to continue wage-price restrictions for the health industry after the Economic Stabilization Act expired April 30.

According to the court, a 6.5% ceiling on price increases conflicted with Medicare and Medicaid statutes requiring that institutions be reimbursed for all "reasonable care" cost increases. The court also declared that the guidelines were "arbitrary and capricous" because they singled out nursing homes without demonstrating they had an inflationary influence on the economy. An estimated 20,000 nursing homes were affected by the ruling.

In other CLC action, wage and price controls were removed from the mobile home, recreational vehicle and semiconductor industries Jan. 21.

Steel producers were allowed to raise prices an additional .5% in action announced Jan. 25. The increase, worth $65 million to the nation's 26 steel companies, brought the total price increases allowed the steel industry since September 1973 to 4.54%, or $756 million. Steel makers had sought a 7.07% increase worth $1 billion.

The CLC also removed a restriction on how much the price of any individual steel product could be raised, but the weighted average price increase remained under Phase 4 guidelines.

Anti-inflationary wage and price controls were removed Jan. 30 from petrochemical feedstocks and products made from feedstocks, such as plastic and synthetic rubber. As a result of the action, it was expected that there would be a 15% increase in production in the industry, which had been hard hit with short supplies and employment layoffs because of the energy crisis.

Wage and price controls were ended at the same time for the rubber tire industry. Five of the largest firms, representing 75% of the industry's output, agreed to limit wholesale price increases to a weighted average of 5% on passenger car tires through Aug. 1. They also agreed to limit retail price increases on small car tires to 4% and increase production in this area.

Higher prices totaling $1 billion were likely to result from decontrol actions in these two sectors of the economy, CLC officials said.

Mandatory wage and price controls were lifted Feb. 11 for Checker Motors Corp.'s vehicle production and for 15 companies that reconditioned steel drums. Price controls were removed from stevedoring and marine terminal operations.

Wage and price restrictions were removed Feb. 12 from makers of rendered products, such as inedible tallow, grease, animal protein and lard.

Manufacturers of nonrubber shoes were freed from wage-price curbs on Feb. 15.

Under fresh decontrol orders, wage and price controls were lifted from the following industries: the $25 million a year postcard manufacturing industry, reported Feb. 20; the $9 billion a year furniture industry (12 of the largest manufacturers pledged to limit price increases to 3% through July 1), reported Feb. 25; the $2 billion a year valve-making industry, the $2.3 billion a year oil-field and mining machinery industries, reported Feb. 27; the $4.6 billion a year eyeglasses and scientific instrument industry and the $2.3 billion a year jewelry and tableware industry, reported March 6.

In action Feb. 28, steelmakers were allowed to implement price increases averaging 5% for costs incurred since mid-November 1973 to Jan. 31. Price adjustments also could be made once a month on a dollar for dollar basis without prior notification to reflect increases in the cost of iron and steel scrap.

A two-month moratorium on increases in auto insurance was lifted March 4. The freeze had been imposed Jan. 17 while the CLC studied the effect of the gasoline shortage on the industry.

In other decontrol actions, wage and price limits were lifted March 6 from fabricated lumber and wood products industry. The makers of industrial fasteners were freed from Phase 4 curbs March 7.

Controls lifted for most retailers—Wage and price controls were removed Feb. 1 for most general merchandise retailers, but those selling food, motor vehicles and parts and petroleum products remained subject to Phase 4 restrictions.

In return for early action on decontrol, the CLC obtained pledges from the nation's 10 largest retail chains that, through Aug. 1, they would hold their pretax operating profit margins at the same level set in the period beginning Feb. 1, 1973 and ending Jan. 31. Industry and government officials said they believed competition would also serve to check an immediate and large rise in prices.

The CLC action affected those businesses employing at least 60 persons and having annual sales of at least $50 million. (Smaller retail outfits comprising 50% of total retail sales had been decontrolled in May 1972.) The group of retail firms decontrolled, with $120 billion in sales, represented 25% of the nation's total retail sales. They handled goods equal to 15% of the Consumer Price Index.

Although mandatory controls were lifted, the group continued to be required to file quarterly reports with the CLC, which would monitor the industry's compliance with price restraint pledges.

Nixon renews 'no recession' pledge. At his press conference Feb. 25, Nixon repeated his pledge of "no recession" in 1974.

Current economic problems did not constitute a recession, Nixon said, "We are going through what I would say is a downturn in the economy at this point . . . [but] for the balance of the year, the prospects are good."

His optimistic predictions were justified, Nixon said, because the energy shortage had passed from the crisis stage to the more manageable problem stage, and because he expected that the nation's food supply would increase over the year, forcing down prices. "Almost two-thirds of the price increase—the increase in prices last year which was at a very high rate—was due to energy and also to the problem of food," Nixon said. By dealing directly with these factors and utilizing the Cost of Living Council in the post-Phase 4 period, Nixon declared, "I believe that we will bring inflation under control as the year goes on."

Nixon conceded that the inflation problem "is still a very nagging one" and that the latest increase in consumer prices was a "troublesome" problem. "We are going to continue to fight it [inflation]," he continued. "It's going to take responsibility on the part of the Congress to keep the budget within the limits that we have laid out. It's also going to take an effort, on the part of our farmers, an effort on the part of the Administration in the field of energy and the rest so that we can get the supplies out, because the answer to higher prices is not simply controls—controls have been tried—and controls have been found wanting."

Nixon said at a televised news conference March 6 that the best advice he was receiving was "that there will not be a recession in 1974."

He reiterated that "the back of the energy crisis has been broken" and he expected by mid-year that the prices of energy would be in check and "even moving downward." A record food crop was predicted, which would tend to bring the price upsurge in food "under control."

While inflation was "a very sticky problem and will remain so for some time, we see the problem being much less difficult as the year goes on," Nixon said.

At a luncheon in Chicago March 15, Nixon said inflation would "go down" the latter part of the year "provided we are responsible in our government spending programs and that the Congress does not go on a wild spending spree." It would go down because the energy crisis had been reduced to a problem and the prospects for food production were good, Nixon said.

Meany cites 'deepening' recession—AFL-CIO President George Meany assailed the Nixon Administration's economic policies April 19, citing recent government reports. "The second Nixon recession, which the President pledged would not occur, is deepening," he said. "The American people are trapped by uncontrolled inflation, tight money and declining production—all the direct result of Nixon economic policies."

"Almost without exception, every economic alarm has now been sounded," Meany said.

Post-Phase 4 controls proposed. The Cost of Living Council (CLC) Feb. 21 published details of the Administration's legislative proposals for economic controls that, if passed by Congress, would take effect upon expiration of the Economic Stabilization Act April 30.

Proposed regulations would maintain controls on certain wages while discarding most price control mechanisms. The Administration bill would grant the President the authority to limit wage increases won by unions on contracts having reopener clauses taking effect after April 30. The legislation also would empower the President to limit full wage increases won in contracts but reduced by the CLC during the period of wage-price controls. Another pay restraint would continue controls on executive compensation for the duration of each company's fiscal year that began before May 1.

Other proposals:

The CLC could monitor wages, prices and inflationary forces in general through 1975, but it would lack the power to limit these factors; however, the CLC could enforce price commitments negotiated during Phase 4 with certain industries in return for early decontrol.

The health care and petroleum industries, and possibly other industries that proved recalcitrant on the issue of voluntary price commitments, would remain subject to controls after Phase 4 ended.

Controls extension killed. The House Banking Committee voted April 5 to postpone indefinitely any action that would extend the Economic Stabilization Act beyond its April 30 expiration date. The Senate Banking Committee had taken similar action to table consideration of a standby controls measure March 26, thus thwarting Administration plans to continue mandatory wage and price restrictions for the health care and petroleum industries. (The CLC had warned that hospital costs would rise 16%–17% a year without federal controls compared with a 10%–11% increase if controls were maintained.)

The Cost of Living Council (CLC) had freed major portions of the economy from economic controls, but in the negotiations leading to early decontrol releases, officials had won pledges of price restraints from many important sectors of the economy. Those industries unwilling to give price restraint pledges had been threatened with a continuation of wage and price controls after April 30, but that bargaining weapon was nullified by Congressional opposition to any form of extended controls.

The committee votes, 21–10 in the House and 11–4 in the Senate, also indicated that most Republicans and many Democrats rejected even a limited research and monitoring role for the CLC after April 30 to enforce the Phase 4 decontrol commitments. Treasury Secretary George P. Shultz and CLC Director John T. Dunlop had lobbied for a compromise that would have salvaged some form of wage and price control machinery.

Meanwhile, action on early decontrols accelerated.

More industries decontrolled. The Cost of Living Council (CLC) continued to release industries from wage and price controls as part of its strategy for gradually decontrolling the economy before expiration of the Economic Stabilization Act April 30.

Immediate decontrol of the $31 billion a year paper industry was announced March 8. According to CLC Director John T. Dunlop, paper and paper product costs were expected to rise 10%–12% by the end of August as a result of the exemption, but he added that the CLC would require manufacturers with annual sales of $150 million to submit written price restraint commitments for a short period. This condition had characterized the lifting of compulsory price controls on most major industries. (Paper prices had risen 7.3% during Phase 4, the CLC said.)

With the decontrol of the paper industry, nearly half the items measured in the Wholesale Price Index had been decontrolled, Dunlop said.

Petrochemical companies with annual sales under $100 million were decontrolled immediately, but the bigger plastics and paint companies remained under Phase 4 restraints, according to a CLC announcement March 13. Certain rubber products makers also were freed from controls in a decision announced the same day. Six of the largest manufacturers agreed to limit increases in the price of industrial rubber hose and related products to 5% through July 1, the CLC said.

Wage and price controls were lifted March 15 for the communications industry, including printing, publishing, broadcasting and advertising. Wages of newspaper employes remained subject to restraints, however, because contract bargaining was under way.

Action on the communications industry was precipitated by the decontrol of the paper industry, whose products represented a "significant portion" of operating costs for the media, CLC officials said.

In the first major decontrol action taken for the food industry, the CLC announced March 18 that fruit and vegetable processors were freed from Phase 4 restraints. Ten major canners agreed to increase crop acreage and maintain present prices for several months in return for the early decontrol. (The move did not apply to retail and wholesale concerns with subsidiaries engaged in canning operations.)

A large portion of the food items that figured in the Consumer Price Index—65%—remained subject to price controls, according to the CLC. Despite Phase 4, however, processed fruits and vegetables had risen more than 20% in price.

A two-step removal of price controls was completed March 21 when the CLC decontrolled ferroalloy manufacturers.

Wage and price controls were lifted March 26 for the twine industry, which employed 8,000 workers and had annual revenues of about $180 million.

The coal industry was freed from wage and price restraints March 27 in exchange for promises to increase its 1974 output by about 3.5%. The CLC also won pledges from 10 of the country's 15 largest coal producers to keep prices below an average $30 a ton through Nov. 12 on contracts running less than five years. The 10 companies also promised to seek the beginning of labor talks soon. The CLC noted that 80% of the coal sold in 1973 (on long term contracts) had been exempted since July 1973.

The aluminum industry was freed from wage and price restraints March 28 and the four major producers immediately raised ingot prices about 8.6%. The same group, however, promised to limit total increases to about 15.5% through July. According to the CLC, the action was required to reduce the price gap between costly foreign aluminum and significantly cheaper domestic aluminum.

Wage and price controls were removed from the aerospace industry March 29 in a move that affected 1,200 manufacturing firms employing more than 600,-000 workers.

36,000 companies in 20 machine manufacturing industries with annual sales of $43 billion were freed from wage and price controls, the CLC announced March 20. It was also announced that day that 33 of the 35 largest paper and paper product firms had pledged to limit future price increases and exports of paper pulp during 1974 in return for early decontrol.

Wage curbs on newspaper employes were lifted April 2.

The CLC announced March 22 that it had allowed American Motors Corp. to raise its base vehicle prices an average $50 above the limit agreed to in

December 1973. The action brought AMC to parity with Ford and General Motors, which had been permitted total increases of $150 compared with AMC's $100 limit.

"No further base price increases are justified for the remainder of the 1974 model year under the terms set forth in the auto industry commitment," CLC officials declared.

Controls lifted for major industries— Wage and price restraints were lifted April 1 on 165 industries. The move—the most sweeping decontrol action yet undertaken by the CLC—was unexpected despite the setback for a planned extension of limited controls suffered in the Senate Banking Committee.

"The sectors exempted aren't those in which serious inflationary pressures remain or are anticipated," CLC Director Dunlop said. Among the industries decontrolled were apparel, banking, real estate, life insurance, securities, much of the wholesale trade industry, restaurants and services.

Curbs were lifted from food retailers and wholesalers April 15 and on 15 other sectors of the economy April 18.

These CLC actions left Phase 4 controls on only nine industries prior to expiration of the economic stabilization program April 30 under current legislation. The nine industries were construction, food-processing, petroleum, health-services, machinery, steel and copper, automobile parts and retail automobile sales.

The April 15 decontrol did not apply to the food manufacturing industry, which processed frozen, canned and packaged food. Controls were lifted on the food distribution industry—retailers and wholesalers—which in 1973 had sales of about $228 billion from 330,500 establishments employing 2.5 million workers.

CLC Director Dunlop said the industry's competitive structure and other factors provided "reasonable" assurance that decontrol "will not result in inordinate rises in food prices in the months ahead attributable to food retailing and wholesaling." Dunlop cited as a complementary action the formation April 12 of a labor-management committee in the retail food industry to investigate wage disputes and other labor problems.

The 15 sectors of the economy exempted from controls April 18 included producers of textiles, glass, soap and detergents, cosmetics, concrete, clay, gypsum, steel and wire springs, coke, lime, metal shipping barrels and drums, metal cans, linseed oil and cake, public warehousing services and truck terminal and maintenance facilities. Wholesale trade activities in the 15 industries also were decontrolled. (Wage controls on some of the industries had been dropped previously.) The April 18 action involved items comprising 6% of the wholesale price index.

The CLC had acted April 11 to permit steelmakers to have an immediate pass-through of higher costs of scrap steel. Steel scrap prices had risen more than 25%, it noted, since the CLC adopted a rule Feb. 28 permitting a price rise once a month to reflect scrap cost hikes.

The CLC released a report April 17 showing that the nation's major steel producers expected their costs to rise an average 13.6% for the six months ending Aug. 1. The report was based on data from 26 large firms and reflected anticipated rises in the costs of fuel and steel scrap, among other things. The data did not include costs of the recent labor pact.

Postal rate increases take effect— Higher postal rates took effect March 2 and Postmaster General E. T. Klassen warned that further increases could be expected because of rising wage and fuel costs. The rate hikes, which averaged 25%, were scheduled to take effect Jan. 5 but implementation was delayed when the CLC pared the proposed increase.

Among the higher rates were a 2¢ boost for first class letters (to 10¢), airmail letters (to 13¢) and postcards (to 8¢).

Truck strike accord reached. Negotiators for independent truckers urged the dissident drivers Feb. 7 to end an eight-day, violence-marked strike and accept an agreement reached with Nixon Administration officials providing for a 6% surcharge on freight rates to cover increased fuel costs. Most of the truckers, indicating acceptance, were back on the roads Feb. 11.

The strike, which was loosely organized by a coalition of 18 regional groups, had been successful in halting deliveries of perishable goods and other items throughout much of the nation.

Major supermarket chains were reported to be airlifting supplies amid reports of panic buying, particularly in urban areas. A tight gasoline supply situation was made worse as protesting truckers set up pickets around oil depots and harassed nonstriking oil truck drivers.

According to the New York Times Feb. 6, the strike had caused at least 75,000 workers to be laid off as the flow of supplies dwindled.

As the effectiveness of the strike mounted, reports of violence also increased. As in past protests by independent truckers, the level of violence was highest in Ohio and Pennsylvania—the nexus of the nation's trucking system and home territory for the most militant drivers—but incidents involving gunfire, stoning, beatings, burned rigs, and bomb threats also were reported in at least 20 states. Two deaths were reported—a driver was killed in Pennsylvania when a boulder was dropped on his cab, causing him to crash; another person was shot to death in Delaware.

Industrial production rebounds. The Federal Reserve Board announced May 15 that industrial production gained a seasonally adjusted .4% in April after declining for four consecutive months. With revisions made in the February and March reports, the index of physical production was at 124.7 in April, based on a 1967 level of 100. The index was .5% higher than in April 1973.

According to officials, a 14% spurt in auto production over the one month period was the most significant factor in reversing the recent downward trend.

College cost rise seen. The College Entrance Examination Board reported March 24 that total student expenses at colleges and universities in the 1974–75 school year would increase 9.4% over the current year. The cost would represent an increase of 35.8% over four years.

The report, based on a survey of 2,200 institutions, said the sharpest increase would be among two-year private colleges, where costs would rise 27.3% to

$3,287 a year. Expenses in two-year "community colleges," long considered the least expensive form of higher education, would also increase sharply and at a higher rate than public or private four-year institutions.

Among the four-year private schools, the average cost (including tuition, room and board and miscellaneous expenses) would be $4,039, up $346. Total expenses in public institutions would be $2,400.

Wage Settlements

San Francisco workers strike. San Francisco municipal workers struck in a wage dispute March 6–15. About 13,000 employes were involved in the strike, which closed hospital, sewage treatment and transit services.

The strike ended with agreement on an $11 million pay raise package which included an average pay increase of 5¼% and a fully paid dental plan.

N.Y. transit pact. A new two-year transit pact for New York City was negotiated March 31, seven hours before a strike deadline. The pact, covering 37,000 bus and subway workers, most of them members of the AFL-CIO Transport Workers Union, called for a 6% wage increase immediately, a 3% increase Dec. 1 and a 5% increase April 1975. Cost-of-living increases also were to be added to the wage base July 1975 and Jan. 1, 1976.

3-year steel accord reached. Agreement on a new three-year contract was reached April 12 by negotiators for the AFL-CIO United Steelworkers of America and the major steel companies. The accord, reached more than three months before expiration of the present contract Aug. 1, was described as a "settlement understanding."

Negotiations were conducted under terms of an Experimental Negotiating Agreement (ENA) signed in 1973, a no-strike agreement calling for binding arbitration of unresolved contract issues. Representatives of both sides—R. Heath Larry, top industry negotiator and vice chairman of U.S. Steel Corp., and USW President I. W. Abel—endorsed the operation of ENA, which was incorporated into the contract for utilization in the 1977 negotiations. This would carry the no-strike status between the union and steel firms into 1980. A $150 lump-sum payment guaranteed by ENA to each of the 386,000 workers covered by the negotiations was part of the accord worked out April 12. Minimum wage increases of 3% in each contract year also were guaranteed under ENA.

The wage agreement reached April 12 called for increases of more than 10% over the three-year period of the pact, a total of 60.9¢. These included a 28¢-an-hour boost May 1, a 16¢-an-hour increase Aug. 1, 1975 and another a year later.

The base pay would also receive a 39¢-an-hour injection May 1 from the cost-of-living (COL) adjustments under the existing contract.

The new pact would have an improved COL formula, effective May 1, to provide a 1¢-an-hour hike for every .35 point rise in the consumer price index (previous boost point was .4).

The new contract did not include the cost-of-living escalator for pension benefits negotiated by USW with other industries. But it did include a flat 5% "inflation adjustment" for those retiring after July 31. Beginning in the third contract year, the adjustment would be applied in the regular monthly pension checks until the contract expired. The minimum monthly pension for new retirees would be increased more than one-third, beginning Aug. 1, 1975, and the retirement age would be lowered from 65 to 62. Workers retired under previous contracts would receive increases of $15–$60 a month.

In addition to U.S. Steel, the pact covered Bethlehem Steel, Republic Steel, National Steel, Jones & Laughlin Steel, Armco Steel, Youngstown Sheet and Tube, Inland Steel, Wheeling-Pittsburgh Steel and Allegheny Ludlum Industries Inc.

Hawaii sugar, pineapple strikes. Hawaii's sugar and pineapple industries were shut down during March and April by new contract disputes involving both cannery and field workers, members of the International Longshoremen's and Warehousemen's Union.

The sugar strike, involving some 9,000 workers, began March 9 and ended April 16. The settlement included a commitment by the companies to remain in business until at least Jan. 31, 1976. The wage provision was an increase of 75¢ an hour, to be paid in four stages by Aug. 1, 1975. The previous scale ranged from $2.85 to $4.805 an hour.

The pineapple strike, involving about 6,-000 workers, began April 7 and ended April 29. Because of the impact of foreign competition, the job security agreement was not as far-reaching as in the sugar pact. The wage increase was 50¢ an hour by August 1975, to be applied to the $2.78–$4.875 base.

Minimum wage raised. President Nixon signed new minimum wage legislation April 8. He had vetoed a similar bill in 1973. The bill was cleared March 28 by votes of 71–29 in the Senate and 345–50 in the House. Preliminary passage in the House was by a 375–37 vote March 20.

The minimum wage would be increased in stages to $2.30 an hour and coverage would be extended to 7–8 million workers not previously covered.

The basic minimum wage, applying to 36 million nonfarm workers, would rise from $1.60 to $2 an hour May 1, to $2.10 Jan. 1, 1975 and to $2.30 Jan. 1, 1976.

For another 19 million nonfarm workers covered under amendments to the basic legislation in 1966, the minimum wage would be $1.90 on May 1, $2 in 1975, $2.10 in 1976 and $2.30 in 1977.

For the more than 500,000 farm workers whose current minimum was $1.30, the new minimum would be $1.60 May 1, $1.80 Jan. 1, 1975, $2 in 1976, $2.20 in 1977 and $2.30 in 1978.

Minimum wage coverage would be extended to an additional seven million workers in federal, state and local government (about 5 million employes), domestic service and retail and service employes of chain store operations.

Money & Interest Rates

Burns affirms credit policy. Federal Reserve Board Chairman Arthur F.

Burns reaffirmed April 22 the board's firm monetary policy against inflation despite soaring interest rates and their impact on the housing industry. "To shape monetary policy with an eye to the fortunes of homebuilding and to neglect the grave and very dangerous problem of inflation would be extremely unwise," Burns said at a news conference.

He indicated that the supply of money and credit had been expanding faster than the Reserve "wished or intended." The Reserve would permit growth to continue, Burns said, "but only at a moderate rate." "We are not going to sit back and clear a monetary path for severe and rapid inflation," he stressed. "Let there be no mistaking our determination in doing this."

Burns conceded that the escalation of short-term interest rates carried danger for the depressed homebuilding industry and that a period of tight mortgage credit "may well be under way." But he said there were "other ways" than monetary policy to encourage homebuilding that could be undertaken by the Administration and Congress.

Burns emphasized his concern about an excessive expansion of the money supply. "We're having a veritable explosion of business loans," he said. "Our monetary aggregates, if anything, had been growing too rapidly. I'm not letting out any secret in saying they have been growing faster than the Federal Reserve System wished or intended." "Excessively rapid expansion of bank loans," he continued, "is a matter of deep concern to me. We aren't going to get inflation under control if that continues." (The Reserve April 24 raised its discount rate—the rate charged member banks to borrow money from the Federal Reserve—to a record 8% from 7½%.)

The news conference was called under a new policy to publish more information on monetary policy targets set by the board's Federal Open Market Committee. The committee's reports of its monthly meetings, released after 90 days, were to include the targets, Burns said. The first such report, covering the Jan. 21–22 meeting, disclosed a 3%–6% annual rate of growth as the target for the January-February period in the narrowly defined money supply, or checking accounts plus currency; a 6%–9% annual growth rate

target in the more broadly defined money supply that included some time deposits; and a range of 8¾%–10% in the average weekly federal funds rate, or the interest rate on overnight loans of excess reserves from one bank to another.

A 10½% prime rate, charged by banks on loans to their major corporate customers, gained strong support April 23 as four more major banks raised their rates to that figure.

Tax cut proposals opposed—Burns stated his opposition to proposals from several Democrats for a tax reduction to stimulate the economy. Asked at his news conference April 22 if he favored a tax cut at this time, he replied, "I do not."

However, the move for a tax cut gained an important advocate the same day when Senate Democratic leader Mike Mansfield (Mont.) issued a statement espousing a tax cut as "something we can do for the average working stiff who's carrying the load in this country."

A call for a tax cut was made by Sens. Edward M. Kennedy (D, Mass.) and Walter F. Mondale (D, Minn.) in a joint statement April 20. The nation was "in the grip of a serious recession," they said, and a tax cut was "the single most important step that Congress can now take for the long-run strength and vitality of the nation's economy."

A statement advocating a tax cut for low- and middle-income families "to stimulate the economy through consumer demand" was issued by Sen. Hubert H. Humphrey (D, Minn.) April 21. He referred to the long-standing economic theory that "a high rate of inflation could not exist side by side in our economy with a drop in economic activity, high levels of unemployment and high interest rates."

Administration opposition to a tax cut was expressed on NBC's "Meet the Press" April 21 by Kenneth R. Cole Jr., President Nixon's chief domestic affairs adviser. "As far as a tax decrease is concerned," he said, "we have an inflation problem. We have too much of an inflation problem and we think that a tax decrease at this particular point in time will inflame that problem rather than resolve the problems that we have in the economy."

The economic problem was "primarily

in the energy-related area," Cole said, and the situation was "picking up" because of the increase in energy supplies flowing from the lifting of the Arab oil embargo and the "picking up" of automobile production and sales. "So I am not so sure that [a tax cut] would solve the problem," he said

White House spokesman Gerald L. Warren said April 22 Cole accurately reflected President Nixon's views on the subject.

Prime rate over 10%. The prime interest rate charged by banks on loans to their major corporate customers reached a record 10.5% April 15 after a precipitous climb from the March 1 8.5% level. The downward movement in the base rate, which had dropped quickly from 9.5% in late January, was reversed after only two weeks at the 8.5% level when First National City Bank raised the lending rate to 8.75% March 15.

Higher short-term interest rates on money used by banks to finance loans and a sharp rise in corporate demand for the funds were cited as factors in the prime rate's turnaround and steady climb.

The upward trend became industry wide March 20 when Bankers Trust initiated a quarter point increase to 9%.

(The earlier drop to 8.5%—the fifth quarter point reduction in the prime rate during 1974—was initiated by First National City Bank but adopted by few other banks. Observers believed that cuts in the lending rate during the first few months of 1974 did not reflect lower demands for bank loans, but rather competitive efforts by banks to halt the recent substantial growth in the use of commercial paper for corporate financing. During the first two months of 1974, there was a $5.7 billion increase in corporate use of the paper money market—a figure that exceeded the last record increase of $2.6 billion set during the first two months of 1970, according to the New York Times March 2.)

After hitting the 9% level, the lending rate rose rapidly—9.25% set March 27; 9.5% set March 28; 9.75% set April 5; 10% set April 8 and equaling the previous record high posted in October and December 1973; 10.1% set April 15 by the First National Bank of Chicago, the nation's 10th largest commercial bank; and 10.25% announced April 15, effective April 12, by the North Carolina National Bank, which ranked 25th in the nation in deposits. Several other large banks joined the move to 10.25% April 16 and 17. The Citizens & Southern National Bank of Atlanta April 17 announced a 10.5% prime rate on new loans to large corporations and a 10.25% rate on existing loans, effective April 15. It became the first bank to announce a differential on minimum base rates.

The Committee on Interest and Dividends, headed by Federal Reserve Chairman Arthur F. Burns, had been swift to challenge banks setting 10% base lending rates in 1973, but the Administration had no immediate comment on the current record levels. The Federal Reserve's alternate anti-recession and anti-inflation efforts in the money market were believed by observers to have had a significant impact on the prime rate's sharp drop and subsequent steep climb. Early in 1974, as fears of a recession were heightened by the worsening energy crisis and evident economic slowdown, the Federal Reserve adopted a less restrictive money policy. But with the ending of the Arab oil embargo, some signs of economic recovery and continued high inflation, a reversal was seen in Washington and the credit market.

With interest levels dropping quickly, the Federal Reserve assumed a strongly anti-inflation position to tighten credit in an attempt to stem the rapid growth in the money supply. Federal Reserve figures showed a record $3.7 billion increase in the money supply (the total of private demand, or checking accounts, deposits, plus cash in public hands) for the week ending March 6, according to the Wall Street Journal March 18. It was one of the largest one-week jumps on record.

The federal government's Export-Import Bank announced Feb. 4 that its lending rates would be increased from 6% to 7%. It was the highest rate ever charged by the group and the first change since August 1966 when the rate was increased from 5.5% to 6%.

The End of Wage-Price Curbs

Wage-price controls expire. The Economic Stabilization Act of 1970 expired at midnight April 30, ending the President's authority to impose most mandatory wage and price controls. Only the petroleum industry would remain controlled under authority granted by the 1973 Emergency Petroleum Allocation Act, which would extend to March 1, 1975. When the act expired, only 12.2% of consumer prices and 31.5% of wholesale prices had not been decontrolled by the Cost of Living Council (CLC). Restraints had remained on machinery, steel, copper, health care and a few other industries.

Nixon warns against price hikes—President Nixon, in an address April 30 to the annual convention of the U.S. Chamber of Commerce, appealed to business leaders to restrain future price increases and warned that continued high inflation would stimulate demands for resumption of controls.

He reiterated his belief that the current economic slowdown would level out in the second quarter of 1974 after which growth would resume. "There will be a very good year in 1975 and the best year in our history in 1976," he said.

In a May 2 statement outlining the final phase of CLC operations, Nixon pledged to combat inflation and reiterated his opposition to any tax cut or to "unnecessary increases" in federal spending. He instructed the CLC to continue monitoring prices through June 30, although it would no longer have power to enforce restraint.

Major price boosts set—The ending of controls was followed May 1-2 by major price increases in the steel, copper and other industries.

Phelps Dodge Corp., Kennecott Copper Corp., Anaconda Co. and other firms increased copper cathode prices from 68¢ to 80¢ May 1.

Phelps Dodge had led the price boost with an announcement April 30. Its president, George B. Munroe, had defended the increase, citing the current world market price for copper of $1.48 a pound and higher production costs. He said the company needed more funds for pol-

lution-control equipment and expansion of copper production.

The U.S. Steel Corp. announced May 2 an average price increase of 5.7% on "a broad range" of products. The price of cold-rolled sheet, the highest volume product, was increased by $20 to $226 a ton, a 9.7% increase. Hot-rolled sheets would rise $17.50 a ton, or 10%, to $191 a ton.

Edgar B. Speer, chairman of U.S. Steel, said the increases covered cost boosts incurred since Jan. 31.

U.S. Steel also announced additional charges, effective May 20, on a number of products. The charges, which could average up to 3.5%, covered pickling, heat treating and other processing.

Wheeling-Pittsburgh Steel Corp. and Youngstown Sheet & Tube also set price increases May 2. Wheeling-Pittsburgh boosted its prices by an average 6%, which would include about a 9.5% increase in its tin-mill products price. Youngstown said its price increases ranged from 10%-25% on tubular products, rigid conduit and electric-metallic tubing.

The first steel price increase had been announced May 1 by National Steel, which raised its tin-mill products by 9.5%.

Among other increases announced May 1-2: Beech Aircraft Corp. increased prices on most of its commercial planes; Revere Copper and Brass, Inc. raised copper from $1.06 a pound to $1.11 and also boosted prices of zinc, tin and lead; Hoffmann-LaRoche raised vitamin prices by 29%-31%; Airco Industrial Gases increased liquid oxygen and nitrogen bulk prices by 10%-15%, plus extra distribution charges; the Linde division of the Union Carbide Corp., raised prices by 10%-15% for industrial gases, including oxygen, nitrogen and hydrogen.

However, the George A. Hormel & Co. announced May 2 a 7%-14% cut in its meat product prices. The firm cited reduced prices of livestock and greater supplies as the reason for its move.

Senate kills CLC monitoring role. In a reversal of preliminary action taken May 1, the Senate voted May 9 to table, postponing indefinitely, a measure giving the Cost of Living Council (CLC) the authority to monitor and enforce Phase 4 price restraint commitments. The move was regarded as a deathblow to the CLC, which was scheduled to disband June 30 with the expiration of its funding.

(The Senate also killed an amendment that would have set a $295 billion ceiling on government spending for fiscal 1975. The measure, proposed by Sen. William Proxmire [D, Wis], was $9.4 billion lower than the spending level budgeted by President Nixon. The CLC and spending ceiling amendments were attached to a bill that would extend the life of the President's Council on International Economic Policy. That bill itself was not rejected and could be brought up again separately.)

Senate vote follows Ford price raise— The 65–19 vote against extending even a limited form of wage-price controls came only one day after the Ford Motor Co. announced that it was raising the retail prices of 1974 model cars and trucks an average $163 (or 3.5%), despite a pledge to the CLC. In December 1973 Ford had promised to limit wholesale price increases for the 1974 model year to $150 in return for the immediate lifting of wage-price restrictions.

CLC Director John T. Dunlop was critical of Ford's move, terming it "unwarranted" and a violation of the company's "voluntary" price restraint pledge, which specified exceptions to the rule only if "unforeseen major economic events" occurred.

According to Ford officials, the increase was necessary to "offset in part unprecedented cost increases," such as recent sharp increases announced in the price of steel. The total increase of $163 per vehicle, composed of a $91 hike in the base vehicle charge, a $15 increase in the cost of optional equipment, a $7 boost in destination charges, and $50 price jump to cover the cost of optional equipment now being offered as standard items, would increase company revenues only by an average $91 per unit, spokesmen said, leaving $98 in "unrecovered costs" incurred since November 1973 to be absorbed by Ford.

In addresses delivered at the firm's annual meeting May 9, Ford officials said

they anticipated no further increases during the 1974 model year, but warned that the retail costs of 1975 models would rise by "hundreds of dollars" "even if cost pressures moderate during the coming months."

An increase of $175 would be required to cover costs for "meeting interim 1975 [emission] standards," Henry Ford 2nd, chairman of the company, told stockholders. Other federal regulations would add nearly $800 to the cost of cars within a few years, according to Ford, beside the $400 in price increases he said had been required to comply with recent government rules.

General Motors Corp., which also had been party to the price restraint pledge given the CLC in December 1973, raised car and truck prices an average 2% May 13. Its action, however drew praise from the CLC for its "restraint," because, unlike Ford's, the increase was not concentrated in the base price. GM's total retail price hike was made up of a $52 increase in the vehicle base price ($41 at wholesale), a $43 increase in the cost of optional equipment and a $10 boost in freight charges.

In a clarification of the December 1973 agreement issued May 13, the CLC explained that the pledge applied only to vehicle base prices at the wholesale level, and since GM had used up only $109 of that sum in a post-December increase, the current price hike was within the limit GM had acceded to.

Chrysler Corp., which had not joined in the price restraint pact although it had been freed from wage-price controls with the rest of the industry, had raised retail prices an estimated $122 a unit May 1— $99 for the vehicle base price and $23 for optional equipment.

*Auto industry profits plummet—*Bleak first quarter earnings reports issued by auto makers reflected the consequences of the interrelated energy and inflation problems facing the country—production cutbacks and sharply higher manufacturing costs.

General Motors Corp. announced April 26 that first quarter earnings were $120 million, their lowest level in 26 years. Profits were down 85% from the record levels reported in the first period of 1973.

Chrysler Corp. coupled its report of a 98.2% decline in first quarter earnings (compared with the same period of 1973) with notice that it would institute sharp new price increases. According to the April 29 report, net income fell to $1.6 million during the January-March quarter.

Ford Motor Co. April 30 reported a 66% drop in first quarter earnings over the same period of 1973. Net income for the 1974 January-March quarter was $124 million, Ford's smallest earnings level since 1967.

American Motors, which was the only auto maker to show increased sales during the energy crisis (because of strength in the small car market), May 1 announced a 58% drop in profits for the January-March period compared with the same 1973 quarter. Net income was $6.9 million for the period.

In contrast, U.S. Steel Corp. showed an 83% increase in first quarter earnings from the year earlier. Net income was $89.5 million, paced by a 29% boost in sales, officials announced April 30. Auto makers had cited sharply rising steel prices in justifying higher retail car prices.

Study cites car cost increases—A study released April 15 by the Federal Highway Administration indicated that the costs of operating a full size 1974 model car were 17% higher than the costs of operating a 1972 car. Operating costs of a 1974 compact car compared with a 1972 model were even higher—19.4%. A rise in gasoline and oil costs, and higher parts, parking, insurance and tax expenses were blamed for the increases.

Chrysler, AMC raise prices again. Chrysler Corp. announced May 17 that it was increasing the prices of 1974 model cars and trucks an average $46, or 1%, effective June 1. Base retail prices and transportation costs would rise across the board but optional equipment being made standard on some models could bring the increase to more than $60 a unit.

It was Chrysler's second price increase in less than a month and the seventh since production began on 1974 vehicles. Overall, the increases totaled about $500 on a 1974 Chrysler vehicle, compared with the previous year's model. Officials of the company said the price hike was necessitated by the recent rise in steel costs.

American Motors Corp. (AMC), citing "unprecedented cost escalation," May 21 announced a $57 increase in the base retail price and a $10 rise in transportation charges for 1974 model cars and trucks, effective immediately. American, which had been party to the price restraint commitment given the Cost of Living Council (CLC) in December 1973, had been allowed a special price increase in March.

The increase was the fourth major pricing move on 1974 models announced by American and set average retail prices $330 above average 1973 prices.

Pay curbs limited. A federal judge in Indianapolis ruled May 13 that the government had no authority to limit pay rates in labor contracts for work performed after April 30, the date federal wage-price controls expired. The judgment was expected to have an immediate effect on wages that had been ordered rolled back despite the fact that the pay rates applied to work performed after April 30.

Mortgage aid announced. President Nixon announced a program May 10 designed to stimulate the home mortgage market with up to $10.3 billion in additional aid.

Among the major actions:

■ The Government National Mortgage Association was authorized to extend its "tandem plan" for below-market interest rates on Federal Housing Administration (FHA) and Veterans Administration (VA) mortgages. An additional $3.3 billion would be committed for purchase of the mortgages at 8% for new construction, up from 7.75%.

■ The Federal Home Loan Bank Board would have the authority to purchase at 8.75% up to $3 billion in conventional mortgages made by savings and loan institutions.

■ Up to $4 billion would be made available to savings institutions to increase their lending capacity. The advances would be made at below-market rates through the Home Loan Bank system.

■ The maximum allowable interest on

FHA and VA mortgages would be raised from 8.5% to a "competitive rate" of 8.75%.

Herbert Stein, chairman of the President's Council of Economic Advisers, noted that the program would not necessarily result in a net addition of $10.3 billion to available mortgage capital. The purpose, according to Stein, was to "shelter" housing from the prevailing high interest rates by shifting money to the mortgage market.

Economy's Health in Dispute

Nixon's economic address. President Nixon presented a midyear economic report May 25 in a nationally broadcast radio address, assuring the nation that recent economic "storms are abating." "The worst is behind us," Nixon said, citing a drop in food prices and a slowing of the fuel price spiral.

No major changes in economic policies were planned, Nixon said, but he announced the appointment of Deputy Secretary of State Kenneth Rush as counselor to the President for economic affairs. Rush, who was sworn in May 29, left the second ranking post at the State Department to coordinate domestic and international economic policy at the White House, where he would have Cabinet rank.

It was also widely reported that Rush was named to the post to fill a policy-making vacuum left by the resignation of George Shultz, who had served as Nixon's top economic adviser as well as Treasury secretary.

Nixon said the Administration's basic economic policies would remain unchanged—opposition to a tax cut backed by Congressional Democrats, support for the Federal Reserve's "tight money" actions, efforts to increase supplies of products, and an attempt to hold the fiscal 1975 federal budget at $305 billion.

Nixon urged Congress to establish a "small flexible organization" in the White House with authority to "monitor wages, prices, industry bottlenecks, supply shortages and other factors bearing on inflation." The task force, which would have only advisory power, would succeed the Cost of Living Council, whose funding expired at the end of June.

Nixon repeated his opposition to a reimposition of economic controls.

The Council of Economic Advisers was directed to establish a "high level group" to evaluate the prospect of a shortage of capital for investment, Nixon said. He also asked the Federal Energy Administration to draw up a plan for phasing out the oil allocation program.

"The requirements for full economic recovery may sound like harsh medicine, but there is no alternative," Nixon cautioned. "We cannot spend our way to prosperity. Neither can we achieve prosperity or price stability by putting America back into a straitjacket of controls," he concluded.

Midyear report to Congress—In an unusual midyear economic report to Congress May 28, the President's Council of Economic Advisers predicted that inflation would drop to a level "in the neighborhood of 7%" by the final quarter of 1974. (As measured by the Consumer Price Index, inflation had expanded at an annual rate of about 12% for the past three months.)

The prediction was based on a belief that increases in food and energy prices would level off. The report called on business and labor to exert "moderation and self-restraint" in raising prices and making wage demands. Both factors could endanger the Administration's fight against inflation, according to the report.

The report contained no new policy initiatives, but like President Nixon's radio address, reflected the Administration's cautious optimism that anti-inflation efforts were easing the price spiral.

Projection of a 6% inflation rate for the final three months of 1974 had been issued several months earlier by the council. An upward revision had been prompted by an unexpected surge in the price of industrial commodities, the report stated. Other forecasts issued previously by the council—that total economic production would rise during the second half of the year but unemployment rates would not exceed 6%—were repeated in the midyear message to Congress.

Despite its optimistic tone, the report did not minimize the dangers of inflation.

"Events have tended to dispel the earlier fear of a recession—either in the U.S. or worldwide—and to focus attention even more heavily on the danger of worldwide inflation," the report warned.

Officials less optimistic—Federal Reserve Board Chairman Arthur F. Burns offered another and considerably more pessimistic analysis of economic conditions. In a commencement address May 26, Burns warned that the "future of our country is in jeopardy" and that a continuation of "debilitating" inflation rates would "threaten the very foundation of our society."

In another departure from the Administration viewpoint, Burns said "rampant inflation" was more a result of "awesome" federal spending levels than of skyrocketing food and fuel costs.

"Individuals have come to depend less and less on their own initiative and more and more on government to achieve their economic objectives," Burns declared.

White House spokesmen rejected Burns' assessment. Press Secretary Ronald L. Ziegler said May 27 that "the President is right and Burns is wrong about economic prospects." Herbert Stein, chairman of the Council of Economic Advisers, May 27 likened Burns to Jeremiah, saying "we don't all talk with the language of an Old Testament prophet."

Treasury Secretary William Simon also called for fiscal restraint. In an interview May 27, Simon termed the nation's inflation rate "totally unacceptable." The key to controlling prices, Simon said, was a balanced budget.

The federal budget had been in deficit for "14 of the last 15 years," according to Simon, who noted that a $9.4 billion deficit was projected for fiscal 1975, beginning July 1. "We are still paying for many of the bold new initiatives that have been proposed over the last 20–30 years," Simon said. A balanced budget would be impossible to achieve in 1975, but he added, "I would certainly aim toward a balanced budget in 1976."

Reuss rebuts Nixon on economy. In a Democratic Party response to President Nixon's economic address, Rep. Henry S. Reuss (D, Wis.) accused the Adminis-

tration June 1 of employing "the same old tired tools—fiscal and monetary restraint" when a new and positive economic policy was required.

"We Democrats reject this passive attitude toward an economic crisis which is undermining the expectations and quality of life of millions of average income Americans—at least two-thirds of a nation," Reuss said in his radio address.

He called for tax cuts for poor and middle income persons and expansion of public service jobs. Reuss also challenged Nixon's assertion that inflation had peaked, accusing the Administration of contributing to inflationary trends by promoting trade subsidies that restricted domestic supplies of scarce commodities.

The public was also critical of Nixon's handling of economic issues, according to a Louis Harris poll published June 3. In a sample of 1,555 households taken May 4–7, 82% of those surveyed said they did not approve of the "way [Nixon] has handled the economy," and 60% said they felt the Administration's economic policies were doing "more harm than good." (Those favoring Nixon in each poll totaled 15% and 20% respectively.)

Those interviewed were critical of the Administration's ties to business—72% said the Administration and the Republican Party were "too close to big business," 38% said the Administration "has given too many advantages, made too many special deals with business," and 69% said the Administration had been "too easy" on big business.

Interest Rates, Pay & Prices Continue to Climb

Interest rates mount. The prime interest rate charged on loans to major corporate borrowers continued its rapid upward movement. The banking industry had moved from widespread adoption of a 10.5% level in late April to an 11.75% prime implemented May 20 by First National Bank of Chicago, the nation's ninth largest commercial bank. The rate rise continued until, by July 8, it had reached a record 12.25%.

There were several signs that the Federal Reserve was determined to maintain a tight money policy despite its effect on the prime rate. It was reported May 23 that the Federal Reserve intervened in the short-term money market during the previous three days to absorb excess funds from the banking system caused by a temporary drop in interest rates for federal funds. (Federal funds were uncommitted reserves banks lend to each other.)

When the federal funds' rate hit 12.5% May 28, the Federal Reserve intervened with purchasing orders to inject cash into the system and reduce the rate. This seesaw policy of injecting funds to reduce the rate and then draining cash from the banking system to bring the lending rate up again was continued throughout the first half of June in an effort to stabilize the interest rate at just under 12% (a record level).

It was announced June 17 that the Federal Reserve's Open Market Committee had voted in March to allow a rise in short-term interest rates, although the group acknowledged that "pursuit of that objective would be likely to entail a further tightening of bank reserve and money market conditions in the near term and some further increases in interest rates in general."

The committee also voted to allow a small expansion in the money supply. The money supply (measured at an annual rate on a quarterly basis) had continued to grow but the amount of increase had been diminishing. A Federal Reserve report for the quarter ending May 29 indicated that the money supply increased at a seasonally adjusted annual rate of 9.2%; for the quarter ending June 5, the annual rate of growth was 8.3%. The Federal Reserve's target annual rate of growth was 6%.

Commercial banks were not the only financial institutions hard hit by tight money conditions. With short-term money yielding such high rates of return, investors were bypassing the lower interest rates offered by banks to attract capital. The lending operations of savings and loan institutions were especially hampered by this process, known as disintermediation, by which investors transferred their deposits from the usual lending mediators, banks and the savings and loan industry, to the short-term money market, where it was not available for mortgages or other consumer loans.

The Federal Home Loan Bank Board announced May 27 that during April savings and loan associations experienced their first net outflow of deposits since September 1973. Thrift institutions lost $335 million, compared with net inflows of $1.751 billion in March and $724 million in April 1973.

The lack of mortgage money was reflected in a drop in housing starts and permits for new housing construction during May. According to the Commerce Department June 18, housing starts were at an annual rate of 1.45 million units, off 11.1% from April and 37.8% below the seasonally adjusted annual rate registered in May 1973.

Permits were at an adjusted annual rate of 1.055 million units, a drop of 18.5% in one month and 42% in 12 months.

Continued heavy demand for bank loans by corporations and high interest rates on the short-term money market accounted for the upward pressure on the prime.

According to Federal Reserve figures, commercial and industrial loans made by the 12 leading New York banks rose $719 million in the week ending June 19, up from the previous week's gain of $421 million; for the week ending June 26, there was a $551 million increase but that figure nearly doubled the following week when loans increased $1.1 billion. It was the fourth consecutive weekly advance and for the period ending July 3, brought total loans outstanding to a level $6 billion above that set 12 months earlier.

The Federal Reserve was forced to inject funds into the tight money market July 2 when the interest rate on federal funds reached 14.25% (after rising briefly to a record 15% the previous week).

The 12.25% prime rate was finally posted by the Central National Bank of Cleveland July 8.

Mortgage rates at record high— Maximum interest rates on federally insured mortgage loans were raised from 8.75% to 9% July 5. It was the third increase in three months on loans insured by the Federal Housing Administration

(FHA) and guaranteed by the Veterans Administration (VA).

Officials said the increase was required to boost the availability of loans. With interest ceilings on the government program so low, lenders had been bypassing federally insured mortgages and investing in the higher yield short-term money market. Financing had been available at the 8.75% rate, officials said, because lenders had charged "points" to make up the difference between the government-backed rate and higher conventional rates. A point was equal to 1% of the face value of the loan, and payment was required in a lump sum in advance, in effect serving as prepaid interest. As many as 8 points had been charged borrowers on some FHA mortgages with interest rates of 8.75%.

Savings and loan institutions, which were the principal sources of home mortgages, had also been victims of the liquidity pinch. The Federal Home Loan Bank Board announced June 27 that although April's net outflow was reversed, the May inflow of funds was the smallest for that month since 1968. The inflow was $423 million, compared with $1.7 billion a year earlier.

Dow average linked to prime rate—Conditions in the troubled stock market were closely linked to the difficulties besetting the banking industry.

The Dow dropped 11.89 points June 26 as several banks increased their interest rates for their most credit worthy customers, causing the Dow to close at 816.96; the slump continued June 27 as the Dow fell 13.3 points and then closed at 790.68 July 2 following a drop of 15.56 points. That marked its lowest level since Dec. 5, 1973.

With a plunge to 770.57 July 8, the market staged a broad-based retreat as 1,-441 stocks dropped in price and 137 were up at the close. More than 600 stocks hit new lows for 1974 that day.

The market continued its steep plunge July 10 when it closed off 10.17 points at 762.12. The Dow was at its lowest point since Nov. 20, 1970.

Prices on the American Stock Exchange reached a four-year low July 8. The Amex market value index dropped

1.95 points to 75.74, its lowest level since July 6, 1970.

Machinists ratify UAL pact. Members of the AFL-CIO International Association of Machinists (IAM) voted May 13–14 to approve a new 26-month contract with United Air Lines. The pact, covering 16,500 employes, called for base pay increases of 15.8% and two cost-of-living adjustments that could boost the total increase to 18.8% over the contract term. The ratification voided a strike call for May 15.

Clothing workers' strike. The AFL-CIO Amalgamated Clothing Workers of America struck manufacturers of men's and boys' clothing June 1. It was the union's first strike since 1921. Negotiators reached agreement on a new contract June 8, and, after a union ratification vote, a return to work began June 12. The strike involved 110,000 workers and 750 manufacturers in 30 states producing 95% of men's and boys' apparel in the country. About 40,000 of the striking workers were employed in the New York area.

The new contract provided for an $1-an-hour wage increase (28%) over a three-year period plus cost-of-living adjustments in 1975 and 1976. The pre-pact average wage was $3.50 an hour.

10% rail freight hike OKd. The Interstate Commerce Commission (ICC) ruled June 4 that the nation's railroads could raise freight prices by as much as 10% over the next 12 months if they ploughed the money back to improve rail service.

The agency said the additional revenues, which could total $1.5 billion, must be used to purchase new equipment, to maintain existing tracks and equipment, or to cover increased material and supply costs other than fuel. (The ICC earlier had allowed railroads to levy surcharges in order to pass on the rising fuel costs.)

The railroads had asked that the increase take effect immediately, but the ICC required that shippers be given 15 days notice.

Car, steel makers raise prices. Car and steel makers instituted another round of price increases in the aftermath of the lifting of Phase 4 controls. General Motors Corp. announced its sixth price hike for 1974 model cars and trucks June 12. A 2.4% increase, averaging about $118 a unit, would take effect June 17, officials said, to cover the cost of making certain optional equipment standard. The move "represents added value" and should not be construed as a price increase, GM spokesmen said. With the latest pricing action, the cost of an average 1974 model vehicle was about $512 more than the cost of an average 1973 model.

The other two major auto firms, Ford Motor Co. and Chrysler Corp., announced smaller price increases. It was reported June 20 that average prices of Ford cars and trucks would be increased by $10.45 a unit to cover higher freight costs. (It was Ford's fifth price hike for 1974 model vehicles.)

The move was followed June 22 by Chrysler's announcement that shipping charges for its cars and trucks would be raised $10.08 a vehicle. Both firms said the actions reflected a direct pass-through of recently-authorized increases in rail transportation charges and would not result in higher corporate profits.

Chrysler instituted another price hike June 27 on grounds of higher steel costs. Chrysler's increase, estimated at 1.4%, or an average $60 a unit, was Chrysler's ninth since 1974 models went on sale in fall 1973 and brought total price increases for the model year well above $500 a unit.

Big increases in the costs of raw materials used in automotive construction were major factors in the 1974 model year price increases and were also having disruptive effects on the industry's ability to project its future costs and prices, according to the New York Times June 30.

The report cited a wide range of material price increases that had contributed to price hikes at the retail level: copper (31 pounds used per vehicle), up 34% since the start of the model year; glass (90 pounds), up 11%; plastic (100 pounds), up 21%; lead (26 pounds), up 30%; steel (3,105 pounds), up 18%; aluminum (62 pounds), up 42%; iron (691 pounds), up 17%; rubber (101 pounds), up 16%; zinc (58 pounds), up 70%. The cost breakdown was based on production costs at Ford Motor Co.

Increases in steel prices had direct effects on the auto industry, as well as other important sectors of the nation's manufacturing industries.

The price increases escalated rapidly: U.S. Steel announced an 8% hike on a wide variety of products June 11; Bethlehem confirmed June 24 that prices of rolled steel products would be raised 5%–15%; subsequent increases announced June 26 by U.S. Steel tended to parallel Bethlehem's move and the remaining portions of the industry joined in the pricing actions June 28.

California nurses strike. A three-week strike by 4,400 nurses at 43 northern California hospitals ended June 28 after ratification of a two-year labor agreement. The agreement called for salary increases averaging about 11%. This would make the top pay scales $1,015 to $1,135 a month.

The strike began June 7 when nurses established picket lines at three private hospital groups—the Associated Hospitals of San Francisco, the Affiliated Hospitals of San Francisco and the Kaiser Permanente Hospital Group. W. J. Usery Jr., head of the Federal Mediation Service, entered the negotiations and an accord reached June 26 was ratified by the membership of the California Nurses Association June 27.

Harper & Row struck. Some 300 employes of Harper & Row Publishers Inc. struck in New York June 17. The 17-day strike was the first against a major publishing house. It ended July 3 with an accord, reached with the help of a state mediator, on a three-year contract for the independent union involved calling for a total $61 weekly gain in wages over the period, $30 of which was in cost of living raises. The pre-strike average weekly pay was $190.

79 A&P stores closed by strike. The Amalgamated Meat Cutters and Butcher Workmen voted June 21 to end its two-week strike that closed 79 Great Atlantic & Pacific Tea Co. foodstores in Massachusetts, Connecticut and Vermont. A two-year contract was approved that would increase the meatcutter's weekly wage from $198 to $250—$22 more immediately, $10 in six months and $20 after one year. Pension benefits would be raised to $300 a month and the retirement age lowered to 62.

Publishers' mail rate hikes delayed. The House passed 277–129 without change June 19 a Senate bill delaying a scheduled series of postal rate increases for magazines, newspapers and nonprofit organizations. President Nixon signed the bill into law June 30.

Under the legislation, the full rate increase scheduled to go into effect in 1976 for newspapers, magazines and other mailers of regular second-class mail was delayed until 1979. Mailers of books, records and other fourth-class items would get the same delay. The new rates for nonprofit organizations and small rural newspapers would go into effect in 1987 instead of the previously scheduled 1981.

'74 wage gains topped 1973. Major collective bargaining agreements negotiated during the first nine months of 1974 for 4.1 million workers exceeded wage gains won in 1973, according to the Labor Department Oct. 25.

During the nine-month negotiating period, wage increases won in the settlements averaged 9.6% for the first year of the contract, compared with 5.8% in 1973, and 7.2% over the life of the contract, compared with 5.1% in 1973. The data applied to 918 settlements in the private nonfarm economy, affecting 1,000 workers or more, and excluded possible cost of living adjustments.

In contracts covering 5,000 workers or more, the wage and benefit gains were greater, averaging 10.1% for the first year, compared with 7.1% in 1973, and 7.5% over the life of the contract, compared with 6.1% in 1973.

Cost of living provisions were adopted in 110 settlements, affecting more than 600,000 workers, during the first nine months of 1974. It was estimated that escalator clauses currently covered 5 million workers in major bargaining units (49% of the total).

Contracts containing cost of living clauses provided annual wage increases (exclusive of potential cost of living benefits) of 5.9% over the life of the contract, compared with wage gains of 4.9% won in 1973. Contracts without cost of living adjustments had annual wage increases averaging 8.9%, compared with 5.3% won during the previous year.

First year negotiated increases and cost of living adjustments already put into effect averaged 11% in settlements containing escalator provisions that were reached during the first nine months of 1974.

Administration Views

Voluntary inflation curbs eyed. President Nixon's two top economic advisers, Kenneth Rush and Herbert Stein, warned July 7 that the Administration might be forced to adopt voluntary restraint machinery for business and labor groups to curb inflation.

In an interview with U.S. News & World Report published July 7, Rush said, "We're working out a plan of consultation and discussion with labor and management." He denied that the Administration planned a return to compulsory economic controls, but warned, "excessive wage and price increases may create irresistable public pressure for reimposition of mandatory wage and price controls."

Rush singled out for criticism "seriously inflationary wage increases negotiated by labor and management." "If such escalation continued," he said, "it would be a very serious matter."

In a television interview July 7, Stein called on the public to exert more discipline in the fight over inflation. Because the public had resisted tax increases in 1965–68 and in 1971, Stein said, the government had been unable to quell rising prices. "Greater discipline," involving the acceptance of austere fiscal and monetary policies, would be required "for a really long time, . . . three or four years, more or less indefinitely," he said.

With excess demand at the root of the inflation problem, Stein declared, "people should understand the limits to what they can demand of the system."

Nixon, businessmen confer. President Nixon conferred for more than two hours July 11 at the White House with a group of corporate executives and economists in a meeting that was described by a senior official as a "listening exercise" for the President to obtain business views on the Administration's anti-inflation efforts.

Participants said no new economic policy initiatives were announced at the meeting, which had been billed as the start of a "national dialogue" between the Administration and segments of the economy on ways to combat inflation.

The businessmen generally expressed support for the Administration's policies but also presented a "strong demand" that the Administration stimulate industrial expansion by providing more tax incentives.

President Nixon's chief economic adviser, Kenneth Rush, who also attended the meeting, said in a later briefing that Nixon "didn't volunteer an opinion" on the group's proposals.

Rush contrasted the inflationary impact of tax concessions for industry and similar concessions for individuals. "A tax cut for individuals means increased demand without increased productivity," Rush said. However, tax incentives for business would be "noninflationary" if they spurred output. "We must have heavy investment in new facilities by industry" to overcome shortages, Rush said, adding that current corporate cash flow was not "nearly sufficient" to spur expansion.

Rush said the group generally expressed an "optimistic" outlook on the economy, but he added, "they are quite unhappy with the prime rate, with the state of the [stock] market, and the weakness in the bond market."

Inflation: No. 1 national concern. Inflation worries had replaced the energy problem as the nation's overriding concern, according to a Gallup Poll published July 14.

Forty-eight percent of those surveyed named the rising cost of living as the nation's paramount problem, followed by 15% who cited "lack of trust in government" and 11% who named "corruption in government" and "Watergate" as the principal areas of concern.

(In a survey conducted in January, 46% of those polled had named the energy crisis as the nation's "most important problem," followed by 25% who cited inflation.)

According to the survey, concern over inflation cut across a wide range of age and income groups, but those most worried about the rising cost of living were concentrated in the $10,000–$15,000 annual income bracket.

Surveys conducted abroad by affiliated organizations also reported that inflation was viewed as a major issue in other nations, the Gallup poll reported: 53% of those surveyed prior to parliamentary elections in Australia cited inflation as the most important issue, as did 49% of those queried in Britain in April.

Nixon economic address. President Nixon reiterated his intention to fight inflation with stringent fiscal and monetary policies—conservative measures that his aides termed "the old time religion"—in an address before four California business groups. The speech, which was delivered July 25 in Los Angeles, was nationally broadcast.

Nixon announced no new policy measures designed to curb rising prices. The answer to combatting inflation, he said, "lies in choosing a sensible, realistic course and sticking to it—whatever the pressures—and that is exactly what we will do." He specifically ruled out "shock treatment" for the economy, such as new deficit spending, or the "discredited patent medicine of wage and price controls," a tax cut—which he said would have the effect of "pouring gasoline on a raging fire," or the fatalistic acceptance of inflation as a "mysterious and incurable disease."

After listing at the outset what his Administration would not do in the fight against inflation, Nixon then cited policies that would be undertaken to control rising prices. He vowed to trim federal spending for fiscal 1975 "toward a goal of $300 billion." He warned that he would veto any Congressional actions that lifted the budget above his goal. There were few specific mentions of where budgetary cuts could be made but he said a savings of $300 million would result from his order to reduce the number of federal employes by 40,000.

Nixon also said that jawboning talks with business and labor groups would continue in an effort to restrain prices and wages. The President endorsed the Federal Reserve Board's strict credit policies, but he also acknowledged that monetary restraint could be carried to the "extreme." The Administration would work to "provide the expansion of money and credit necessary to support moderate growth of the economy at reasonable prices," Nixon said, assuring the business group that "there will not be a credit crunch in which the money for essential economic activity becomes unavailable."

In a message aimed at consumers, Nixon said, "We have worldwide inflation because people's demand too often is translated into a supply of votes, not a supply of work, saving, initiative and innovation." People believed that "the way to get more is to have the government spend more even though no more is produced," he said.

Nixon appealed to consumers to save an additional 1.5% of their income, families were urged to "reduce or defer some expenditure," businesses were urged to trim the "fat" from their operations, and all groups were invited to join an ad hoc "anti-inflation lobby" organized to counteract the pressures of special interest groups in Washington.

"In the longer run, we can focus more on increasing the growth of output—on producing more rather than demanding less . . . so that we can have more goods and services without higher prices," Nixon said.

Achieving prosperity without inflation, Nixon continued, would entail an overhaul of "obsolete" regulatory policies that "stifled" the "creative energies of our economic system." He was ordering a "sweeping review" of these policies, Nixon said. He also called for Congressional passage of the proposed trade reform bill and a restoration of the "idea that the way to have more is to produce more."

In one of the few controversial aspects of his speech, Nixon also said, "We must re-evaluate the trade-off between in-creasing supplies and certain other objectives, such as improving the environment and increasing safety. These are important, but we often have a tendency to push particular social goals so fast or so far that other important economic goals are unduly sacrificed."

Nixon's call for a 1.5% reduction in consumer spending prompted a debate among his aides July 26. When it was pointed out to Sidney L. Jones, a senior White House official, at a news conference that such a cutback would reduce consumer spending by more than $12 billion a year, Jones replied, "I don't want to see it. We don't want a consumer boycott." In an effort to clarify the President's remarks, Jones said, the Administration sought "more discretion" in consumer spending, meaning greater resistance to items that had shown large increases in price recently.

Herbert Stein, whose resignation as chairman of the President's Council of Economic Advisers was announced July 19, was less willing to disavow the appeal for reduced consumer expenditures. The proposal presented no "danger of causing a recession," Stein said, adding that a $12 billion cut in consumer spending would have the same salutary effects as a similar cut in the budget.

Rush, Stein, Burns assess policies— President Nixon's three chief economic advisers defended Administration policies but offered gloomy economic predictions in Congressional testimony July 29 and 30.

Kenneth Rush had declined previous invitations to testify before Congress on grounds that as economic adviser to the President, his relationship with Nixon was "confidential" and that their need for a "candid and uninhibited" exchange of views could be hampered by Congressional examinations. Rush relented when Sen. William Proxmire (D, Wis.), chairman of the Joint Economic Committee, threatened to hold up action on appropriations for Rush's salary.

Rush revealed little July 29 during the Joint Economic Committee's annual hearings on the mid-year state of the economy. He endorsed the Administration's policies of "moderate" budget and monetary restraint and rejected Proxmire's charge that the White House had "no policy" on economic matters because the President "cannot cope" with inflation problems while he was preoccupied with Watergate and impeachment problems. "I see no problem of leadership," Rush responded. No new economic policies were being utilized to combat rising prices, he said, because "what people need now is certainty, a period of feeling that we're on the right track and plan to stay on the right track."

(Rush altered his views July 31 when, following the House Judiciary Committee's vote, he observed that the threat of impeachment was exerting a "disturbing influence" on the economy by generating uncertainty within the business community.)

In testimony July 30 before the committee, Herbert Stein also endorsed the Administration's policies and said "our troubles are due to failure to follow this prescription." Stein conceded that Nixon's economic planners had not anticipated how long it would take to conquer inflation, adding that this had been reflected in "policies which were too weak in dealing with inflation or were abandoned too soon."

Stein predicted that inflation would taper off during the last half of 1974 to a "neighborhood of 7%" and that unemployment could rise to about 6% by the end of the year. But he admitted that the Administration's previous economic forecasts had "underestimated the future inflation rate."

The House Banking and Currency Committee heard testimony July 30 from Arthur Burns, who charged that inflation problems were caused by "loose fiscal policies" and called for a budget surplus for fiscal year 1975, ending June 30, 1975. (In another appearance before Congress July 15, Burns had said he favored a $10 billion cut in federal spending, lower capital gains taxes and reimposition of voluntary wage-price controls to combat inflation.)

Burns also defended the Federal Reserve's decision to reduce the rate of monetary and credit expansion. Tight credit policies over the past year, Burns said, had caused the rate of growth in the nation's money supply to slow to about 6% annually, but he added such a pace was "still too high for stability of average prices over the long term" and said efforts would be made to reduce it further.

Democrats offer policy rebuttal—In an official response to Nixon's speech from Congressional Democrats, Sen. Lloyd Bentsen (D, Tex.) charged the Administration with engaging in "too many trials and far too many errors" in devising economic policy.

Bentsen's rebuttal, which was broadcast nationally July 31, accused Nixon of telling the nation that current economic troubles "are everyone's fault except his and his advisers." Nixon "blamed international conditions, wild spending by Congress, the extravagance of citizens who spend money rather than save it," Bentsen said. "I felt that I was hearing the language of the economic cover-up."

In place of Nixon policies, which he said were characterized by "high interest rates, tight money, slow growth—business as usual," Bentsen advocated a program to meet short and long term economic needs. Proposals included repeal of tax provisions encouraging U.S. businesses to build factories abroad, repeal of "tax shelters for unproductive investments," "selective" credit allocations that would channel investments to areas in need of funds, such as housing, creation of a cost of living task force "to keep track of price increases and wage settlements," and reduced federal spending, including cuts in defense areas.

Wage-price monitoring group sought. President Nixon asked Congress Aug. 2 to establish a "cost of living task force" that could monitor wage, price, supply and productivity developments. According to the Administration's proposed legislation, however, the new group would not have enforcement powers to delay or reduce wage and price increases—powers that had been held by the defunct Cost of Living Council.

The proposal had wide bipartisan support in Congress. Joint Economic Committee members of both parties expressed support for a similar plan during hearings conducted Aug. 2 when Treasury Secretary William P. Simon was questioned about the Administration's efforts to curb inflation. In a television interview Aug. 4, Simon indicated that the White House would persist in its application of stringent policies of fiscal and monetary restraint even if the unemployment rate exceeded 6%, a level generally regarded as recessionary.

Simon maintained that rising prices, rather than rising unemployment, was the nation's principal economic problem. He opposed a shift away from "fiscal restraint," which he said was "just now beginning to bite," and added, "unemployment inching up does not mean that we are having a recession. . . . We can deal with the unemployment . . . with a welfare and unemployment [compensation] system."

Nixon urged to give way to Ford. Two opponents of President Nixon's economic policies called on him to relinquish his office to Vice President Gerald Ford in an effort to restore leadership during a time of economic crisis. Sen. William Proxmire (D, Wis.), chairman of the Joint Economic Committee, said Aug. 4 that Nixon should step aside under provisions of the 25th Amendment of the Constitution because impeachment developments would make it "extremely hard" for Nixon to "pull the country together" to "appeal to labor . . . [and] management" in a sustained fight against inflation.

AFL-CIO President George Meany criticized the Administration's policies Aug. 5 and suggested that Ford could cope with the current economic problems better than Nixon. While noting that he was not impressed by Ford's previous Congressional voting record or by his performance as vice president, Meany said Ford was a "conservative with integrity [and that] is far better than what we have today in the White House."

"All I want is for the President to go away," Meany declared. The Administration's tight money policies had pushed the economy to "the brink of disaster," Meany added.

"A depressed home-building industry, declining national production and increased unemployment had added to runaway inflation," Meany said. "The threat of business failures, drawn-out recession and continuing inflation hang over the nation as the result of the present money crunch."

Final action. Among his last actions as President Aug. 8, Nixon vetoed a $13.5 billion bill providing appropriations for the Agriculture Department, the Environmental Protection Agency, the Consumer Product Safety Commission, the Federal Trade Commission and the National Water Quality Commission. The measure would also have provided relief to the drought-stricken farmers of the Midwest. The bill posed a "distinct threat to our fight against inflation," Nixon said, because the amount authorized exceeded his fiscal 1975 budget by "some $540 million."

Nixon resigned as President Aug. 9.

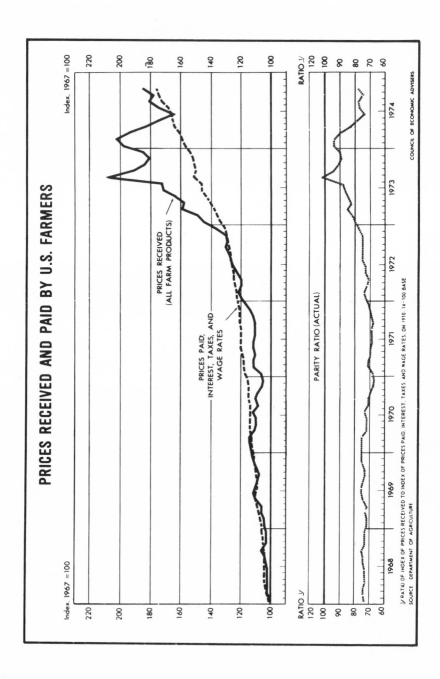

PRICES RECEIVED AND PAID BY U.S. FARMERS

PRICES RECEIVED
(ALL FARM PRODUCTS)

PRICES PAID,
INTEREST, TAXES, AND
WAGE RATES

PARITY RATIO (ACTUAL)

1/ RATIO OF INDEX OF PRICES RECEIVED TO INDEX OF PRICES PAID, INTEREST TAXES AND WAGE RATES, ON 1910-14=100 BASE

SOURCE DEPARTMENT OF AGRICULTURE

COUNCIL OF ECONOMIC ADVISERS

Food & Energy

Food Costs Rise

Bakers see $1 a loaf for bread. The American Bakers Association warned Jan. 9 that a spring wheat shortage could force prices up to $8–$12 a bushel and cause retail bread costs to climb to $1 per 1.5 pound loaf. (Wheat prices reached a new high of $5.93 a bushel in trading Jan. 9 on the Chicago commodities market. Large-sized loaves of bread currently were selling for an average 50¢.)

Bill O. Mead, chairman of the association, urged the Administration to set export controls because contracts already negotiated for wheat exports could cause a deficit in U.S. supplies before the 1974 crop became available. Mead traced the shortage to the U.S. sale of grain to the Soviet Union in 1972 when U.S. grains stocks were drastically depleted. Consequently, carryover supplies and the 1973 wheat harvest had proven insufficient to meet export demands during 1973 as well as current domestic requirements.

Assistant Agriculture Secretary Carroll G. Brunthaver termed the bakers' fears "irrational" but he conceded that the government was seeking to delay grain export shipments and that negotiations were under way with Canada to increase U.S. wheat purchases. (The Agriculture Department announced Jan. 11 that the Soviet Union had agreed to a delay in delivery of 18.4 million bushels of wheat until after the start of the summer harvest. The U.S. was still obligated to deliver 38.7 million bushels to the U.S.S.R. by June 30.)

Brunthaver accused the bakers of alarming the public with "scare tactics" but Mead said at his news conference that the warnings were issued directly to consumers because the Agriculture Department had ignored its requests for export controls.

Wheat import quota suspended. President Nixon Jan. 25 lifted the import quota on wheat for five months to provide a "stabilizing effect" on domestic wheat prices, which were at record levels. Nongovernmental analyists predicted, however, that the Administration's use of higher priced foreign wheat, principally from Canada, to stabilize domestic prices would cause further increases in the cost of wheat for U.S. consumers.

A White House spokesman denied that the action signaled an impending grain shortage, although he conceded that some "regional dislocations" were possible in the spring because of dwindling wheat supplies.

(New Agriculture Department figures released Jan. 30 showed that 714 million bushels of wheat were exported during the last six months of 1973. Their record shortages, hoarding and black marketing developed. The government's annual goal value was $2.62 billion, more than triple the value of exports during the same period of 1972. China was the largest single purchaser within the six-month period, buying 95 million bushels worth $272.4 million.)

The Tariff Commission said in a Jan. 24 report that the 1973 crop, which totaled 1.7 billion bushels, and supplemental carry over supplies would be nearly exhausted by June because of the combination of domestic consumption and a record export total of 1.2 billion bushels. According to the Agriculture Department, less than 200 million bushels of wheat—equivalent to a seven-week domestic and export supply—would remain from the 1973 crop when the 1974 harvest was ready for market. It would be the lowest carry over level since 1946, officials said. (As of Jan. 1, only 934 million bushels were on hand—the smallest amount in storage on that date since 1952.)

The U.S. had set wheat import levels at 800,000 bushels annually but the quota had not been met since 1965 when the U.S. support price was higher than the world price. Since July 1, 1973, less than 100,000 bushels had been imported.

Canadian grain prices raised. The Canadian Wheat Board announced Feb. 23 that the prices paid to farmers for wheat and barley would be raised March 1 by at least 50%. Minister of Justice Otto Lang, who was responsible for the board, said initial payments for wheat would rise from $2.25 to $3.75 a bushel, while barley prices would increase as much as 75¢ to $2.25 a bushel. The price adjustments would be temporary, applying only to the remainder of the 1973-74 crop year.

The higher payments would be instituted to induce farmers to increase deliveries to elevators and to put additional acreage into production. Canada had fallen behind in sales and shipment of grains and the board had earlier requested the farmers' cooperation in helping to meet current export and domestic commitments to maintain the nation's reputation "as a dependable grain supplier."

Despite large production increases, slackening deliveries had caused wheat exports to decline sharply during August-December 1973 (down 24% from the comparable 1972 period), Statistics Canada reported Feb. 18.

The shrinking deliveries were explained by the severe prairie winter whose snows hampered access to storage bins, absence of incentive caused by a good 1972-73 crop year and the anticipation that wheat prices would continue to be high, and, according to several farm organizations, low initial delivery payments.

Late planting due to heavy spring rains and cold weather resulted in an estimated 20% cut in the wheat crop, the Canadian Wheat Board said May 31. A June 25 assessment reported as much as a 25% reduction in the wheat harvest. A crop shortfall of the magnitude predicted could limit Canada's wheat exports to only 400 million bushels in the coming crop year.

The Wheat Board had dropped export wheat prices almost a dollar a bushel to a range of $4.75—$7.13 a bushel, it was reported May 17. The price cut preceded a major wheat sale to China by a month.

Higher world grain prices in 1973 had more than doubled the 1973 income of farmers in Saskatchewan, Alberta and Manitoba, it was reported June 6. Agriculture Minister Eugene Whelan defended the rise and continued July 10 to call for higher food prices in order to push farm incomes even higher.

U.S.-Soviet grain deal scored. The Senate Permanent Investigations Subcommittee issued a final report July 28 of its study of the controversial sale of massive supplies of U.S. grain to the Soviet Union in 1972.

Agriculture Secretary Earl Butz and two former assistant secretaries, Clarence Palmby and Carroll Brunthaver, were singled out for special responsibility for what the subcommittee termed a "$300 million error in judgment" that had resulted in depleted U.S. grain reserves, farm product shortages, higher food prices and the current crisis in the livestock industry.

"At virtually every step, from the initial planning of the sales to the subsidy that helped support them, the grain sales were ineptly managed," the subcommittee declared.

The panel, which was chaired by Sen. Henry M. Jackson (D, Wash.), found no fault with President Nixon's decision to use trade as a means of improving U.S.-Soviet relations, but the subcommittee was critical of the Administration's handling of the grain sale. "The Russians and the large [U.S.] grain [exporting] companies reaped the major benefits," Jackson said.

Subsidies costing $300 million were paid to the six exporting firms serving as middlemen in the deal. These payments were "unjustified," according to the committee, which added that the government's Commodity Exchange Authority was "derelict in its oversight responsibility" when it mishandled an investigation into possible market manipulation by the exporting companies.

The subcommittee urged Congress to pass legislation barring imposition of export subsidies unless public hearings were held. In other recommendations, the report asked creation of an independent commodity exchange commission patterned after the Securities and Exchange Commission; creation of a task force, made up of members drawn from government agencies concerned with economic policy, to coordinate future transactions like the grain deal; and preparation of a five-year projection of the nation's grain supplies and demands, beginning in 1975.

Two grain exporting firms that participated in the Soviet sale subsequently were directed by the Agriculture Department to "cease and desist from willfully submitting any false or misleading information in reports required under the Commodity Exchange Act." The orders, similar to an injunction, were served on the Louis Dreyfus Corp. Aug. 6 and the Continental Grain Co. Aug. 9.

Both firms consented to the order but denied allegations of willful violations. Dreyfus was accused of understating its cash position by 900,000 to 25 million bushels of wheat between July 7, 1972 and Oct. 20, 1972 when arrangements were being made to sell grain to the Soviet Union. Similar charges were filed against Continental, the nation's largest grain exporting firm.

The General Accounting Office had concluded Feb. 13 that there was no evidence that the exporting firms had reaped excessive profits from the Soviet deal or profited from inside information. Three of the companies lost money on the sale, according to the GAO.

However, the exporting companies eventually profited from the sale, the GAO said, because the Soviet transaction pushed up domestic grain prices and subsequently, federal subsidies paid to exporters.

Food riots in India. Scores of people died in India in January riots over food shortages and rising prices in the adjacent States of Maharashtra and Gujarat. The cost of basic items, especially food and fuel, had risen by 20% in the past six months, the greatest increase in India's cost of living in 26 years.

The first outbreak occurred Jan. 2 when a 24-hour strike in Bombay, Maharashtra closed factories, railways, restaurants and markets. A union leader said the walkout was an expression of "the people's anger and resentment at the failure" of the government to hold down prices. Six persons were killed at Wani, 350 miles north of Bombay, when police opened fire at a mob trying to burn a government office.

A rally at Nagpur was cut short when demonstrators disrupted a speech by Prime Minister Indira Gandhi.

Rioting, looting and arson in 16 cities and towns in Gujarat Jan. 11–13 left 12 persons dead and an unspecified number injured. At least 380 persons were arrested, according to police.

Food Riots in Gujarat cost at least 15 more lives Jan. 18–25.

Five persons were shot to death by police Jan. 18 in Rajkot after a mob burned or looted 50 shops and houses. Four more persons were slain Jan. 24 and another six died Jan. 25. Much of the violence was centered in the state capital of Ahmedabad, which was placed under a 24-hour curfew Jan. 24.

Police gunfire took the lives of seven participants in food riots in Bombay Feb. 22. Thousands of persons had marched in protest against rising food prices and shortages. The demonstrators burned shops, public buses and police vehicles and stoned police.

In an action aimed at speeding up food production, the Cabinet decided March 28 to abandon government control of wheat distribution. The old policy had been adopted in April 1973 to keep the price of wheat low and stable. Instead, the cost of wheat increased by 36% in one year and of 14.7 million tons of food for ration distribution had fallen short by more than six million tons.

India had been forced to purchase 1.8 million metric tons of foreign food grain during the current financial year, Economic Affairs Minister M.G. Kaul announced Aug. 1.

The crisis was further pointed up Aug. 12 by Food Minister Chidambara Subramaniam, who told Parliament that the government was having difficulty distributing wheat to the cities, where about a third of the population lived. The system under which the government purchased food for its ration shops in the cities was said by officials to be failing because of inflation, shifting policies, hoarding, corruption and the failure of state governments to deal with farmers.

Food prices climb in U.S. The Agriculture Department announced Feb. 26 that the market basket costs for a theoretical household of 3.2 persons rose 1.8% in January to total $1,680 at an annual rate. Over a 12-month period, retail prices rose 22%.

The department had predicted Feb. 14 that supermarket food prices would rise 12% throughout 1974 with most of the increase occurring in the first six months of the year. Prices were expected to stabilize during the third quarter and decline slightly in the final period.

Average supermarket prices increased 16% in 1973. The government had anticipated only a 6.5% gain.

The government's figures were based on year to year measures. When expressed in month to month terms, i.e., December 1972–December 1973, the increase in supermarket food prices was 22.1%.

In 1973, most of the higher food prices went to the farmer; in 1974, however, middlemen—processors, shippers, and distributors—were expected to receive the bulk of the increases.

Officials said sharply higher prices accounted for the 11% jump in food expenditures totaling a record $139 billion in 1973. Consumers' per capita purchases declined for the first time in years, dropping 2% from 1972. All of the cutback was in livestock related areas—meat, poultry and dairy products.

One of the principal commodities showing dramatic price increases during 1973 was wheat, which set new price records in January 1974. The closing price of a 60-pound bushel of wheat scheduled for March delivery was $6.315 in trading Feb. 15 on the Chicago commodities market. Steady high demand from foreign buyers and fears of shortages in basic foodstuffs caused other products (potatoes, sugar and cocoa) to rise the daily permissible limit in bidding.

The index of prices received by farmers climbed 1.5% in the 30-day period from mid-January to mid-February, officials announced Feb. 28. Since mid-February 1973, prices paid to farmers had risen 36%.

In a related action, Agriculture Secretary Earl L. Butz increased federal price supports for dairy products to $6.57 per hundredweight for the marketing year beginning April 1, the Wall Street Journal reported March 11. The current level was $5.61.

Butz assured consumers that the action would not cause dairy product prices to rise because their actual retail price had been near or above the support level.

Prices of food then fell, registering one-month declines but little price diminution over 12 months. The price of raw farm products fell 4% in the 30-day period from mid-February to mid-March, according to the Agriculture Department March 29. Livestock and wheat prices led the decline, each dropping 8% in that period.

It was the first decline reported in four 30-day periods, but prices received by farmers remained 22% above the comparable period of 1973. Prices paid by farmers rose 17% over the same 12-month span.

By March, the market basket's annual cost had mounted to a record $1,747. This was up $15 (or .9%) from February and 19.8% higher than in March 1973. It was the fifth consecutive month of increases, although lower meat prices helped to slow the March price spiral.

The annual cost of the market basket then declined 1.1% from March to April—to $1,728—but remained 16.8% higher than during the same period of 1973. In this first decline in market basket costs since October 1973, the consumer's weekly food bill dropped less than 40¢, and farmers absorbed most of the decline as middlemen increased their margins 1.5%.

During March, farmers' share of the dollar spent in retail stores fell from 45.9¢ in February to 43.6¢. Their returns from market basket foods were off 4.2% in one month. The middlemen's share, however, continued its steady upward movement, rising 5.2% in 30 days.

The Agriculture Department updated its raw farm price report April 30, announcing that costs were down 6% in the 30-day period ending April 15, despite the fact that farm prices generally were 17% higher than during the same period of 1973. Prices paid by farmers gained 2% in the period, and were 16% above last year's level.

Livestock and wheat price drops paced the index again; livestock costs fell 6% in 30 days and 9% from the comparable period of 1973. Wheat was off 18% from mid-March to mid-April but remained 86% higher than in mid-April 1973.

U.S. intervenes, bolsters beef prices— Agriculture Secretary Earl L. Butz announced March 27 that the government's Commodity Credit Corp. would move to bolster sagging beef prices by buying $45 million worth of hamburger made from prime, grain-fed cattle for use in the 1974–75 school lunch program.

That figure did not represent a significant increase over similar purchases made for the 1973–74 year, which totaled $43.4 million, but officials hoped their action would have an impact on market conditions because the purchases were made far ahead of schedule and involved a much better grade of meat than was usually bought.

Cattle prices had slumped to $40–$42 per hundredweight from the year's record high of $50.50 per hundredweight, set in January. Chaotic supply conditions were resulting from the immediate oversupply of animals ready for slaughter: in protest against the low prices, cattle feeders were withholding fattened livestock from market and choosing to sell their grain rather than use it to feed young animals. The problem could come full circle in six months when insufficient numbers of cattle went to slaughter because of drastic cutbacks in the herds and prices soared.

The Texas Cattle Feeders Association, which represented the top ranking cattle feeding state in the U.S., reported April 3 that the nation's cattle feeders had lost nearly $900 million in the past six months. The estimate was based on a "very conservative" estimate of an average $75 loss per head of cattle, spokesmen said.

The group attributed the losses to "government interference in the form of a discriminatory price freeze last July; the energy crisis which caused a recession psychology resulting in consumers buying less beef; the truckers' strike and increased feed costs." Other analysts placed the blame on cattle feeders who had miscalculated six months earlier and put too many cattle in feeder stations, inundating the market with cattle ready for slaughter.

Consumer groups were highly critical of the government's decision to intervene.

Farm price cuts bypass consumer. Wholesale and consumer price indexes indicated that a curious pattern was developing with food prices—significant declines were apparent at the farm level but these large price drops were not being passed along to consumers. In a roundup of regional supermarket prices June 17, the Wall Street Journal reported that wholesale choice beef prices were down 28% from their February high, but consumers were paying only 10% less. In other Journal comparisons, wholesale pork prices were down 27% but retail prices fell only 19%; frying chickens were down nearly 58% from Jan. 1 wholesale levels but supermarket customers were paying only 46% less; similar price relationships were noted for other commodities.

Agriculture Secretary Earl Butz urged food chains to reflect the downward trend in the price of farm products, according to the Journal. "It's high time that these lower farm prices show up more fully in lower retail store pricing," Butz said. Supermarket officials countered however, saying that the industry's net profit during 1973 fell to .49% of sales, its lowest margin in years.

Most of the pricing controversy centered on livestock, which had plummeted in price, and meat, which had shown considerably smaller declines at the retail price level.

A meeting for cattlemen, meat packers and supermarket officials was held at the White House June 17 to discuss the price squeeze threatening cattle feeders, who faced soaring grain prices and falling livestock prices. (Prices in Midwest markets fell $30-$35 in one week for an average 1,100 pound prime steer, the Washington Post reported June 13.)

Following the meeting, food chain executives promised to spur consumer demand by reducing meat prices and promoting sales for the glutted meat market. There was little indication, however, that the Administration would accede to cattlemen's demands and impose meat quotas. But in Congressional testimony June 20, Butz warned importing and exporting nations that the U.S. would be forced to use retaliatory trade measures "unless major exporting nations agree to voluntary restraints on [meat] shipments to this country and unless other countries, particularly Canada, reduce barriers to U.S. shipments."

In subsequent developments, it was announced June 18 that the government would increase its purchases of beef and pork for the school lunch program. Officials said that up to $100 million would be set aside for immediate purchases while meat prices were cheap, the market glutted and cattlemen were threatening further dislocations in the market by withholding livestock from slaughter until price conditions improved.

In other agricultural trade developments, the White House announced June 26 that President Nixon had lifted wheat and wheat product import quotas indefinitely. The quota had been suspended Jan. 25 in an effort to stabilize record prices for flour but only small amounts of Canadian wheat was imported and had little effect on domestic prices.

The Agriculture Department announced June 10 that it would begin to buy surplus cheese to bolster the price of milk used in making cheese.

Farm prices resume rise. The price of farm produced food increased by mid-July, the Agriculture Department announced July 31, after registering declines in the four preceding reporting periods. Officials said there was little prospect that the downward trend could be resumed because severe drought conditions in the Midwest had caused sharp reductions in the summer harvest of grain crops.

The 6% increase in prices paid to farmers for the 30-day period ending July 15 brought prices to a level 1% above 12 months earlier. Prices paid by farmers also increased 1% during the one-month period, but over 12 months, farmers' costs showed a 15% rise.

Officials attributed the price rebound to an extremely wet spring that delayed the planting of several grain crops and a period of dry weather that retarded their growth, sharply higher costs for fuel and fertilizer resulting from the recent energy crisis, and continued high demand for U.S.-produced foodstuffs on international markets.

The turnaround came after significant price drops were reported for the mid-April to mid-June period. Farm prices fell 4% in the 30-day period ending May 15, although they remained 7% above the level set in 1973. In its announcement May 31, Agriculture Department officials charged that middlemen were not passing the price declines on to consumers, citing a 30% drop in the farm price of hogs over a 12-month period and a 3% drop in the retail cost of pork. The price of steers fell 12% from the previous year, but retail beef prices were off less than 1%, according to the government.

Farm prices declined 6% from mid-May to mid-June and were 4% below the year earlier figure, officials said June 28. It was the first time in three years that farm prices showed a drop over a 12-month period. However, inflation caused farmers' costs to rise by 14% over the same one-year period. (In another report June 13, the Agriculture Department announced that the value of farmland jumped 25% during the past year—the largest annual increase since 1920. "A record high net farm income in 1973 and considerable optimism regarding future levels of net farm income set the stage for the jump," officials said.)

A continued slump in cattle and hog prices by mid-June contributed to the pressure on Congress to pass emergency credit legislation for livestock producers.

Weather conditions threaten prices— The nation's Midwest grain belt experienced a severe drought during July that was followed by heavy damaging rains in early August, conditions that were expected to have an adverse effect on meat supplies and consumer food prices over the next year, Agriculture Department officials warned.

In its latest revision of the 1974 corn crop forecast, officials said Aug. 12 that the harvest would be 12% below the 1973 level.

The nation's soybean crop was also damaged. New forecasts put the expected harvest at 1.3 billion bushels, down 16% from 1973's record level. Estimates of the wheat crop were reduced by 4% from previous forecasts, but the output—1.84 billion bushels—would still be 8% above the 1973 level.

Officials said Aug. 14 that reduced grain harvests "will have a substantial impact on the livestock and poultry industry and could set off a chain of events that may reverberate through the livestock industry for several years" as higher feed grain prices forced cattlemen to curtail the number of animal being fattened for slaughter.

Consequences of the smaller grain harvests were not limited to U.S. consumers. The U.S. ordinarily exported two-thirds of its wheat crop, a fifth of its corn and half of its soybean production. Smaller supplies of grain available for export were coinciding with periods of bad weather in food exporting nations, increases in fertilizer costs, and rising demand for foodstuffs. As a result, the pressure on the U.S. as the world's major food exporting nation was intense.

A&P guilty on meat prices. A federal court jury in San Francisco July 25 found the Great Atlantic & Pacific Tea Co. (the A&P supermarket chain) guilty of conspiring to fix wholesale and retail beef prices. The jury awarded actual damages of $10.9 million to six livestock producers, and the damages were automatically trebled under antitrust law.

The verdict came in a suit filed in 1968, in which the plaintiffs accused A&P of conspiring with other major food chains to set high, noncompetitive retail prices and low wholesale prices paid to packers. The suit had also charged that A&P conspired to restrain trade by allocating geographical territories to preclude competition.

Two other defendants, Safeway Stores Inc. and Kroger Co., had settled out of court in 1973, agreeing to pay only plaintiffs' attorneys fees.

The damages covered the 1964-68 period, although the plaintiffs had contended that the practices continued through early 1973. The company said it would seek a new trial.

Another suit charging A&P and Safeway with conspiring to fix meat prices had been filed in Lincoln, Neb. federal district court June 10. The plaintiff, Loren Schmit—a cattleman and Nebraska state senator—filed the suit as a class action for other state meat producers and claimed $507 million in actual damages.

Hunger, poverty found worsening. The Senate Select Committee on Nutrition and Human Needs was told during hearings June 19-21 that the nation's needy were getting hungrier and poorer and that government programs dealing with hunger were ineffective.

A report prepared for the committee by a panel of outside experts cited steeply rising food costs and inequities in federal food programs, particularly food stamps, as the major problems.

The panel noted that between December 1970 and March 1974, food stamp benefits for a family of four had increased 34% while the cost of foods in the Agriculture Department's "economy" food plan—the basis for food stamp allocations—had increased 42%. Since it was the cheapest foods that underwent the sharpest price increases during that period (124% for rice, 256% for dried beans), the poor did not have the "spending down" option available to higher-income groups.

'Banana war' developments. A conflict between members of the fledgling Union of Banana Exporting Countries (UPEB) and the U.S. firms United Brands Co. and Standard Fruit & Steamship Co. intensified during May–August.

The trouble stemmed from an UPEB decision in March to impose an export tax of up to $1 per 40-pound crate on the producing companies. Standard and United Brands retaliated by halting exports and cutting production in three of the four countries which actually imposed the tax—Costa Rica, Honduras and Panama—prompting charges by Panamanian officials that the firms were plotting against those nations' governments.

Leaders of the affected nations met several times to discuss the companies' action. Representatives of all UPEB countries except Ecuador met in Panama July 15-17 and agreed to formally constitute UPEB by Sept. 17. Ecuador did not participate or impose the export tax because it said that as an oil producer, it was not suffering from the rise in world oil prices—the chief reason given by UPEB members for trying to increase their banana export revenues.

Panama, which exported 32 million crates of bananas in 1972, was the only nation to impose and maintain the full $1 tax, putting it into effect April 1. United Brands retaliated by starting court action against the tax, and, according to banana workers' leaders, by reducing cutting of fruit from five to two days a week, it was reported June 13.

United Brands halted exports from Panama July 28, after the government demanded payment of the tax in cash, rather than in guaranteed certificates.

Panama's ambassador to Costa Rica, David Pere, charged June 3 that United Brands and Standard were involved in plots to assassinate Panama's strongman, Brig. Gen. Omar Torrijos, and to overthrow the Costa Rican and Honduran governments.

Torrijos had donated $1 million each to Honduras and Costa Rica May 27 to help them through their conflicts with the U.S. firms. He said Aug. 1 that Cuba had offered to buy bananas from Panama, despite lack of need, to help Panama in its conflict with United Brands.

Costa Rica, which exported 53 million crates of bananas in 1972, imposed the $1 tax in April but was forced to reduce it to 25¢ a crate Aug. 1, after various retaliatory actions by both Standard and United Brands.

Standard initially reacted to the Costa Rican export tax by halting exports, cutting production and firing local workers, according to press reports.

United Brands at first paid the Costa Rica tax, estimating it would affect its rival Standard more seriously, the London newsletter Latin America reported July 12. However, it changed tactics after President Daniel Oduber decided to tax unfarmed land owned by foreigners (United Brands was the largest landowner in Costa Rica, but used little of

its property, according to Latin America). In June, the U.S. firm refused to settle a strike by workers for its banana subsidiary, effectively matching Standard's production cutback. The strike was halted July 8.

Honduras, which exported 45 million crates of bananas in 1972, imposed a tax of 50¢ a crate April 25. Standard halted exports, cut production and, according to labor union leaders, was destroying 145,-000 crates of bananas and other fruit each week in May, it was reported May 21. Standard initially denied the destruction but finally admitted it, according to the Miami Herald May 27. Standard resumed exporting bananas from Honduras at one-third its normal output, it was reported May 31, but the exports went to new markets—chiefly Belgium and Morocco—where the tax did not apply.

Colombia, which exported only 10 million crates in 1972, imposed a 40¢ tax May 8.

International Energy Developments

U.S. seeks foreign ministers' meeting. Secretary of State Henry A. Kissinger Jan. 10 called on oil-producing and oil-consuming nations to seek a long-term multinational agreement to deal with the energy shortage.

Kissinger's appeal followed an announcement by the White House Jan. 9 that President Richard M. Nixon had asked foreign ministers of eight oil-consuming nations meet in Washington Feb. 11 to discuss world energy problems. Invitations were sent to the heads of government of Britain, Canada, France, Italy, Japan, the Netherlands, Norway and West Germany. Nixon also had sent messages to the 13 states belonging to the Organization of Petroleum Exporting Countries (OPEC), inviting them to join in the discussions with the consumer nations at a later date.

The President said the purpose of the foreign ministers' meeting would be to analyze the situation and then "establish a task force" to "formulate a consumer action program." The program, he said, would "deal with the explosive growth of global energy demand" and would "accelerate the coordinated development of new energy sources." According to Nixon, the oil-consuming nations would seek to "meet the legitimate interests of oil-producing countries while assuring the consumer nations adequate supplies at fair and reasonable prices."

Kissinger's remarks on the fuel crisis were made at a joint news conference with William E. Simon, head of the Federal Energy Office. The secretary said the goal of multilateral agreements lay behind President Nixon's proposal for the Feb. 11 energy conference. Kissinger advised the oil-consuming nations not to seek individual agreements with oil-producers to protect their supplies because such "unrestricted bilateral competition will be ruinous for all countries concerned."

France proposes world energy meeting— French Foreign Minister Michel Jobert, in a letter to United Nations Secretary General Kurt Waldheim dated Jan. 18, proposed the urgent convening of a world energy conference under U.N. auspices. Jobert wrote that the conference should aim at determining the general principles of future cooperation between the energy producers and consumers and to devise practical steps likely to achieve such cooperation. The planning would seek to forestall difficulties between nations or groups of nations, and would be of particular interest to developing countries hurt by energy shortages.

OPEC delays price changes. The Organization of Petroleum Exporting Countries (OPEC) announced Jan. 9 after a three-day meeting in Geneva that there would be no "increase or decrease in the [basic] price of crude oil until April 1."

Iranian Finance Minister Jamshid Amouzegar, who issued that statement, said the OPEC would raise its prices after April 1 if import costs continued to rise. According to Amouzegar, a four-point agreement reached at the OPEC meeting provided for continued pricing studies, a decrease in the fixed relationship between posted prices and actual market prices, possible creation of a development bank to assist underdeveloped countries to pay their higher oil bills and a renewed plea to consumer nations to combat inflation.

Canada's oil export tax. Canada's Parliament passed a bill setting an oil export tax of $6.40 a barrel for February and March, but rejected a government request for authority to extend and adjust the tax every month to a maximum of $10, it was reported Jan. 9.

Opposition members said a permanent tax should only be imposed after long-term pricing policies had been determined, and after a scheduled federal-provincial energy conference was held. Members were also in dispute over federal equalization payments to non-oil-producing provinces, to match export tax funds going to oil producing provinces.

The new export tax rise would raise the cost of Canadian crude oil to U.S. purchasers to $10.50 a barrel, roughly in line with world prices.

France raises fuel prices. France Jan. 10 announced sharp increases in the price of gasoline, heating and industrial fuel oil, effective the following day, to reflect recent price raises by oil-producing nations.

The price of a liter of high-test gasoline rose by nearly 30% to 1.75 francs (about $1.30 a U.S. gallon), the second highest rate in Western Europe after Italy. The price of heating fuel rose by 45%.

Finance Minister Valery Giscard d'Estaing, in the first of planned monthly television talks, said Jan. 8 that the petroleum price increases by producer nations would cause a French trade deficit in 1974 for the first time since 1969 by adding 31 billion francs (about $6 billion) to France's annual import bill. This would result in an anticipated 18 billion franc deficit instead of the previously expected eight billion franc surplus. The producer price increases would also cause French retail prices to rise by an additional 1.5%–2%.

French mission to Arab states. French Foreign Minister Michel Jobert visited Saudi Arabia, Kuwait and Syria Jan. 24–29 in a move aimed at establishing French economic, political and military influence in the region.

In his meetings with Saudi Arabian King Faisal Jan. 24–26, Jobert discussed a proposed 20-year agreement in which France would receive 800 million tons of oil in return for sophisticated arms and industrial equipment.

Jobert was said to have sought a similar oil-arms agreement in his discussions in Kuwait Jan. 27–28. Kuwait government sources reported Jan. 28 that France was ready to supply fighter planes, tanks and anti-aircraft missiles without political conditions. Jobert, the sources said, offered French participation in petrochemical and oil refinery projects in Kuwait in return for a yearly guarantee of oil delivery.

The French foreign minister conferred in Damascus Jan. 29 with Syrian President Hafez al-Assad and Foreign Minister Abdel Halim Khaddam.

Iran, U.K. approve oil deal. Iran would supply Great Britain with five million additional tons of crude oil in exchange for about $240 million worth of industrial goods under an agreement concluded Jan. 25. The accord was reached in St. Moritz, Switzerland, where British Chancellor of the Exchequer Anthony Barber and Trade and Industry Secretary Peter Walker conferred with the shah of Iran, who was on vacation.

The British goods would include textile fibers, steel, paper and petrochemicals, but no arms, according to British spokesmen. However, Iranian officials had recently discussed possible weapons purchases in London.

On their return to London, Walker and Barber said the extra oil, representing about 5% of Britain's oil imports in 1973, would mean that Britain would now receive 25% of its oil from Iran. The price of the five million tons would be about $7 a barrel, less than Iran received from concessionary oil firms.

Bonn accord with Iran discussed—West Germany announced Jan. 27 that it had agreed in principle to finance and build a $1.2 billion oil refinery in Bousair, Iran, in return for 182.5 million barrels of Iranian oil for five years. The refinery, to have an annual capacity of 25 million tons, would be totally owned by Iran after 15 years.

The agreement was reached after talks in St. Moritz between the shah and West German Economics Minister Hans Friderichs. They also discussed Iranian proposals for a German-financed billion-dollar chemical plant in Iran.

Algeria raises oil price. Algeria announced Jan. 17 that the posted prices of its oil would be increased 75% effective Jan. 1. The boost raised the price of a barrel from $9.25 to $16.21.

Saudis pledge oil price cut. Saudi Arabian Petroleum Minister Sheik Ahmed Zaki al-Yamani said Jan. 27 that King Faisal was preparing to "take very important steps" aimed at reducing the price of crude oil to avoid harming the world economy.

Yamani made the statement in Tokyo where he had arrived Jan. 26 on a five-day mission to explain his government's oil policy to Japanese officials. He told a news conference that although Saudi Arabia regarded current prices as "fair and reasonable," it was concerned that the "present prices of oil will create some serious problems in the balance of payments of so many nations, whether they are developing nations or industrialized nations."

Algerian Industry and Energy Minister Belaid Abdelsalam, who accompanied Yamani, expressed disagreement and said he was opposed to any cut in petroleum prices. He said the current high rates were necessary in view of Algeria's balance of payments deficit and its heavy indebtedness to foreign countries.

The two Arab officials held discussions Jan. 27 with Japanese leaders, including Deputy Premier Takeo Miki and Finance Minister Takeo Fukuda.

Yamani said Jan. 28 that any cut in oil prices must be taken jointly by the oil producers. "If we can convince the others, we will reduce our prices," Yamani said. He reiterated his warning against participation by other countries in the forthcoming U.S.-sponsored world energy conference to be held in Washington Feb. 11. Yamani said Japan and other oil-consuming nations "cannot afford any sort of confrontation."

Venezuela doubles oil price. Venezuela Feb. 6 doubled to about $14 a barrel the price it charged petroleum companies for royalty oil. The increase, retroactive to Feb. 1, affected the one-sixth of each firm's output which accrued to the government either in cash or in kind.

Posted prices for Venezuelan oil remained stable in February, but not because of pressure from the Organization of Petroleum Exporting Countries (OPEC), according to the government. Mines Minister Hugo Perez La Salvia had denied Jan. 15 that there was an OPEC agreement to freeze oil prices until April 1, asserting there was instead an agreement by six OPEC members from the Persian Gulf to hold prices in January–March.

Increases in posted prices for Venezuelan oil through December 1973 had increased the nation's international monetary reserves to $2.418 billion, according to International Monetary Fund statistics reported Feb. 2.

Jesus Soto Amesty, chairman of the Venezuelan Senate Foreign Relations Committee, charged Jan. 30 that a U.S. Senate warning on oil prices was an "act of arrogance." The U.S. Senate Jan. 29 had passed a resolution saying that further oil price increases by Venezuela, Canada and Middle Eastern states might result in "reciprocal economic action" by the U.S.

"For many years," Soto asserted, "[developed countries] have sacked underdeveloped people throughout the world, carrying away their raw materials at laughable prices."

"Moreover," he continued, "still at present the importing countries have to bear the tremendous expenses that the United States incurs in countries such as Vietnam, Korea or Cambodia, paying at high prices for ... indispensable articles. Thus, when the exporting countries unite to charge a just price for their oil, they are doing nothing less than defending themselves from the voracity of giants."

Senate panel probes secret oil deals. The Senate Foreign Relations Committee's subcomittee on multinational corporations held public hearings Jan. 30–31 to examine the pattern of relationship that developed over more than 20 years among major oil companies, the U.S. government and oil producing states in the Middle East.

Testimony at the first day's session concerned international tax aspects of the oil industry, including a secret Truman Administration decision and negotiations with Arab states over royalty payments, which gave the oil companies the opportunity to realize enormous after-tax profits.

Subcommittee Chairman Sen. Frank Church (D, Ida.) described the transactions, which had been detailed by tax analysts and former government officials in private subcommittee hearings.

In the summer of 1950, Church said, the National Security Council decided in "secret session" to make arrangements that would insure stable, pro-U.S. government in the Arab world. Accordingly, at the urging of the State Department, the Treasury Department "agreed to a system in which the [oil] companies would increase their payments to the oil producing governments and the American government would permit them to reduce their U.S. tax payments correspondingly," Church said.

The tax credit program proved mutually advantageous to the Arab governments and to the oil industry. According to Church, "the result of this arrangement was to abruptly reduce the taxes paid by the companies to the U.S. Treasury while dramatically increasing the tax revenues accruing to the oil producing governments." (If the royalty payments had been regarded as business expenses subject to deduction from gross earnings rather than as foreign taxes suitable for a dollar for dollar writeoff, the oil companies' after-tax profits would have been drastically reduced.)

Tax credits derived from the oil industry's highly profitable foreign operations had exceeded their U.S. tax liabilities since 1962, Church said. In 1973, when the five major U.S. oil companies— Exxon, Texaco, Mobil, Standard (California) and Gulf—made $4.5 billion abroad, they paid negligible amounts of U.S. taxes, he said.

The subcommittee also released private cable traffic from the London Policy Group, an oil industry association, and its New York advisory committee. In one cablegram, oil officials conceded that the "artificiality" of the posted price system used for setting royalty payments and computing tax credits was "obvious and well known, but it has not been challenged by the IRS."

The subcommittee staff pointed out that despite the artifically high price for Middle East oil, neither the producing states nor the oil companies had any incentive to reduce it because royalty payments enriched Arab treasuries and U.S. tax credits enabled the companies to write off their expenses.

Origins of escalating price hikes—Sen. Church charged Jan. 31 that the oil companies' inability to present a united stand against demands from oil producing countries for a larger share of oil profits, together with "indifference" expressed by the State Department and Justice Department over consequences of escalating prices, permitted the recent trend toward "leap frog" prices increases to reach chaotic and dangerous proportions.

Testimony from Henry M. Schuler, vice president of Hunt International Petroleum Corp., third largest independent oil producing venture in Libya, supplemented Church's charges.

Schuler described oil policy and negotiations since 1971 as an "unmitigated disaster" which had created the "unstoppable momentum" within the Arab world for higher prices.

Unless the oil companies and oil consuming nations stood firm in the face of these escalating prices, Schuler said, "there will be such serious economic and political dislocation for the entire world that demands for military intervention will become inevitable."

"If a political and economic monster has been loosed upon the world [by the oil crisis]," Schuler continued, "it is the creation of Western governments and companies. Together we created it and gave it the necessary push, so only we, acting in harmony, can slow it down."

Schuler began his testimony with the observation that since August 1970, the price of Libyan crude had increased 1,- 100% from $1.50 a barrel to $16.

After the Libyan revolution in 1969, Schuler said, the government decided to seek a larger proportion of oil revenues than the 50-50 split, which had been in effect for 20 years, by raising prices and limiting production.

Occidental Petroleum Corp., the most vulnerable oil company for such a strategy because Libya was its only source of crude, was selected as the first target.

When Exxon refused to provide Occidental with an alternative source of petroleum to withstand the Libyan pressure, Occidental capitulated to Libya's demands and in September 1970 agreed to turn over 58% of its total profits.

With the Occidental precedent established, the oil "companies were picked off one by one," Church said. According to Schuler, the final breakdown in efforts to maintain industry unity before the "leap frog" strategy of negotiating separate price increases occurred in January 1971. At a meeting in London, the major companies and all but two independents— Hunt and a German firm—surrendered to the Middle East nations' price demands. (The London Policy Group evolved out of this unsuccessful effort to present a unified front in negotiations.)

On the basis of Schuler's testimony and numerous government documents on the issue, several senators charged that the oil companies' efforts were "undercut" by the U.S. government that lacked even "the foggiest notion" of the price crisis' implications. The Justice Department had agreed to waive antitrust reprisals against the industry during its period of joint negotiations, but, Church declared, the Nixon Administration "waffled" the opportunity for presenting a united front when in January 1971 federal officials suggested that the price talks be divided into separate discussions with the Persian Gulf states and with Libya and Algeria. "We were seen to back off and off," Schuler said. "The oil producing states realized there was no way to stand against them. This is why we are in the position we are in today."

McCloy's antitrust efforts—John J. Mc-Cloy, a longtime presidential adviser, told the subcommittee Feb. 6 about his 10-year efforts to lay the groundwork for protection from antitrust prosecution for the oil industry in its joint bargaining with Middle East nations and the industry's stunning setback suffered in 1971 negotiations with oil producers.

McCloy, a Wall Street lawyer representing 23 oil companies, told of his talks with President John F. Kennedy in 1961 soon after producing nations formed the Organization of Petroleum Exporting Countries (OPEC). He mentioned the need for similar "concerted action" by the oil companies, McCloy said, adding that he personally had reminded every attorney general from 1961 to 1972 of the industry's problems in dealing jointly with foreign oil producing nations while constrained by U.S. antitrust laws.

McCloy said his efforts resulted in an informal agreement in which the government allowed the oil companies to bargain collectively. In 1971, McCloy continued, he sought and obtained a formal letter of enforcement intention disavowing any government challenge to the industry position as additional protection; his preparations proved fruitless, however, when presidential emissary John N. Irwin 2nd, and Douglas MacArthur 2nd, ambassador to Iran, agreed to a suggestion by the shah of Iran that the oil companies conclude separate price agreements with producing states. His fears that a "chain reaction inherent in separate [price] negotiations" would result were realized, McCloy said.

(The Justice Department gave preliminary approval Jan. 29 to the oil companies' plan to negotiate jointly with OPEC. The department stressed that the action did not constitute immunity from future antitrust prosecution. The oil companies had sought an advisory opinion, called a business review letter, on the matter. The opinion they received allowing them to proceed with joint talks represented only an "expression of present enforcement intention," officials said. The ruling was similar to that won in 1971 by McCloy.)

In testimony released Feb. 9, John N. Irwin 2nd, currently ambassador to France and former undersecretary of state, described negotiations he attended in 1971 between representatives of oil companies and OPEC nations. Irwin had been accused of failing to back up the oil companies in their efforts to present a unified negotiating front with Middle East nations seeking higher oil prices. Irwin was President Nixon's special representative at the talks, which resulted in a period of staggering, "leap-frogging" price increases when the participants failed to reach a stable pricing agreement.

According to Irwin, he was prepared to support the oil companies in their desire to negotiate as a single group with OPEC. He said he agreed to split the talks between the Persian Gulf state producers and Libya and Algeria as another group after being persuaded by the shah of Iran. The U.S. ambassador to Iran, Douglas MacArthur 2nd, concurred in the decision, Irwin said.

The oil companies were not informed of the change in strategy, which effectively undercut their position, until after Irwin accepted the shah's proposal, he added.

Price hike tied to oil company dispute— Sen. Church charged Feb. 18 that a dispute between a major U.S. oil company and a large U.S. distributor forced up prices paid for petroleum by public utilities along the eastern seaboard. Customers, principally those served by Consolidated Edison of New York and Long Island (N.Y.) Lighting Co., paid $50 million more annually in higher prices as a result.

The charges were based on testimony taken in December 1973 from Edward M. Carey, president of New England Petroleum Co. (NEPCO), which sold fuel to the utilities.

NEPCO accused Standard Oil Co. (California) of breaking a long-term contract to supply it with crude oil, forcing the company to charter other tankers at a higher cost to import the fuel.

The dispute arose in 1973 when Libya seized 51% of Standard's oil operations. After Libya's action, Standard, which operated a refinery in the Bahamas with NEPCO to process the Libyan crude, notified NEPCO that it would suspend deliveries from Libya as part of its tough new policy aimed at denying Libya a market for the oil it had seized.

NEPCO, faced with the need to supply its customers and meet payments on the Bahamas refinery, negotiated a separate deal with the Libyan National Oil Co. and arranged for tankers to ship the "hot" oil Standard refused to deliver.

Carey explained the decision: "We did not feel that we could prudently sit and wait for the major oil companies to negotiate something with the Libyan government because [in the interim] ... you would have substantial blackouts and brownouts in the northeast part of the U.S."

After the deal was negotiated with Libya, NEPCO officials said they received two phone calls from Texaco and Standard executives warning the firm not to proceed with the import arrangement. (Texaco oil fields also had been seized.) Immediately thereafter, Frank A. Mau of the State Department's Office of Fuel and Energy, called NEPCO officials.

Mau's "conversation was essentially the same as the previous two except instead of saying that legal actions would be taken to preserve the rights of these two companies, we were told that the State Department felt this was the wrong thing for New England to do, that this would have repercussions in the Middle East and that the State Department opposed this action," Richard Manning, NEPCO's attorney, testified.

Manning said he returned the phone call to protest the government intervention: "If the State Department wanted us to stop picking up the oil and shut down the utilities on the East Coast," he said, "we would have to be notified by the elected representative of the people."

The oil industry pressure tactics proved unsuccessful over the long term as well. They were not able to shut off the world market in "hot" oil and Libya nationalized the remaining U.S. oil operations Feb. 11. The Wall Street Journal reported Feb. 15 that Libya continued to sell oil to NEPCO as a "gesture of gratitude" for defying the big oil companies.

By the latter part of 1973, however, electricity rates for utilities served by NEPCO rose 18.5% and their fuel prices soared 74%, according to Church. Standard had charged 40¢ a barrel to transport the oil to the jointly owned refinery but tankers chartered to ship the "hot" oil charged $1.90 a barrel, Carey said.

Joint action planned. A U.S. proposal for international cooperation to combat the world's energy crisis was endorsed in a communique adopted Feb. 13 at the conclusion of a three-day conference in Washington of 13 major oil-consuming nations. France, one of the participants, objected strenuously to several key points of a 17-point proposal.

Attending the U.S.-sponsored meeting were the foreign ministers of Belgium,

Britain, Canada, Denmark, France, West Germany, Ireland, Italy, Japan, Luxembourg, the Netherlands, Norway-and the U.S. The finance ministers of all those countries, except France, also were present.

The proposals opposed by France:

■ "A comprehensive action program to deal with all facets of the world energy situation." This included several U.S. proposals that called for joint measures in conserving energy, in allocating oil supplies in times of emergency and in speeding research for new energy sources.

■ Establishment of a coordinating group to prepare for a conference of oil-producing and oil-consuming countries "at the earliest possible opportunity."

■ Formation of a coordinating group of senior officials "to coordinate the development of the actions" recommended by the conference.

■ Adoption of financial and monetary measures to avoid "competitive depreciation and the escalation of restrictions on trade and payments or disruptive actions in external borrowing."

French Foreign Minister Michel Jobert criticized the conference, asserting that energy matters were used by the U.S. as "a pretext." The parley's real purpose, he said, was a "political" desire by the U.S. to dominate the relationships of Western Europe and Japan.

Despite France's objections to the key elements of the communique, U.S. Secretary of State Henry A. Kissinger called the meeting a success and possibly a major step toward "dealing with world problems cooperatively."

Jobert had said in a speech at the opening session Feb. 11 that the conference should not take specific action, that it should be confined to merely an exchange of views. He criticized West German Finance Minister Helmut Schmidt for going too far in supporting the U.S. position at the meeting.

The final communique adopted was based largely on a seven-point program Kissinger had submitted in an address to the Feb. 11 session. Calling his plan "Project Interdependence," the secretary said the U.S. was prepared to share its technological expertise with others in the development of new energy sources and in arranging for improved cooperation between oil producers and consumers.

The proposals set forth by Kissinger:

■ The U.S. would join other consumer nations in studying conservation methods to cut down on the use of energy.

■ In order to cushion the impact on major industrial nations, an international program would be set up to handle any interruption in, or manipulation of fuel supplies.

■ The U.S. would make "a major contribution" toward international research and development of new technology in energy programs.

■ The U.S. would be willing to share its energy with other consumers in times of shortages if those nations would offer to do the same.

■ International cooperation, including "new mechanisms," must be carried out to deal with distribution of capital from oil revenues.

■ New foreign aid programs were required to help less wealthy consumers that suffered even more from high oil prices.

■ Consumers and producers should discuss what constituted a "just price" for oil and how to insure long-term investments.

Kissinger said his proposals were aimed at making certain of future "abundant energy at reasonable cost to meet the entire world's requirements for economic growth and human needs."

At a dinner in honor of the foreign ministers later Feb. 11, President Nixon emphasized that bilateral deals caused the price of oil to increase. He said that while such transactions might be "good short-term politics," they were "bad long-term statesmanship."

Financial aspects of oil price rise—The U.S. Feb. 14 released the text of Treasury Secretary George P. Shultz's address to the Washington energy conference.

In his speech on the world financial ramifications of soaring oil prices, Shultz warned that current price levels "spell misery and even starvation" to developing countries unable to pay for needed oil. Since industrial nations already faced severe payments crises because of higher oil prices, and "can't be expected to pay for the cost of increased oil" for developing nations, Shultz said, "that responsibility must fall primarily on the oil producers."

Any basic solution to the financial dilemma confronted by industrial and developing nations alike, Shultz said, involved a reduction in oil prices. "Cooperation is essential . . . [but it] is not a substitute for changing the problem so that it is more manageable. There is no way to print up money and use it to 'paper over' a real problem," Shultz declared. To deal with the special problems of developing countries, Shultz said industrial nations must maintain their "historical levels of aid," but that the newly affluent oil-producing countries should "take immediate steps to greatly expand their aid programs." He also proposed establishment of "a kind of multinational joint venture," a mutual fund in which Arabs could safely invest their surplus wealth and also facilitate the redistribution of their profits for the benefit of poorer nations hardest hit by oil price increases. Investor and recipient nations would share in the management of the organization, according to Shultz's plan.

Other U.S. suggestions for dealing with money problems arising from the oil price crisis included increased use of reciprocal currency arrangements or swaps among central banks, increased Arab involvement in international financial organizations, a "rechanneling" of World Bank money from oil-producing states to poorer countries and early repayment of existing bank loans by petroleum-exporting nations.

Arabs assail energy conference—The conference in Washington was criticized Feb. 10 by the major Arab oil-producing states of Libya, Kuwait and Saudi Arabia.

Tripoli radio called the meeting "an aggressive act against the oil-producing states, particularly the Arab states." It said the parley was "an American trap to sanction an American tutelage in Europe and internationalize oil resources by means of force."

Kuwaiti Petroleum Minister Abdel Rahman Atiki said his government approved of the conference in principle, but opposed "the idea of allowing opposing blocs to discuss such an important topic."

Prince Saud of Saudi Arabia said "if the aim of the Washington conference is to mount pressure on the producing states, then we do not think it will be fruitful." He questioned whether the meeting would produce a unified position of the oil consumers in view of "the discrepancy in the attitudes of the participants."

Algerian President Houari Boumedienne had said Feb. 4 that the conference was "directed toward creation of an imperialist protectorate over energy resources." He said it would bring no results "because the oil-producing states are opposed to it."

The Soviet Communist Party newspaper Pravda described the conference Feb. 11 as a U.S. attempt "to create a coalition of industrial states against the oil-exporting developing countries."

Islamic conferees discuss oil crisis. A summit meeting of heads of state and government of 38 Moslem nations was held in Lahore, Pakistan Feb. 22–24 to discuss Israel's occupation of Arab territories, the future status of Jerusalem and the oil crisis.*

A "Declaration of Lahore" established an eight-nation committee to study ways of easing the pressure of high oil prices on developing Moslem nations in Africa and Asia. However, the delegates rejected a proposal that would have provided a specific aid program by the Arab states to those nations.

Oil issue hurting third world—Several black African nations were reported questioning the wisdom of siding with the Arabs on the Middle East conflict in exchange for the promise of an Arab boycott of Rhodesia, Portugal and South Africa, according to the New York Times March 3.

Petroleum prices in the undeveloped countries had risen 30% and the Arab states had rejected requests for price reductions.

Shah says U.S. continues to get oil. Shah Mohammed Riza Pahlevi of Iran said Feb. 24 that the U.S. was importing at

---

*Participants in the conference: Afghanistan, Algeria, Bahrain, Bangla Desh, Chad, Egypt, Gabon, Gambia, Guinea, Guinea Bissau, India, Indonesia, Iran, Iraq, Jordan, Kuwait, Lebanon, Libya, Malaysia, Mali, Mauritania, Morocco, Niger, Nigeria, Oman, Pakistan, Palestine Liberation Organization, Qatar, Saudi Arabia, Senegal, Somalia, South Yemen, Sudan, Syria, Tunisia, Turkey, Uganda, United Arab Emirates and Yemen.

Among the heads of state attending were King Faisal of Saudi Arabia, and Presidents Anwar Sadat of Egypt, Muammar el-Qaddafi of Libya, Houari Boumedienne of Algeria and Hafez al-Assad of Syria.

least as much oil as it did before the Arabs imposed their embargo during the October 1973 war in the Middle East and indicated that the American oil industry may have deliberately manipulated gasoline shortages in the U.S. to increase their profits.

The shah's statement was made to interviewer Mike Wallace and broadcast on WCBS-TV. Suggesting that the U.S. may be getting oil surreptitiously, the Iranian leader told of tankers changing their destinations "two or three times" in mid-ocean and of oil being sold for one destination and being delivered somewhere else.

The shah predicted that oil-producing countries would raise their prices further but the extent depended on whether the industrial consumers adopted "a hostile or a cooperative attitude." He said the degree of the price increase would also depend on whether the industrial nations would control their inflation. "The bills [for their goods] that they are presenting us every day is something ridiculous," the shah said.

7 nations end embargo of U.S. Seven of nine Arab petroleum-producing countries agreed at a meeting in Vienna March 18 to lift the oil embargo they had imposed against the U.S.

One of the seven nations, Algeria, said it was removing the ban provisionally until June 1. The Arab producers were to meet again on that date in Cairo to review their decision. The embargo was to remain in effect against the Netherlands and Denmark. The delegates placed Italy and West Germany on the list of "friendly nations," assuring them of larger supplies.

The Arab action, taken at a meeting of the Organization of Petroleum Exporting Countries (OPEC), was approved by Algeria, Saudi Arabia, Kuwait, Qatar, Bahrain, Egypt and Abu Dhabi. Libya and Syria refused to join the majority. Iraq boycotted the talks.

The OPEC meeting, which had begun March 16, confirmed the Arab decision which had been approved in principle at a conference in Tripoli, Libya March 13. The Vienna delegates had agreed at the March 17 meeting that oil prices would not be rolled back, despite protests and appeals from consumer nations. A communique said the oil ministers would convene a new meeting if any of the countries asked for one before July "with a view to revising the posted prices" for oil. The posted price for the next three months was to remain at $11.65 a barrel for Arabian light crude oil, in effect since Jan. 1.

Saudi Arabia was the only country which pressed for a lower price for oil. Other countries, led by Indonesia, Algeria, Nigeria and Iran, sought an increase above the $11.65 posted price.

With the announcement of the agreement to end the oil embargo, Saudi Arabia pledged March 18 an immediate production increase of a million barrels a day for the U.S. market.

A formal statement on the Arab decision did not mention the restoration of production cutbacks. The communique explained that a shift in American policy away from Israel had prompted the producers to terminate the embargo.

Algerian Petroleum Minister Belaid Abdelsalam said March 18 his country believed the U.S. had shown enough "goodwill" in using its influence to get Israel to carry out military disengagement with Egypt and to agree to contacts with Syria to negotiate a similar pullback to warrant lifting the embargo. Libya and Syria, however, were not convinced of this and decided not to go along with the majority opinion, Abdelsalam said.

Saudi Arabia Petroleum Minister Sheik Ahmed Zaki al-Yamani said March 18 the decision against resuming the flow of Arab oil to the Netherlands and Denmark was taken because these two countries "have not made clear their position on asking for a full [Israeli] withdrawal from occupied territories."

OPEC official accuses oil consumers— OPEC Secretary General Abderraham Khene of Algeria charged March 19 that major oil-consuming nations were "conspiring" to force down the market price of oil. He asserted that the alleged conspiracy had resulted from a meeting of the major oil-consuming nations in Washington in February.

Khene said: "We had doubts about the meeting in Washington, and now we are concerned about some of the results . . . we have the facts that big pressure has already been put on the oil companies by all consumer nations to resist the market price asked for."

Major oil firms' profits soar. British Petroleum Co., which was 49% owned by the British government, announced March 14 that profits rose 332% in 1973 to a record $760 million, despite a drop in the sale of crude oil and refined products. Higher oil prices and changes in currency values accounted for the increase, officials said.

Fourth quarter profits increased an estimated 250% to total $289 million. Revenue rose 60% in the final three months of 1973.

■ Standard Oil Co. (Ohio) announced Jan. 27 that its operating profits in the final quarter of 1973 dropped 40% on a 7% increase in revenue, but operating profits for the entire year rose 24% on an 8% gain in revenue. Net income for the October-December period was $11.6 million, down from operating profits of $19.3 million and net income of $17.1 million in the final period of 1972. Total operating profits for the year were $74.1 million, up from operating profits of $59.7 million. Net income over the same period climbed from $57.5 million to $89.4 million, a 55% gain.

■ Standard Oil Co. (Indiana) Jan. 28 reported a 53% gain in earnings during the fourth quarter of 1973 and a 36% increase for the entire year. Net income in the final period was $121.4 million, up from $79.5 million. Revenue totaled $1.9 billion, a gain of 26%. For the year, net income rose to $511.2 million from $374.7 million on an 18% gain in revenue to $6.5 billion. Earnings from U.S. operations were 32% higher than in 1972.

■ Standard Oil Co. (California), the nation's fifth largest oil company, reported Jan. 30 that its fourth quarter earnings were $283.1 million, up 94% from $145.8 million. For the year, earnings increased 54% to total $843.6 million. The 1973 return on net investment was 15%, up from 10.8% in 1972.

■ Phillips Petroleum Co. posted a 128% increase in earnings during the final quarter and a 55% gain in profits for the entire year, officials said Jan. 29. In the December quarter, Phillips earned $86.7 million, up from $38.1 million. For the year, net income was $230.4 million, up from $148.4 million. Domestic operations accounted for 19% of 1973 earnings, according to the company.

■ Sun Oil Co. reported Jan. 29 that its earnings for the final period were 60% above year earlier levels, reaching $75 million. Full year earnings were $230 million compared with $155 million in 1972—a gain of 48%.

■ Because of a change in accounting procedures, Marathon Oil Co. released only full year profits statistics. Officials said Jan. 29 that net income for 1973 was $143.3 million. Earnings before extraordinary items in 1973 rose 62.2% in one year.

■ Amerada Hess Corp. posted fourth quarter earnings of $104.5 million, compared with $18.3 million in the final period of 1972. Net income for the year showed an even greater increase: up from $26 million in the previous year to $245.8 million for 1973. Revenues were up 42.2% over 12 months.

■ Gulf Oil Corp. announced that its operating revenues had increased 153% in the final quarter of 1973 (compared with year-earlier figures).

Data for the full year showed operating profits gained 79% to total $800 million. Revenues were up 29%, with the bulk of the increase from foreign operations. Earnings from U.S. operations were up 14% while foreign earnings climbed to $560 million from $150 million in 1972.

■ Atlantic Richfield Corp. announced a 41% increase in fourth quarter profits (compared with the same period in 1972). Earnings totaled $91.7 million. Figures for the full year put earnings at $270 million, up 38% from $195.6 million.

■ Occidental Petroleum announced Feb. 20 that its fourth quarter earnings were up 172% in 12 months, reaching $24.3 million compared with $8.9 million in the final three months of 1972.

For the entire year, profits soared more than 300%. Earnings were $79.8 million.

Treasury Secretary George P. Shultz submitted a report to Congress Feb. 4 rebutting the oil industry's contention that 1973 profits merely appeared high because earnings in previous years had been unusually low. Averaged earnings of the 22 largest oil companies were higher in 1973 than any of the preceding 10 years, based on an analysis of return on stockholders' equity, according to the report.

In 1973, the return was 15.1% com-
pared with 9.7% in 1972, 11.8% in 1968 and 10.9% for the average over 10 years.

OPEC bars price hike, boosts royalties.
The 12-nation Organization of Petroleum Exporting Countries (OPEC) agreed June 17 after a three-day meeting in Quito, Ecuador to continue the posted price of oil at current levels for three months, from July 1. In another action, all OPEC members, except Saudi Arabia, announced a 2% increase in royalties levied on Western oil companies.

The dual decision on prices and royalties would have the effect of curbing the oil companies' profits unless they could pass the added cost on to consumers.

Saudi Petroleum Minister Sheik Ahmed Zaki al-Yamani, who had blocked OPEC attempts to raise prices, explained that his government was opposed to increasing royalties because of its forthcoming negotiations with the Arabian American Oil Co. (Aramco) "to establish a new relationship. Therefore, we cannot associate ourselves with any fiscal changes which might contradict the future arrangement we will have with Aramco."

An OPEC communique said the organization's economic commission had complained of "the excessive profits earned by the international major companies" and of their failure during January–June "to contain the alarming rate of inflation while the level of posted prices was kept constant by OPEC countries." OPEC's decision not to raises prices for at least three months was designed to give the companies "another opportunity to adopt the necessary measures in these respects," the communique said.

The OPEC meeting June 16 had rejected an appeal by the European Economic Community (EEC) against new taxes on oil exports. An EEC note circulated among the delegates had argued that the taxes to absorb excess profits would only increase oil prices in Europe and harm the world economic situation.

Venezuela raises oil price—Venezuela June 30 increased posted prices of oil exports by an average 5%, to $14.43 a barrel. Foreign oil companies operating in Venezuela would pay an additional 21¢ a barrel in taxes.

The increase in the government's oil income was higher than the 10¢–14¢ rise endorsed by OPEC.

Arabs end oil ban against Holland. The Organization of Arab Petroleum Exporting Countries (OAPEC) decided at a meeting in Cairo July 10 to lift its nine-month old oil embargo against the Netherlands.

OAPEC had decided to end the ban because it was now "convinced the Dutch government's attitude toward the Middle East had changed," Saudi Arabian Petroleum Minister Sheik Zaki al-Yamani said.

World oil surplus seen. A U.S. government study predicted that reduced demand for oil and a modest increase in production would result in a world-wide oil surplus, estimated at 1.5 billion barrels a day by the second half of 1974 and rising to 2.7 million barrels a day during the first half of 1975.

According to the study, which was submitted to the 12-nation Energy Coordination Group meeting in Brussels and reported in the New York Times July 1, this surplus would exert a downward pressure on world oil prices and create cracks in the unity of the Organization of Petroleum Exporting Countries (OPEC). Oil industry estimates generally confirmed the U.S. study, but anticipated a slightly larger surplus in future months than did the government report. Oil companies, whose stocks had been severely depleted during the Arab oil embargo, had been completely resupplied.

Oil prices already had dropped in European markets because of the increase in supplies—the wholesale price of a metric ton of gasoline ranged from $134–$139 in Rotterdam June 28, compared with a $174–$183 price spread two months earlier.

A similar downward movement in price had not occurred in the U.S., however, because the nation relied more heavily on domestic supplies of oil, which was increasing in price as oil from OPEC nations was declining, according to industry spokesmen.

"The present combination of free world oil production and price levels is unsustainable. Reduction in output, prices or both seems likely this summer," the

U.S. study declared. Saudi Arabia had based its objections to an OPEC proposal to raise prices on this ground, contending that severe economic dislocations in oil importing countries caused by dramatic price increases necessitated a reduction in price and they threatened to increase production to force down prices in order to achieve this goal.

Other OPEC nations had rejected the Saudi argument, saying that oil prices should keep pace with worldwide inflation. They also threatened to cut production in an effort to negate the effects of the Saudi boost in production levels.

U.S. Energy Price Problem

Airlines warn of fuel price increases. In a letter Jan. 8 to energy czar William Simon, the Airline Transport Association asked him to place jet fuel under "effective fuel price control" before escalating petroleum prices put the cost of air travel "beyond the reach of millions of citizens to whom it is essential."

The industry's concern over rising fuel costs also was evident in a warning Jan. 4 from Eastern Airlines President Floyd D. Hall, who said airlines faced bankruptcy or the need for massive government subsidies unless fare increases were authorized.

According to the industry, its fuel bill for 1974 could range from $2 billion–$4 billion, up from $1.3 billion in 1973.

Cost saving devices already adopted by carriers, in addition to extensive employe layoffs and curtailments in flight schedules, included grounding of the jumbo jets and other expensive equipment and abolishing cut rate and special fares.

Air fares rise as fuel costs increase. The Civil Aeronautics Board (CAB) March 22 authorized a temporary 4% increase in domestic air fares, effective April 16 through Oct. 31, citing a "precipitous" rise in the price of jet fuel. The CAB also indicated that airlines could raise fares an additional 2% at the same time if they wished.

Action came on a petition to raise fares filed by United Air Lines.

The International Air Transport Association, meeting in Switzerland March 22, announced agreement on a decision to raise air cargo rates on North Atlantic routes by 5% and Mid and South Atlantic routes by 4%, effective June 1 and subject to government approval.

Oil price rises probed. A subcommittee of the House Select Committee on Small Business held hearings Jan. 17–18 to elicit testimony from government officials on oil industry data and Administration-approved price increases.

At the first session, Interior Department officials admitted that statistics supplied by the oil and natural gas industry had formed the basis of government projections and policy on fuel production. The government had agreed to keep the records secret in order to insure voluntary compliance with its request for information, officials added.

As a result of this information policy, officials said they believed there was evidence that the industry was "seriously underestimating" gas reserves. They also conceded they were unable to gather evidence to determine whether oil and gas wells on government land had been capped to drive up prices.

Subcommittee members questioned Federal Energy Office (FEO) officials Jan. 18 about the Cost of Living Council's recent approval of a $1 barrel increase in "old" oil prices.

Rep. Henry Reuss (D, Wis.) termed the action "unjustified." "The drilling equipment is in place, the derricks are pumping, and oil is flowing out of the ground," Reuss said. He won admissions from two FEO officials that they had no firm evidence that oil companies were reinvesting the amount of increase in new production sites.

Subcommittee Chairman John D. Dingell (D, Mich.) charged that the price increase guaranteed oil companies a $4.75 billion annual "bonanza."

Artificial shortage charged. New York State filed suit Feb. 6 against Shell Oil Co. and three other members of the Royal Dutch/Shell Group, accusing them of diverting and withholding home heating oil in a scheme to inflate prices and eliminate competition during a period of contrived winter fuel shortages.

According to the civil complaint, the defendants arranged to divert 1 million barrels of oil normally imported by Shell and store it in New Jersey under customs bonds. Fuel stored under bond technically was not regarded as imported until the bond was removed. The supply was never reported to the American Petroleum Institute, an industry group whose assessment of the extent of the shortage until recently gave federal officials their only measure of the supply crisis. The stored fuel was not reported to the Federal Energy Office until Jan. 15, New York charged, adding that one of the defendants "indicated . . . its intention to issue a fraudulent invoice" and conceal its true inventory position while the state investigation was taking place.

The fuel remained "hidden in New Jersey" until after the Arab oil embargo was imposed and then was sold in November 1973 at "exorbitant prices," New York charged.

While this oil was in bond, Shell customers were unable to receive their full supplies of oil, according to New York. The state also charged that when the disputed oil was sold to distributors, they paid up to 49.5¢ a gallon and passed on the increase to homeowners. Shell charged other wholesalers 18.35¢ a gallon for oil imported through other terminals, the complaint stated.

Named as defendants with Shell were the Asiatic Petroleum Corp., Cia. Shell de Venezuela, Ltd., and Shell Curacao, N.V.

In other legal action related to the fuel crisis, it was reported Jan. 22 that the federal government had brought civil suits against 13 gasoline stations in cities from Chicago to New York. The dealers were accused of price gouging.

Six holders of oil company credit cards filed two class action suits against the American Petroleum Institute and eight oil companies, it was reported Jan. 15. The suits, filed in superior and federal courts in Los Angeles on behalf of an estimated 4 million California credit card holders, accused the firms of antitrust violations and of a massive conspiracy to hoard oil and drive up the price of gasoline.

Propane price rulings. The Federal Energy Office issued proposals Jan. 30 to control retail propane prices by limiting refiners' pass through increases to actual crude oil price hikes. No provision for a price rollback was included in the program, despite charges by Georgia Gov. Jimmy Carter (D) that the cost of propane, which was widely used in the rural South, had risen an average 310% in one year.

Record natural gas price OKd. The Federal Power Commission (FPC) Feb. 2 allowed an interstate pipeline to buy natural gas at 55¢ per 1,000 cubic feet. It was the highest purchase price ever approved by the FPC and 22% above the previous record—45¢—set in May 1973, and itself a 73% increase over 1971 prices. The price of gas sold interstate averaged 26¢. The price of federally regulated natural gas had tripled between 1954 and 1972. (Gas sold intrastate was not subject to federal regulation.)

Under the ruling, Southern Natural Gas Co. was authorized to buy Alabama-produced natural gas under a 20-year contract. The FPC staff had recommended a 38¢ purchase ceiling. The difference between the staff-approved rate and that set by the commission would total $1.8 million, an amount that could be passed on to distributors and customers.

In its 3–2 ruling, the commission appeared bitterly divided over the question of allowing further price increases as an incentive to producers to stimulate exploration and development.

In dissent, William L. Springer charged that the majority had "capitulated to the prescription of an industry-established price . . . rather than a just and reasonable rate set by regulatory review."

Another opponent of the price increase, Commission Chairman John N. Nassikas, joined Springer in denouncing the decision as a "travesty of regulatory justice." They noted, however, that because no interested parties had intervened to oppose the increase when it was before the FPC, a reversal on court appeal was not possible.

Energy bill vetoed, Nixon upheld. President Nixon vetoed an emergency energy

bill March 6. In action the same day, the Senate sustained the veto on a 58–40 vote that was eight short of the two-thirds majority required to override the President's action.

Despite the veto, there was no indication that the issue was dead. Sen. Henry Jackson (D, Wash.), a principal supporter of the legislation which included a provision for reducing oil prices, warned that "the rollback provision is going to be an ongoing fight."

Shortly after the Senate vote, the House voted 218–175 to insert a nearly identical price rollback measure into a bill to form a Federal Energy Administration. But the House reversed itself March 7 and voted 216–163, to kill the proposal.

In his veto message, Nixon said the bill would "set domestic crude oil prices at such low levels that the oil industry would be unable to sustain its present production of petroleum products, including gasoline. It would result in reduced energy supplies, longer lines at the gas pump" and increased unemployment.

Jackson termed the veto a "flagrant show of contempt for the impact of fuel shortages and soaring fuel prices." By his action, Nixon "defends and advocates higher oil prices," Jackson declared.

The rollback would have cut prices of crude oil from "new" wells and "stripper" wells producing less than 10 barrels a day to $5.25 a barrel. The current price of "new" oil, which was not under price controls, was $10.35 a barrel.

Crude oil price changes proposed. The Federal Energy Office issued proposed changes May 16 for its petroleum price regulations. One of the revisions, which would disallow some of the costs oil companies had claimed for crude and refined products purchased abroad from their affiliates, could result in a price rollback by a number of oil companies because these overseas costs had been used to compute domestic prices under government guidelines.

Use of these "transfer prices" to the "disadvantage of American consumers" "may explain in part the significant increases in international profits reported by the major oil companies," FEO Administrator John Sawhill said.

The FEO earlier had accused Gulf Oil Co. of overcharging itself, and indirectly, its U.S. customers by overstating the costs of buying oil from an African affiliate.

The proposed rule changes resulted from an audit of 30 large refiners undertaken since January by the FEO and the Internal Revenue Service. The change in regulations governing calculation of domestic U.S. oil prices, under which the FEO asserted its authority to intervene in companies' cost accounting procedures, could establish an important precedent.

Sawhill revealed April 25 that the joint FEO-IRS investigation was considering 47,000 cases of alleged price gouging by the energy industry at the wholesale and retail level. The evidence indicated that U.S. consumers may have been overcharged by as much as $100 million, Sawhill said. He added that $14.2 million in wholesale and retail refunds had been ordered as a result of price violations uncovered during the continuing investigations.

'73 oil price increase disputed. Consumer advocate Ralph Nader made public June 7 internal documents from the Cost of Living Council (CLC) indicating that the CLC had authorized a $1 a barrel increase in the price of "old" oil despite the objections of its staff and an independent consultant hired by the CLC.

The new information was obtained from the CLC when Nader invoked the Freedom of Information Act.

The documents pertained to the CLC's decision, announced Dec. 19, 1973, to allow a $1 increase to $5.25 a barrel in the price of crude oil that was produced in the U.S. at pre-1972 production levels.

According to the newly released documents, the CLC staff felt that the increase was "arbitrary" and unjustified. Since production of domestic oil already was near maximum levels, the staff paper declared, no additional increase in oil supplies could be expected as a result of the price hike. Secondary and tertiary recovery methods of oil could be stimulated by a price increase, the staff added, but these supplies were likely to increase

regardless of any pricing decision, and in any case, would produce no immediate rise in supply.

The CLC's independent consultant, the Stanford Research Institute, asserted that the $4.25 price ceiling was not holding down production—the bottleneck was occurring because of an equipment shortage, and a price increase would not alleviate that problem.

The effort to reduce soaring demand by making oil products more costly had been a basic tenet of Administration policy since the imposition of the Arab oil embargo.

Other CLC documents obtained by Nader showed that Herbert Stein, chairman of the President's Council of Economic Advisers, favored a $12 a barrel ceiling, coupled with a windfall profits tax limiting the oil companies' yield to $6.50. A $7-to-$8 ceiling was reportedly favored by other high officials.

CLC Director John T. Dunlop, who supported a price ceiling of $5 a barrel, successfully opposed this upper limit, documents showed. In a memo to George Shultz, then Treasury secretary, Dunlop wrote, "If a price of $7-$8 is now established, I recommend full decontrol of the economy because even orderly phasing out of a controls system cannot be viable under such a shock."

The CLC staff and the Stanford group also warned that higher domestic prices could trigger a new round of price increases by oil exporting countries.

John Sawhill, administrator of the Federal Energy Office until the agency was superseded by the Federal Energy Administration July 1, defended the $1 a barrel price increase June 7 at Senate hearings considering his nomination as administrator of the FEA.

Sawhill opposed an oil price rollback and said "circumstances have changed since" December 1973. "The [$5.25] price looks much smaller now relative to the world price of oil," Sawhill said.

New natural gas price set. The Federal Power Commission (FPC) June 24 authorized a single national price for "new" natural gas pumped from wells that began operation after Jan. 1, 1973. The ruling, which the FPC termed a "landmark decision," affected new gas sold in interstate commerce and replaced the FPC's current policy of setting ceiling prices for separate geographic areas under limited term and emergency sales rate procedures.

The new rate—42¢ per 1,000 cubic feet—eventually would mean sharply higher prices for gas wholesalers and consumers. Area gas prices established in previous FPC rulings had ranged from 19.9¢ to 34¢ per 1,000 cubic feet. The average price of gas sold nationwide, including gas that the FPC had said could be sold at prices above the regulated ceiling level, was 27¢ per 1,000 cubic feet in March.

The new rate also allowed for an automatic annual price increase of 1¢ per 1,-000 cubic feet, a "gathering allowance" for certain producing areas of 1¢–2.5¢ per 1,000 cubic feet, and an additional 1¢ per 1,000 cubic feet increase for producers who transported gas from offshore to onshore. Rate reviews were planned every two years, the FPC said. The agency also noted that its "optional" pricing procedure adopted in 1972, allowing producers to apply for rates above the area ceilings, was not abrogated by the new national price policy.

The pricing action was necessitated, according to the FPC, by a "national emergency" in which consumer demand for natural gas was expected to exceed supplies into the 1980s while at the same time national reserves of the fuel continued to decline. All five FPC commissioners agreed that higher wellhead prices were justified by costs and were needed to spur exploration and production in order to increase natural gas supplies. (The new rate was expected to provide producers with a 15% rate of return on capital and thus stimulate drilling and production capacity.)

Four commissioners voted to establish the uniform price at 42¢ but one member, Rush Moody Jr., was in partial dissent, claiming that the 42¢ rate was too low. The natural gas industry was critical of the FPC action for similar reasons.

Moody's view was echoed June 25 by Federal Energy Office Administrator John Sawhill, who said the FPC's new rate was a "step in the right direction" but was still too low "to stimulate exploration needed to provide adequate supplies of natural gas." Sawhill urged Congress to remove all federal price controls from natural gas and allow market conditions to determine prices. Gas sold intrastate and hence not subject to federal regulations had been selling as high as $1.30 per 1,000 cubic feet on the free market.

FEA Administrator John Sawhill, in a letter to the nation's 20 major oil firms Aug. 5, accused the industry of making "efforts to coax the public into buying gasoline that it has indicated it doesn't want or need" while the government was urging stepped up conservation efforts. Sawhill called for an end to "hard sell tactics" and warned that the agency would take "strong action" to hold down fuel consumption.

Sawhill cited letters sent by Gulf and Standard Oil (Ohio) to their dealers urging service stations to remain open longer to sell more gasoline.

The FEA announced Aug. 20 it had brought administrative proceedings against 14 oil companies accused of inflating prices by $194.4 million. It was announced the next day that four of the firms—Continental Oil Co., Ashland Oil Inc., Koch Industries Inc. and Charter Oil Co.—had complied with the government's orders to make up $58.2 million in overcharges by rolling back prices or delaying planned price increases. The price violations occurred between late 1973 and April when the firms passed through costs in the same month they were incurred rather than in the next month, as specified by law.

Six other firms, the FEA said Aug. 20, had voluntarily agreed to roll back price increases totaling $45.5 million without a formal order from the government. The firms were not identified. Four other oil companies were under investigation for alleged overcharges totaling $90.7 million.

Gasoline supply, price controversy. According to a New York Times report July 29, the nation's major oil companies were cutting back production of gasoline and operating refineries at levels 6%–7% below the previous year's capacity. Industry critics charged that the actions taken were to maintain artificially high prices and avoid costly price wars.

According to American Petroleum Institute statistics, for the week ending

July 19, inventories of gasoline totaled 222 million barrels, up 9% from the previous year. Crude oil reserves were up by the same percentage. However, refineries produced 6.81 million barrels of gasoline a day, compared with 6.88 million in July 1973. Total refinery capacity utilization for the week ending July 19 was 92.5%, compared with a 98.8% rate of utilization for the same week in 1973.

International Problems

Deficits Resumed in U.S. Trade & Payments

The U.S. enjoyed a surplus in foreign trade and in its "basic" balance of payments during 1973. But the first half of 1974 produced deficits in both the trade balance and in payments balance measurements.

'73 trade surplus first since '70. The Commerce Department reported Jan. 28 that a seasonally adjusted $942.1 million trade surplus in December 1973 contributed to the full year surplus of $1.68 billion. It was the largest one-month increase since March 1965 and the first annual surplus since 1970.

December figures showed exports up 1.6% to $6.93 billion; imports fell 11.1% to $5.99 billion. For the full year, exports totaled $70.8 billion (a gain of 44%) and imports reached $69.12 billion (a gain of 24%).

The "overriding factor" in the $8.4 billion turnaround from 1972, officials said, was the competitive edge given U.S. goods by two dollar devaluations undertaken in December 1971 and February 1973. Farm exports, especially of grain, also surged in 1973 as their export value increased 88% over a 12-month period. The export of manufactured goods and other non-agricultural products rose 33%,

partly because of the effects of U.S. price controls which diverted U.S.-made goods to the higher priced foreign markets.

Over the year, oil imports rose by $3.4 billion to $8 billion as prices rose tremendously in the fourth quarter. Officials warned that further increases in the value of oil imports threatened to return the trade account to deficit in 1974.

First annual payments surplus. The Commerce Department announced March 20 that the U.S. posted a $1.21 billion surplus in 1973 in its "basic" balance of payments. It was the first yearly surplus on record since statistics were first compiled in 1960 and a vast improvement over the $9.84 billion deficit registered in 1972.

The "basic" balance, regarded by many analysts as the most stable and reliable guide in determining trends in the nation's payments position, reflected trade, government grants, long-term corporate investments and the flow of other long-term funds, but did not include measures of short-term capital flow. Other payments measures which did reflect the sometimes volatile movement of short-term funds, had showed sizable deficits for 1973.

Officials warned that the dramatic turnaround from deficit to surplus could be reversed again if the U.S. were unable to offset higher prices paid for imported oil by encouraging oil-producing nations to invest a portion of their trade receipts in the U.S.

There was a $24 million surplus in the nation's fourth quarter "basic" balance, officials said. The surplus was reduced over the last three months because of an increase in direct investment abroad by U.S. firms, a decline in foreign direct investment in the U.S. and a rise in the net outflow of other net long-term private capital transactions, according to officials. A strong showing in the merchandise trade balance and services account (including travel and tourism) served to offset these negative effects.

U.S.-Soviet trade doubles. Two-way trade between the U.S. and the Soviet Union more than doubled in 1973, to $1.4 billion compared with $642 million in 1972, it was reported Feb. 6.

The trade balance heavily favored the U.S., which had a bilateral surplus of $976 million in 1973. The volume of trade was seven times what it had been in 1970.

Americas trade record. The value of Latin American exports rose by 30% in 1973, to a record $26 billion, it was reported Jan. 16. Latin countries reported a positive trade balance of $1 billion, and their hard currency reserves reached a record $17 billion.

The trade boom was spurred by sharp increases in international prices for many basic materials, including petroleum, copper, iron ore, cotton, beef, sugar, coffee and cocoa. These products, in short supply, were exported by Latin nations. Latin America was also selling more manufactured goods overseas, led by Brazil with exports of $2 billion in products such as automobiles, trucks, computer parts and shoes.

More foreign trade problems forecast. In his second annual international economic report to Congress, President Nixon warned Feb. 7 that the U.S. "has moved from an era of near self-sufficiency to one of rising dependence on foreign resources with a concomitant need to earn more foreign exchange to pay for these imports."

But, Nixon added, it was unlikely that nations producing these vital raw materials could exploit their advantageous trade position by forming a cartel or "monopoly" similar to the Arab control of the petroleum market.

Nixon cited four obstacles to the formation of such a cartel:

■ Extractive (or producing) nations would experience significant unemployment if any attempt were made to cut back production and hence control supply while forcing up prices. Arab countries, successful in this strategy, were unaffected by unemployment troubles during the period of production cutback.

■ Arab countries were able to absorb the losses caused by a reduction in sales volume during this production slowdown period (and during the later embargo) because they had ample supplies of foreign reserves to cushion the drop in revenues. Extractive states, which in most cases were also the poorer, developing nations, lacked the foreign reserves to carry them through this tight period of curtailed production.

■ While the demand for oil has continued to rise, the demand for certain other raw materials has been more closely associated with worldwide economic trends and in the course of an international slowdown, demand could decline.

■ In a period of reduced demand, producing countries lacked a strong bargaining position. It was possible that the situation could be reversed as extractive nations competed for markets.

(A State Department analysis, which also discounted the likelihood of commodity cartels being formed, listed two other obstacles faced by exporting countries: commodity stockpiles existing in consuming nations and the possibility that steep price increases would force importers to seek other, more profitable sources of supplies and to use substitute materials. According to the Washington Post, which published the report Feb. 8, the State Department was "eager to disseminate the results of its study" to discourage developing nations from forming cartels and to "cool what the department considers an overreaction to the threat of such combines by the Interior Department and other agencies.")

A concern with the oil crisis and its repercussions was expressed elsewhere in Nixon's report. According to the President, oil imports in 1974 could cost the U.S. $25 billion, $16 billion more than in 1973, an assumption that was based on 1974 prices and volume remaining constant with 1973 levels.

Because of these added costs, Nixon said, the U.S. faced a "basic" payments deficit of $3 billion–$5 billion. Peter Flanigan, a presidential aide, executive director of the Council on International Economic Policy and principal author of the White House report, said the turnaround, which could total $8 billion because of an estimated $2.7 billion surplus in 1973, was "a problem but a manageable problem."

June trade deficit erases '74 surplus. The Commerce Department reported July 26 that imports exceeded exports during June by $255.8 million, an amount that wiped out a small five-month trade surplus and left the nation with a $254.3 million deficit for the first half of 1974.

The U.S. trade surplus had shrunk from $643.8 million in January to $213.1 million in February. A $171.3 million deficit was reported in March, a $92.8 million surplus in April and a $776.9 million deficit in May.

The shift in the trade balance from surplus to deficit was attributed to the cost of oil imports following the lifting of the Arab oil embargo.

Imports of crude oil and petroleum products declined from a level of 208.7 million barrels in November 1973 and 169.2 million barrels in December 1973 to 164 million barrels in January, figures which officials said indicated that the Arab oil embargo had become increasingly effective.

The price of imports rose inversely as supplies declined. In January, the cost of oil imports was $1.3 billion, compared with $1.03 billion in December 1973. In January 1973 when oil imports were roughly equivalent to current levels, costs totaled $532.2 million. According to the department, the price of crude oil in January averaged $6.71 a barrel, compared with $5.28 in December 1973 and $2.73 in January 1973.

Sharply higher petroleum prices and a rise in imports during the post-embargo period were offset by a steep reduction in nonpetroleum imports. (Petroleum imports cost $2.24 billion in April, up from $1.77 billion in March and $470.8 million in April 1973.)

Exports rose 9.5% from May to June, reaching $8.36 billion; imports increased 2.4% to $8.61 billion. For the first six months, exports totaled $46.61 billion, up 45% from the same period in 1973, and imports totaled $46.87 billion, up 42% from 1973. Officials said the large increases were chiefly a reflection of inflation, rather than a real gain in trade volume.

Calculated according to methods used by most other nations (c.i.f., or cost, insurance and freight), the U.S. deficit was $3.58 billion in 1974's first half.

The U.S. imported 175.1 million barrels of petroleum imports during June. That figure was off slightly from the previous June, but costs soared over the 12-month period, rising from $578 million to $2.04 billion. A barrel of oil that had cost $3.07 in June 1973 was currently selling for $11.63, the government report added.

The U.S.' monthly trade deficit was the third worst on record in July ($728.4 million) and a record $1.13 billion in August.

Worsening trade figures were directly related to rising fuel costs, spokesmen said. A 15% surge in fuel imports from June to July, combined with a record price for foreign oil—$11.69 a barrel, added $300 million to the nation's oil bill for the month. Total oil costs in July were $2.3 billion. Since January, the cost of oil had soared to $13.2 billion, which was far in excess of the $3.6 billion paid during the same period of 1973.

Oil imports rose 2.9% to 206.6 million barrels in August. Increased consumption plus a record cost of $11.73 a barrel raised the August fuel bill to $2.52 billion.

U.S. doubles arms sales abroad. U.S. arms sales abroad during fiscal 1974 (July 1, 1973–June 30, 1974) were double that of the previous fiscal year, the Pentagon reported July 9. The bulk of some $8.5 billion in sales was to Middle East and Persian Gulf nations. This total did not include $1.5 billion in arms given to Israel or smaller arms grants to Lebanon and Jordan.

According to the Pentagon, Iran had purchased over $4 billion in arms, Israel over $1 billion, Saudi Arabia $700 million and Kuwait $100 million. In other parts of the world, sales were $320 million to nations in East Asia and the Pacific, $655 million to Western Europe, $35 million to Africa and $220 million to Latin America.

Balance of payments in deficit. Two measures of the nation's balance of payments were in deficit during the second quarter of 1974, the Commerce Department announced Aug. 15.

When measured on the "official reserve transactions" basis, the deficit for the June quarter totaled a seasonally adjusted $4.49 billion, which was in sharp contrast to the $287 million surplus reported for the same period of 1973 and the $1.04 billion surplus recorded in the first three months of 1974 (revised).

On a "net liquidity" basis, the payments deficit was an adjusted $6.28 billion. That figure also marked a substantial deterioration from the 1973 second quarter, when the deficit was $1.71 billion, and from the $873 million deficit posted in the 1st quarter of 1974 (revised).

The figures were heavily influenced by the flow of "petrodollars" (revenue from oil exporting countries). There was a "significant" increase in short-term investments in the U.S. from these countries, spokesmen said. Another factor contributing to the deficit figures was a sharp rise in U.S. bank loans to foreigners. The increase, from $2.8 billion in the first quarter to $6.1 billion in the second period, was a partial reflection of the lifting of government controls on such lending early in 1974.

Jack Bennett, undersecretary of the Treasury for monetary affairs, said the official reserves transactions figure was a "totally useless number." It was intended to measure changes in the dollar holdings of foreign central banks. In the period before floating exchange rates, large dollar purchases by these government banks indicated that the par value of a weak dollar was being supported against the foreign currency. But under current conditions, Bennett said, governments were using dollars to purchase costlier oil—evidence that the dollar had renewed strength in exchange transactions.

The "basic" balance of payments, reported Sept. 18, was in deficit by $2.74 billion in the second quarter, as compared with the revised surplus of $1.79 billion in the first quarter.

Court voids 1971 Nixon import surcharge. The U.S. Customs Court in New York City ruled July 8 that President Nixon had exceeded his constitutional authority in 1971 when he imposed a 10% import surcharge tax. In its unanimous decision, the three-judge panel ordered the Treasury Department to refund the $481 million it had collected during the last four months of 1971 when the tax was in effect.

Designed to reverse the U.S.'s deteriorating international balance of payments position, the surcharge was imposed Aug. 15, 1971, the same date that Nixon announced a 90-day wage-price freeze.

In a strongly worded opinion, Chief Judge Nils A. Boe concluded that Nixon's action "exceeded authority delegated to the President." The court could not "fail to recognize the efforts of the President to achieve stability in the international trade position and monetary reserves of this country." But, Boe wrote, "neither need nor national emergency will justify the exercise of a power by the executive that isn't inherent in his office nor delegated by Congress."

After imposing the surcharge, the government allowed importers to pass on the tax to consumers through higher prices. The Customs Court ruling did not require the importers to make refunds to consumers.

Eximbank to end fixed loan rate. The U.S. Export-Import Bank announced July 8 that its fixed interest rate policy was being abandoned because of tight money conditions and political criticism and replaced with a system of flexible rates ranging from 7%–8.5%.

The bank's flat rate had been 6% until February, when it was raised to 7%. Despite the increase, the move evoked Congressional criticism because the rate remained considerably below the prime interest rate of 9% and higher available to major U.S. businesses at that time. Legislators accused the Eximbank of subsidizing foreign borrowers in their purchases of U.S. goods and services.

The new flexible rate plan would result in higher interest charges for many borrowers. Eximbank Chairman William J. Casey disclosed that the average cost of money to the bank in financing its loans exceeded 7% for the first time in May.

Casey also said the bank would seek to limit its participation in export transactions in an effort to make the bank's resources go further. Previously, the bank had put up 45% of the cost of export goods, with private banks putting up the same amount and the borrower sharing 10% of the cost. Casey said that for the first time in its modern history, the bank had more "good" loan applications on hand at the end of fiscal 1974 (ending June 30) than could be met under its legal lending ceiling.

Monetary Problems

Monetary system buffeted by oil crisis. As representatives of the International Monetary Fund's (IMF) member nations were meeting in Rome Jan. 14–18 to discuss an overhaul of the world's currency system, shock waves caused by drastic increases in the price of Middle East oil were registered in world money markets. Gold soared to record levels, the pound plunged to new lows, and France was forced to float the franc.

Pound sinks—The pound hit record lows Jan. 15 and 16 in the face of "persistent and general selling" as investors reacted to Britain's worsening industrial strife and general economic weakness evidenced by the report of a large drop in the trade index.

Despite intervention Jan. 15 by the Bank of England, the pound lost 4¢ against the dollar. In London Jan. 16 the pound traded at $2.1630 and closed at $2.1760. Since the Smithsonian currency realignment of December 1971, the pound's effective rate of devaluation was at the worst level ever—20.4%.

The dollar continued to show uneven strength, gaining against the pound but dropping Jan. 16 against the West German mark to close at 2.803 marks as

the West German Central Bank intervened to support currency levels. (On a trade-weighted average Jan. 17, the dollar had depreciated only 1.41% from the Smithsonian level, its best showing yet.)

Gold, however, showed consistent and dramatic gains. In London Jan. 17, an ounce of gold traded at $128.50, but closed off 15¢. Gold was quoted at $132.30 an ounce on the Paris bullion market Jan. 17 and one day later, closed at $136.58, the highest price ever recorded.

Finance ministers meet—Confidence in the pound had been undermined by persistent reports that Britain would be forced to negotiate a loan from the International Monetary Fund (IMF) to overcome a massive payments imbalance generated partially by higher fuel bills. IMF Managing Director Johannes Witteveen's presence in London at a world banking conference lent credence to these fears. It was reported Jan. 16 that Witteveen believed the world's oil problems added a "sharp twist" to current inflationary trends and would result in a "staggering disequilibrium in the global balance of payments" situation.

Against this background of extreme currency instability, finance ministers and their deputies representing the IMF's Committee of 20, met in Rome to continue discussions on a long awaited package of money reform measures.

However, the question of reform was quickly overshadowed by the prospect of large current account deficits facing nearly every country in the world (with the U.S. as a possible exception) because of abrupt and enormous increases in the price of fuel. At the conclusion of the conference, the finance ministers issued a cautious 1,000 word communique calling for the "closest international cooperation and consultation" to ease the payments burden rapidly overtaking industrial and developing nations.

It was agreed that "countries must not adopt policies which would merely aggravate the problems of other countries" in managing their international payments. "Accordingly," the group "stressed the importance of avoiding competitive depreciation and the escalation of restrictions on trade and payments."

The group emphasized the payments

problems faced by non-oil producing developing countries. According to estimates prepared by the Organization of Economic Cooperation and Development (OECD), developing countries would be required to spend $10 billion more in 1974 over 1973 to pay for their oil supplies—a figure equivalent to the annual aid provided them by richer nations.

During the conference, Witteveen proposed that the IMF borrow money directly from the oil-producing nations to meet the needs of any nation facing an unmanagable payments deficit.

Treasury Secretary George P. Shultz, who led the U.S. delegation at the meeting, said Jan. 18 the conference was "decisive and constructive." But despite the urgency of the circumstances, no substantive decisions were made on the question of basic currency reforms and no final steps were adopted to deal decisively with the payments problem because major disagreement was expressed over the long-term implication of skyrocketing oil prices.

Shultz appealed for a rollback of "staggering" oil price increases that he said had brought about a "change in economic circumstances without precedent in magnitude and suddenness in peacetime." He asked oil-producing states to recognize the "simple fact" that a rollback was in their ultimate self-interest because a "capricious manipulation of [oil] supplies or prices" could lead to national recessions and international financial turmoil. Shultz asked them to "cooperate with the rest of the world in scaling down the magnitude of financial problems," but an Arab spokesman labeled the call for a price rollback "naive."

Valery Giscard d'Estaing and Anthony Barber, spokesmen for France and Britain, the only countries to engage in bilateral arms-for-oil deals with the Arabs since the embargo was imposed, argued that the IMF should accept the current high prices and act within those terms.

West Germany's finance minister, Helmut Schmidt, was especially critical of France's "go it alone" trade policy concerning the Arabs and French resistance to a common front against the "fantastic explosion" in oil prices.

At the meeting's end, nations which had been divided on the issue of a systematic overhaul of monetary arrangements, also appeared to be in basic conflict over a strategy for dealing with rising oil prices and the payments crisis, issues which underlined the urgency for achieving a reordering of international currency relationships.

France floats franc—In a move that further reflected France's "go it alone" policies and the IMF meeting's inability to allay deepening financial fears, Giscard d'Estaing announced Jan. 19 that the French government would undertake a de facto devaluation of the franc (estimated at 4%–5%) by allowing it to float for six months.

Giscard d'Estaing offered two reasons for the decision to suspend support for the franc by the French Central Bank whose intervention had been required recently to prop up fixed rates set in March 1973 by six members of the European Economic Community under a limited joint float pact.

Action was taken, Giscard d'Estaing said, because "there is no chance that the international monetary system will be reformed in 1974 or 1975," especially since six major world currencies already were floating—the U.S. dollar, the British pound, the Canadian dollar, the Italian lira, the Japanese yen and the Swiss franc.

"The second factor is that the events of last fall, and in particular, the oil crisis, have created throughout the world, and will continue to create in 1974, very large payments deficits in most countries." Financing of these deficits was uncertain, Giscard d'Estaing said. Under conditions of a "disturbed and unstable monetary system, if a country retains the obligation to supply its own reserves to meet the demands presented through speculation, this country runs the risk of losing its reserves," he declared.

The five remaining EEC nations participating in the joint float announced Jan. 21 that they were determined to "maintain the existing margins" between the West German, Dutch, Belgian, Luxembourg, and Danish currencies. The group also announced extended plans to facilitate a coordinated monetary policy.

Reaction to the French decision was generally restrained. The Bonn government Jan. 20 expressed "deep regret" over the float, adding however, "we also view it with a great deal of understanding." U.S. Treasury Secretary Shultz said Jan. 21 that the French action was "realistic" in view of its worsening reserve position. He emphasized that the U.S. did not consider the float to be a competitive devaluation but other U.S. officials said privately that one major result of the float would be a reduction in the dollar's strongly competitive position in world trade.

Participants at the IMF meeting had expressed fear of such a "competitive depreciation and the escalation of restrictions on trade and payments." Giscard d'Estaing said the decision to float the franc was made immediately after his return from the Rome meeting.

Although Giscard d'Estaing said in his statement that the decision was made "coldly, calmly, by ourselves, without any pressure from the outside and without any speculation," there were unofficial reports that the Bank of France had spent $130 million in support of the franc during the previous week. Pressure on the franc had caused its value to drop from 3.8 francs to the dollar during the preceding summer to close at 4.97 francs to the dollar in trading Jan. 18 on the commercial market.

Credit curbs dismantled. In three actions designed to eliminate controls on the flow of dollars abroad, President Nixon Jan. 29 ended the interest equalization tax on the purchase of foreign securities by U.S. citizens by reducing the tax rate to zero; the Commerce Department lifted restraints on direct investments abroad by U.S. companies; and the Federal Reserve Board removed limits on lending and investment abroad by U.S. banks and financial institutions.

According to the Treasury Department, the Administration abolished the barriers to credit outflow, which had been in effect since the mid-1960s, because of "the recent improvements in the U.S. balance of payments position [and] the strong position of the dollar in the exchange market," as well as a desire to lessen the burden of other nations imperiled by large payments deficits.

In a Chicago speech Jan. 29, Treasury Secretary George P. Shultz said the actions were also designed to attract inves-

tors to the U.S. "Apparently many foreign investors hesitated to invest in a country that needed a fence around it to keep money in," Shultz said. "They were afraid the controls would somehow, someday prevent them from getting their money out when they wanted it."

The dollar devaluation announced in February 1973 was another Administration effort to deal with deepening payments deficits brought on in part by a huge trade imbalance. At that time, Shultz had pledged that the three credit curbs would be "phased out" by the end of 1974.

Currencies remain unstable. The international money markets were exceptionally tumultuous in reaction to news of France's decision to float the franc, an end to credit barriers announced by the U.S. government, a strike vote by British miners and the widespread payments crisis precipitated by high oil prices.

Jan. 21: On the first day of the float, the financial franc lost 4% against the dollar, closing at 5.35 francs. (The Bank of France intervened to prevent a drastic drop in the franc's value by selling $150 million in currency reserves.) The dollar was strong against most currencies (closing at 2.84 West German marks). The pound closed at $2.173 after falling 1.45¢. Gold closed at $142 an ounce in Zurich and $152.16 in Paris.

Jan. 22: The Spanish currency was allowed to float against the dollar, and closed off at 59.15 pesetas to the dollar.

Jan. 23: Massive intervention by the governments of Japan and France was required to check their currencies' drop against the dollar. The Bank of Japan was reported to have spent at least $650 million to maintain the rate of 300 yen to the dollar.

Jan. 25: In Paris, gold sold at $145.86 an ounce (and rose to $152.62 Jan. 28).

Feb. 4: An end to the U.S. credit curbs caused the dollar to take a tailspin against most currencies, trading off at 2.748 marks, and 4.9963 commercial francs. Gold dropped to $133.50 an ounce on the London bullion market.

In the only exception to its decline, the dollar gained against the pound, trading at $2.2653, as news of the strike vote reached investors.

Gold price peak, paper money declines.
Gold prices continued to hit record levels during February, falling off sharply only on Feb. 28. The trend toward higher prices was also seen in renewed investor interest in silver and other metals and commodities—basic trading items that had been traditional hedges against inflation.

Despite its resiliency in recent months, the dollar declined in value as gold moved higher, reflecting a widespread lack of confidence among traders in paper currencies.

Feb. 20—In London, the price of gold rose to $150 an ounce. The dollar declined to 2.6815 West German marks and 288.65 Japanese yen.

Feb. 21—Gold in London closed at $157.25, and at $163.35 commercial dollars in Paris. The dollar was weak, falling 5.35% below the December 1971 currency rates and 16.08% below its value in the summer of 1970.

Feb. 22—In London, gold traded at $164 but closed down at $163. The dollar was off against most currencies ($2.315 to the British pound, 2.649 marks, 4.72 francs, 281.75 yen)

Feb. 25—Gold in London sold for $170 and in Paris at $173.17.

Feb. 26—Gold traded up at $184 in London before closing down at $175.50. It was the first indication of extensive selling and a signal that the dramatic upward pressure on gold had begun to abate. In Paris gold sold at $188.15. The dollar weakened. Its effective devaluation against December 1971 levels of 14 major currencies was 5.15%. Silver prices soared in London, closing at $6.77 an ounce. Contracts on immediate delivery climbed 80.9¢ in one day. Leading silver refiners and distributors in the U.S. set the price at $6.70 an ounce, up 62.5¢ in one day. Refined copper prices for March delivery were offered at $1.27 a pound, up 5.5¢ in one day. On the Commodities Exchange in New York, the price of silver bullion rose for the 18th consecutive session.

Feb. 27—In London, gold traded at $180 and closed down at $174. Commodities prices also fell sharply after weeks of unprecedented advances. Correspondingly, the dollar gained in strength.

Feb. 28—Gold dropped $11.50 in London, trading at $162.50. Despite the

selloff, the price of gold was nearly $50 higher than at the beginning of 1974 and almost four times the "official" price set by foreign central banks—$42.22. Although the dollar recouped some of its losses, it remained 5.1% below the December 1971 level.

Gold traded at a record high of $179.50 an ounce on the London bullion market April 3 following the death of French President Georges Pompidou. In Paris, where gold prices were ordinarily higher than elsewhere, the political uncertainty caused the price to soar to $197 an ounce April 3.

The record London price exceeded the previous high of $175 an ounce set Feb. 26. Gold fever had seized major European markets in the intervening period as speculators sought protection from inflation and widespread political disarray.

Gold prices sagged, however, during most of the next two months, declining to $154 an ounce in London and $158.41 in Paris May 28. The price rose abruptly May 30 in London to $162 an ounce on news that the U.S. Senate had approved a bill allowing private U.S. citizens to own gold.

The dollar exhibited unusual weakness over a four-month period. The wave of selling reflected a general fear that inflation would further undermine paper currencies, as well as specific U.S. difficulties, such as high interest rates, shrinking trade and payments surpluses, the continued outflow of dollars from U.S. banks and Nixon's political troubles.

The dollar closed at 2.645 West German marks March 13 and continued to drop during the rest of the month. On March 19, the dollar traded at 280.9 yen in Tokyo. On March 21, following France's decision to abandon its two-tiered exchange system, the dollar closed at 4.7975 French francs.

The dollar moved lower during April. On April 2, the dollar was worth 4.7775 French francs, 2.532 marks and 274.25 yen. Its trade-weighted devaluation, which measured the dollar's trading value against a level set at the 1971 Smithsonian meeting in Washington, was 7.46%. On Jan. 23, at the height of the dollar's resurgence, its rate of exchange had been only .52% below its 1971 value.

The dollar's slide continued during May, hitting values of 627.67 lira May 6;

2.3925 marks and 4.7825 French francs May 13; but rallying slightly May 30 to levels of 2.54 marks and 280.83 yen.

The U.S. Federal Reserve System revealed June 5 that the government had intervened actively in support of the dollar from February to April. An estimated $4.27 million in foreign currencies (mostly borrowed West German marks) was sold.

Austria announced a de facto revaluation of the schilling May 16 when the government withdrew as an unofficial participant in the five-member joint float.

Austria's move, allowing the schilling to fluctuate upward by 4.5%, was seen as an effort to limit inflation by restricting imports from West Germany—Austria's principal trading partner—without formally revaluing the currency.

Although other participants in the float reaffirmed the partnership, West Germany was forced to intervene May 17 in support of the Danish, Swedish and Norwegian currencies to offset any consequent instability. (The dollar traded at 17.65 schillings May 17.)

In an unrelated move, Iceland announced May 17 that it was devaluing the krona by 4% because of financial difficulties in the fishing industry. (Under the new exchange rate, the dollar was worth 92.8 kroner.)

Although Great Britain continued to report poor trade figures and rising inflation rates, the pound was generally strong. The advance was partially a reflection of the dollar's weakness, and partly an indication of sterling's value in the multinational economy of Middle Eastern oil.

The pound traded at $2.3485 in London March 13; at $2.394 March 29; at $2.415 April 15; at $2.4345 May 8; and at $2.392 May 28.

IMF group sets reform goals. The International Monetary Fund's (IMF) Committee of 20 adopted interim rules dealing with reform of the international monetary system and postponed for "some time" efforts to devise a permanent solution to the currency crisis. Agreement on the interim guidelines was reached at the group's sixth and final meeting, held June 12–13 in Washington. An "outline of reform" describing long-range plans for

modernizing the monetary system was published June 14.

Final agreement on a permanent framework of reform promoting financial harmony and stability had eluded the committee and its deputies since their work, subject to a two-year deadline, had begun in September 1972. At its meeting in Rome in January, the committee finally abandoned its attempt to devise a thorough overhaul because of new tensions introduced into the already strained monetary relationships by the effects of soaring inflation and quadrupled oil prices on trade and balance of payments problems.

"Economic vicissitudes have dictated changes in objectives, approach and timing," IMF officials explained. Instead of designing a thoroughly revised monetary structure, they resigned themselves to drawing up a plan that featured the "managed float"—a device that had been adopted on a temporary basis in early 1973 to deal with recurrent instability in exchange rates.

Interim measures—The limited interim measures adopted by the committee were directed at current problems, and especially those of developing nations faced with paying large oil import bills. "Immediate action" was required on these short term measures, the committee declared.

Lengthy complex guidelines were developed to deal with the management of floating exchange rates. Central banks were urged to intervene in the buying or selling of their own currencies "as necessary to prevent or moderate sharp and disruptive fluctuations."

The committee stressed that "close international consultation and surveillance of the adjustment process" was required during this period of "exceptional and widespread payments imbalances."

The group issued several warnings to members to avoid competitive devaluation or undervaluation of currencies, and asked them to take a voluntary pledge barring trade restrictions as a means of improving their balance of payments problems.

Another of the measures adopted would set a new value for Special Drawing Rights (SDRs), which had been developed by the IMF as a new monetary standard to replace gold or the dollar. Effective July 1, the value of one SDR would be based on a "basket" of currencies of the following composition (equal to 100%):

U.S. dollar	33%
West German mark	12.5%
British pound	9%
French franc	7.5%
Japanese yen	7.5%
Canadian dollar	6%
Italian lira	6%
Dutch guilder	4.5%
Belgian franc	3.5%
Swedish krona	2.5%
Australian dollar	1.5%
Spanish peseta	1.5%
Norwegian krone	1.5%
Danish krone	1.5%
Austrian schilling	1%
South African rand	1%
	100%

According to the IMF, "The currencies included in the SDR basket are those of the 16 countries that had a share in world exports of goods and services in excess of 1% on average over the 5-year period 1968-72. The relative weights for these currencies were set broadly proportionate to the share of these countries in international transactions, using as proxy for this purpose average exports of goods and services in the period 1968-72 but modified, particularly with respect to the United States, in recognition that the proxy does not necessarily provide an adequate measure of a currency's real weight in the world economy in all cases. Accordingly, the U.S. dollar was assigned the weight of 33% of the basket. The IMF will collect exchange rates of the basket currencies daily in order to calculate a daily rate of the SDR in terms of each of the 16 currencies."

Another interim proposal called for establishment of a temporary "oil facility" providing loans to member nations hard hit by increased fuel costs. According to the IMF, 3 billion units of SDRs already had been pledged by Abu Dhabi, Canada, Iran, Kuwait, Libya, Oman, Saudi Arabia, and Venezuela.

Long-term proposals—The committee also published an "outline of reform" describing the general form a permanently reformed monetary system would take. Few new agreements were reached that had not already been accepted in previous meetings, including the IMF's 1973 annual meeting in Nairobi, Kenya.

Highlights of the long-term reform proposals: the central feature of the new system would be a "stable but adjustable" currency exchange rate system; most countries would maintain fixed "par values" and intervene frequently to maintain those rates within an agreed upon margin on either side of the value to correct balance of payments deficits and surpluses.

Countries in financial troubles could seek IMF approval to make major adjustments by instituting floating exchange rates.

"Objective indicators" would be used to warn governments when to make adjustments in its exchange rates. No agreement was reached on the question of "automatic" adjustments, under which nations would be compelled to institute changes.

"Convertibility" would be restored to the new monetary system, allowing nations to turn in their dollar holdings for "primary" reserve assets, such as gold or SDRs.

SDRs would replace gold or the dollar as the main reserve asset and also would serve as the "numeraire" or standard of value in which currency values were expressed.

At a press conference June 13, C. Jeremy Morse, chairman of the Committee of 20's deputies, said the proposed system would have four characteristics: it would choose a "middle" path between floating and fixed exchange rates "with a bias toward par values"; the system would be based on SDRs; the IMF's role would be greatly increased in an "internationally managed" system; and, he said, "the reformed system aims to take a step forward to greater international authority in all the main areas, but not a frighteningly large step."

Gold prices slide, rebound. Gold prices hit a six-month low July 4, closing at $129 an ounce in London. Observers attributed the bullion market's steady decline over the previous few months to world economic uncertainties that clouded trading in currencies and metals. Other experts also noted that large numbers of speculators had purchased gold on margin during the early period of 1974 when gold hit record high levels in European markets.

With prices falling, investors were now selling rather than putting up the cash required to cover their purchases. In a period of high interest rates, other monetary experts added, investors were unwilling to buy gold that paid no income.

Gold prices recovered slowly during the next three weeks and then jumped to $158 an ounce July 29 in the wake of the votes taken by the Judiciary Committee of the U.S. House of Representatives recommending the impeachment of President Nixon.

Gold suddenly became attractive again, observers said, because investors feared that the U.S. was entering a period of political instability and sought a safe haven for their investments. The price reached $159.40 in London Aug. 1 in what some brokers said was a delayed reaction to the prospect that U.S. citizens soon would be able to buy and sell gold.

Gold prices declined slightly during the short period of political crisis in the U.S. culminating in Nixon's resignation as gold and the U.S. dollar underwent a turnaround in roles. The dollar, which was traditionally weak during periods of uncertainty, rebounded with every political development moving Nixon toward removal from office, and gold weakened.

Dollar posts gains on Nixon resignation. Events in Washington continued to exert a strong influence on the position of the U.S. dollar in foreign markets. The dollar gained on nearly all markets Aug. 7 as the early departure of Richard M. Nixon from the U.S. Presidency grew certain. In Tokyo, the dollar closed at 302.10 yen, its highest level since February 1973, and posted strong gains against most European currencies.

Demand for the dollar strengthened Aug. 8 as resignation rumors mounted and investors signaled their belief that a new Administration would restore confidence in the U.S. economy and exercise its customary leadership in world affairs. In Frankfurt, the dollar reached its highest level since March, closing at 2.5998 marks.

On the day of Nixon's resignation, Aug. 9, the dollar was traded at 2.6 marks in Frankfurt, 4.765 francs in Paris and 2.9745 Swiss francs in Zurich. The dollar also moved higher in Tokyo.

Widespread Inflation

'73 inflation rates published. The Organization for Economic Development and Cooperation (OECD) published 1973 annual inflation rates Feb. 26. No reduction in inflation from December 1972–73 was reported for any member country, although Luxembourg showed the smallest percentage gain—6.1%. Prices rose most rapidly during the year in Greece, where the inflation rate was 30.6%.

Price increases over a 12-month period: Iceland 28.4%; Portugal, 20.1%; Turkey, 19.9%; Japan, 19.1%; Finland, 15.6%; Spain, 14.3%; Australia, 13.2%; Denmark and Ireland, 12.6%; Italy, 12.5%; Switzerland, 11.9%; Great Britain, 10.6%; Canada, 9.1%; United States, 8.8%; France, 8.5%; the Netherlands, 8.2%; Austria and West Germany, 7.8%; Norway, 7.6%; Sweden, 7.5%; and Belgium, 7.3%.

Italian regime falls. Premier Mariano Rumor's center-left coalition, Italy's 35th government since World War II, resigned March 2, one day after the small Republican Party withdrew in a dispute over economic policy. (Rumor later formed a new Cabinet, which took office March 15.)

The crisis was sparked by the resignation Feb. 28 of Treasury Minister Ugo La Malfa, a Republican, over the terms of a proposed standby credit of 1 billion Special Drawing Rights (SDRs) ($1.2 billion) from the International Monetary Fund. After expressing full support for La Malfa, the Republican Party pulled out of the coalition March 1. The IMF credit was sought to support the declining value of the lira and help finance Italy's expected record trade deficit for 1974. (The IMF announced approval of the credit April 10.)

La Malfa and the governor of the Bank of Italy, Guido Carli, had promised the IMF in February that Italy would curb domestic credit and government spending, a deflationary program opposed by Budget and Economic Planning Minister Antonio Giolitti, a Socialist, on grounds it would increase unemployment and economic stagnation and prevent investment in structural social reforms.

La Malfa's Republican Party had issued a statement Jan. 24 stating that the 1973 trade deficit amounted to about 2.7 trillion lire and could rise to over 5 trillion lire (about $7.5 billion) in 1974 because of the huge increase in oil prices. Previously the highest deficit had been 1.6 trillion lire, recorded in 1963. The 1972 trade deficit had totaled 434 billion lire.

(An unprecedented 9.2 trillion lire deficit was projected in Italy's 1974 budget, approved by the Chamber of Deputies Feb. 20. La Malfa warned in the debate that public spending was at "an almost unsupportable limit." He said Italy had, in relation to its national income, the biggest deficit among industrialized nations; borrowed the most on foreign markets as a result of its monetary imbalances; and registered the biggest increases in prices in 1973.)

The Rumor Cabinet had agreed Feb. 7 to establish a fund of some 100 billion lire ($150 million) to maintain current price levels of certain basic food products, particularly through subsidizing imports.

Bakers and government officials agreed on a compromise to increase bread prices Feb. 10, two days after the chairman of the bakers' union was charged and given a month's suspended jail sentence for breaking the price freeze. The bakers had decided to raise prices unilaterally.

A 50% surcharge was imposed April 30 on all imports of manufactured goods, including those from the European Economic Community (EEC). The measure was designed to curb inflation and help improve the balance of payments deficit.

Italy March 22 had ended its two-tier foreign exchange system after the rate differential between the "commercial" and "financial" lira had declined to 2.5%. The Treasury Ministry acknowleged that the move resulted from similar action by France March 21.

Inflation statistics. Two series of statistics measuring inflation and economic output were released by the Organization for Economic Development (OECD) and the International Monetary Fund (IMF). According to the OECD report issued July 23, the industrialized nations of the West recently had undergone the "most exceptional deceleration of growth ever experienced" but were expected to begin a "modest recovery" over the next 12 months and show a gradual decline in the inflation rate.

As a group, the seven major industrial nations—the U.S., Canada, Japan, France, West Germany, Italy and Britain—registered a 1.25% drop in their output of goods and services in the first half of 1974 (after adjustments were made for inflation). The decline was in contrast to the group's 8.1% rise in output over the first half of 1973 and a 3% increase in the last six months of the year.

Inflation figures released by the IMF Aug. 12 showed a sharp acceleration in price increases during the second quarter of 1974 compared with the same period of 1973. The average world inflation rate was over 12.5%. Consumer prices in industrial countries rose an average 13% from the second quarter of 1973 to 1974. Japan showed the highest rate of 21.9% through June. Inflation figures for other countries for the 12-month period ending June: U.S., 11.2%; Canada, 11.4%; Britain (through May), 16%.

Declines in the inflation rate were registered in West Germany, where prices rose by 6.9% through June compared with 7.2% in the 12-month period ending in May; Norway, 8.2%, down from 8.7%; and Switzerland, 9.6%, down from 9.9%.

The OECD reported Sept. 13 that the inflation rate for non-Communist industrial countries was a record 13.3% for the 12-month period ending July 31, but declined to 12% at an annual rate during May–July.

Inflation had increased at an annual rate of 7.7% in 1973, 4.7% in 1972 and an average 3.7% during 1961–71.

Inflation rates from July 1973–July 1974 for the OECD's 24 member states: Iceland, 43.8%; Greece, 31.8%; Turkey and Portugal, 25.9%; Japan, 25.2%; Italy, 18.9%; Britain, 17.1%; Finland, 16.4%; Ireland, 16.2%; Denmark, 15.9%; Spain, 15.2%; France and Australia, 14.4%; Belgium, 13.7%; U.S., 11.7%; Canada, 11.3%; Luxembourg, 10.1%; New Zealand and Austria, 10%; Switzerland, 9.8%; Netherlands, 9.6%; Norway, 8.8%; Sweden, 8.4%; and West Germany, 6%.

Index